In July of 2011, my pet dog Edu, who lived with my parents, passed away from old age. Thank you for the long eighteen years we spent together, Edu. Rest in peace. I wonder if he's romping around in Heaven right now. Oh, Edu! (My current weight...72 kg!! It's not changing at all!! Oh no!)

–Mitsutoshi Shimabukuro, 2011

Mitsutoshi Shimabukuro made his debut in **Weekly Shonen Jump** in 1996. He is best known for **Seikimatsu Leader Den Takeshi!** for which he won the 46th Shogakukan Manga Award for children's manga in 2001. His current series, **Toriko**, began serialization in Japan in 2008.

TORIKO VOL. 16
SHONEN JUMP Manga Edition

STORY AND ART BY **MITSUTOSHI SHIMABUKURO**

Translation/Christine Dashiell
Adaptation/Hope Donovan
Touch-Up Art & Lettering/Maui Girl
Design/Matt Hinrichs
Editor/Hope Donovan

TORIKO © 2008 by Mitsutoshi Shimabukuro
All rights reserved. First published in Japan in 2008 by SHUEISHA Inc., Tokyo.
English translation rights arranged by SHUEISHA Inc.

Printed in Canada

Published by VIZ Media, LLC
P.O. Box 77010
San Francisco, CA 94107

10 9 8 7 6 5 4 3 2 1
First printing, June 2013

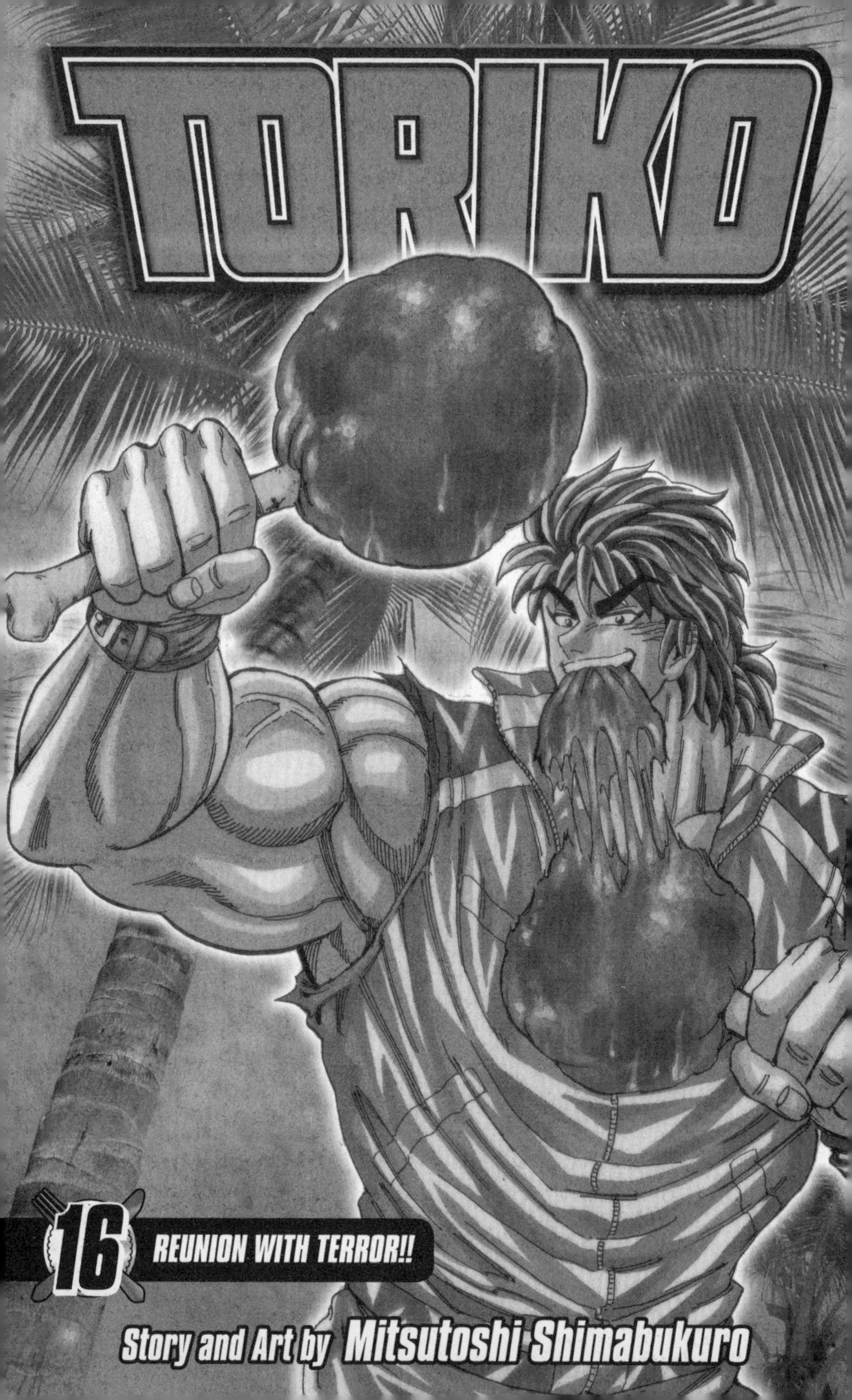
TORIKO
16
REUNION WITH TERROR!!
Story and Art by Mitsutoshi Shimabukuro

TORIKO

THE ULTIMATE GOURMET HUNTER WHO'S ON A NEVER-ENDING QUEST TO FIND AND SCARF UP THE RAREST FOODS ON EARTH! HE FIGHTS WITH A KNIFE (HIS FIST), A FORK (HIS FIST), AND SPIKED PUNCH (ALSO HIS FISTS).

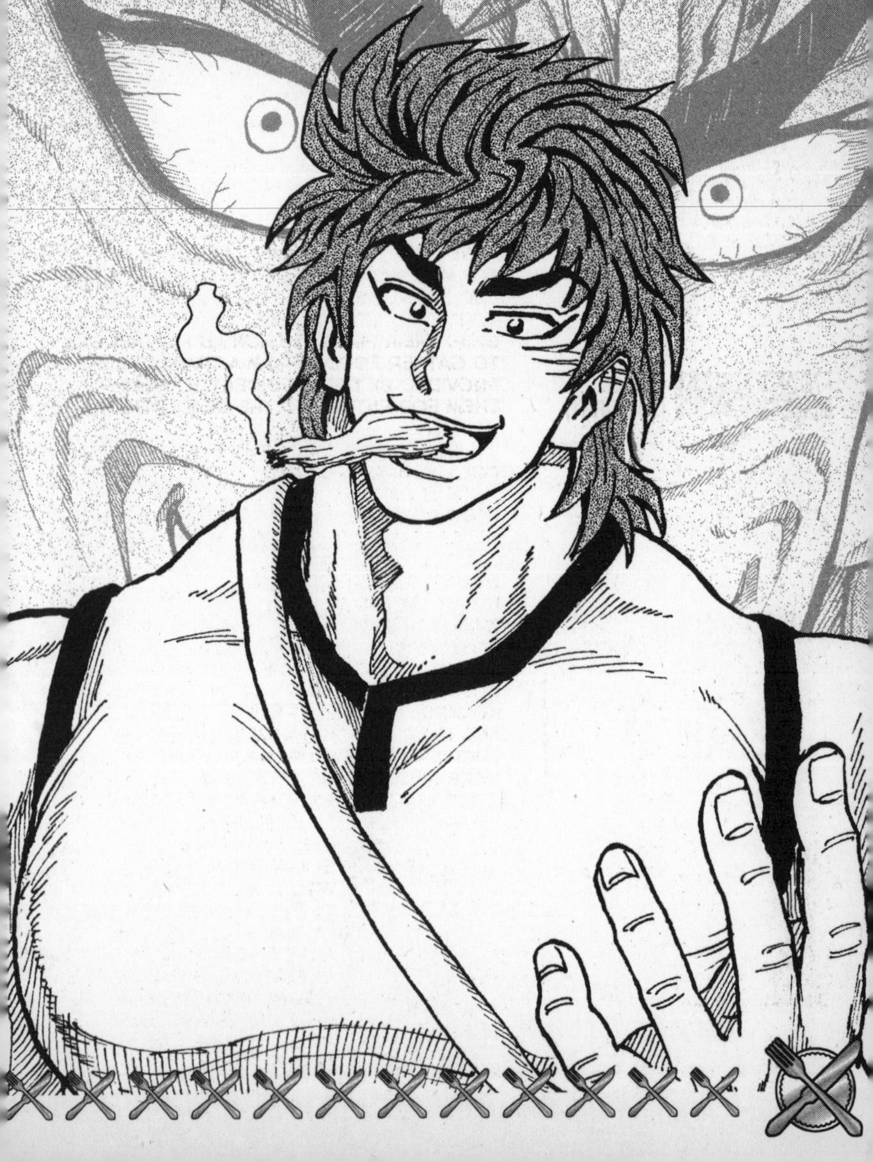

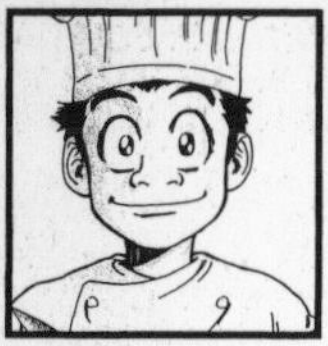

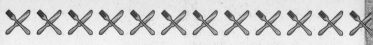

●KOMATSU
TALENTED IGO HOTEL CHEF AND TORIKO'S #1 FAN.

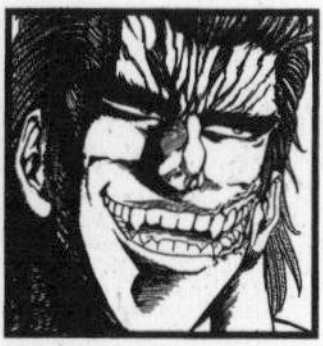

●ZEBRA
A GOURMET HUNTER AND ONE OF THE FOUR KINGS. A DANGEROUS PERSON WITH SUPERHUMAN HEARING AND VOCAL POWERS.

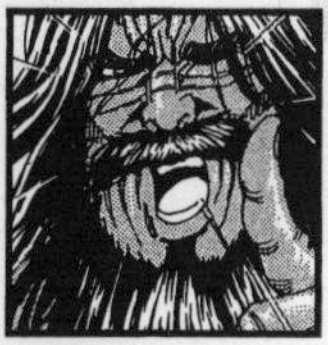

●MELK (THE FIRST)
WORLD'S MOST TALENTED AND INFLUENTIAL CUTLER. A FRIEND OF THE IGO PRESIDENT.

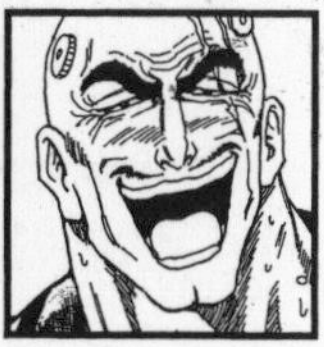

●MANSOM
IGO DEVELOPMENT CHIEF & GOURMET LABORATORY DIRECTOR. SUPER STRONG AND A BIG DRINKER.

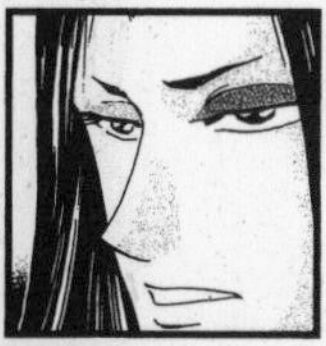

●RAY
IGO DEFENSE BUREAU CHIEF

WHAT'S FOR DINNER

IT'S THE AGE OF GOURMET! KOMATSU, THE HEAD CHEF AT THE HOTEL OWNED BY THE IGO (INTERNATIONAL GOURMET ORGANIZATION), BECAME FAST FRIENDS WITH THE LEGENDARY GOURMET HUNTER TORIKO WHILE GATOR HUNTING. NOW KOMATSU ACCOMPANIES TORIKO ON HIS LIFELONG QUEST TO CREATE THE PERFECT FULL-COURSE MEAL.

TORIKO AND KOMATSU GO ON MANY ADVENTURES TOGETHER, ONE OF THE MOST NOTABLE BEING THE QUEST FOR CENTURY SOUP. ALTHOUGH THEY COME AWAY EMPTY-HANDED, KOMATSU RE-CREATES THE SOUP TO WORLDWIDE ACCLAIM. AT THE URGING OF THE IGO PRESIDENT, TORIKO AND KOMATSU FORM THE ULTIMATE HUNTER-CHEF PARTNERSHIP. THEIR FIRST MISSION AS PARTNERS IS TO GATHER FOODS FROM A TRAINING LIST PROVIDED BY THE PRESIDENT TO READY THEM FOR ENTRY INTO THE DEADLY GOURMET WORLD.

THE THIRD ITEM ON THE LIST IS MELLOW COLA. ZEBRA, THE MOST VIOLENT OF THE FOUR KINGS, IS RELEASED FROM JAIL TO TACKLE GOURMET PYRAMID WITH THEM. HOWEVER, IN A TRICKY PART OF THE DESERT CALLED DESERT LABYRINTH, KOMATSU GETS SWEPT UP IN QUICKSAND AND IS SEPARATED FROM THE OTHERS. LUCKILY, HE ENDS UP JUST WHERE THEY WERE HEADED: THE BASEMENT LEVEL OF GOURMET PYRAMID! TORIKO AND ZEBRA USE UP PRECIOUS ENERGY HURRYING TO REACH HIM. MEANWHILE, THE SOUND ARMOR ZEBRA WRAPS AROUND KOMATSU PROTECTS HIM FROM THE WILD ANIMALS HE RUNS ACROSS UNTIL HE FINALLY ENTERS THE HEART OF THE PYRAMID AND FINDS HIMSELF IN A MYSTERIOUS ROOM COVERED IN DRAWINGS!

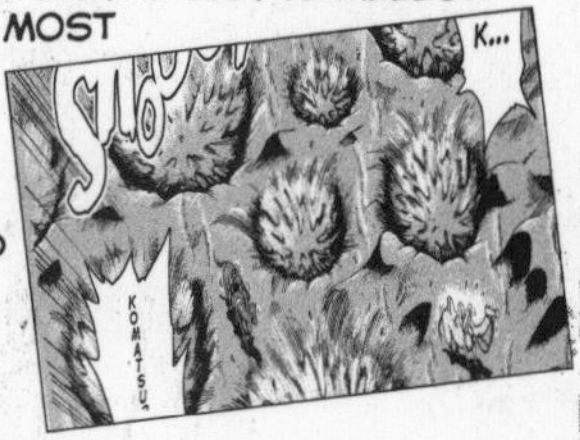
K...
KOMATSU

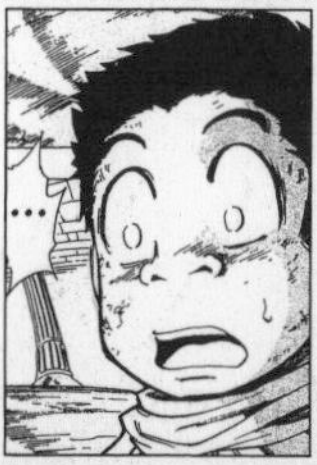
...

Contents

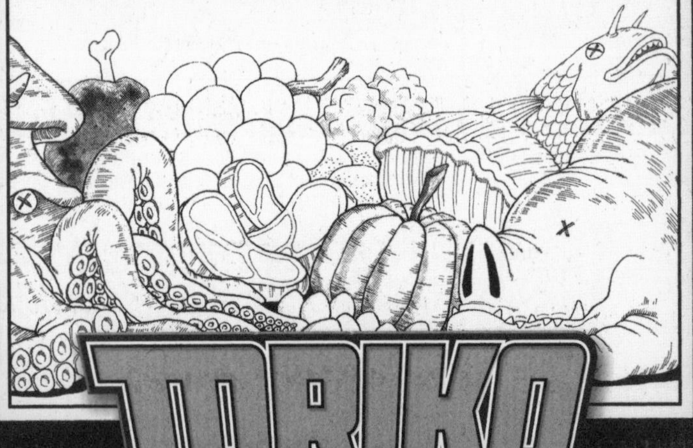

TORIKO

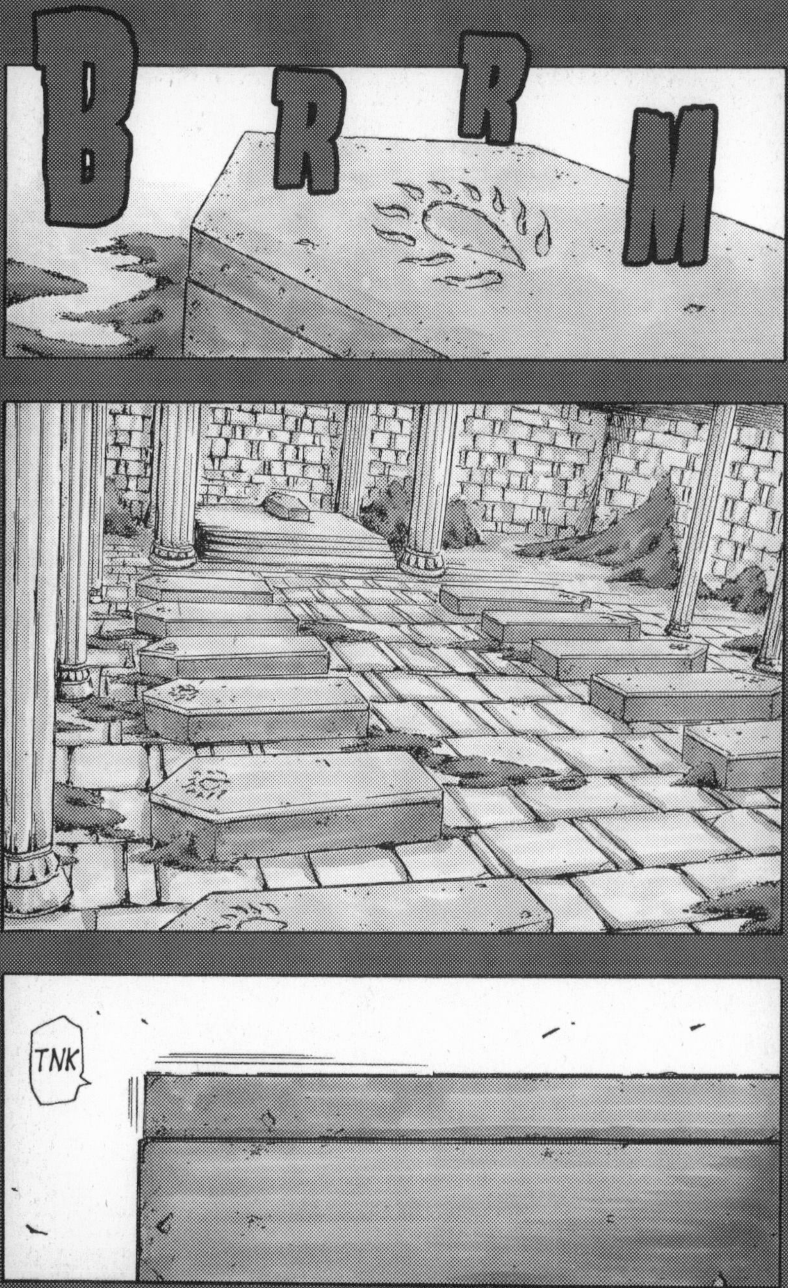
BRRM
TNK

GOURMET 135: RECOVERY!!

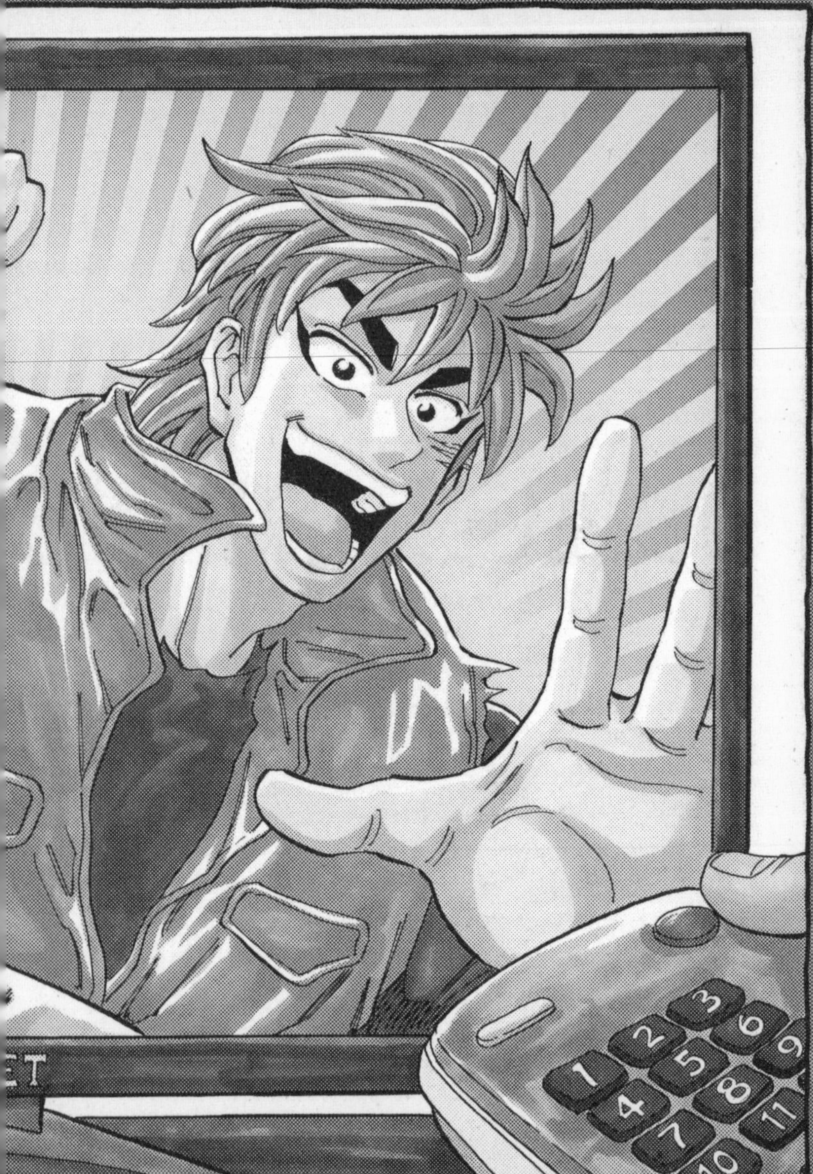

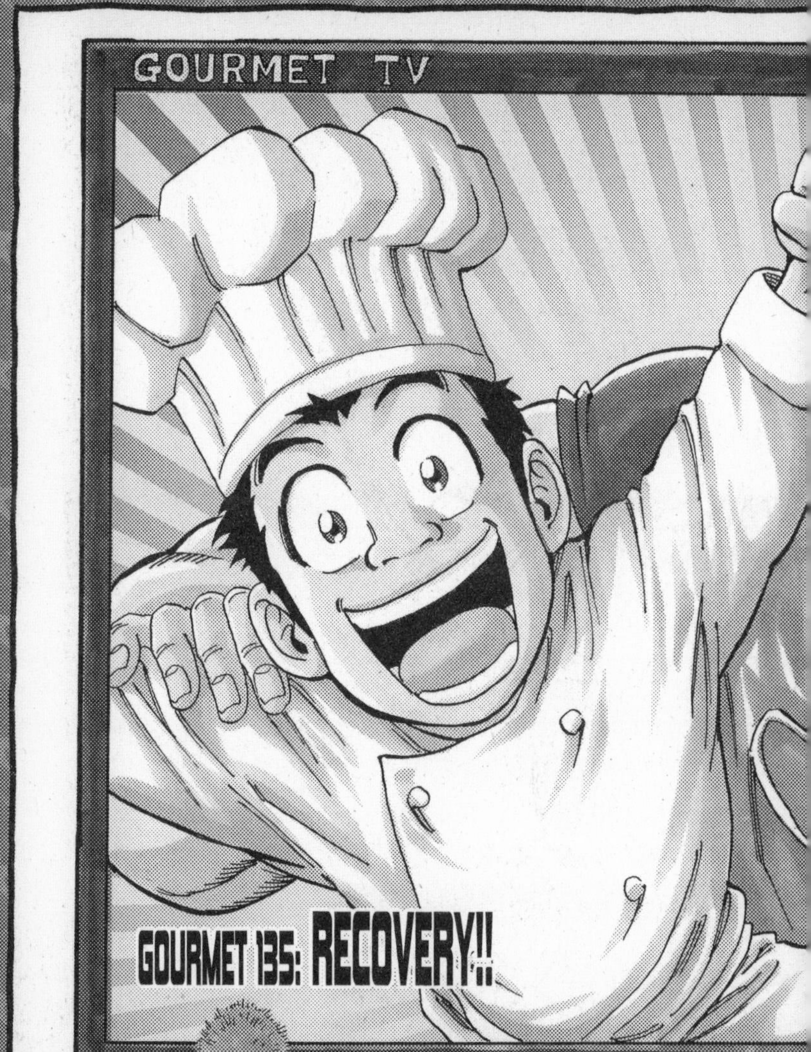
GOURMET TV
GOURMET 135: RECOVERY!!
GOU

TORIKO

GOURMET CHECKLIST

Vol. 155

POTATO SPRING
(VEGETABLE)

CAPTURE LEVEL: 3 (ON EARTH);
30 (IN VEGETABLE SKY)

HABITAT: VEGETABLE SKY

SIZE: SPRING IS 10 METERS WIDE, 1 METER DEEP; FRIES ARE 30–50CM LONG

WEIGHT: ---

PRICE: 50 YEN PER FRY

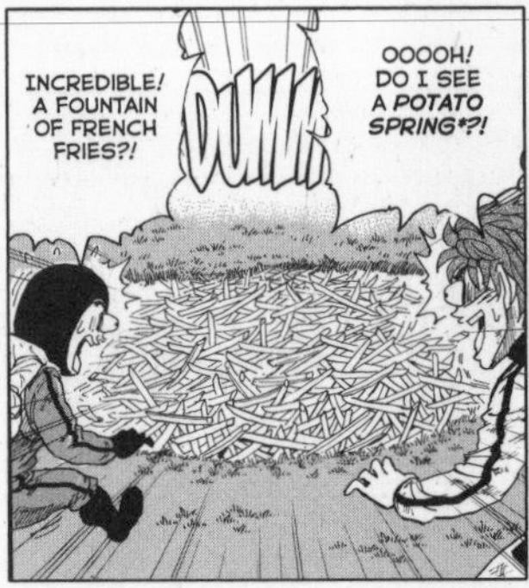
OOOOH! DO I SEE A *POTATO SPRING**?!
INCREDIBLE! A FOUNTAIN OF FRENCH FRIES?!

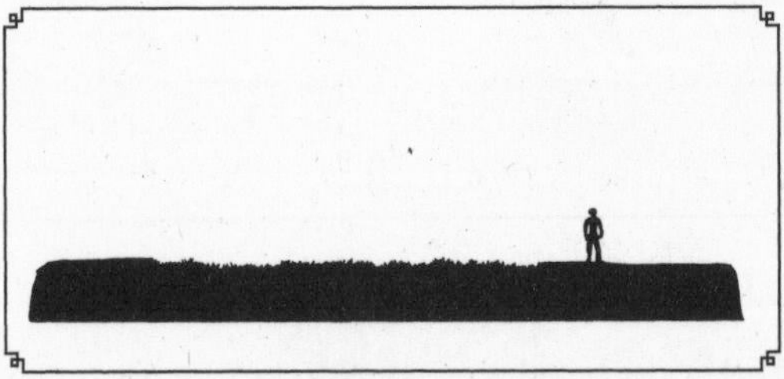

SCALE

A LONG, SKINNY PERENNIAL IN THE NIGHTSHADE FAMILY. GEOTHERMAL HEAT WARMS THE OIL OF NEARBY RAPESEED PLANTS, CREATING CONDITIONS AKIN TO BOILING OIL. NO SEASONING IS NECESSARY AS THEY HAVE A NATURAL SALTINESS. SINCE MOST OF THE VEGETABLES IN VEGETABLE SKY HAVE A CRISP, REFRESHING TASTE, THIS FOOD OFFERS THE PERFECT GUT-BUSTING ALTERNATIVE.

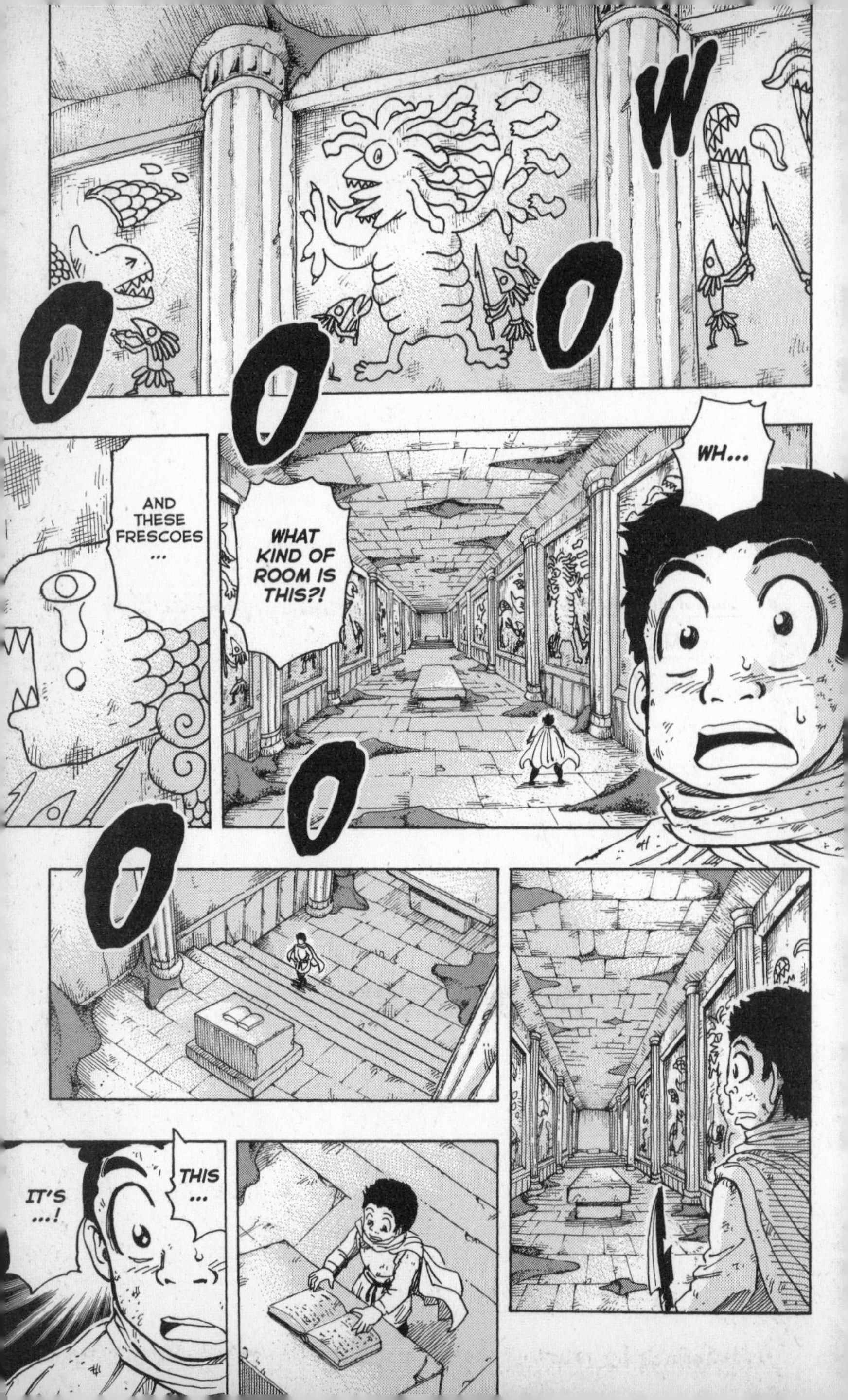
WOOOOOO
WH...
WHAT KIND OF ROOM IS THIS?!
AND THESE FRESCOES ...
THIS ...
IT'S ...!

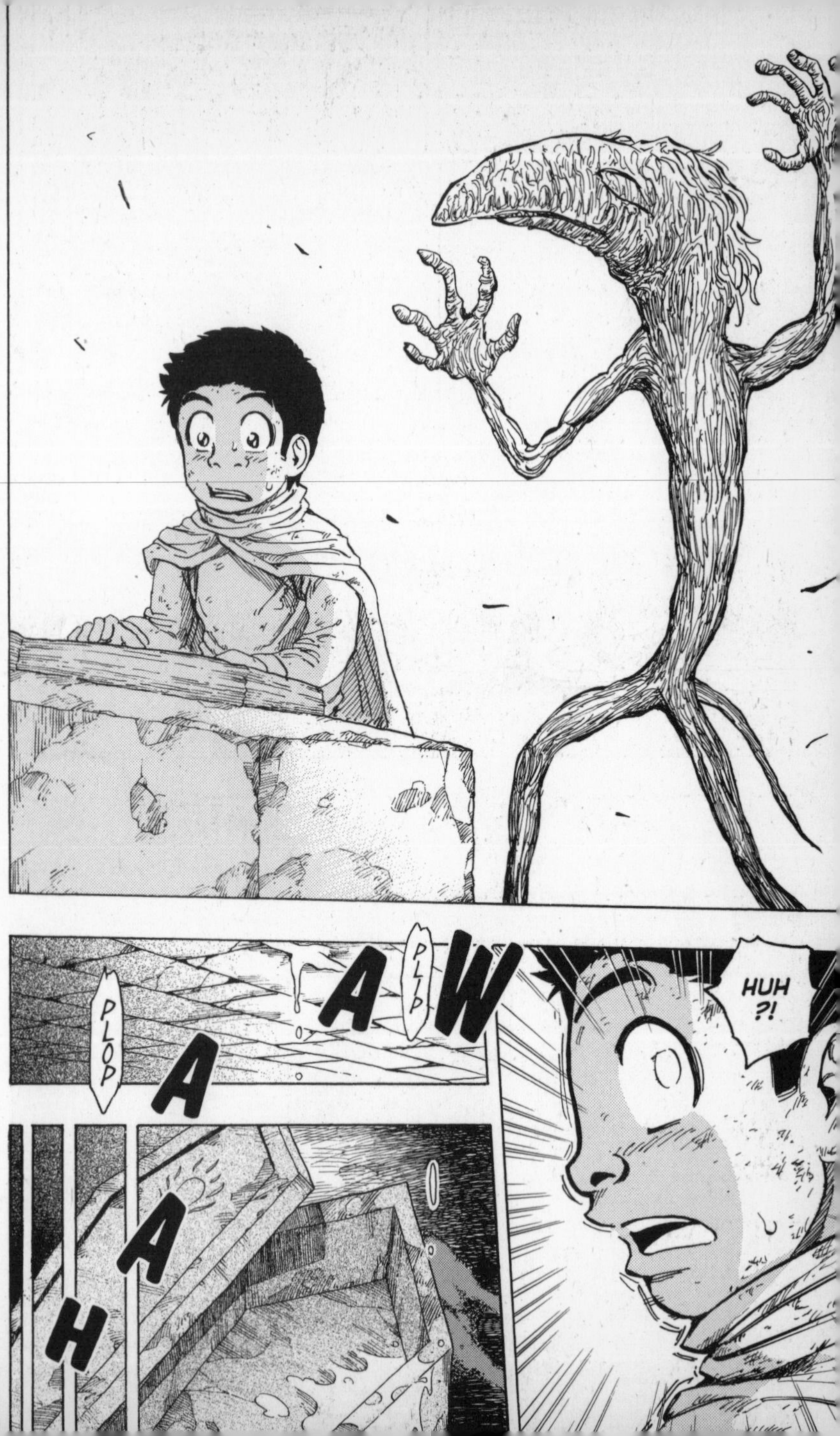
HUH ?!
PLIP
PLOP
WAAAH

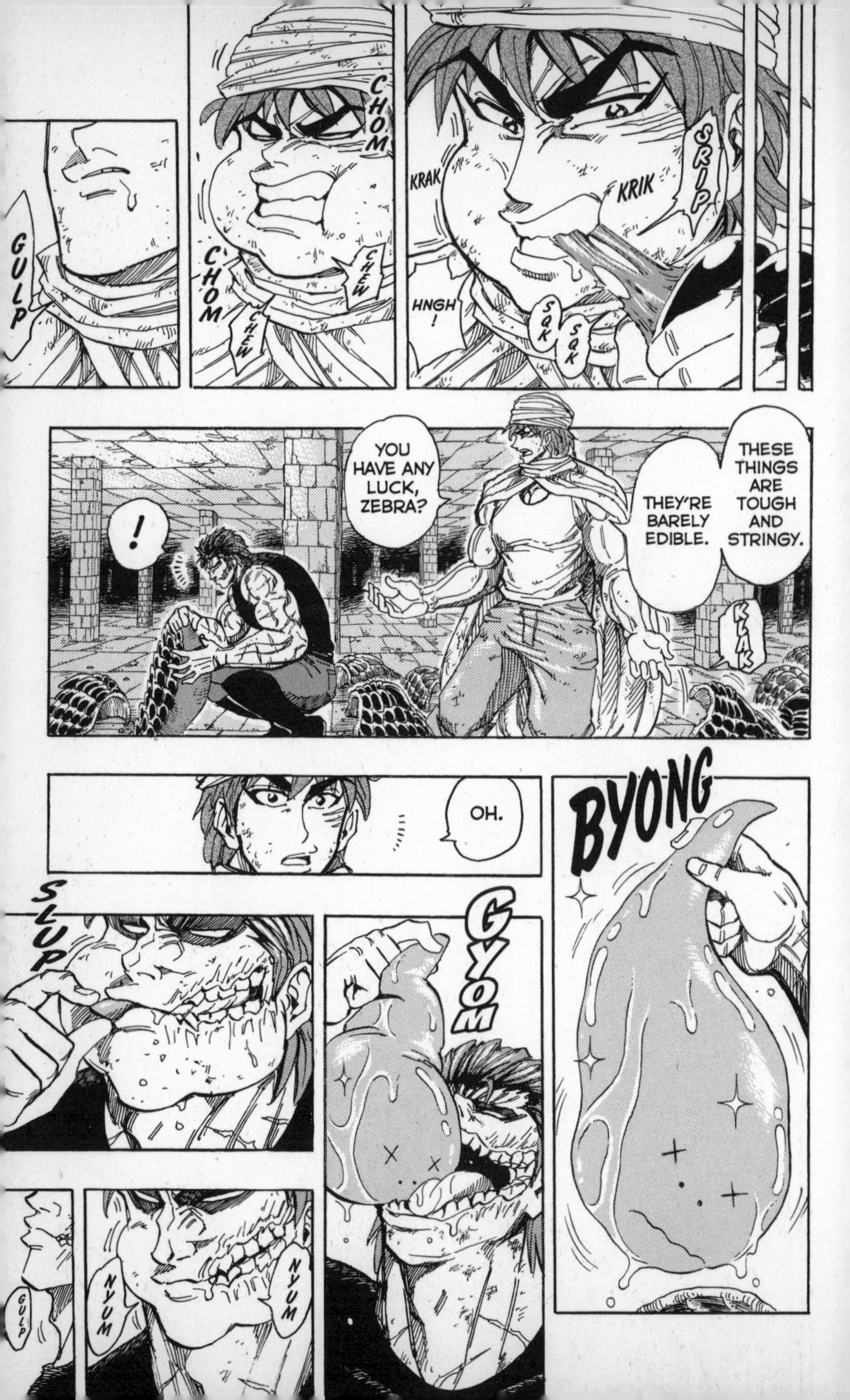
SRIP
KRIK
KRAK
HNGH!
SQK
SQK
CHOM
CHOM
CHEW
CHEW
CHOM
GULP
THESE THINGS ARE TOUGH AND STRINGY.
THEY'RE BARELY EDIBLE.
YOU HAVE ANY LUCK, ZEBRA?
!
KLAK
BYONG
OH.
GYOM
SLUP
NYUM
NYUM
GULP

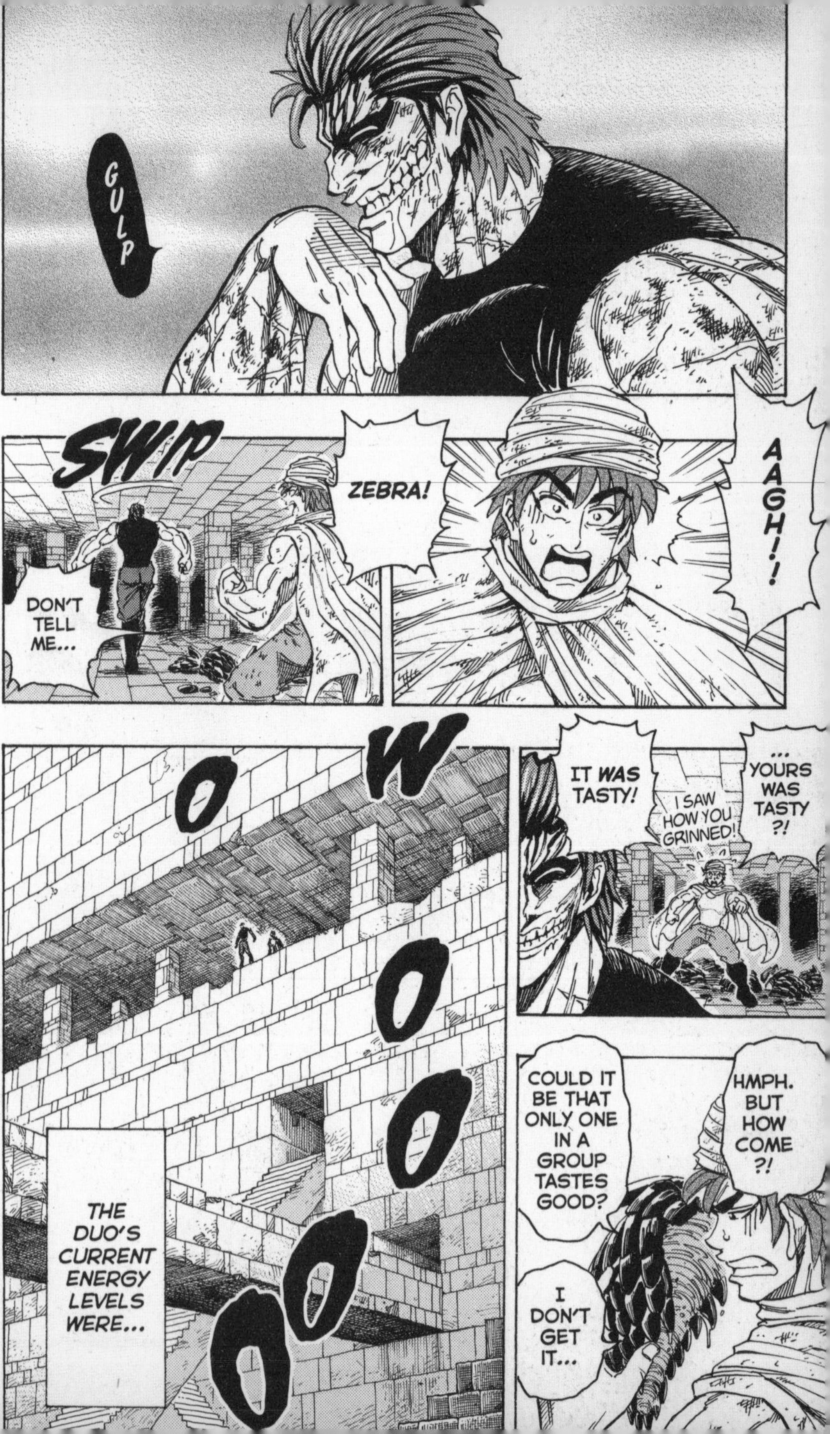
GULP
AAGH!!
ZEBRA!
SWIP
DON'T TELL ME...
...YOURS WAS TASTY?!
I SAW HOW YOU GRINNED!
IT WAS TASTY!
HMPH. BUT HOW COME?!
COULD IT BE THAT ONLY ONE IN A GROUP TASTES GOOD?
I DON'T GET IT...
OWOOOO
THE DUO'S CURRENT ENERGY LEVELS WERE...

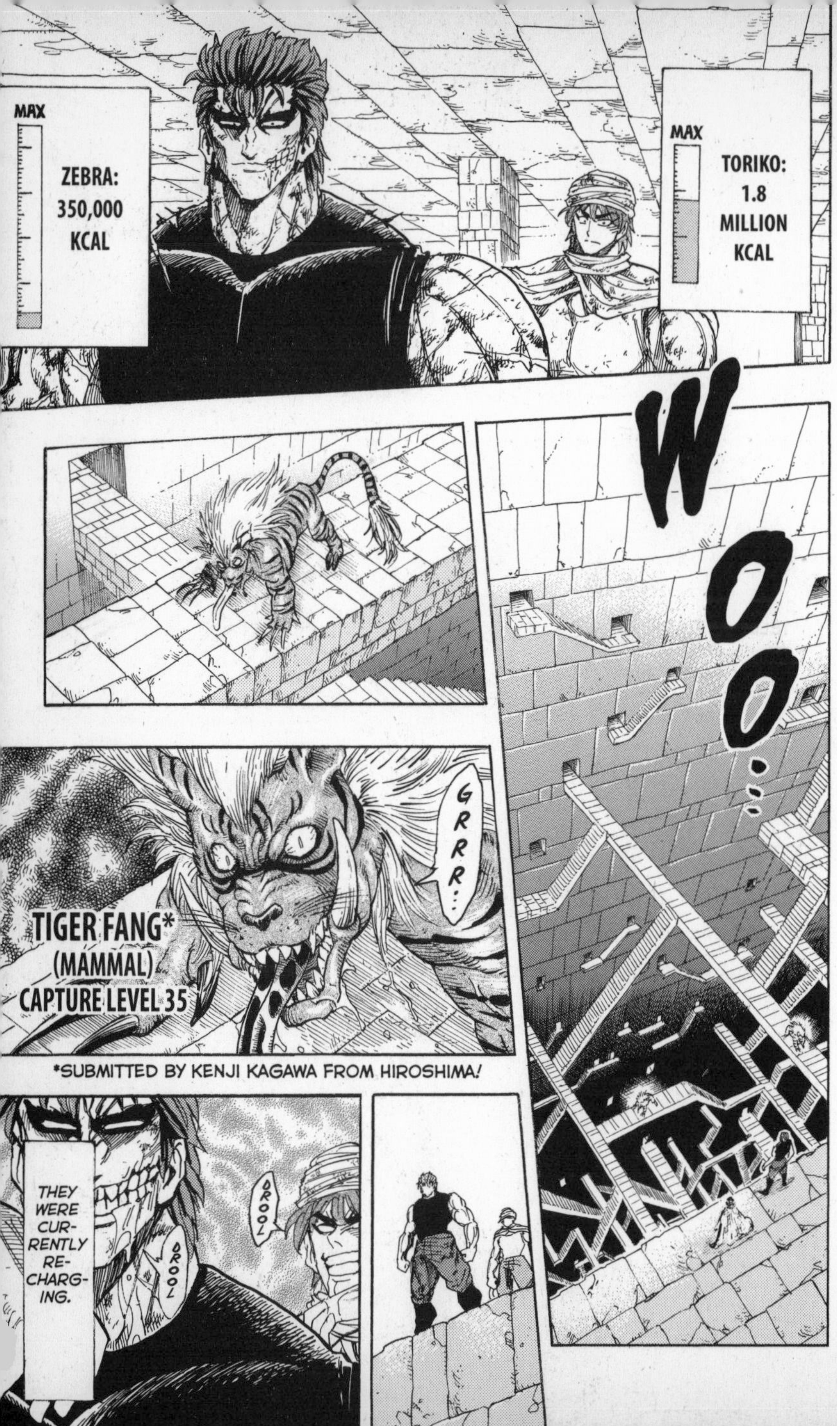
MAX
TORIKO: 1.8 MILLION KCAL
MAX
ZEBRA: 350,000 KCAL
WOOO...
GRRR...
TIGER FANG* (MAMMAL) CAPTURE LEVEL 35
*SUBMITTED BY KENJI KAGAWA FROM HIROSHIMA!
DROOL
DROOL
THEY WERE CUR-RENTLY RE-CHARG-ING.

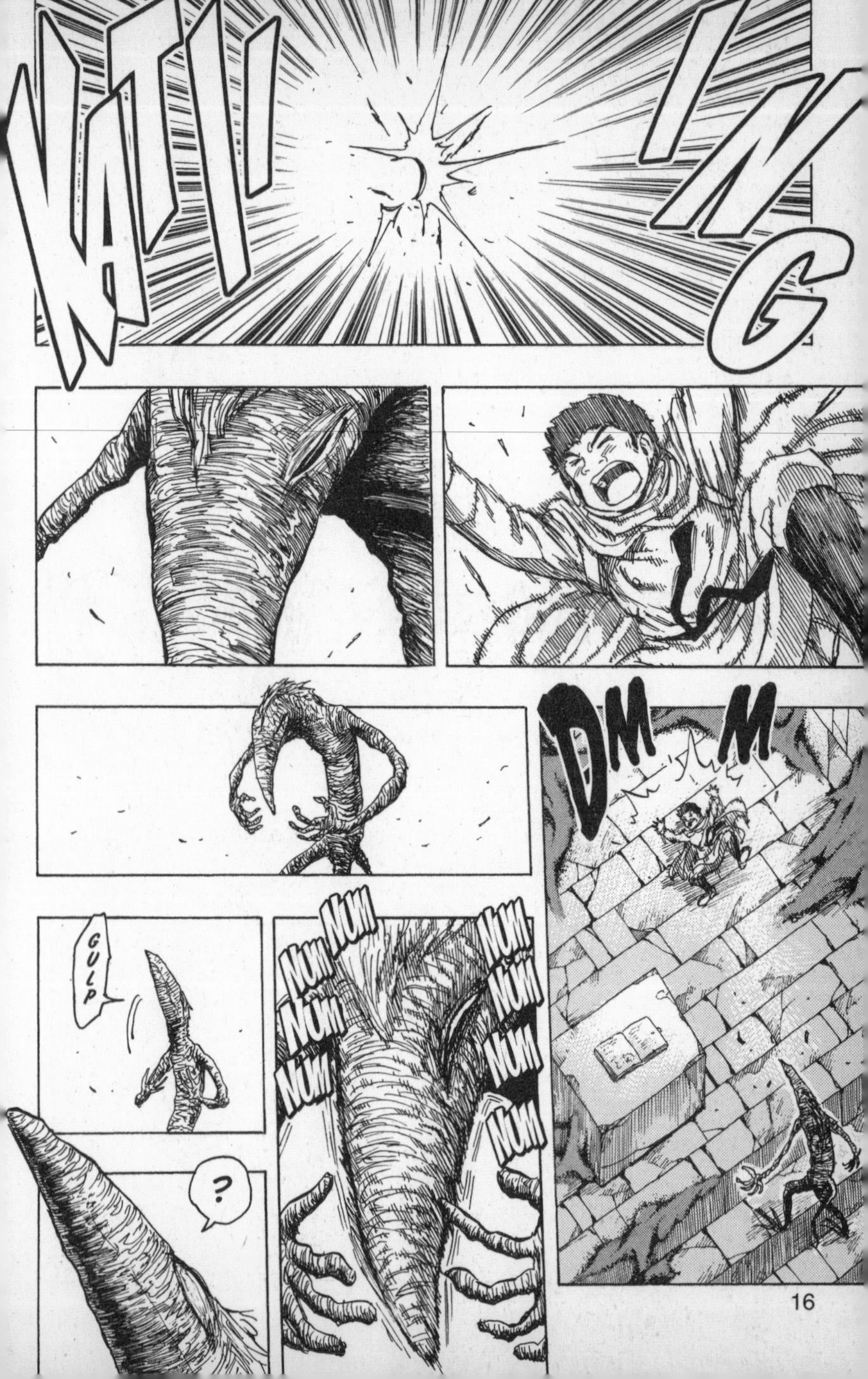
KATII
ING
DM M
NUM NUM NUM NUM NUM
NUM NUM NUM NUM NUM
GULP
?

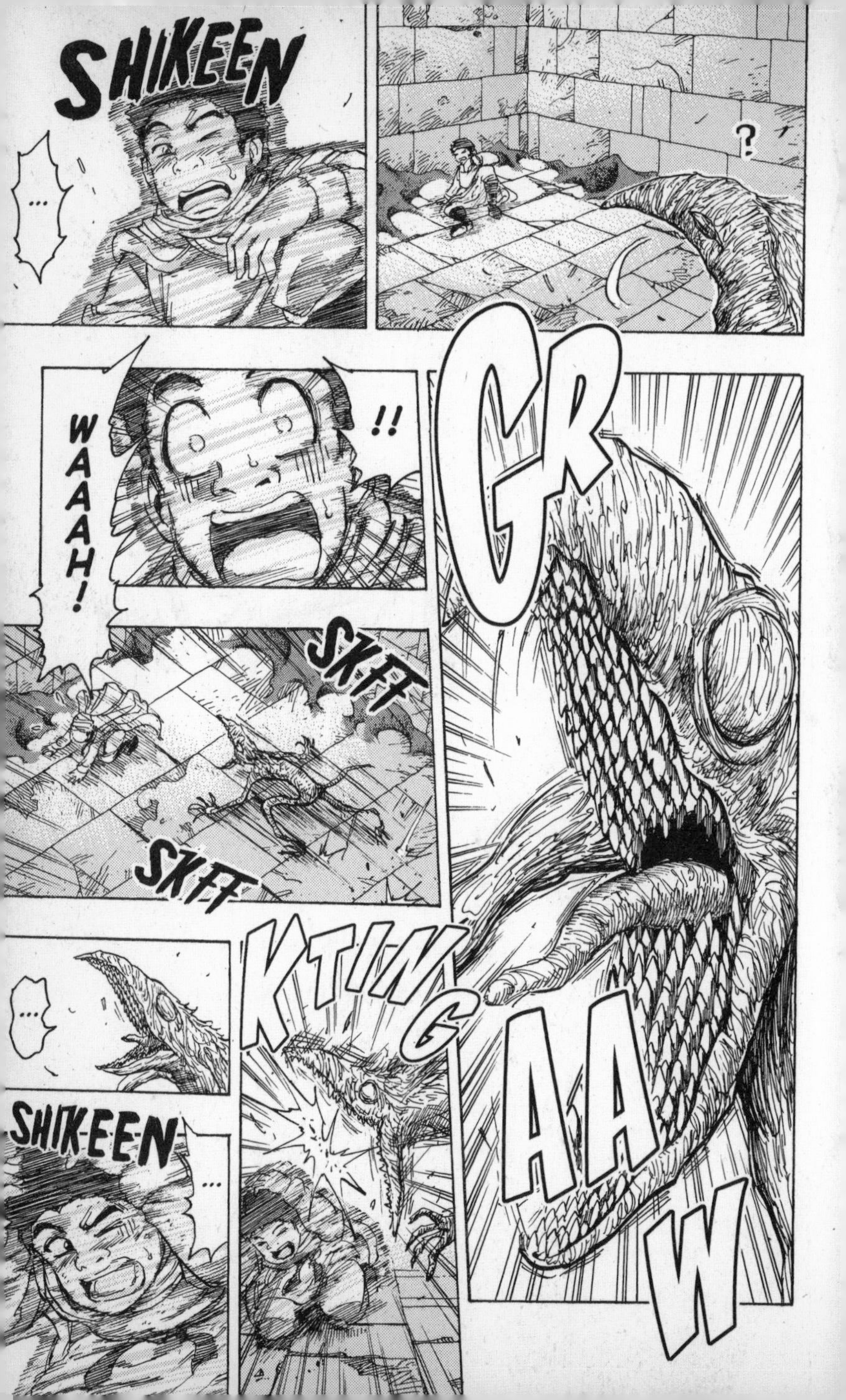
?
SHIKEEN
...
GRAAAW
!!
WAAAAH!
SKFF
SKFF
KTING
...
SHIK-E-EN
...

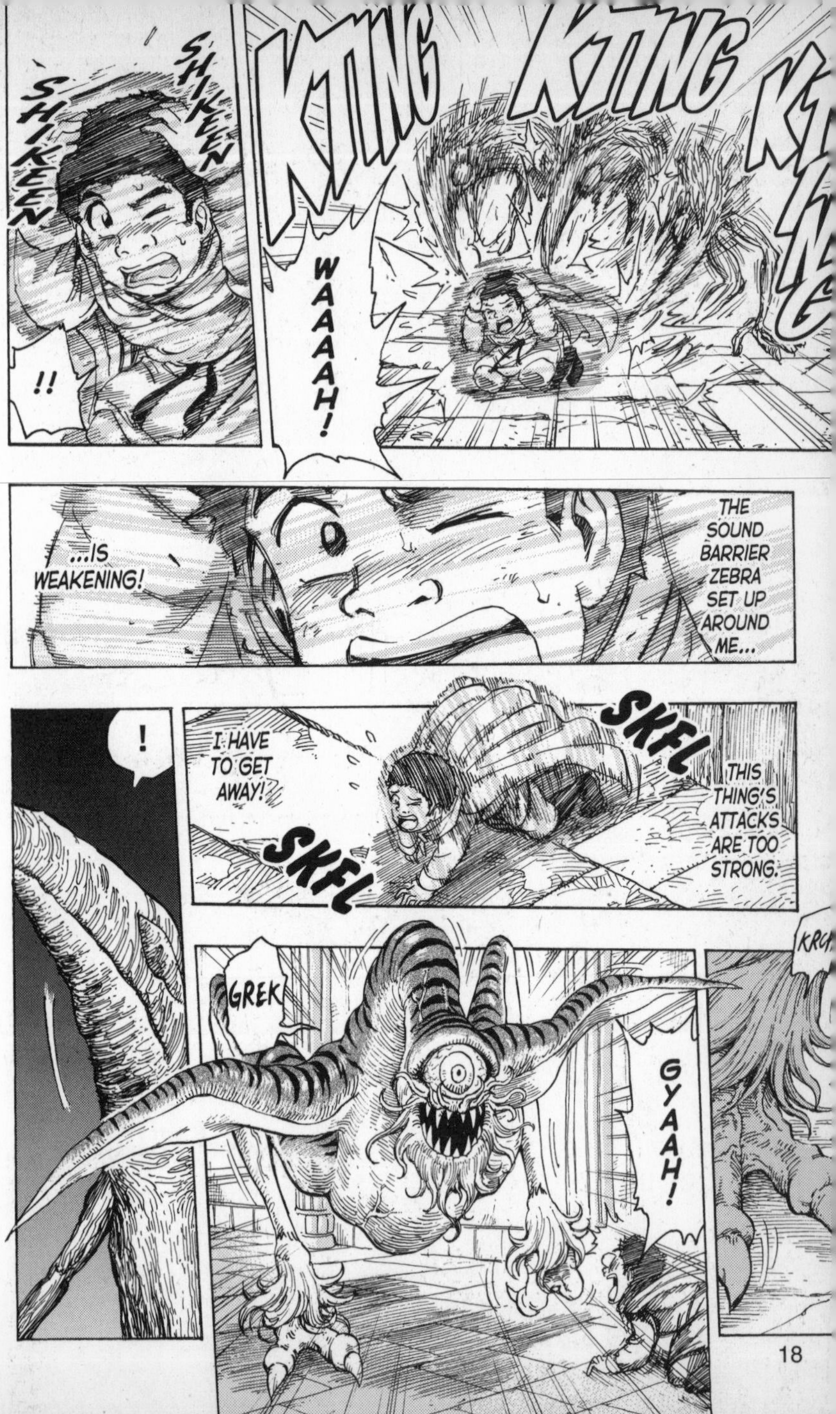
KTING
KTING
KTING
KTING
WAAAAAH!
SHIKEEN
SHIKEEN
!!
THE SOUND BARRIER ZEBRA SET UP AROUND ME...
...IS WEAKENING!
THIS THING'S ATTACKS ARE TOO STRONG.
SKFL
SKFL
I HAVE TO GET AWAY!
GYAAH!
GREK
!

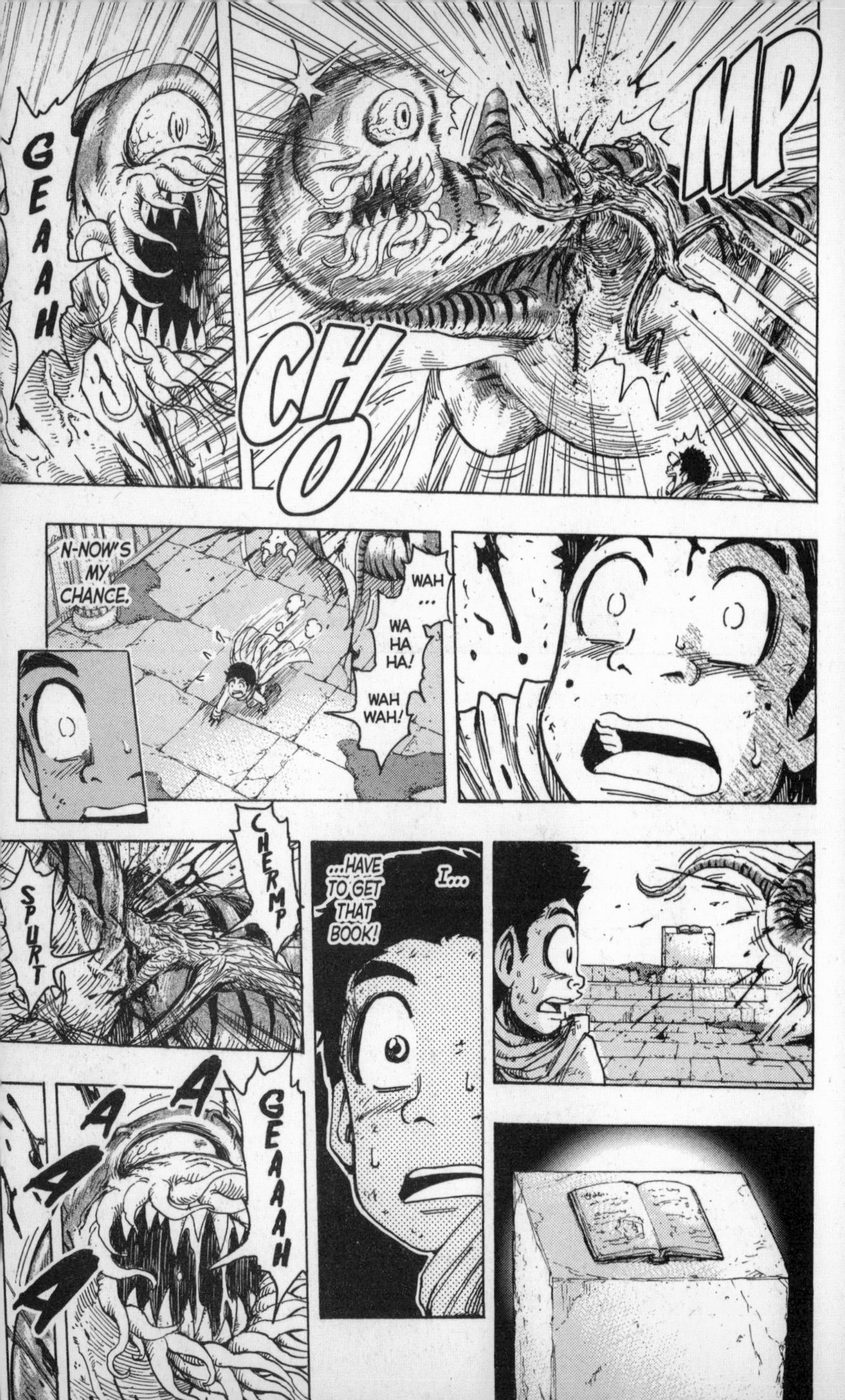
CHOMP
GEAAH
WAH ...
WA HA HA!
WAH WAH!
N-NOW'S MY CHANCE.
I...
...HAVE TO GET THAT BOOK!
CHERMP
SPURT
GEAAAAH
AAAAA

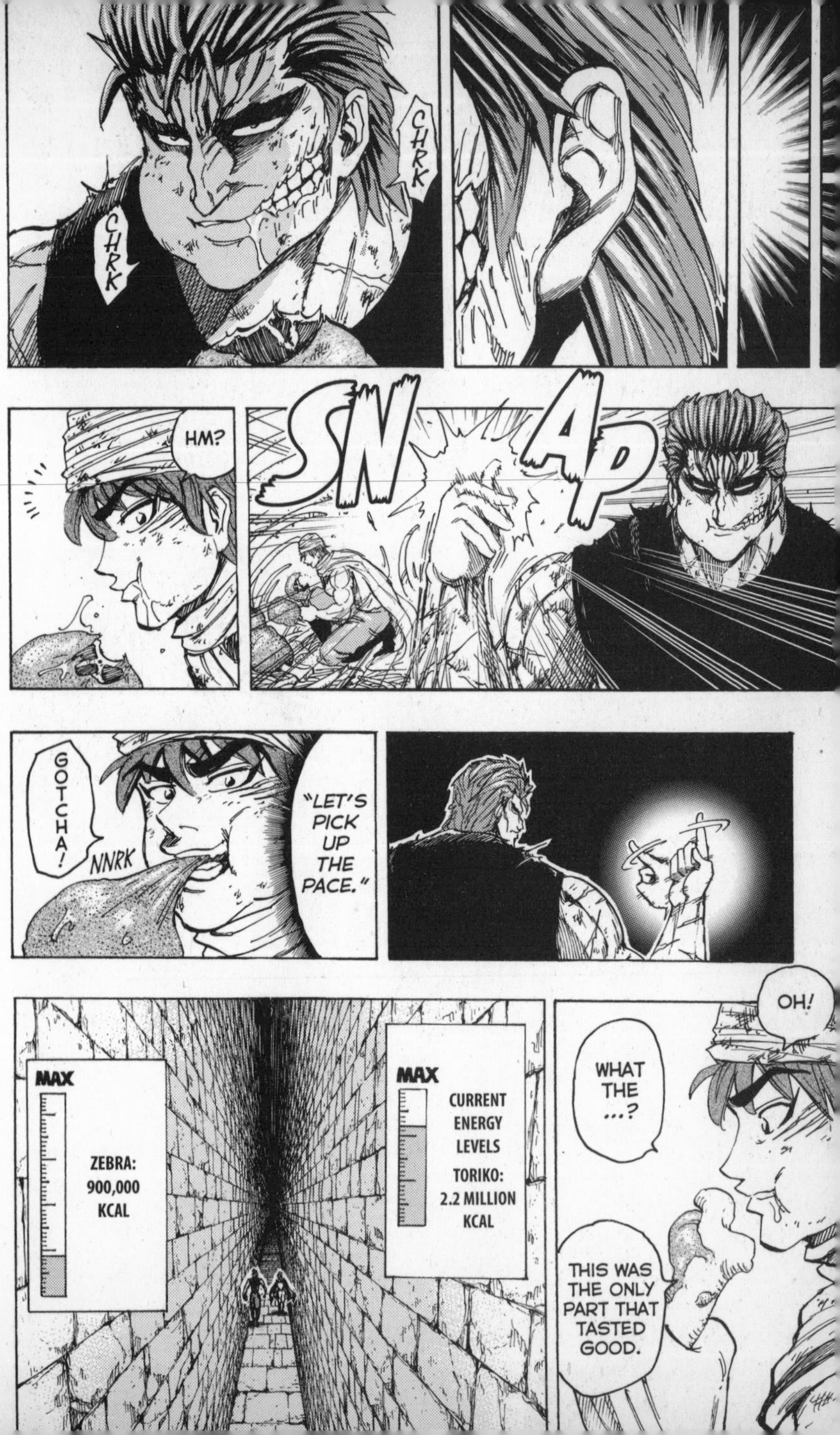
CHRK
CHRK
SNAP
HM?
"LET'S PICK UP THE PACE."
GOTCHA!
NNRK
OH!
WHAT THE ...?
THIS WAS THE ONLY PART THAT TASTED GOOD.
MAX
CURRENT ENERGY LEVELS
TORIKO: 2.2 MILLION KCAL
MAX
ZEBRA: 900,000 KCAL

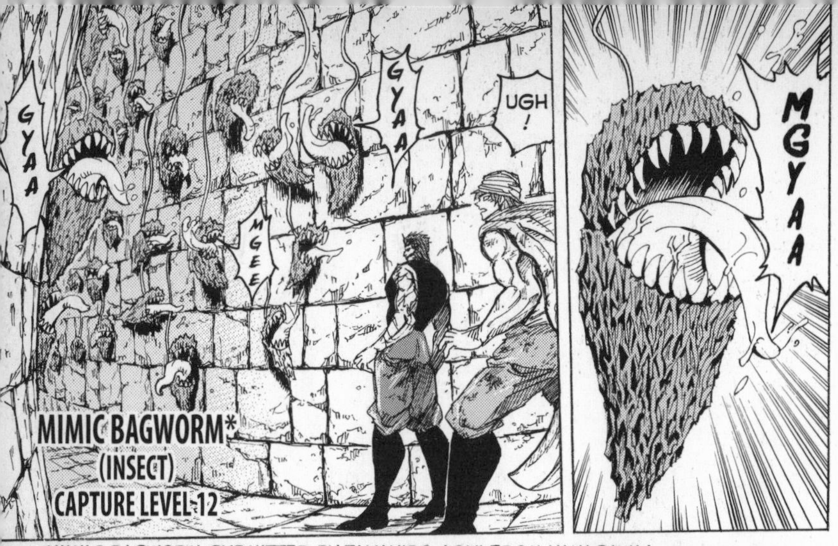
MGYAA
UGH!
GYAA
MGEE
GYAA
MIMIC BAGWORM*
(INSECT)
CAPTURE LEVEL 12

*MIMIC BAGWORM SUBMITTED BY TAKAHIRO AOKI FROM KANAGAWA!

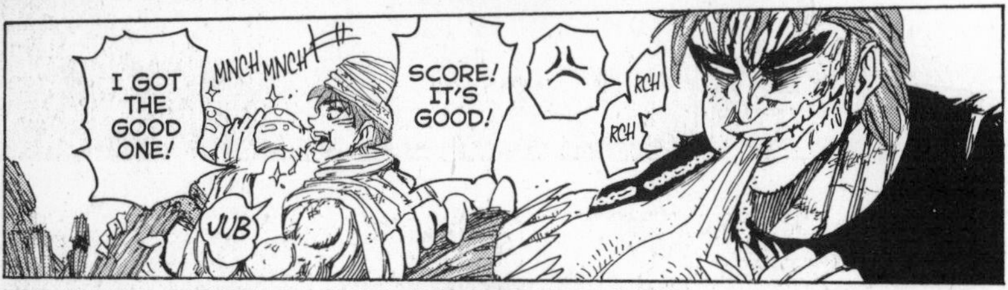
RCH
RCH
SCORE! IT'S GOOD!
MNCH MNCH
I GOT THE GOOD ONE!
JUB

*EVIL HUNTER CREATED BY GENTA YAMAMOTO FROM FUKUI!

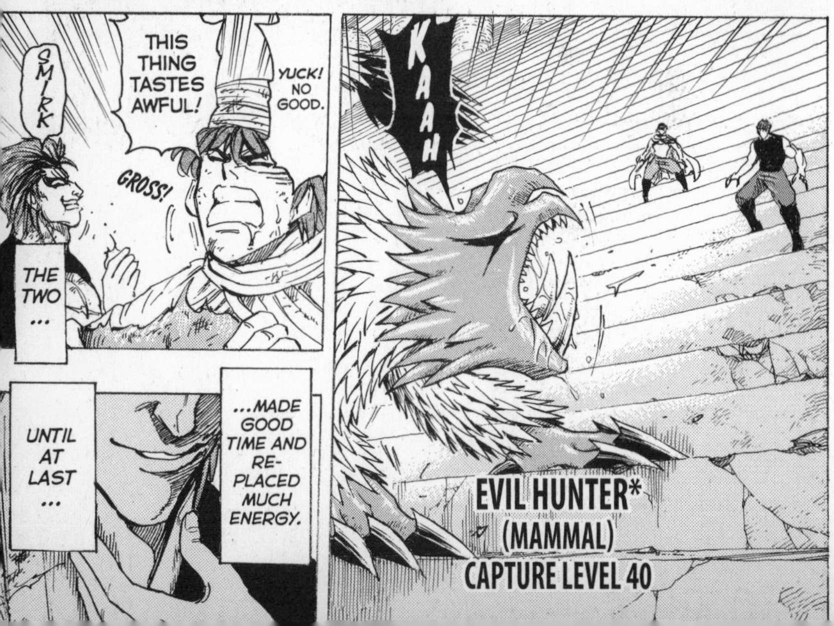
KAAAH
EVIL HUNTER*
(MAMMAL)
CAPTURE LEVEL 40
YUCK! NO GOOD.
THIS THING TASTES AWFUL!
SMIRK
GROSS!
THE TWO...
...MADE GOOD TIME AND RE-PLACED MUCH ENERGY.
UNTIL AT LAST...

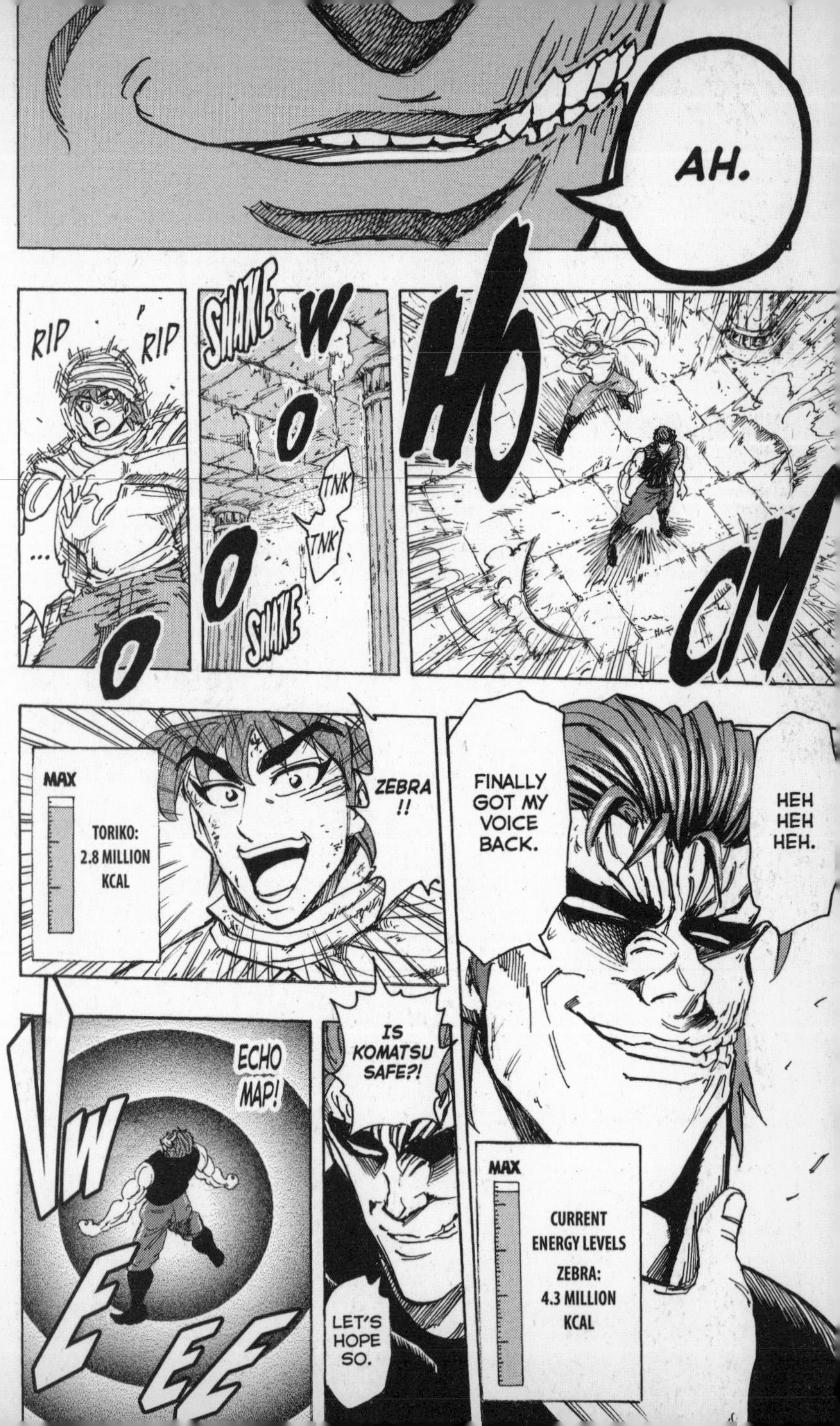
AH.
HO
OM
SHAKE
W
O
TNK
TNK
O
SHAKE
RIP
RIP
...
O
HEH HEH HEH.
FINALLY GOT MY VOICE BACK.
MAX
CURRENT ENERGY LEVELS
ZEBRA: 4.3 MILLION KCAL
ZEBRA!!
MAX
TORIKO: 2.8 MILLION KCAL
IS KOMATSU SAFE?!
LET'S HOPE SO.
ECHO MAP!
VWEEE

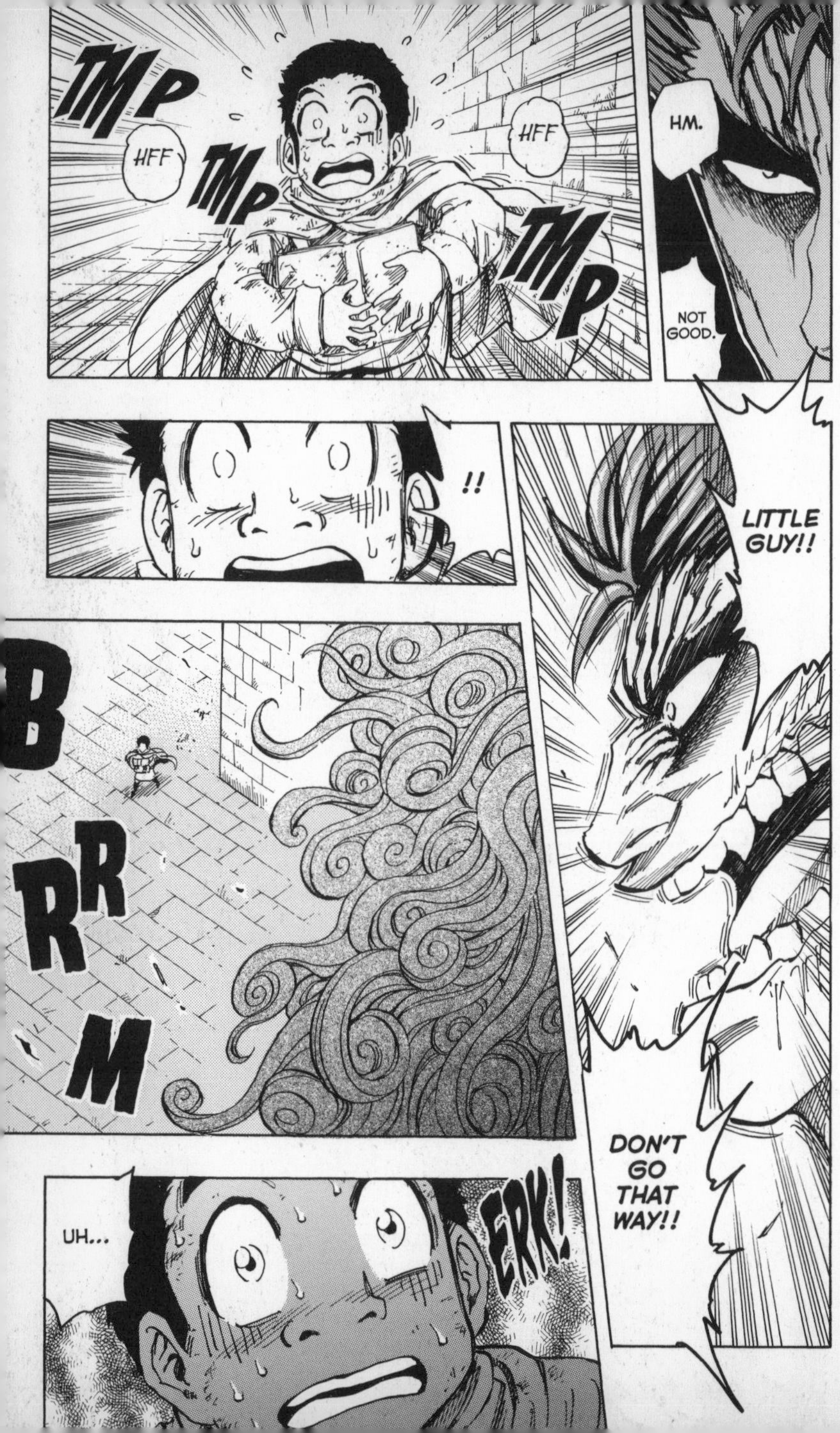

HM.
NOT GOOD.
HFF
TMP
TMP
HFF
TMP
LITTLE GUY!!
DON'T GO THAT WAY!!
!!
BRRRM
UH...
ERK!

TORIKO

GOURMET CHECKLIST

Vol. 156

OZONE GRASS
(VEGETABLE)

CAPTURE LEVEL: 68

HABITAT: VEGETABLE SKY

LENGTH: 50 CM; OUTER LEAVES

APPR. 15 METERS

HEIGHT: ---

WEIGHT: 1.5 KG

PRICE: 1 BILLION YEN PER LEAF

SCALE

THE KING OF VEGETABLE SKY'S VEGGIES. ITS CAPTURE LEVEL NEVER DIPS BELOW 60 THANKS TO ITS REMOTE HABITAT AND COMPLICATED CAPTURE PROCEDURE. THE ONLY WAY TO REACH THE JUICY PART OF OZONE GRASS IS TO PEEL THE EXTERIOR LEAVES AWAY TWO AT A TIME, STARTING WITH THE SMELLIEST. TWO PEOPLE MUST EAT IT AT THE SAME TIME, OR ELSE IT WILL ROT ON THE SPOT. THEREFORE, IT REQUIRES SPECIAL PREPARATION AS WELL AS SPECIAL CONSUMPTION. THIS FOOD SUITED TORIKO SO WELL THAT ITS DIVINE TASTE ADVANCED THE LEVEL OF HIS GOURMET CELLS. TORIKO AND KOMATSU FORMED THEIR PARTNERSHIP AROUND OZONE GRASS, AS THEY WOULD NOT HAVE BEEN ABLE TO CAPTURE OR EAT IT IF THEY HAD NOT COMBINED THEIR STRENGTHS. OZONE GRASS SYMBOLIZES THEIR PARTNERSHIP.

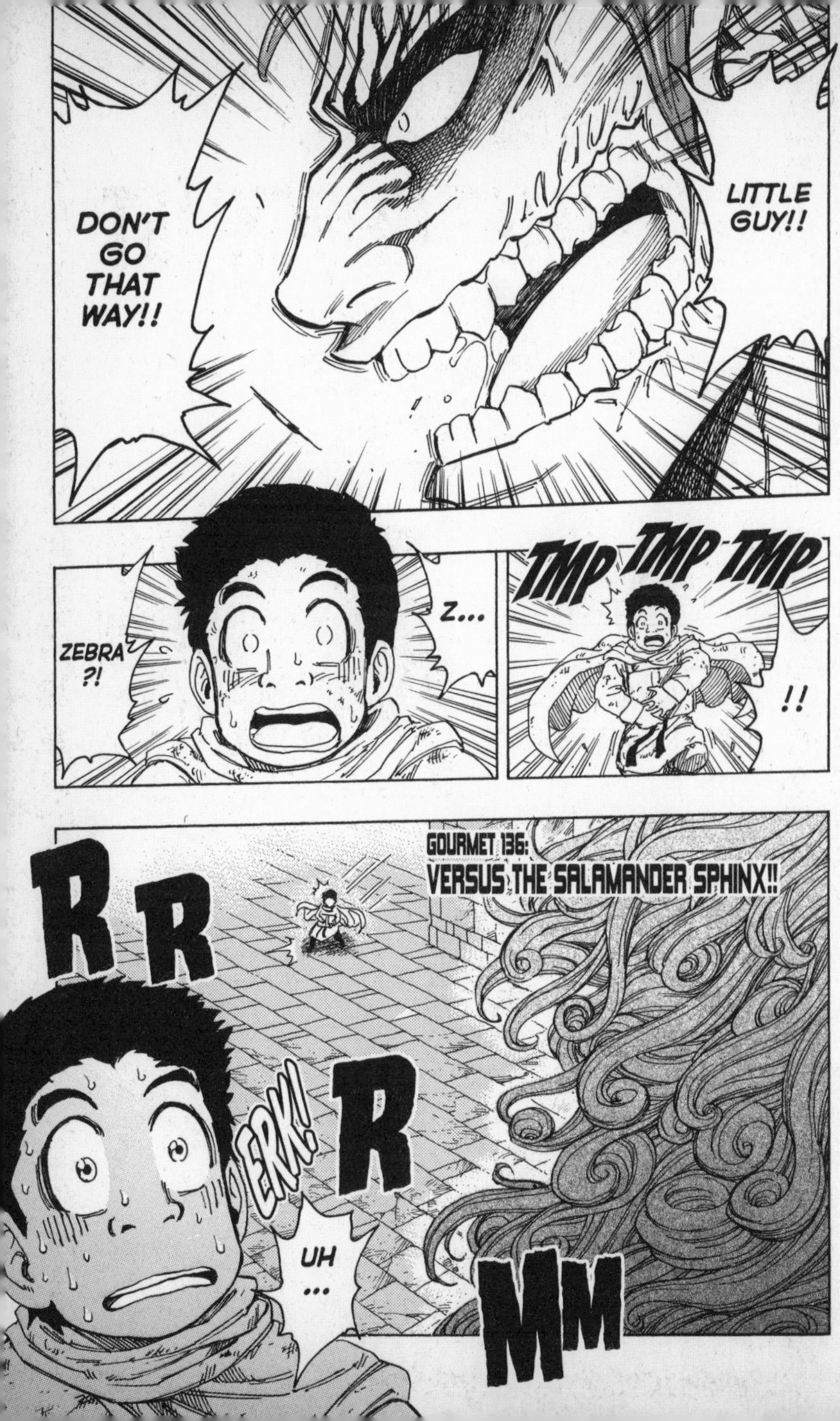
LITTLE GUY!!
DON'T GO THAT WAY!!
TMP TMP TMP
!!
Z...
ZEBRA ?!
GOURMET 136:
VERSUS THE SALAMANDER SPHINX!!
RRRMM
ERK!
UH ...

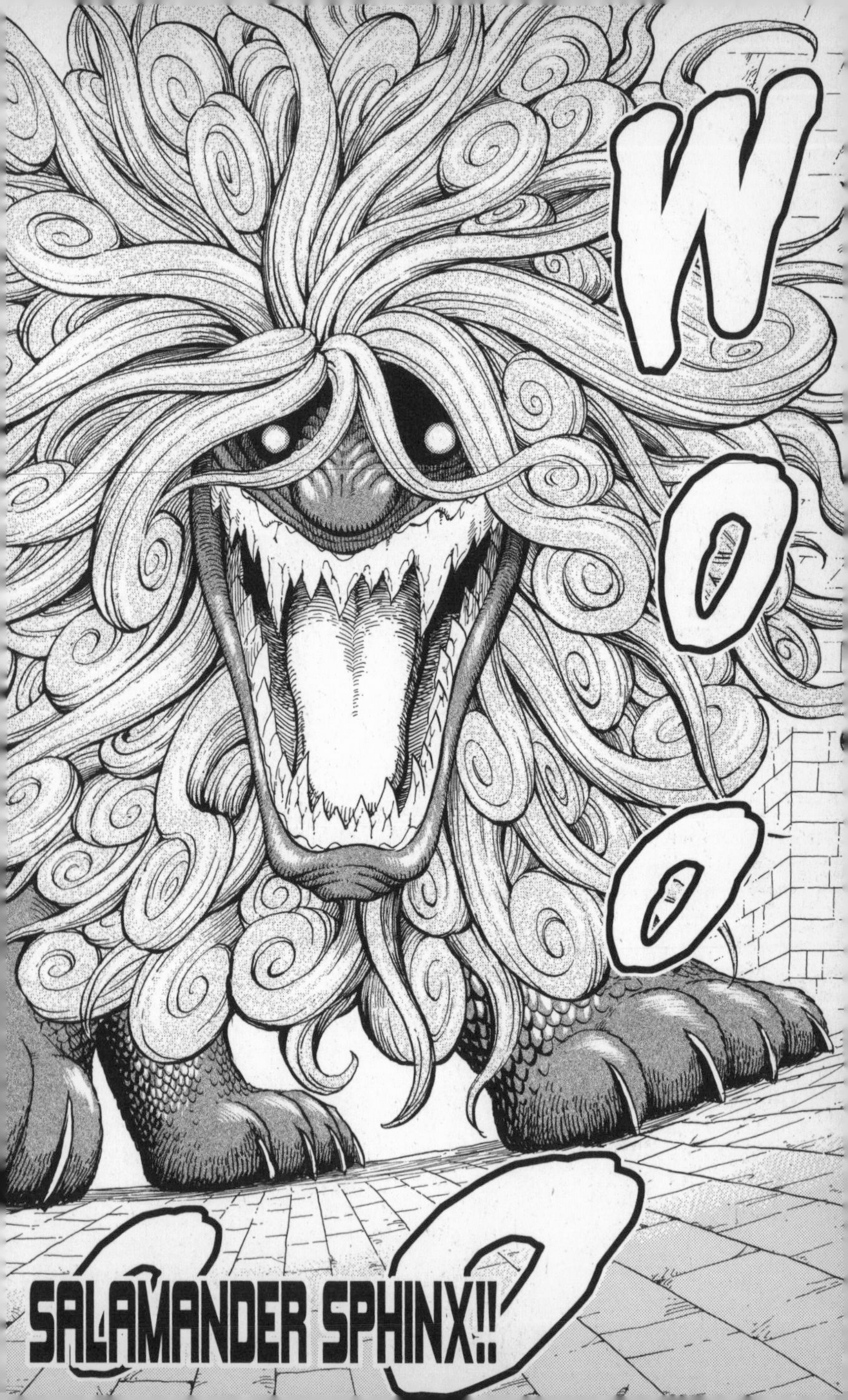
WOOOO
SALAMANDER SPHINX!!

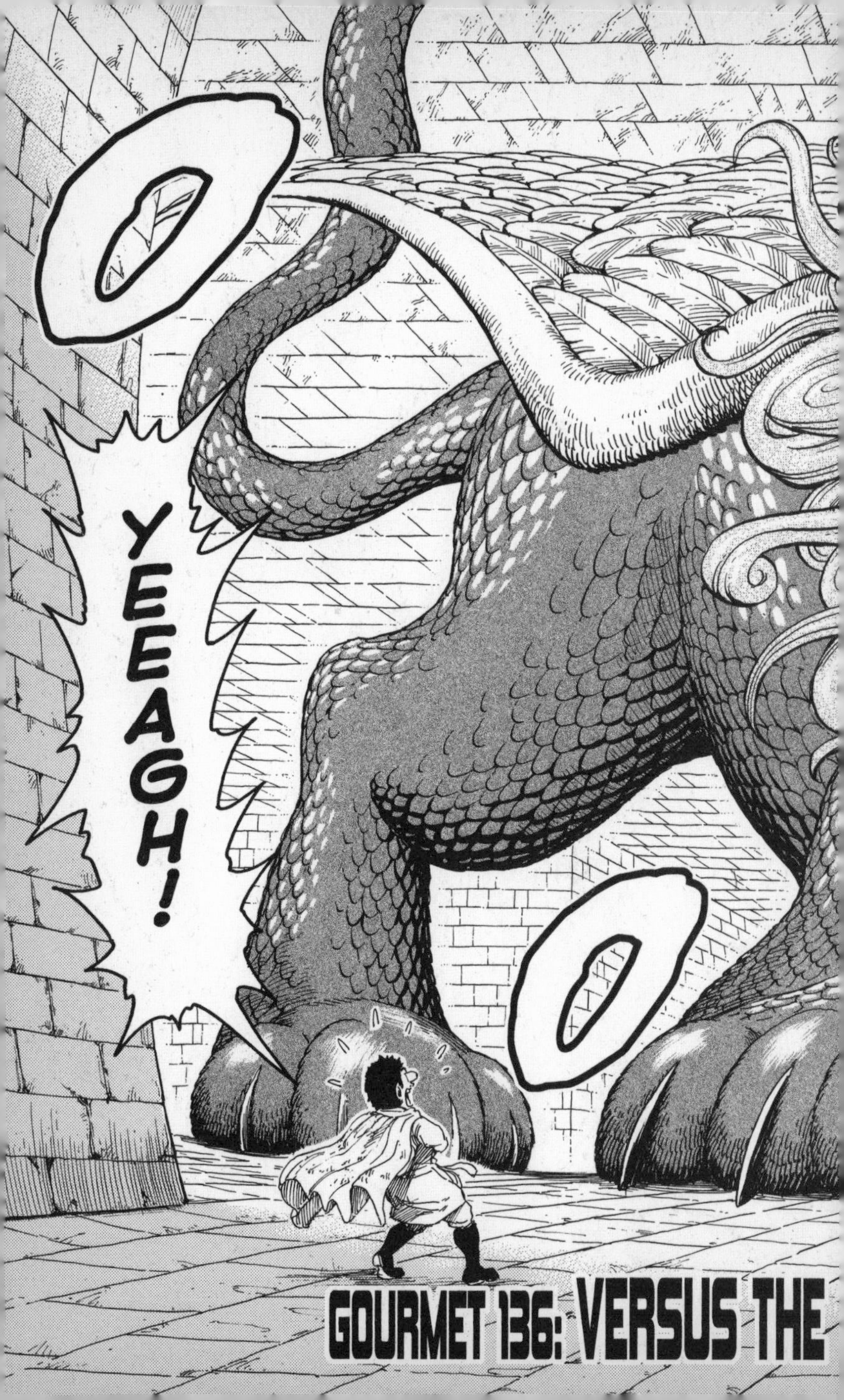
YEEAGH!
GOURMET 136: VERSUS THE

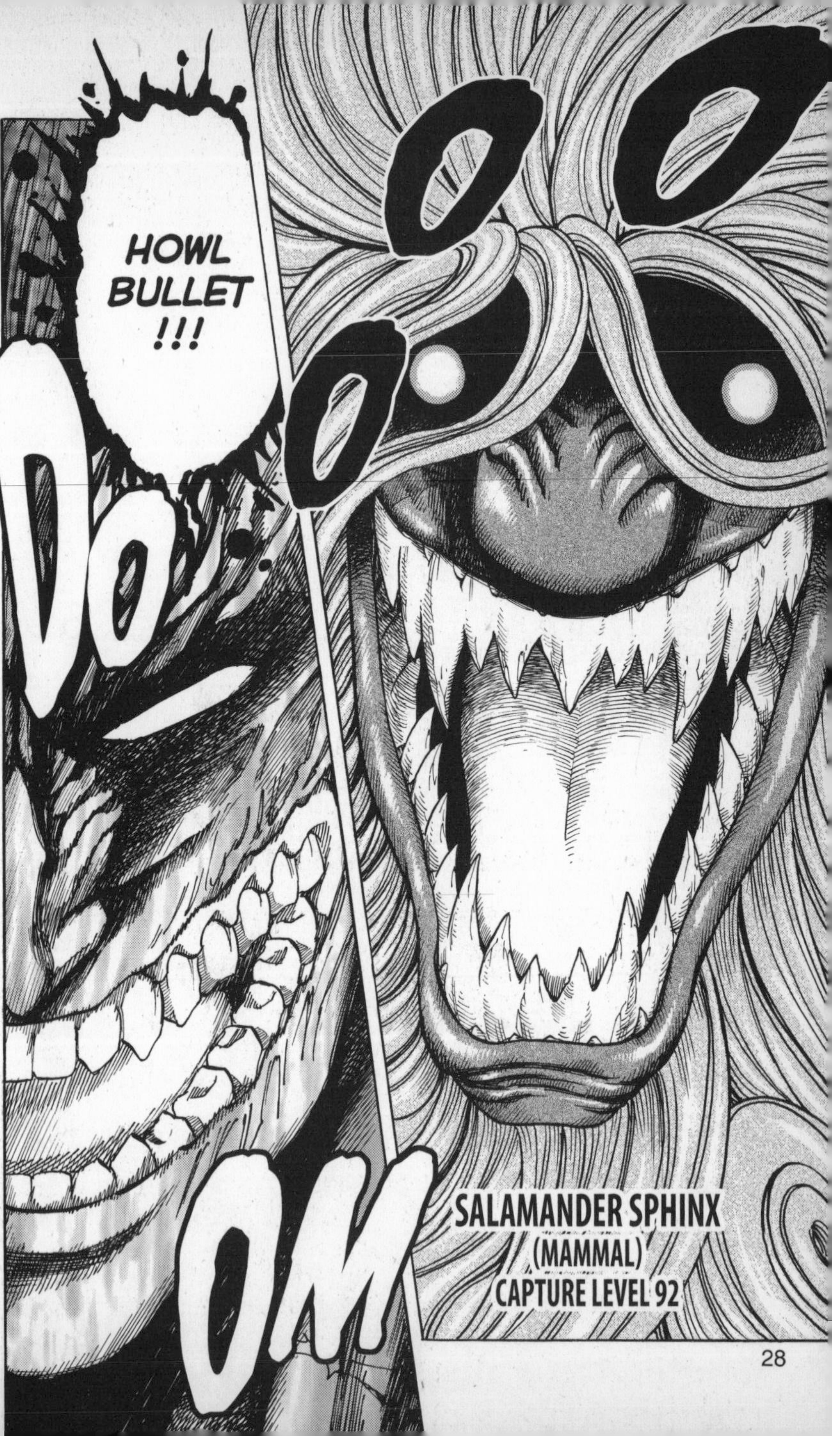
SALAMANDER SPHINX
(MAMMAL)
CAPTURE LEVEL 92
HOWL BULLET !!!

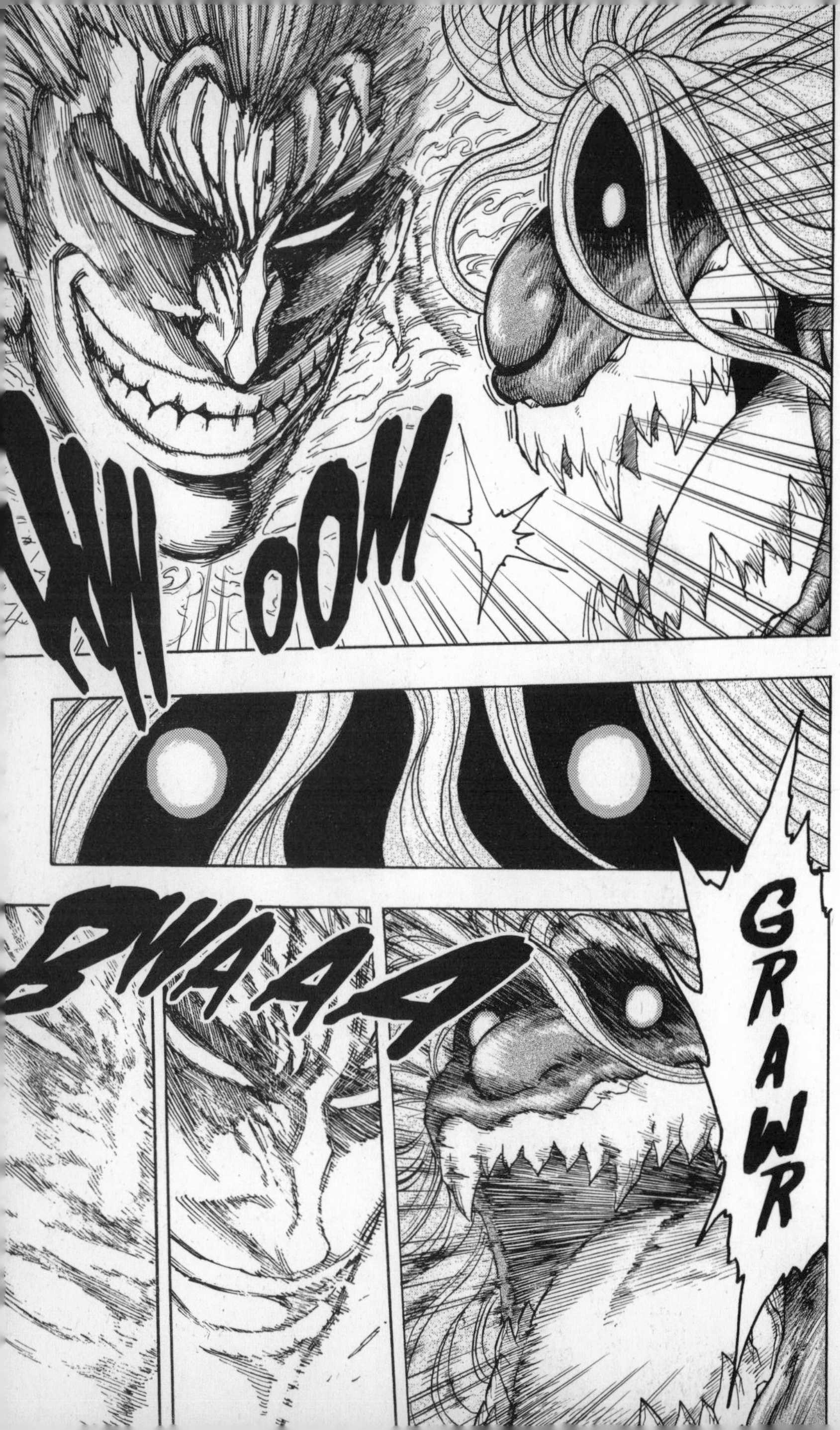
WHOOM
GRAWR
BWAAAA

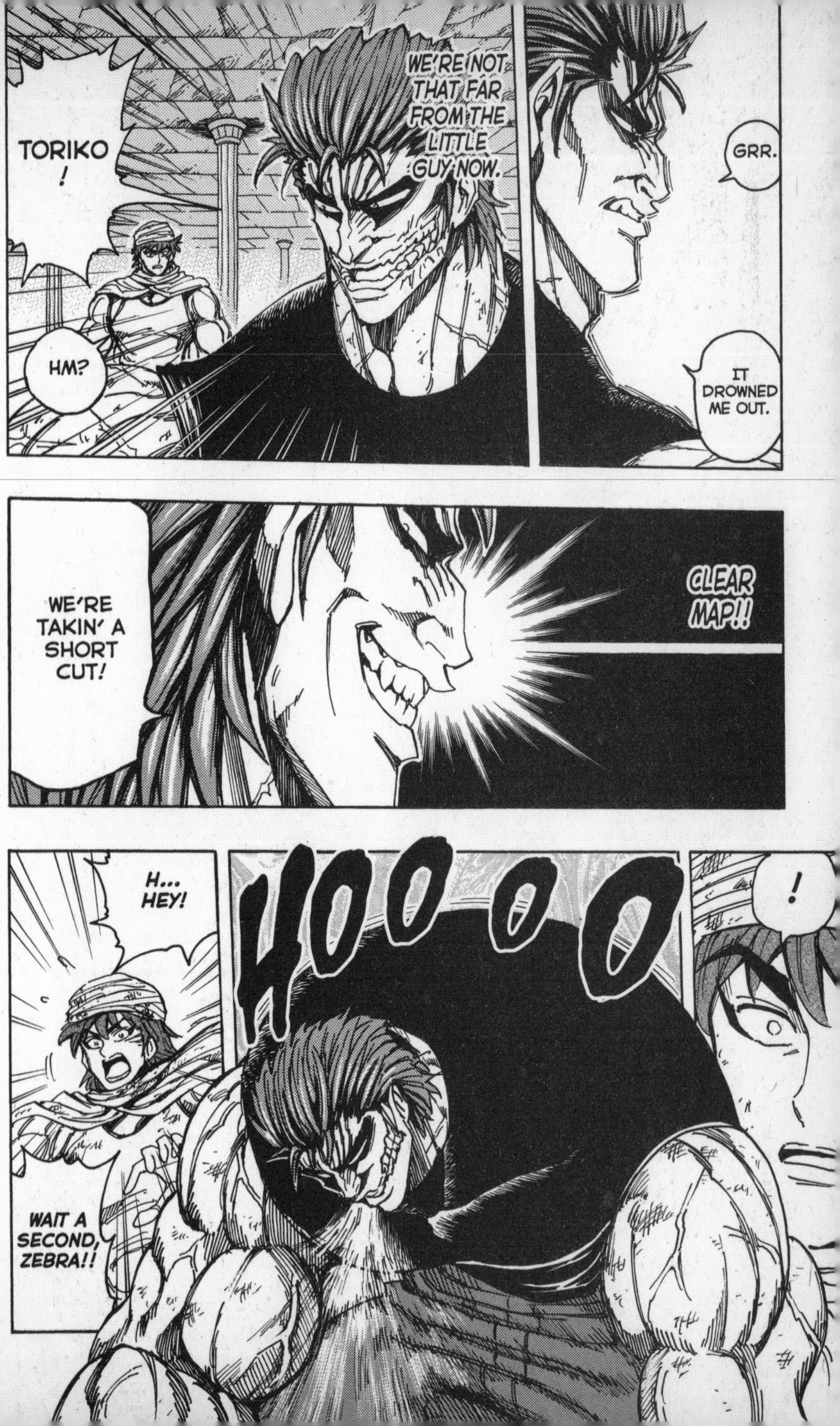
GRR.
IT DROWNED ME OUT.
WE'RE NOT THAT FAR FROM THE LITTLE GUY NOW.
TORIKO!
HM?
CLEAR MAP!!
WE'RE TAKIN' A SHORT CUT!
!
HOOOO
H... HEY!
WAIT A SECOND, ZEBRA!!

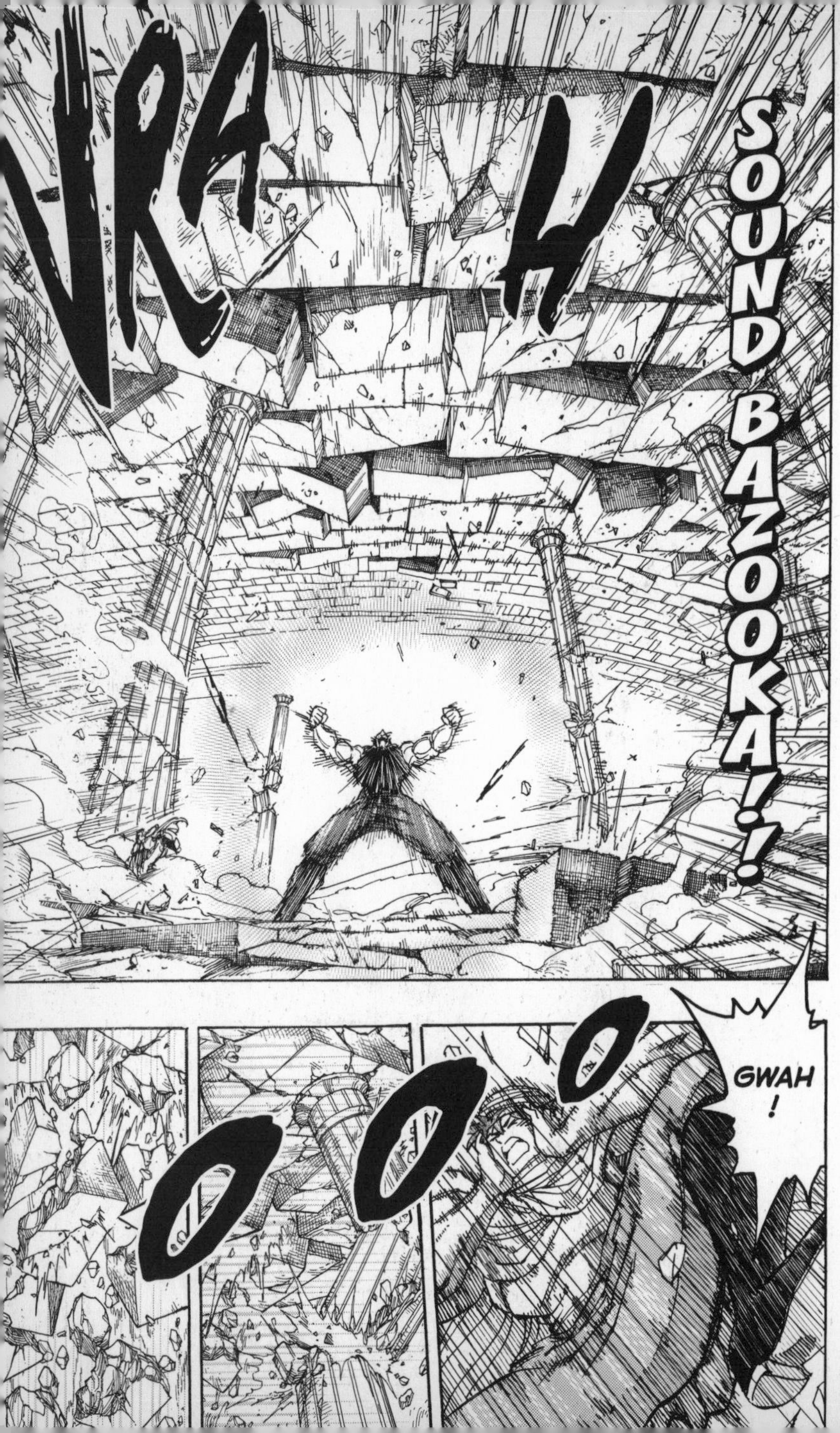

SOUND BAZOOKA!!
VRAA
GWAH!
OOOO

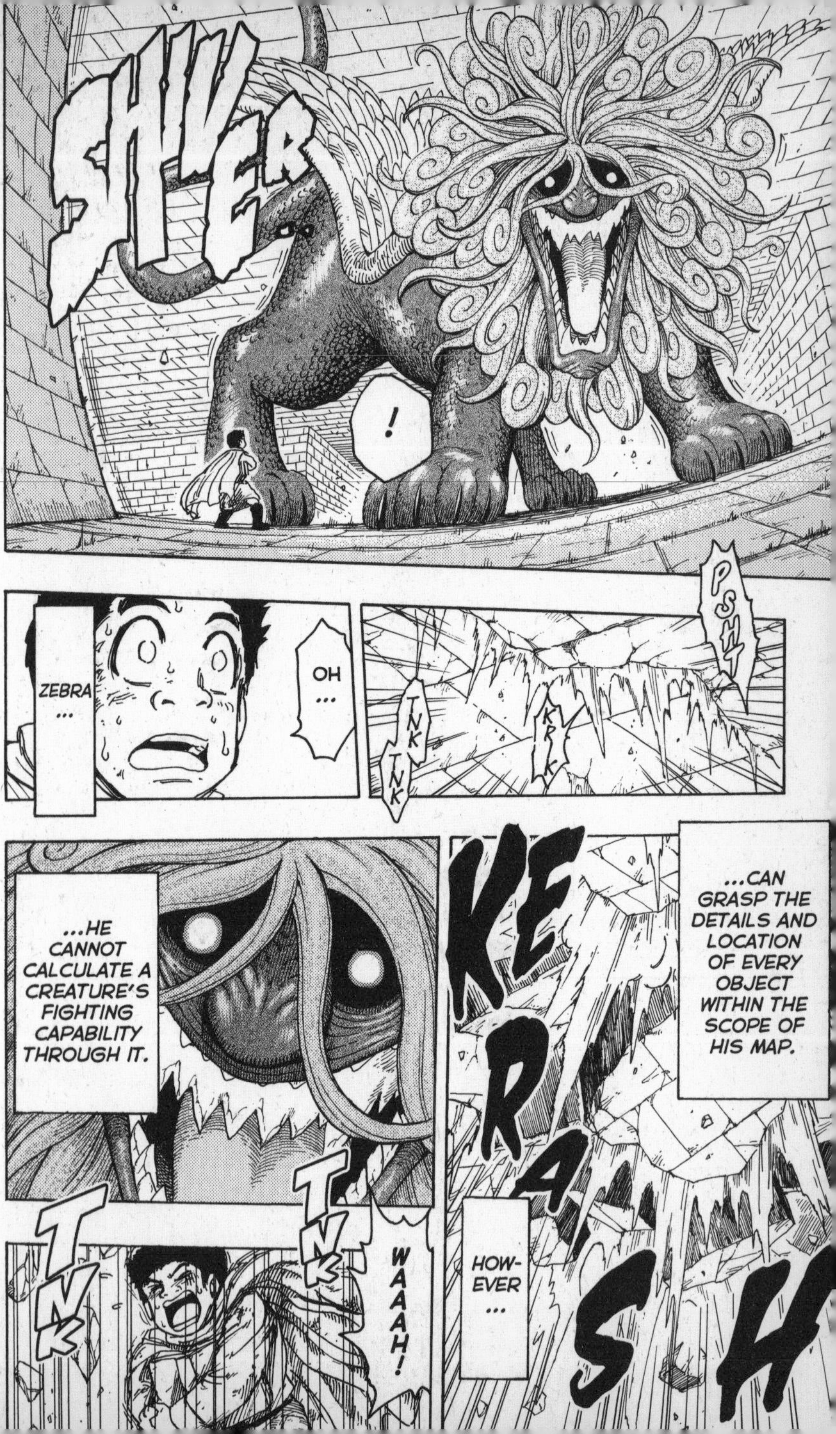
SHIVER
!
PSHT
KRK
TNK TNK
OH ...
ZEBRA ...
...CAN GRASP THE DETAILS AND LOCATION OF EVERY OBJECT WITHIN THE SCOPE OF HIS MAP.
KERRASH
HOW-EVER ...
...HE CANNOT CALCULATE A CREATURE'S FIGHTING CAPABILITY THROUGH IT.
TNK
WAAAAH!
TNK

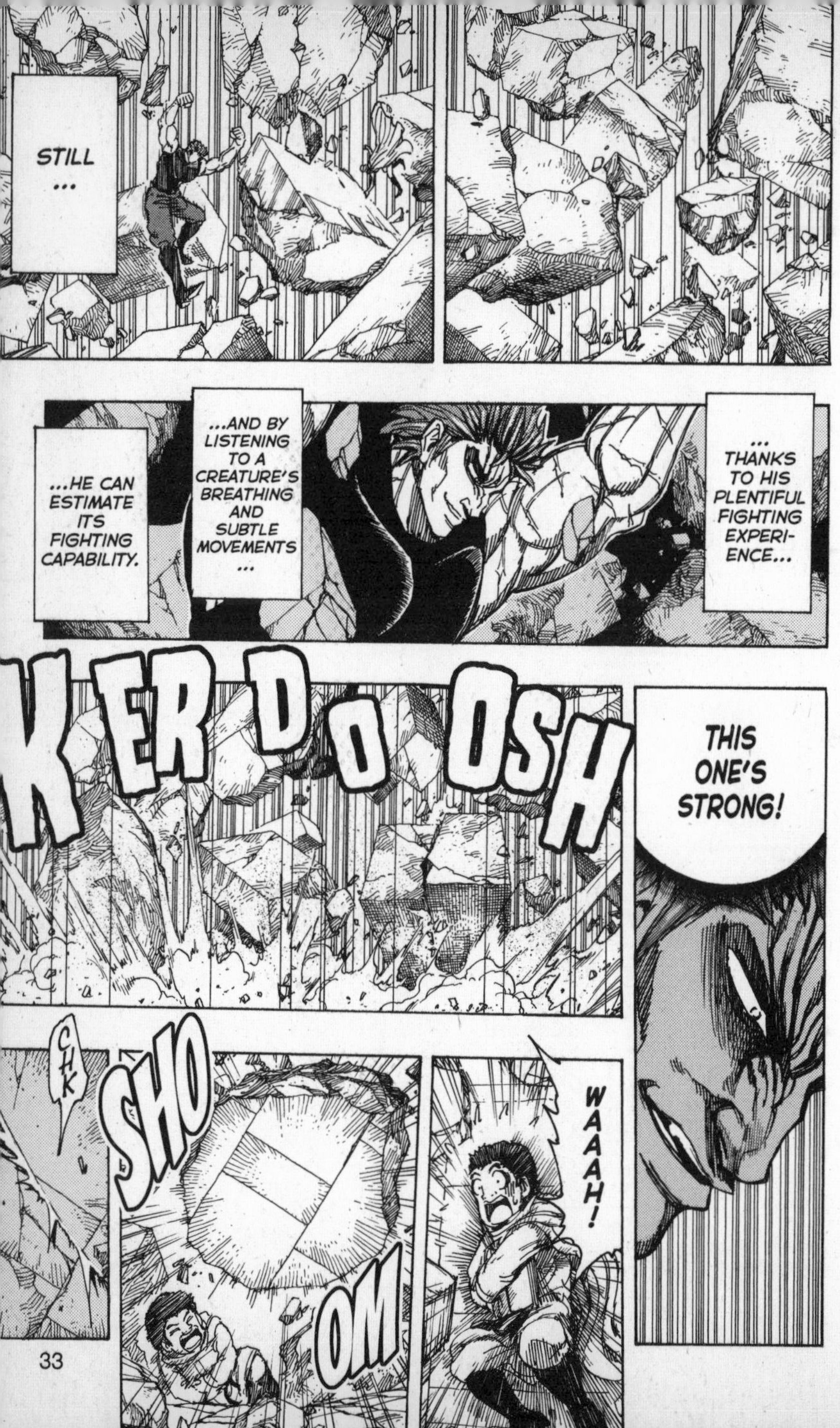
STILL ...
... THANKS TO HIS PLENTIFUL FIGHTING EXPERIENCE...
...AND BY LISTENING TO A CREATURE'S BREATHING AND SUBTLE MOVEMENTS ...
...HE CAN ESTIMATE ITS FIGHTING CAPABILITY.
THIS ONE'S STRONG!
KERDOOSH
WAAAH!
SHOOM
CHK

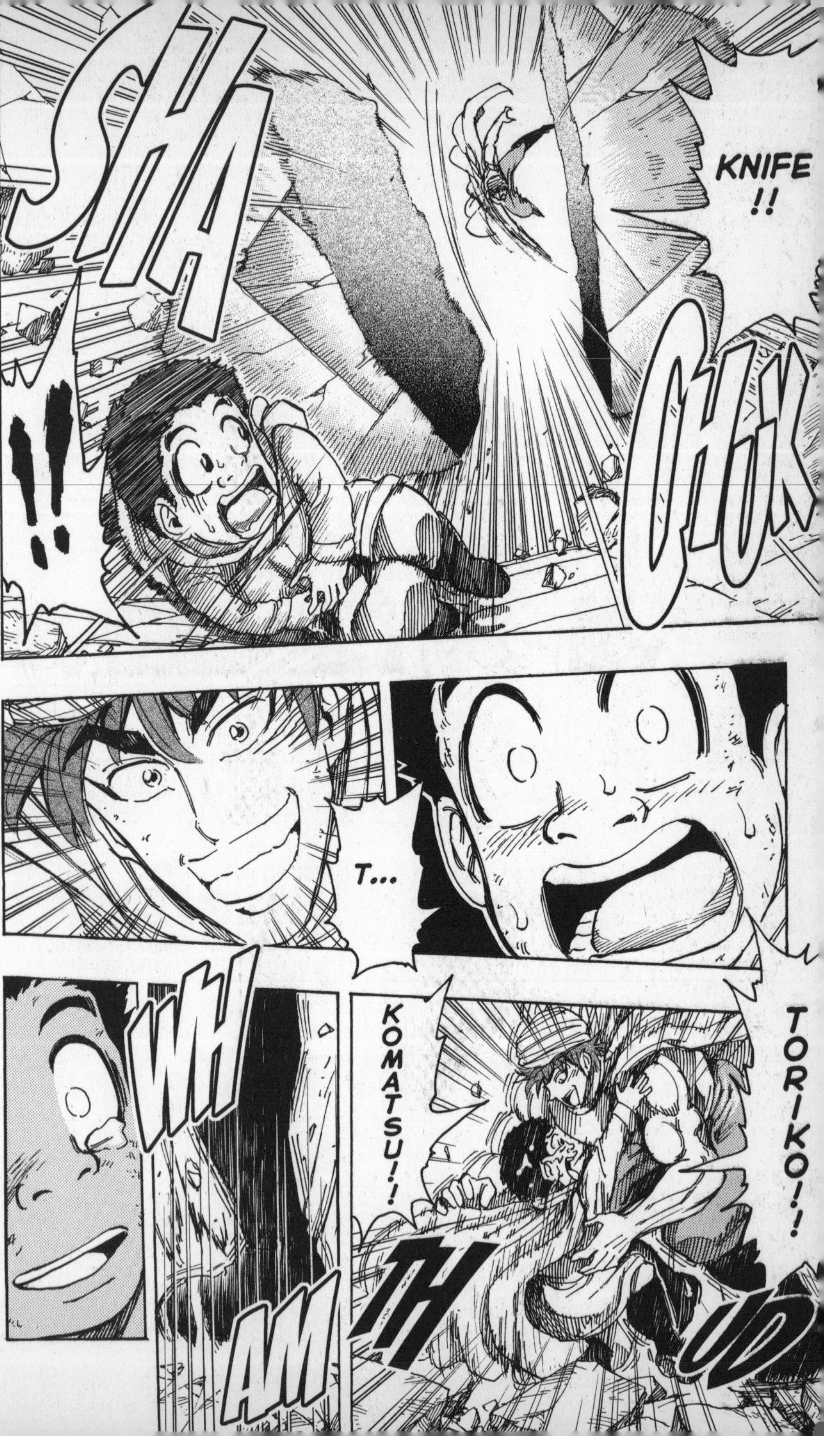
KNIFE !!
CHIN
SHA
!!
T...
TORIKO!!
KOMATSU!!
THUD
WHAM

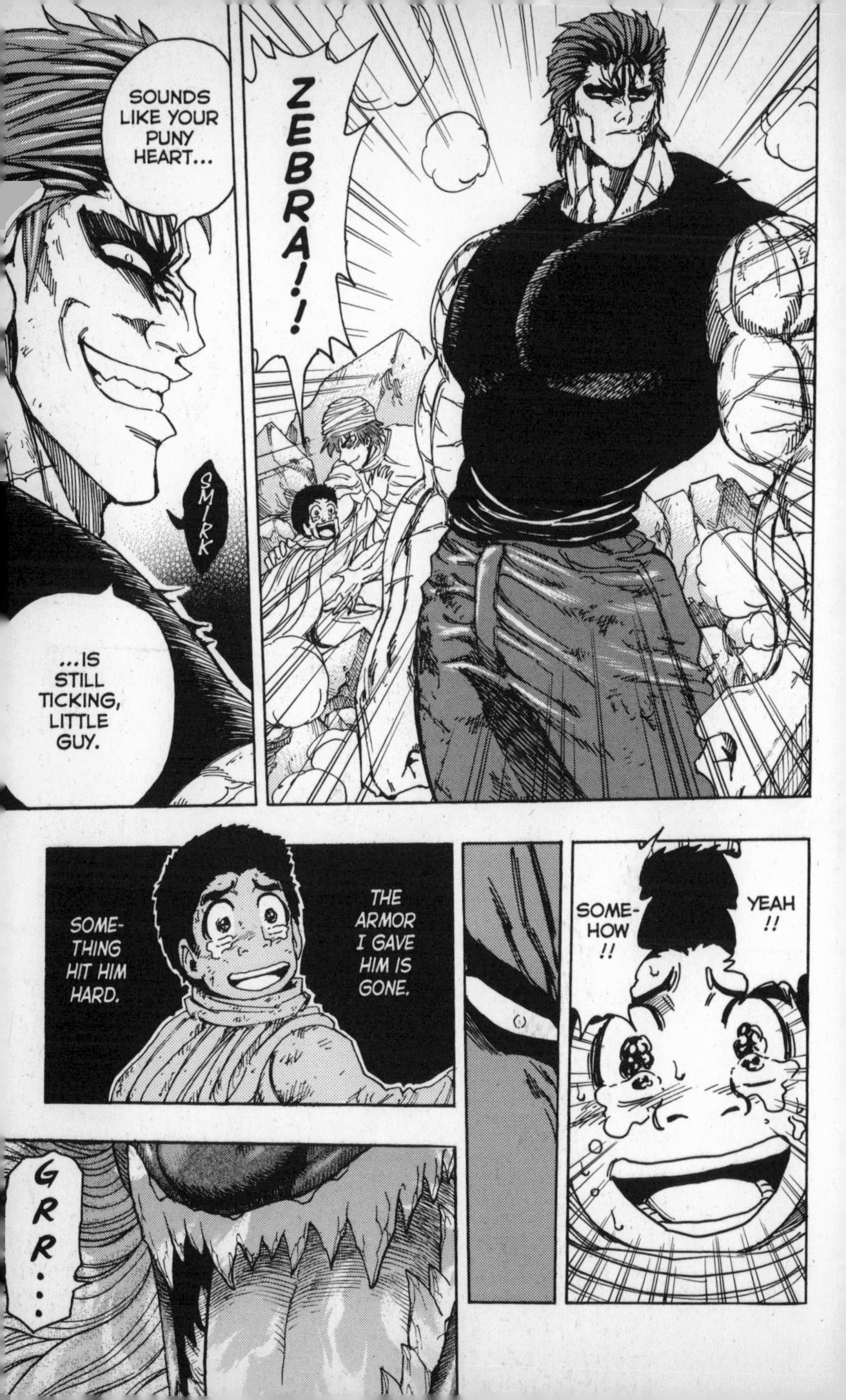
ZEBRA!!
SOUNDS LIKE YOUR PUNY HEART...
SMIRK
...IS STILL TICKING, LITTLE GUY.
YEAH!!
SOMEHOW!!
THE ARMOR I GAVE HIM IS GONE.
SOMETHING HIT HIM HARD.
GRR...

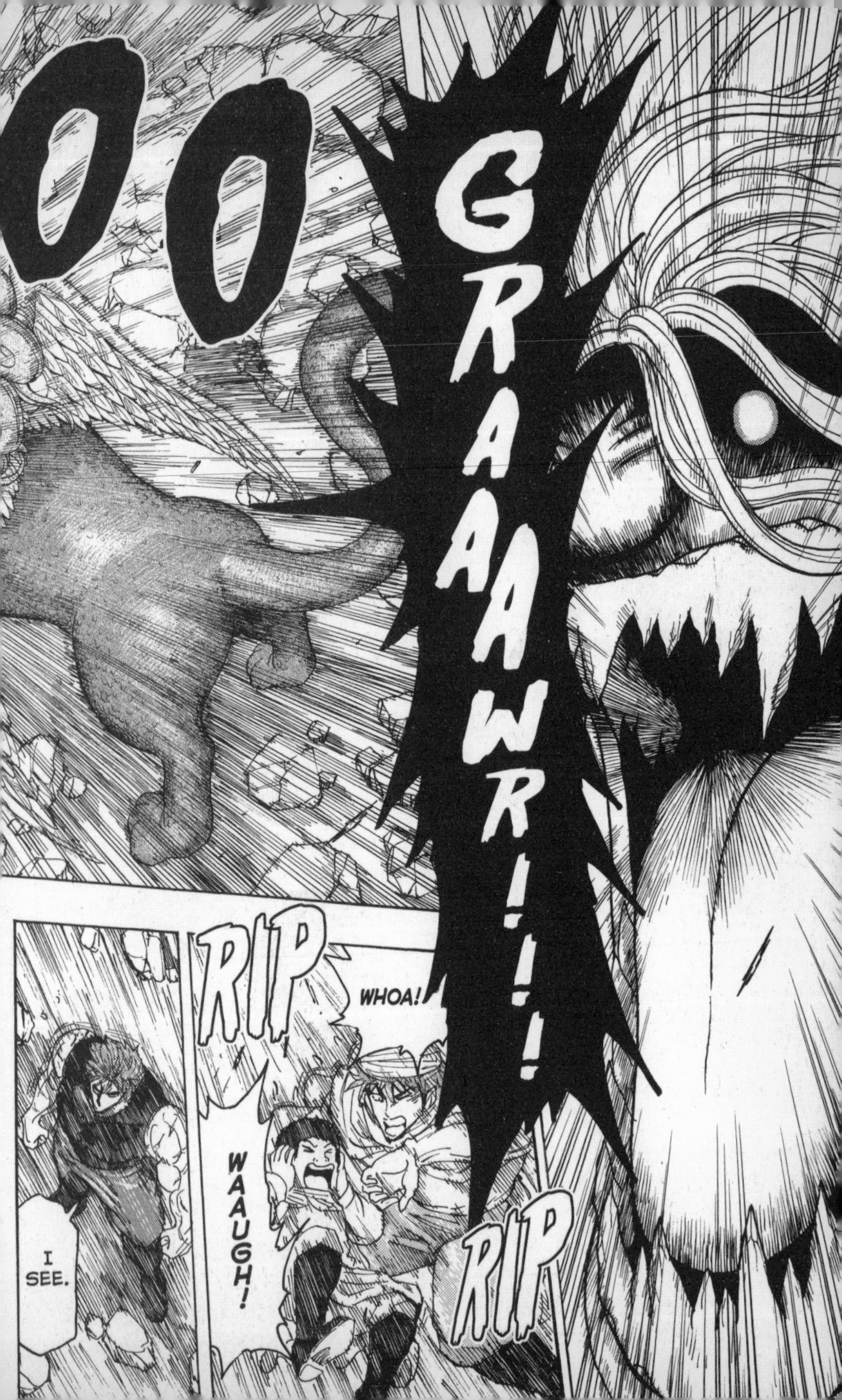

GRAAAWR!!!
OO
WHOA!
RIP
WAAAUGH!
RIP
I SEE.

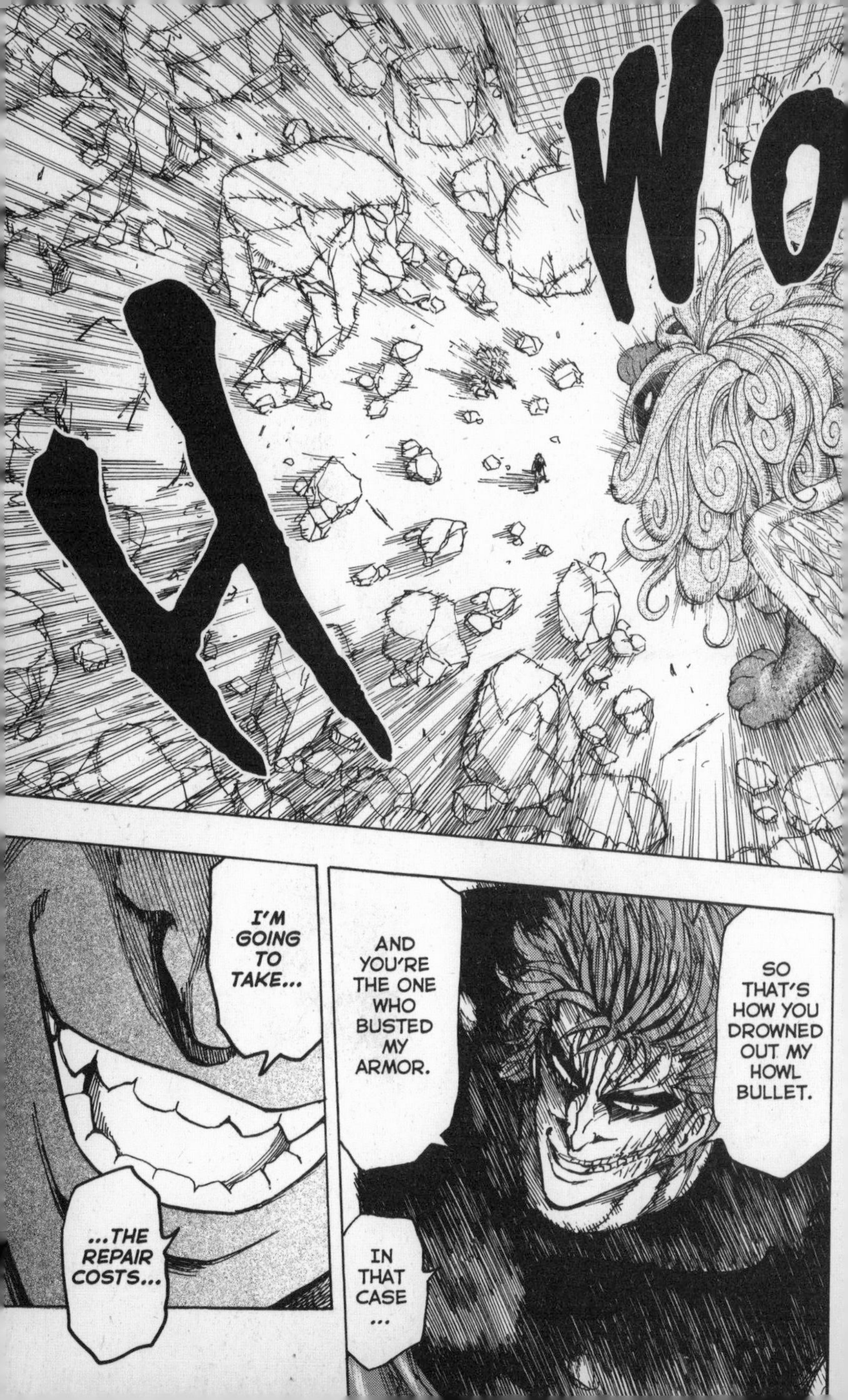
WOH
SO THAT'S HOW YOU DROWNED OUT MY HOWL BULLET.
AND YOU'RE THE ONE WHO BUSTED MY ARMOR.
IN THAT CASE...
I'M GOING TO TAKE...
...THE REPAIR COSTS...

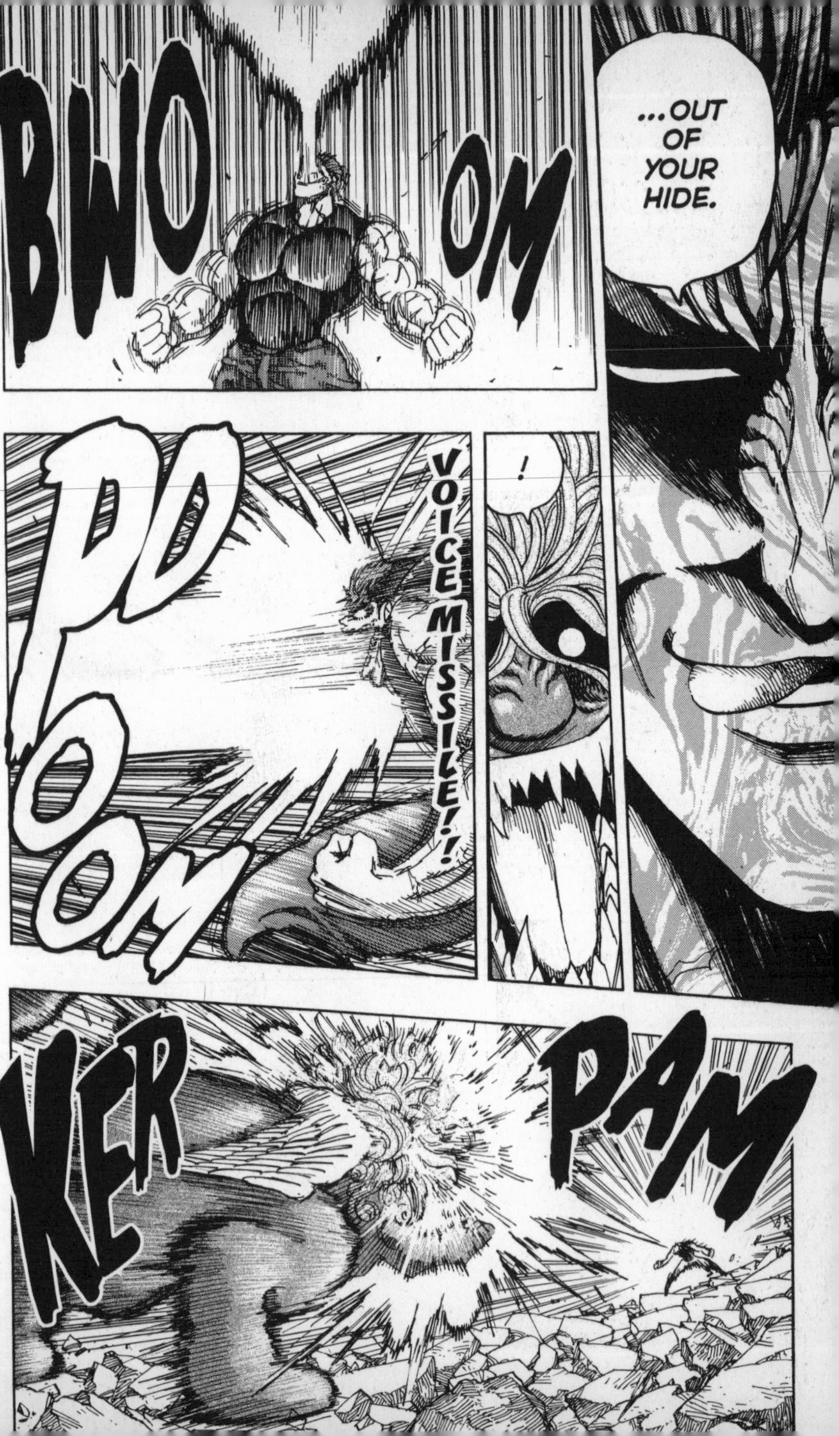
...OUT OF YOUR HIDE.
BWOOM
!
VOICE MISSILE!!
PDOOM
KERPAM

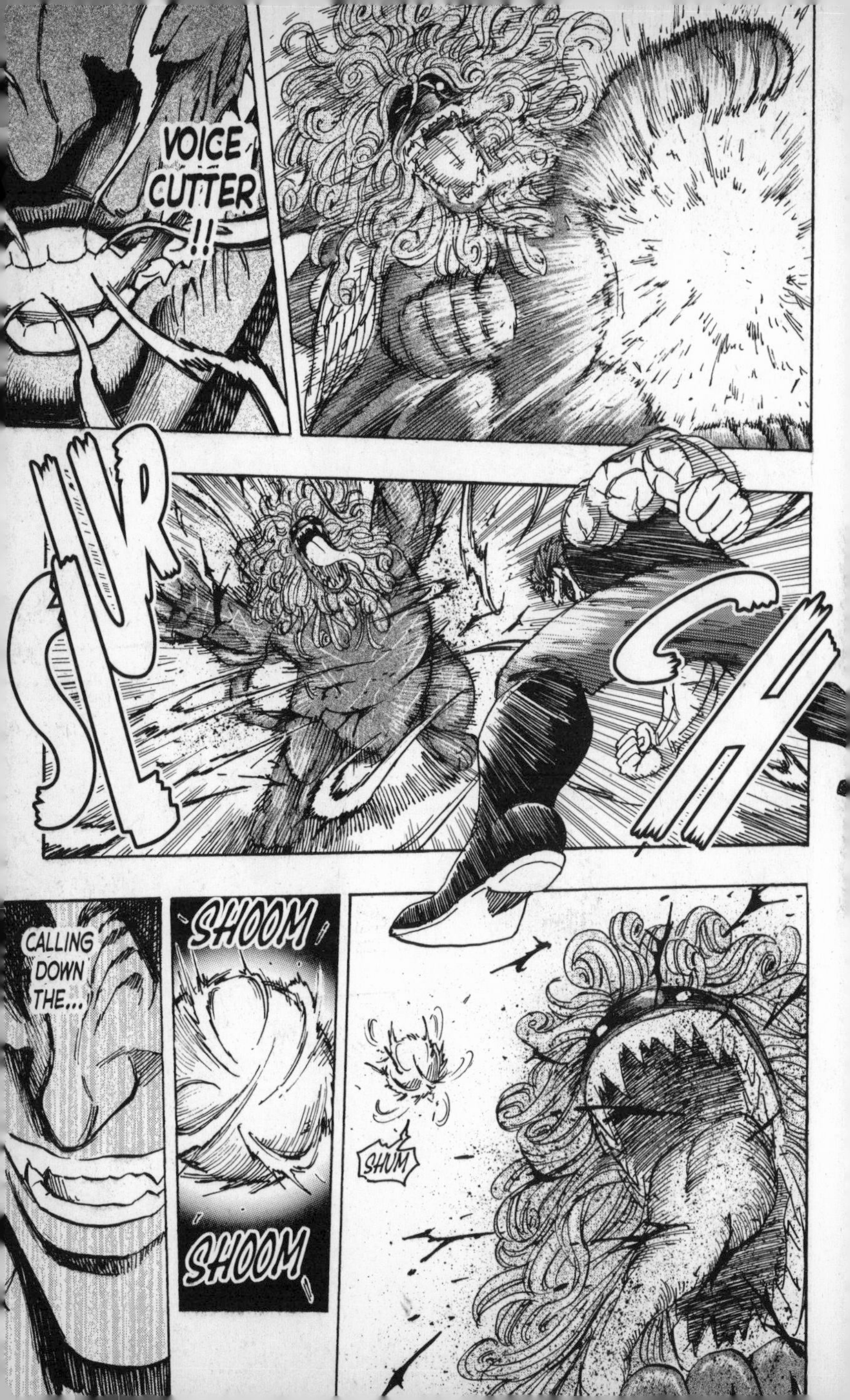
VOICE CUTTER!!
SUR
CH
CALLING DOWN THE...
SHOOM
SHOOM
SHUM

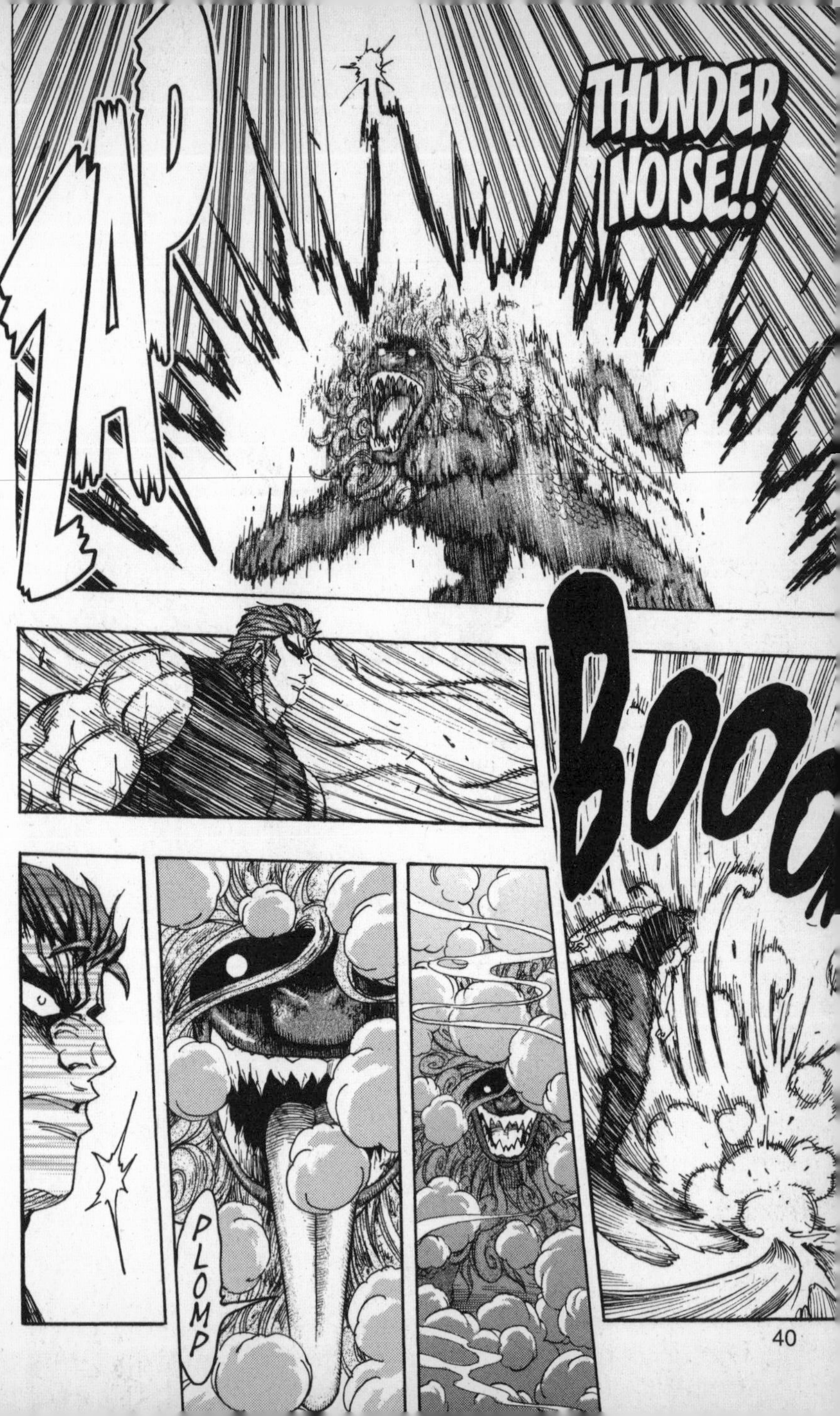
THUNDER NOISE!!
ZAP
BOOO
PLOMP

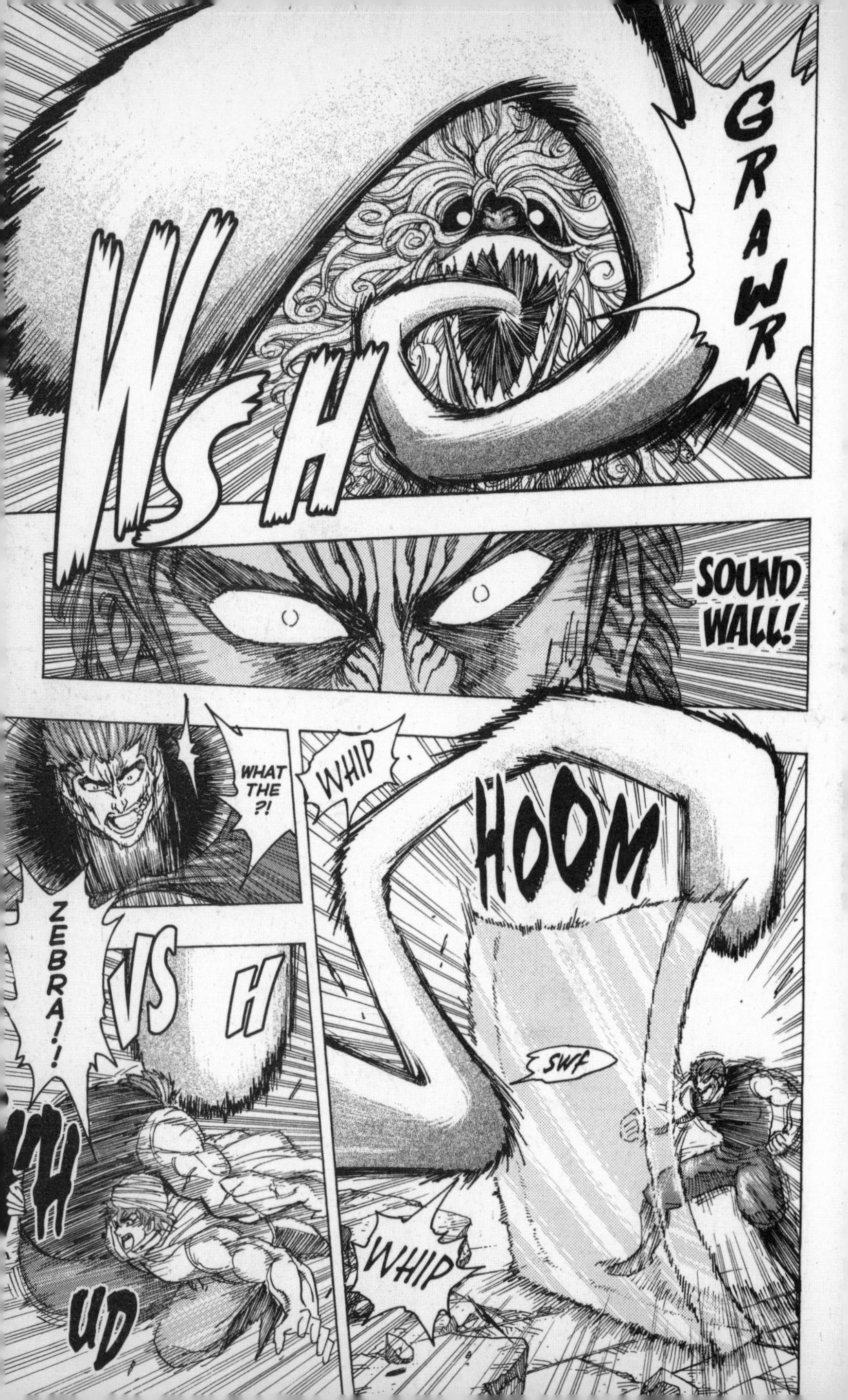
GRAWR
WSH
SOUND WALL!
WHIP
HOOM
SWF
WHIP
WHAT THE ?!
ZEBRA!!
VSH
THUD

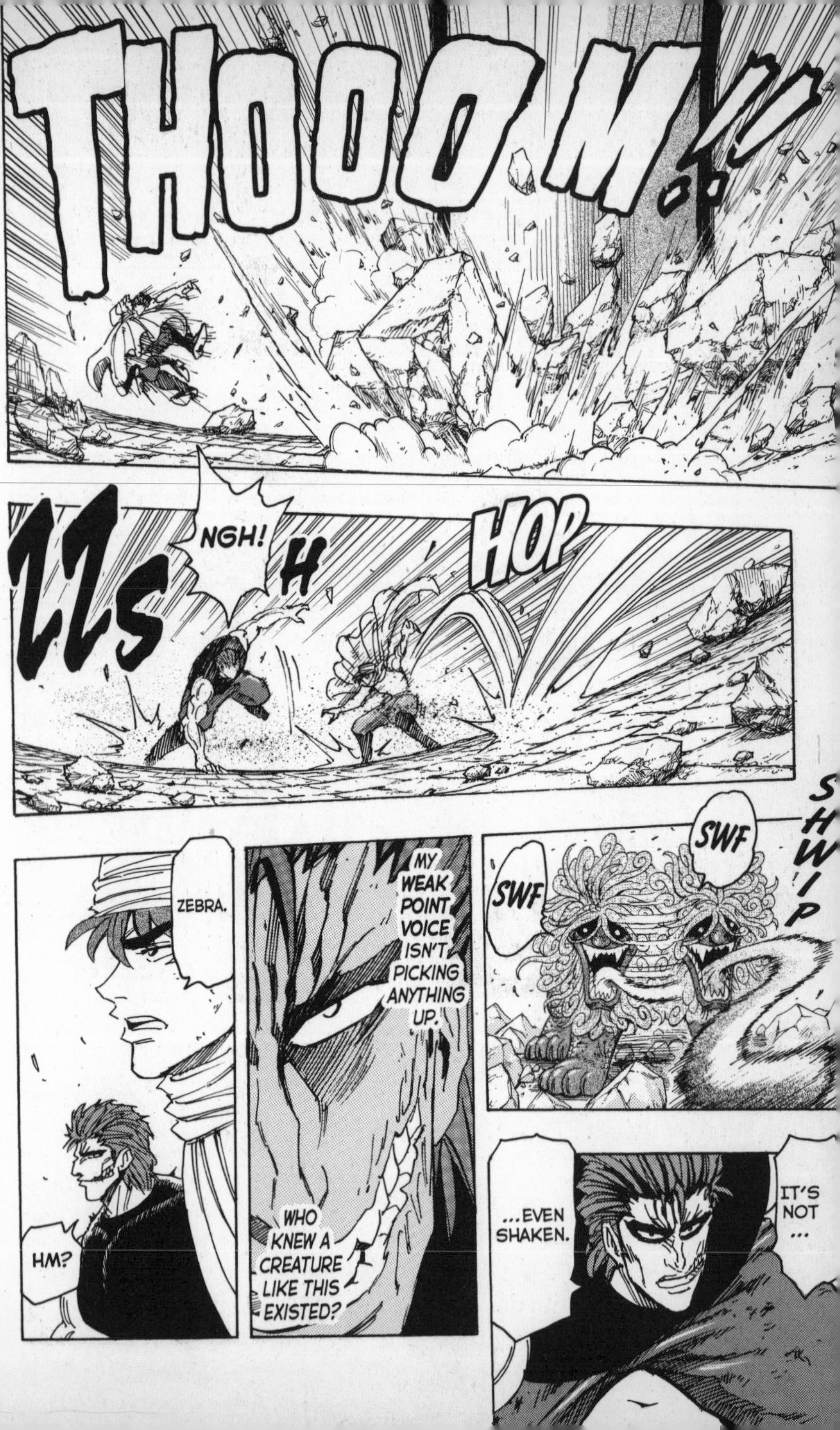
THOOOM!!
HOP
NGH!
ZZSH
SHWIP
SWF
SWF
IT'S NOT...
...EVEN SHAKEN.
MY WEAK POINT VOICE ISN'T PICKING ANYTHING UP.
WHO KNEW A CREATURE LIKE THIS EXISTED?
ZEBRA.
HM?

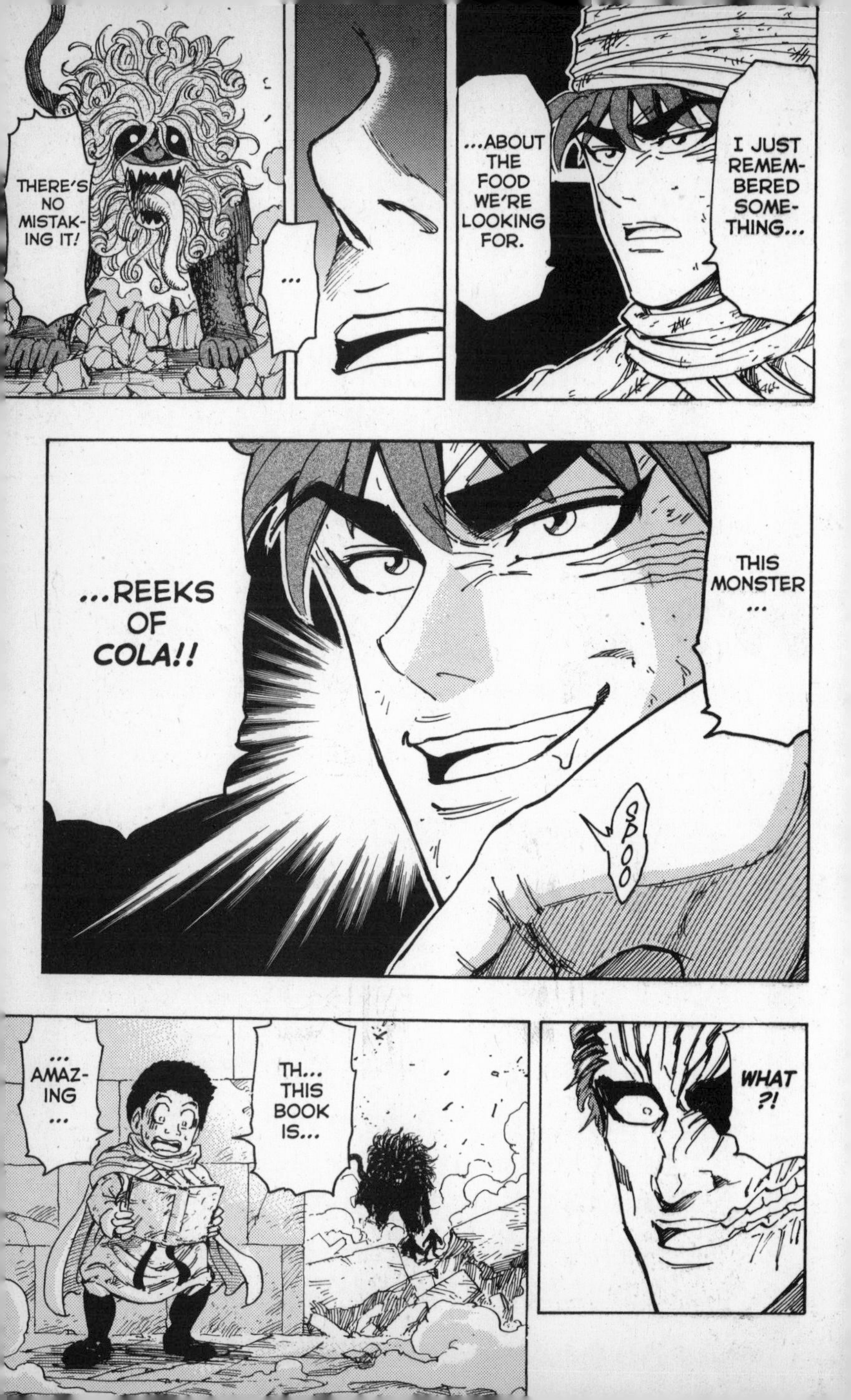
I JUST REMEMBERED SOMETHING...
...ABOUT THE FOOD WE'RE LOOKING FOR.
...
THERE'S NO MISTAKING IT!
THIS MONSTER...
...REEKS OF COLA!!
SPOO
WHAT?!
TH... THIS BOOK IS...
...AMAZING...

TORIKO

GOURMET CHECKLIST

Vol. 157

CHESTNUT SEA URCHIN
(MARINE ANIMAL)

CAPTURE LEVEL: 4

HABITAT: MOST OCEANS

LENGTH: 12 CM

HEIGHT: --

WEIGHT: 400 G

PRICE: 4,500 YEN PER URCHIN

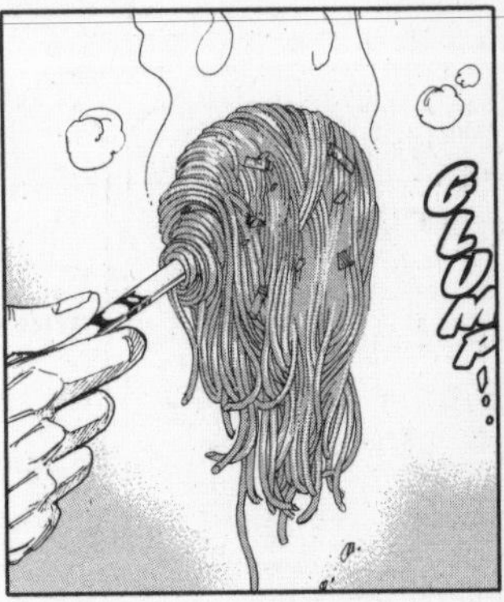
GLUMP!..

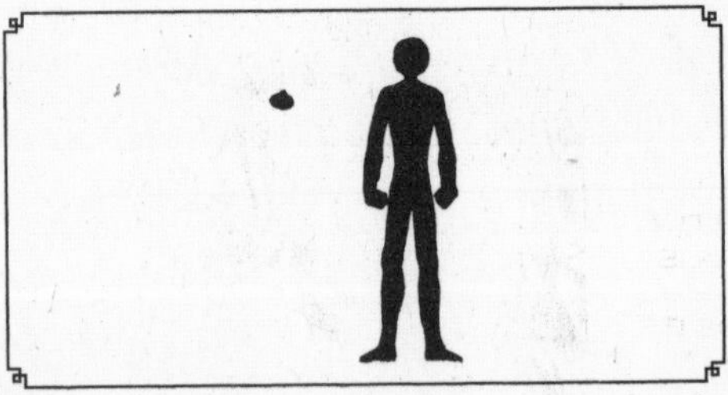

SCALE

AN ECHINODERM THAT LIVES IN THE OCEANS. ITS SHELL IS HARD; ITS NATURE SIMILAR TO THE GORI LEEK. ITS NEEDLES CAN BE USED AS ICE PICKS BUT ITS FLESH IS SOFT AND PUFFY. CHESTNUT SEA URCHIN TASTES RICH AND SMOOTH, MAKING IT A PERFECT BASE FOR PASTA NOODLES.

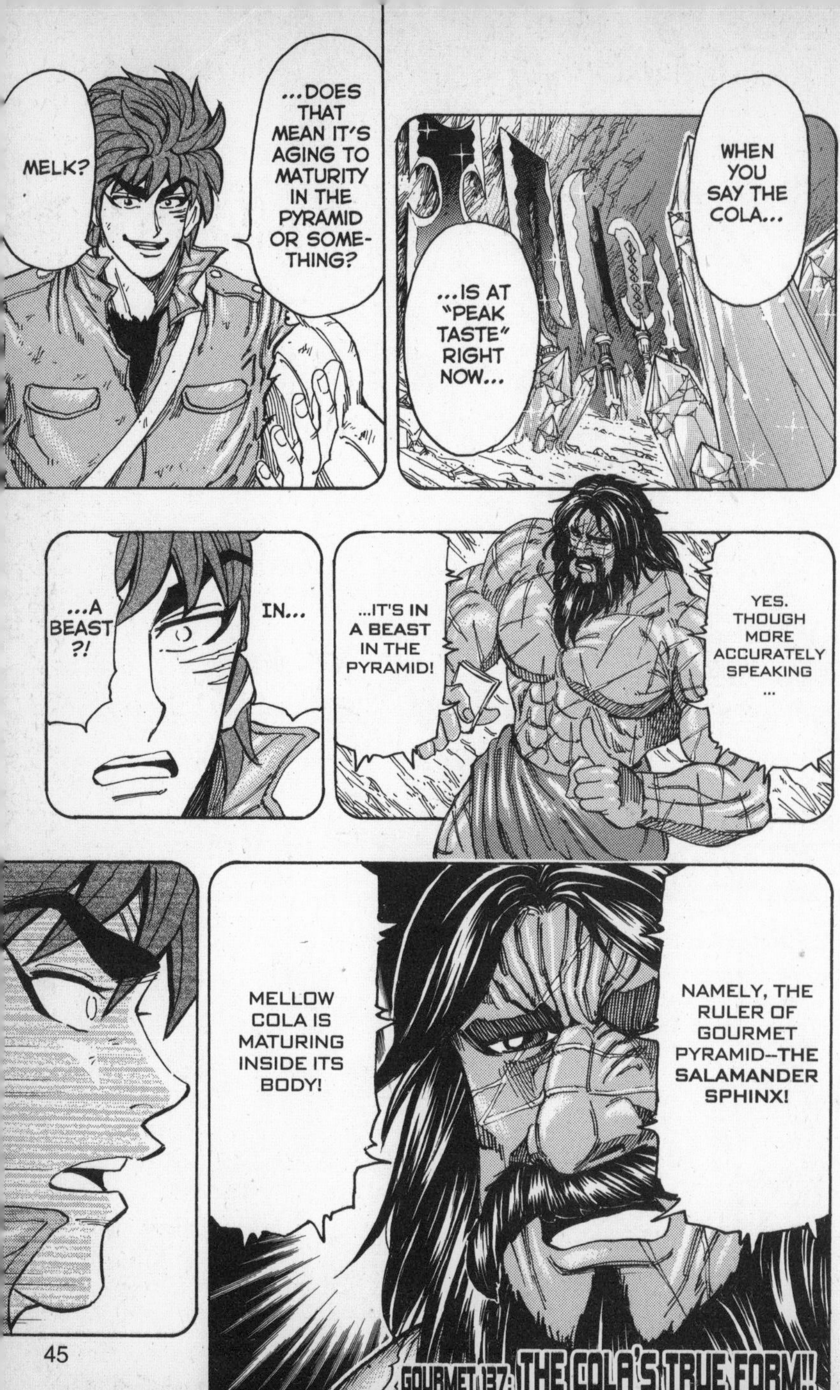
WHEN YOU SAY THE COLA...
...IS AT "PEAK TASTE" RIGHT NOW...
...DOES THAT MEAN IT'S AGING TO MATURITY IN THE PYRAMID OR SOMETHING?
MELK?
YES. THOUGH MORE ACCURATELY SPEAKING...
...IT'S IN A BEAST IN THE PYRAMID!
IN...
...A BEAST?!
NAMELY, THE RULER OF GOURMET PYRAMID--THE SALAMANDER SPHINX!
MELLOW COLA IS MATURING INSIDE ITS BODY!
GOURMET 137: THE COLA'S TRUE FORM!!

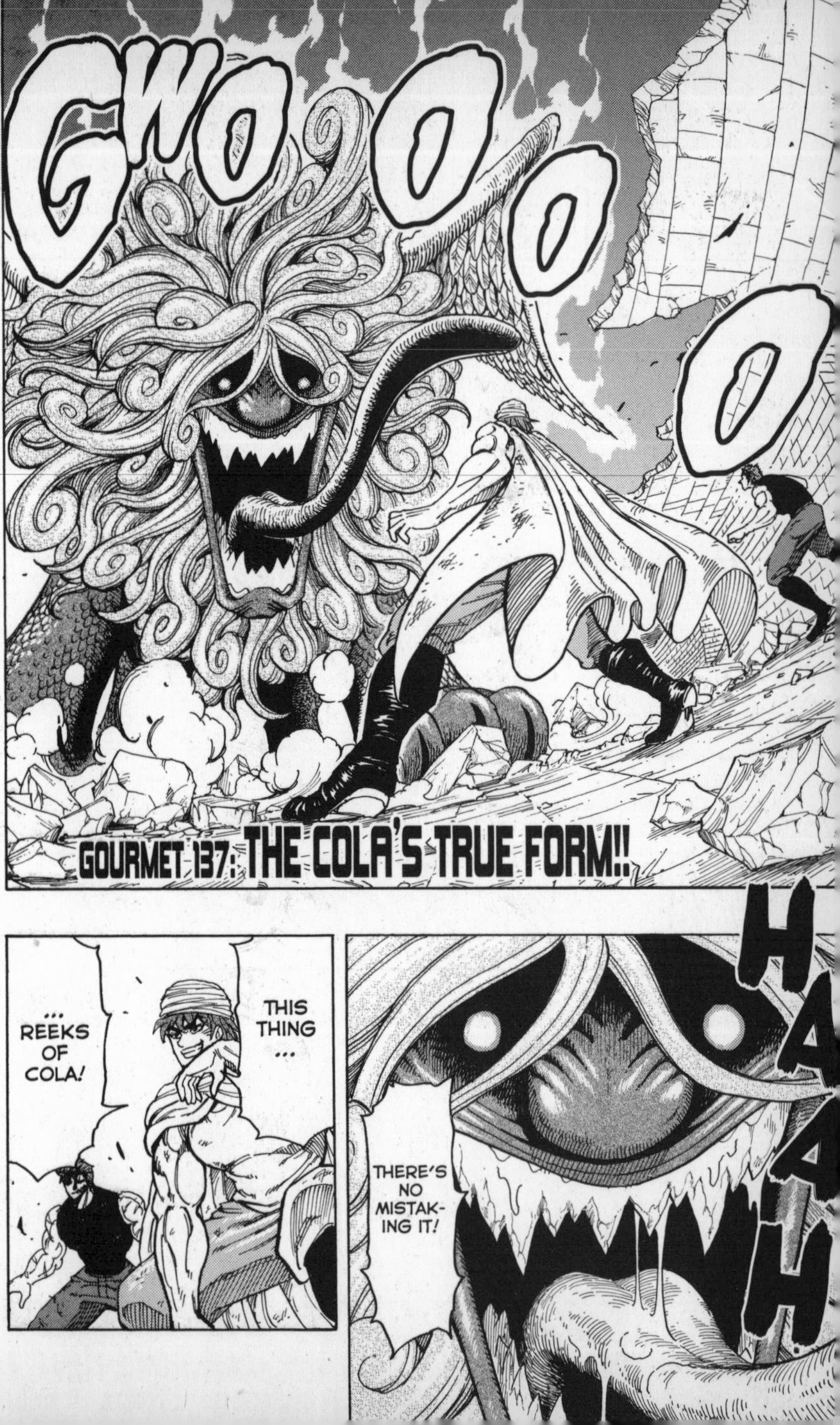
GWOOOOOO
GOURMET 137: THE COLA'S TRUE FORM!!
HAAH
THERE'S NO MISTAKING IT!
THIS THING...
...REEKS OF COLA!

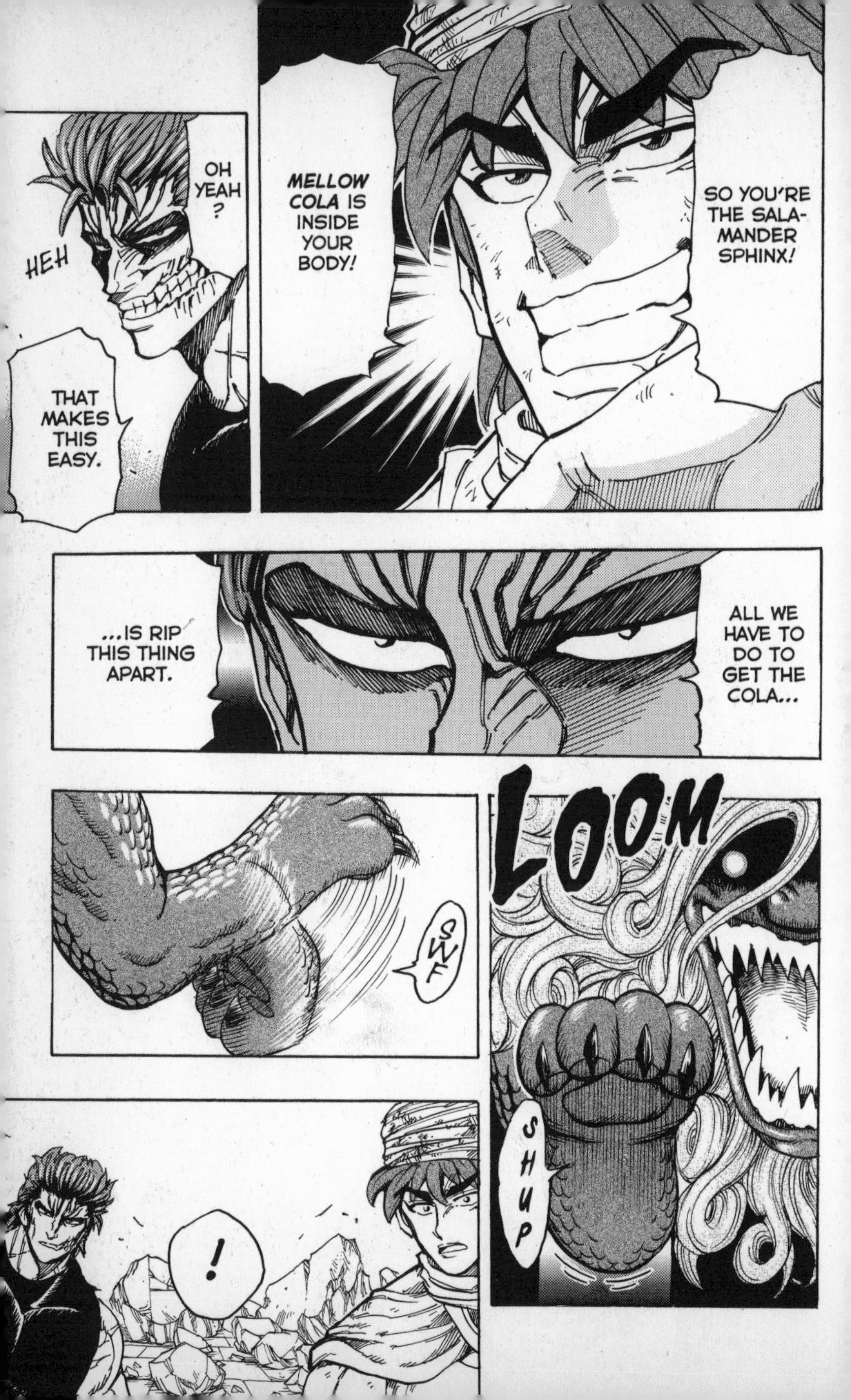
SO YOU'RE THE SALA-MANDER SPHINX!
MELLOW COLA IS INSIDE YOUR BODY!
OH YEAH?
HEH
THAT MAKES THIS EASY.
ALL WE HAVE TO DO TO GET THE COLA...
...IS RIP THIS THING APART.
LOOM
SHUP
SWF
!

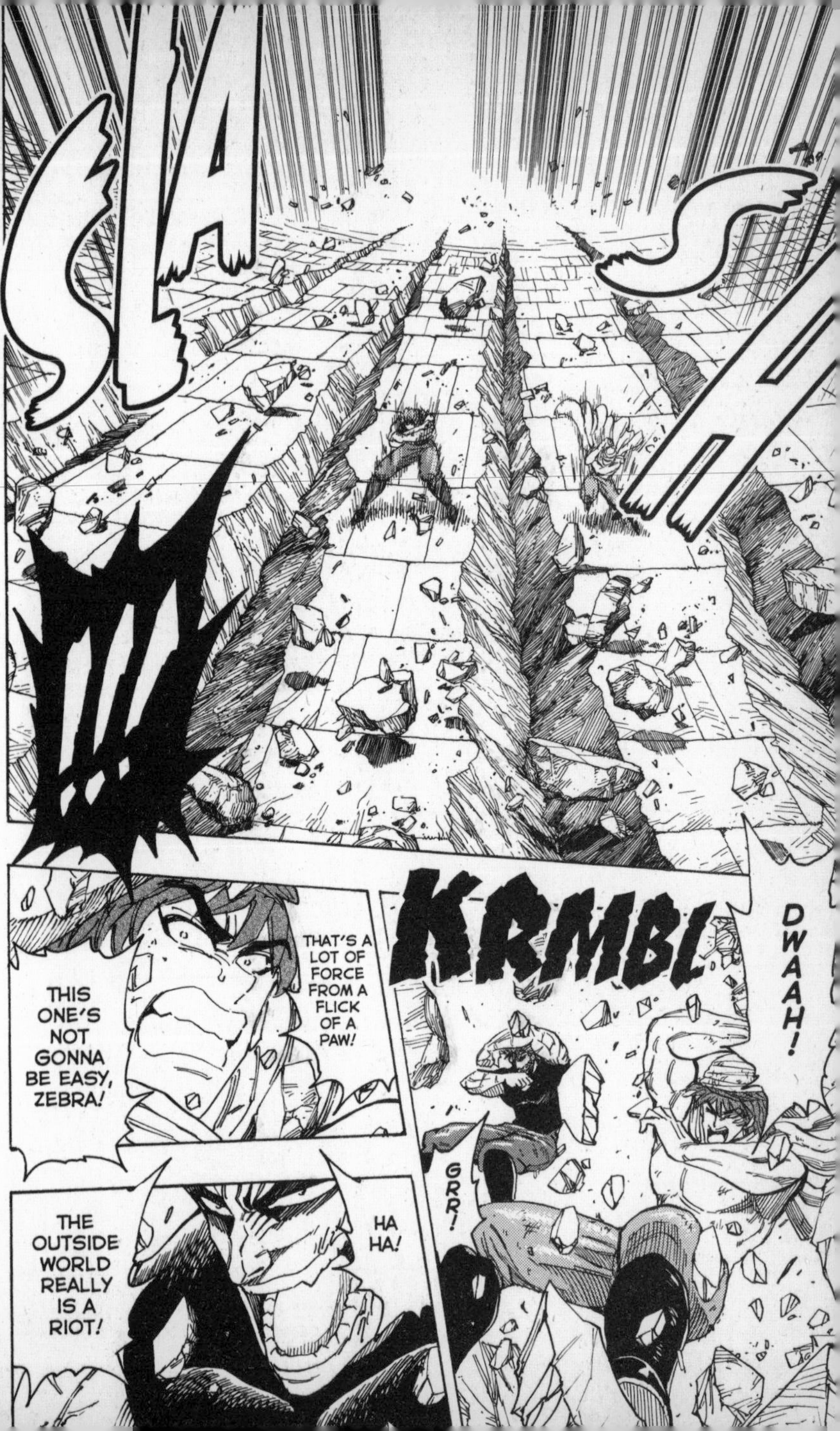
SLASH
KRMBL
DWAAH!
GRR!
THAT'S A LOT OF FORCE FROM A FLICK OF A PAW!
THIS ONE'S NOT GONNA BE EASY, ZEBRA!
HA HA!
THE OUTSIDE WORLD REALLY IS A RIOT!

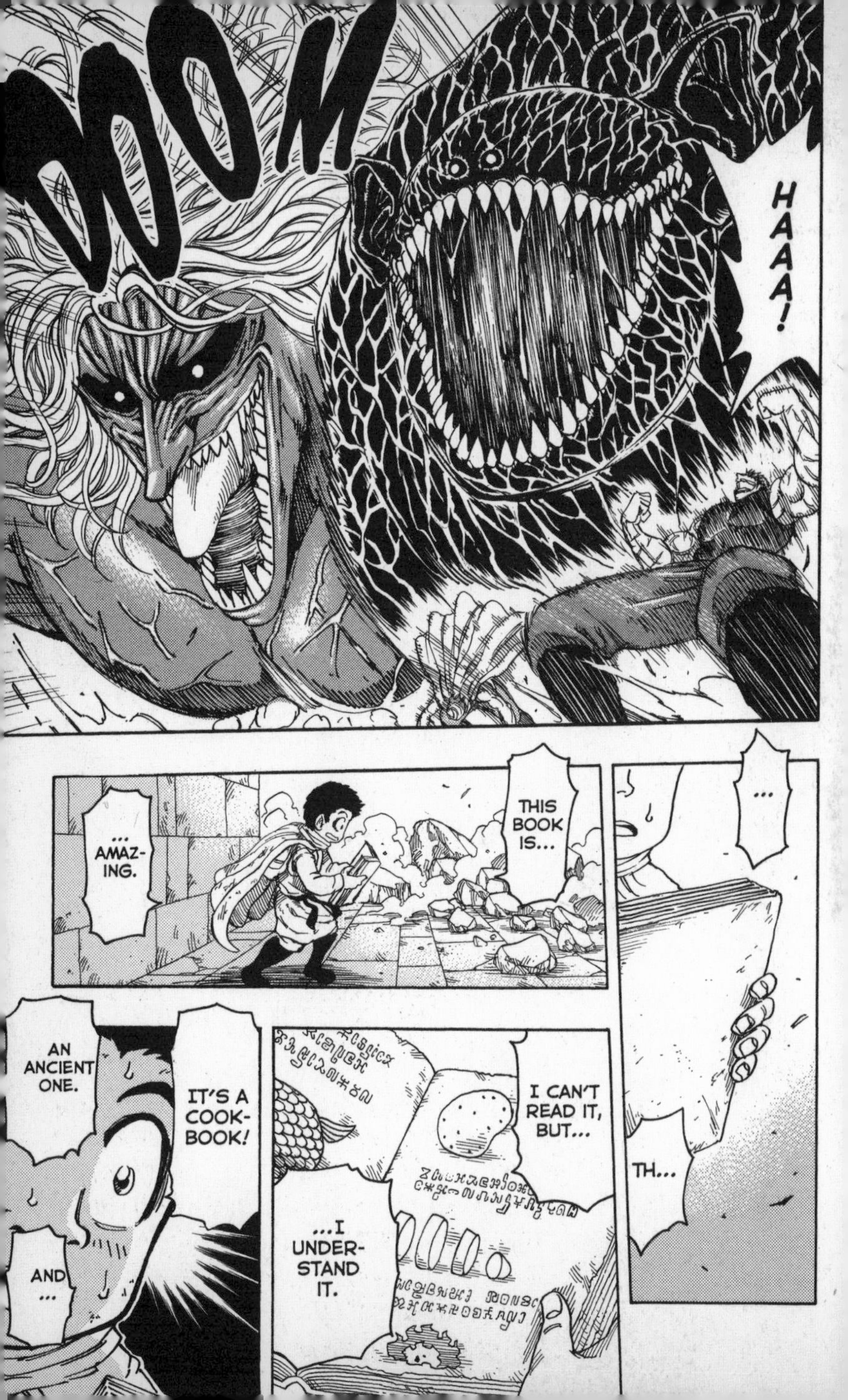
HAAAA!
DOOM
...
TH...
THIS BOOK IS...
... AMAZ-ING.
I CAN'T READ IT, BUT...
...I UNDER-STAND IT.
IT'S A COOK-BOOK!
AN ANCIENT ONE.
AND ...

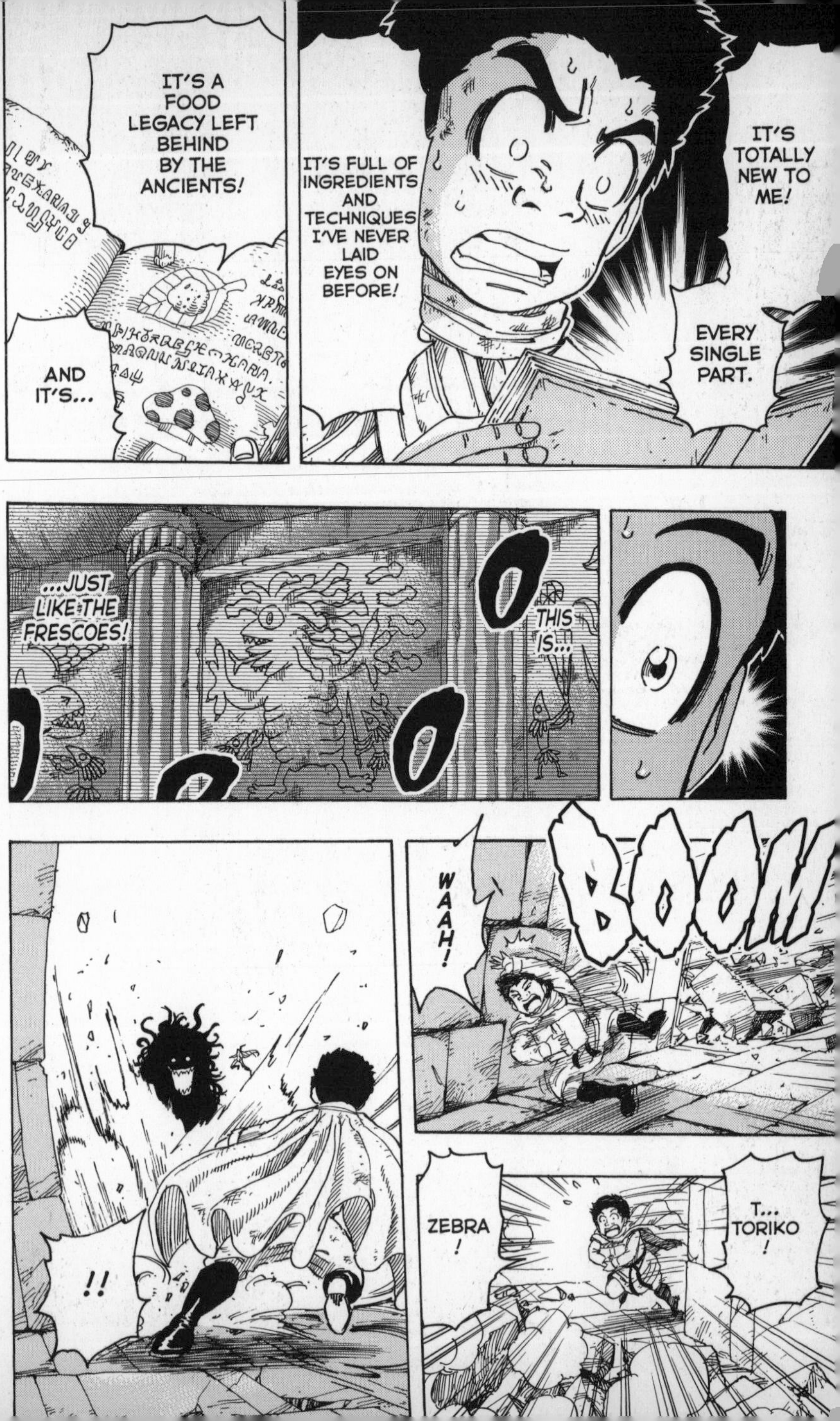
IT'S TOTALLY NEW TO ME!
EVERY SINGLE PART.
IT'S FULL OF INGREDIENTS AND TECHNIQUES I'VE NEVER LAID EYES ON BEFORE!
IT'S A FOOD LEGACY LEFT BEHIND BY THE ANCIENTS!
AND IT'S...
THIS IS...!
...JUST LIKE THE FRESCOES!
BOOM
WAAH!
T... TORIKO!
ZEBRA!
!!

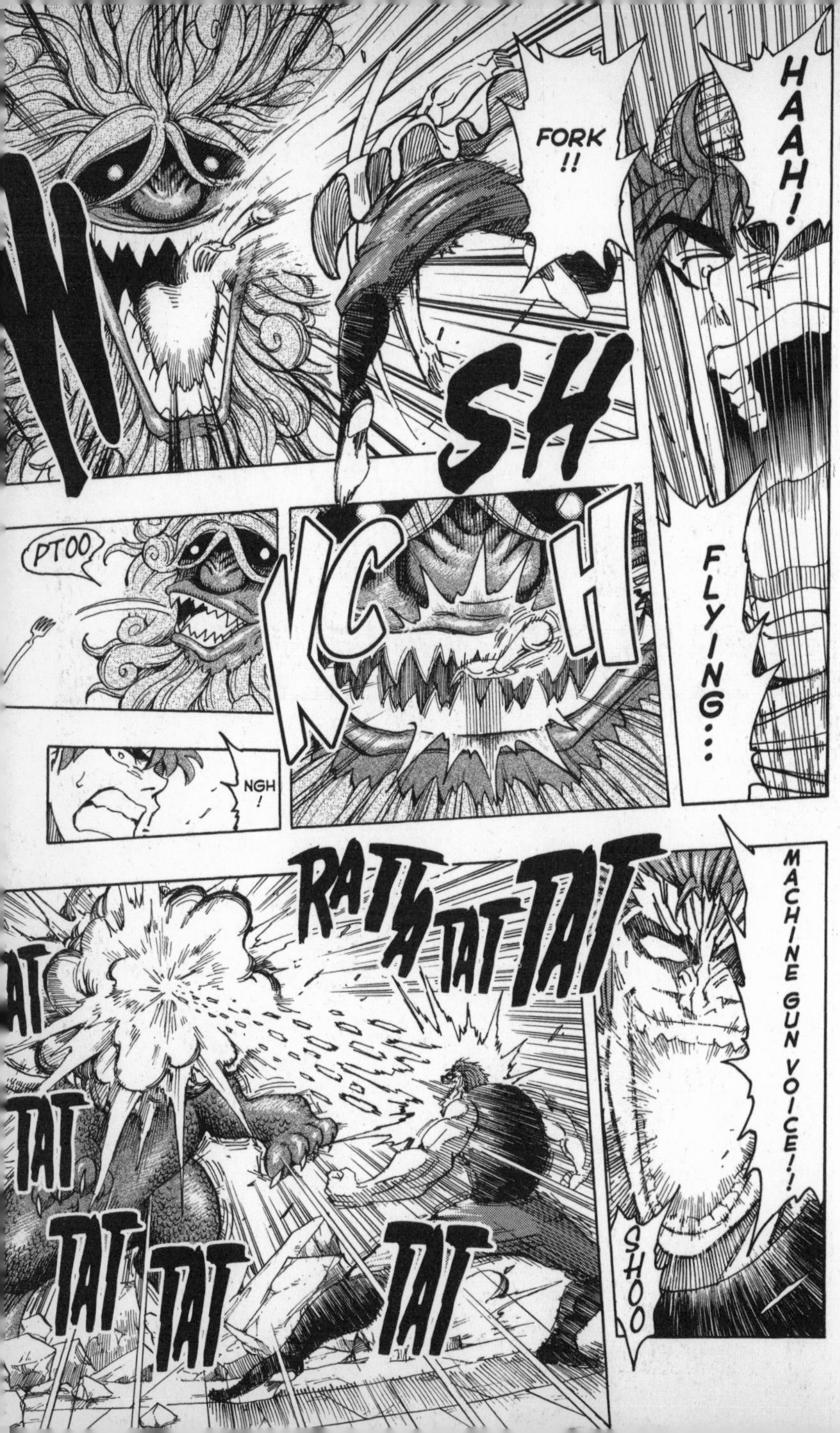

HAAAH!
FORK !!
WSH
FLYING...
KCH
PTOO
NGH !
MACHINE GUN VOICE!!
SHOO
RATATAT TAT TAT
TAT TAT TAT TAT TAT TAT

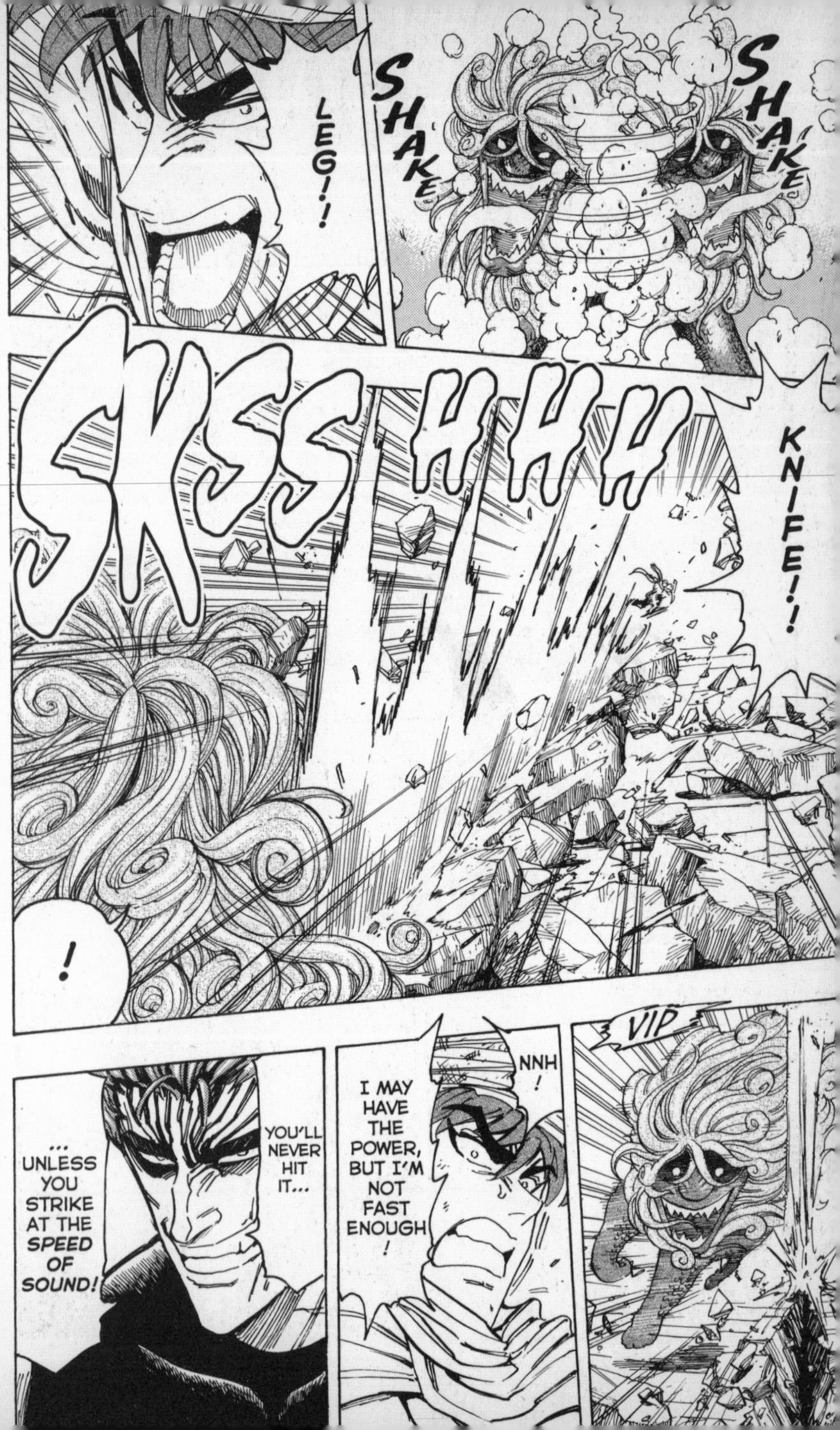
SHAKE
SHAKE
LEG!!
KNIFE!!
SKSSHHHH
!
VIP
NNH!
I MAY HAVE THE POWER, BUT I'M NOT FAST ENOUGH!
YOU'LL NEVER HIT IT...
...UNLESS YOU STRIKE AT THE SPEED OF SOUND!

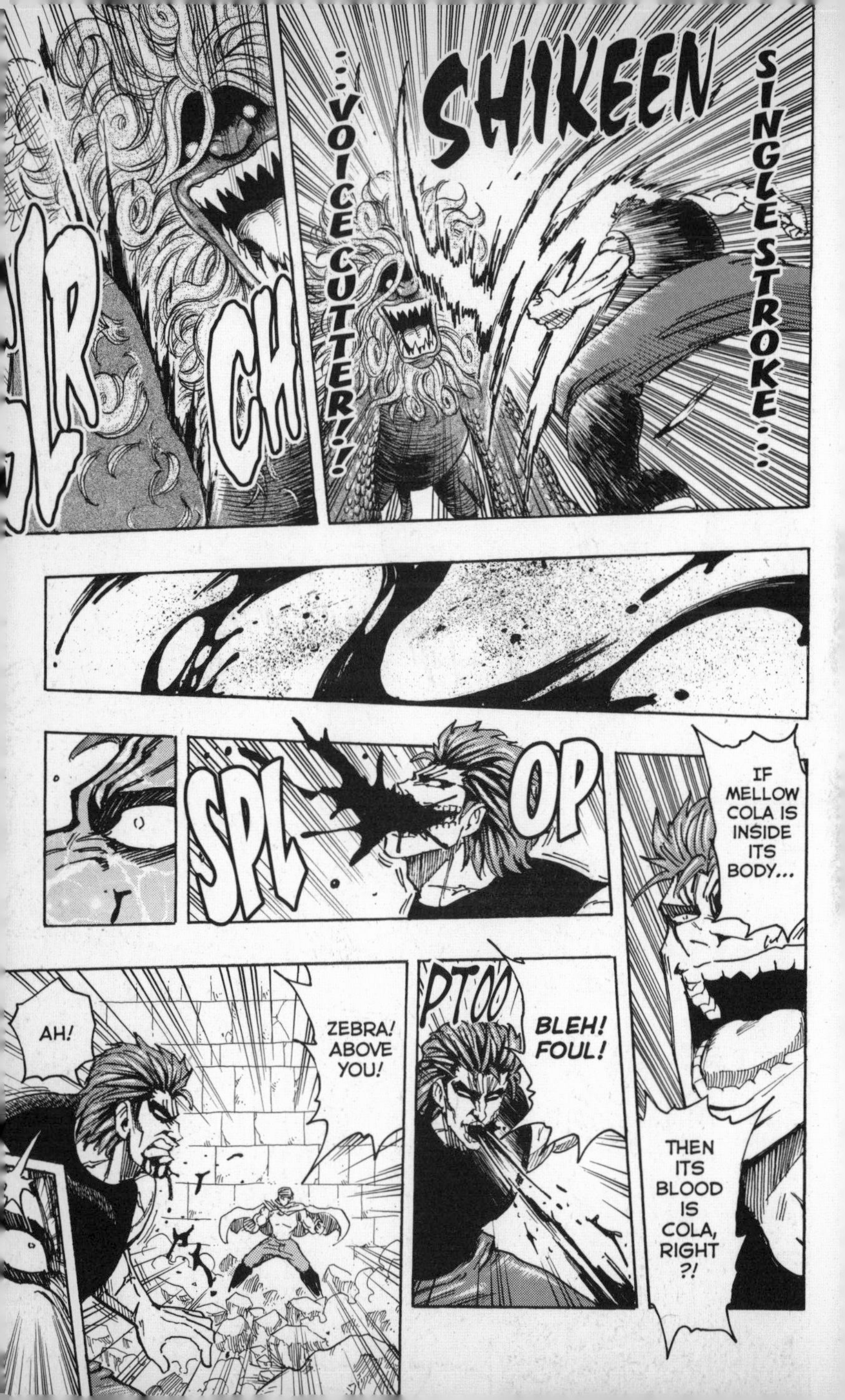
SINGLE STROKE...
SHIKEEN
...VOICE CUTTER!!
CH
IF MELLOW COLA IS INSIDE ITS BODY...
THEN ITS BLOOD IS COLA, RIGHT?!
SPLOP
PTOO
BLEH! FOUL!
ZEBRA! ABOVE YOU!
AH!

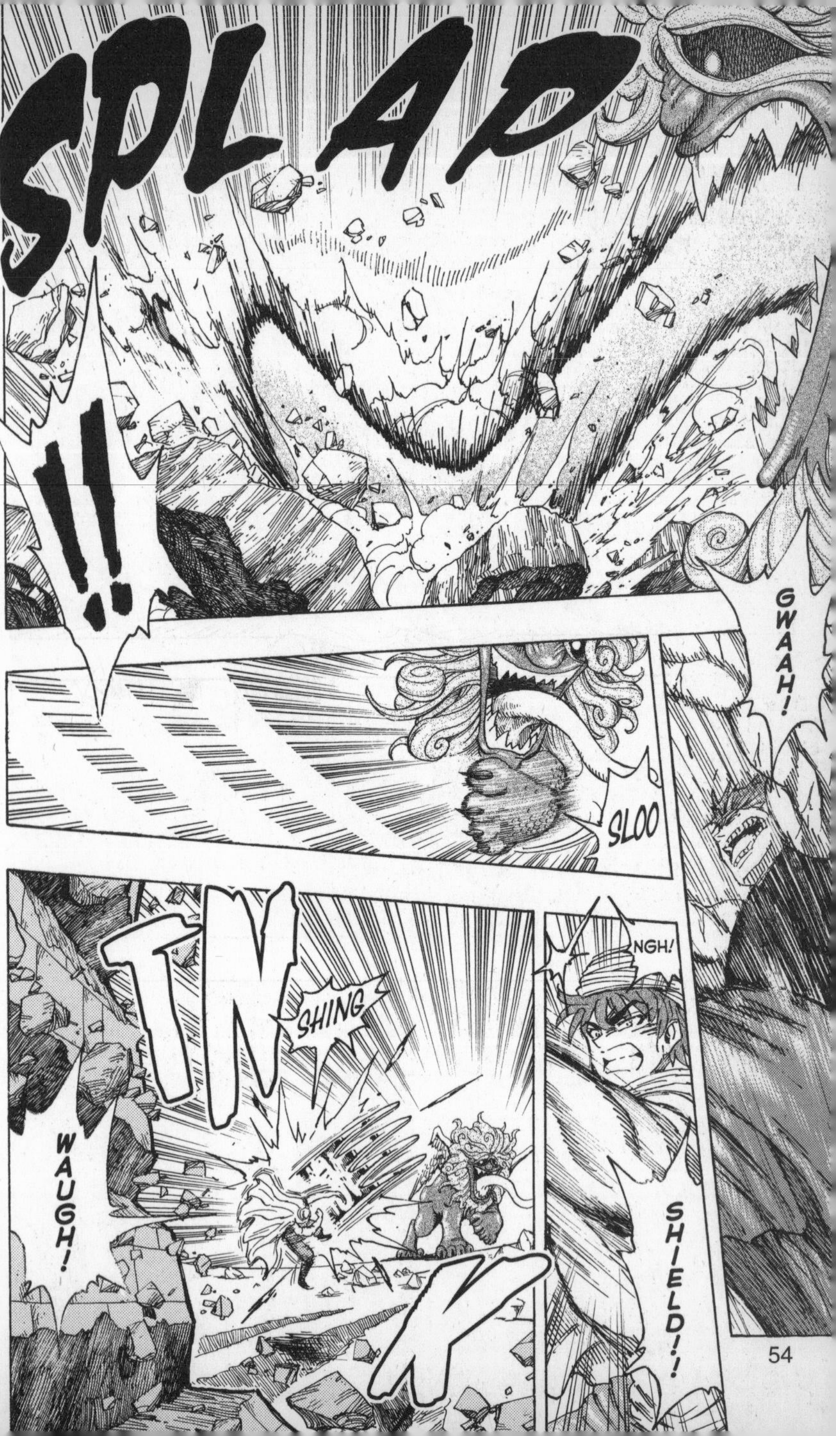
GWAAH!
SPLAD
!!
SLOO
NGH!
SHIELD!!
SHING
TN
K
WAUGH!

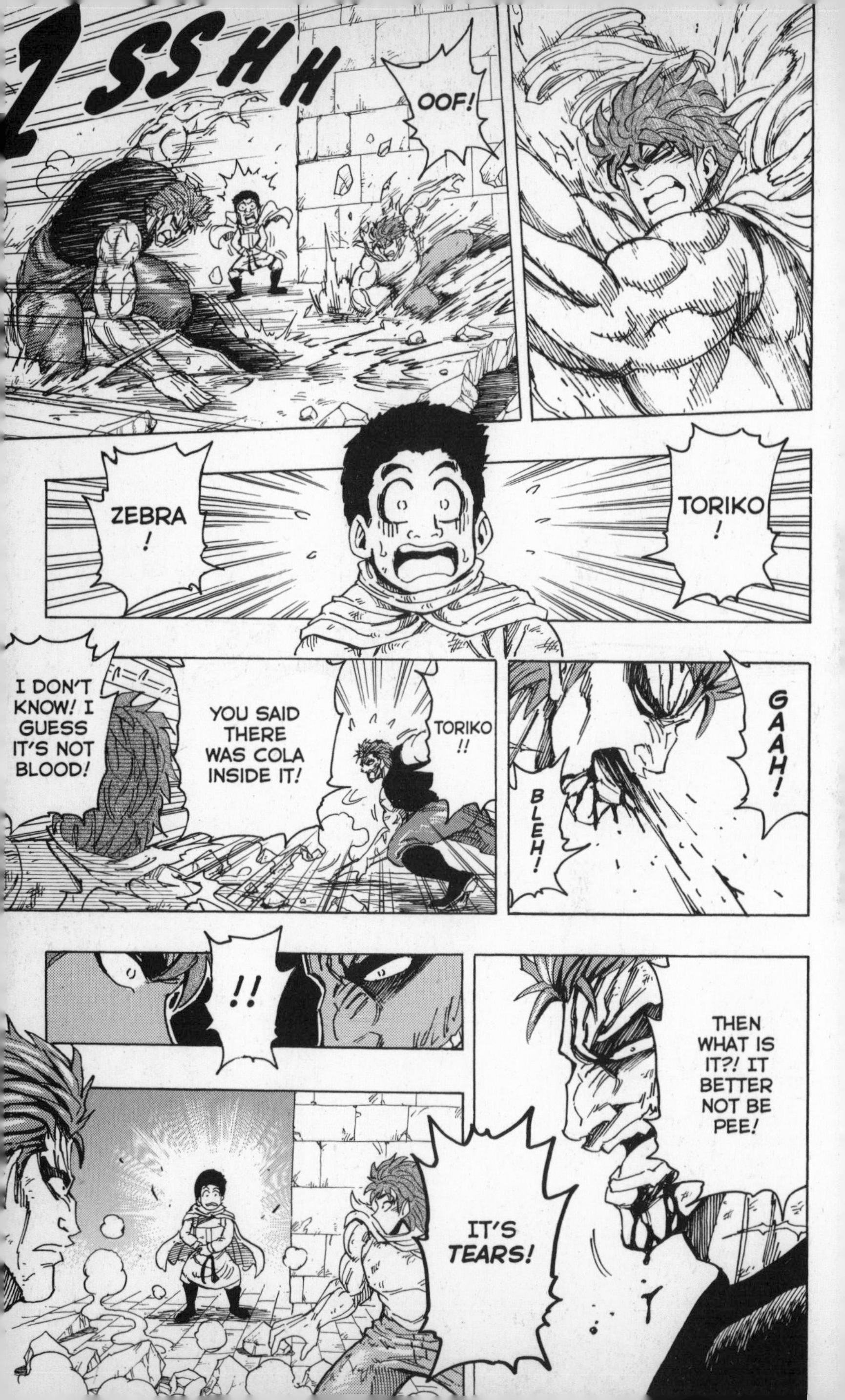
ZSSHH
OOF!
TORIKO!
ZEBRA!
GAAH!
BLEH!
TORIKO!!
YOU SAID THERE WAS COLA INSIDE IT!
I DON'T KNOW! I GUESS IT'S NOT BLOOD!
THEN WHAT IS IT?! IT BETTER NOT BE PEE!
!!
IT'S TEARS!

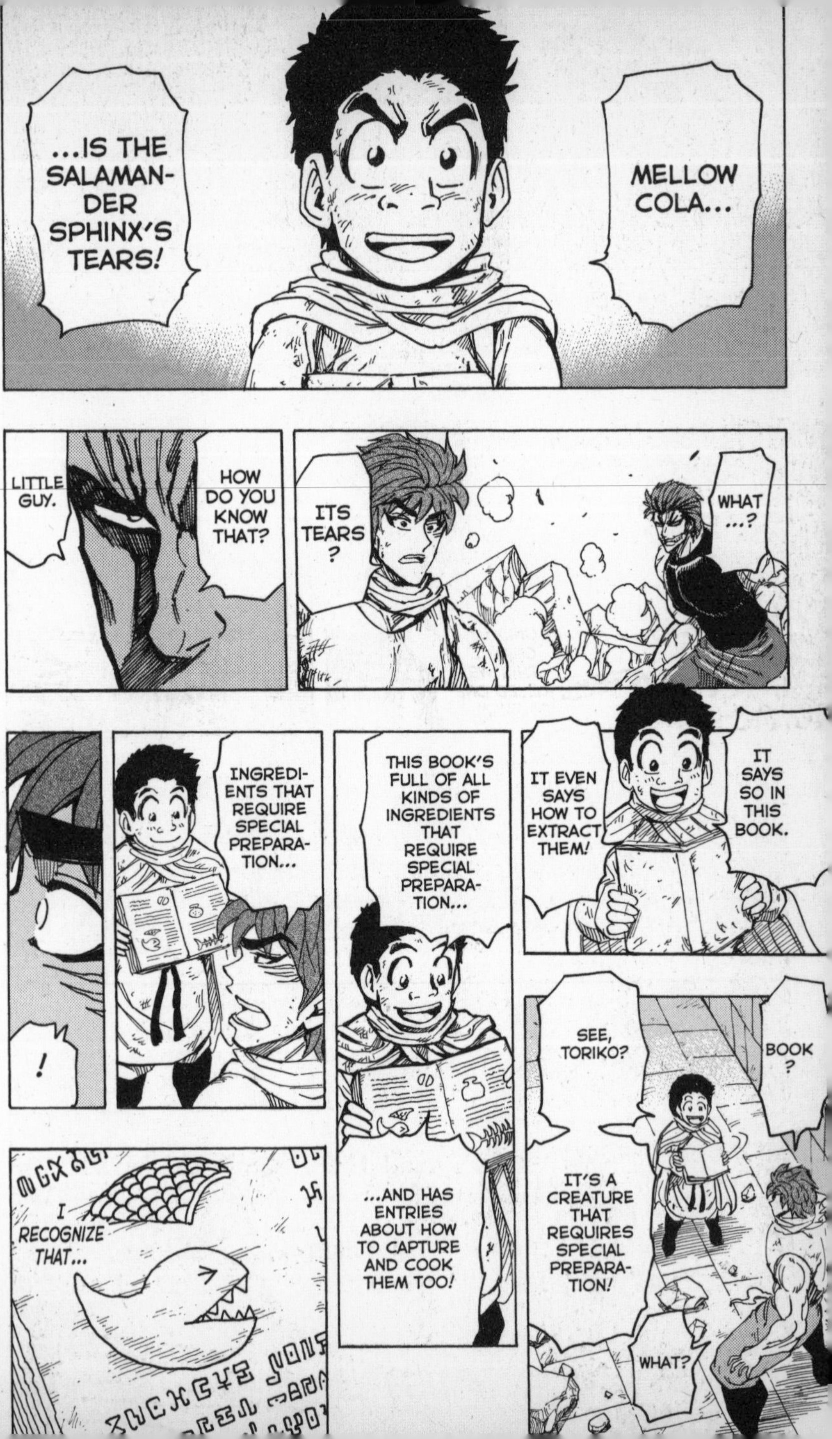
MELLOW COLA...
...IS THE SALAMANDER SPHINX'S TEARS!
WHAT ...?
ITS TEARS?
HOW DO YOU KNOW THAT?
LITTLE GUY.
IT SAYS SO IN THIS BOOK.
IT EVEN SAYS HOW TO EXTRACT THEM!
BOOK?
SEE, TORIKO?
IT'S A CREATURE THAT REQUIRES SPECIAL PREPARATION!
WHAT?
THIS BOOK'S FULL OF ALL KINDS OF INGREDIENTS THAT REQUIRE SPECIAL PREPARATION...
...AND HAS ENTRIES ABOUT HOW TO CAPTURE AND COOK THEM TOO!
INGREDIENTS THAT REQUIRE SPECIAL PREPARATION...
!
I RECOGNIZE THAT...

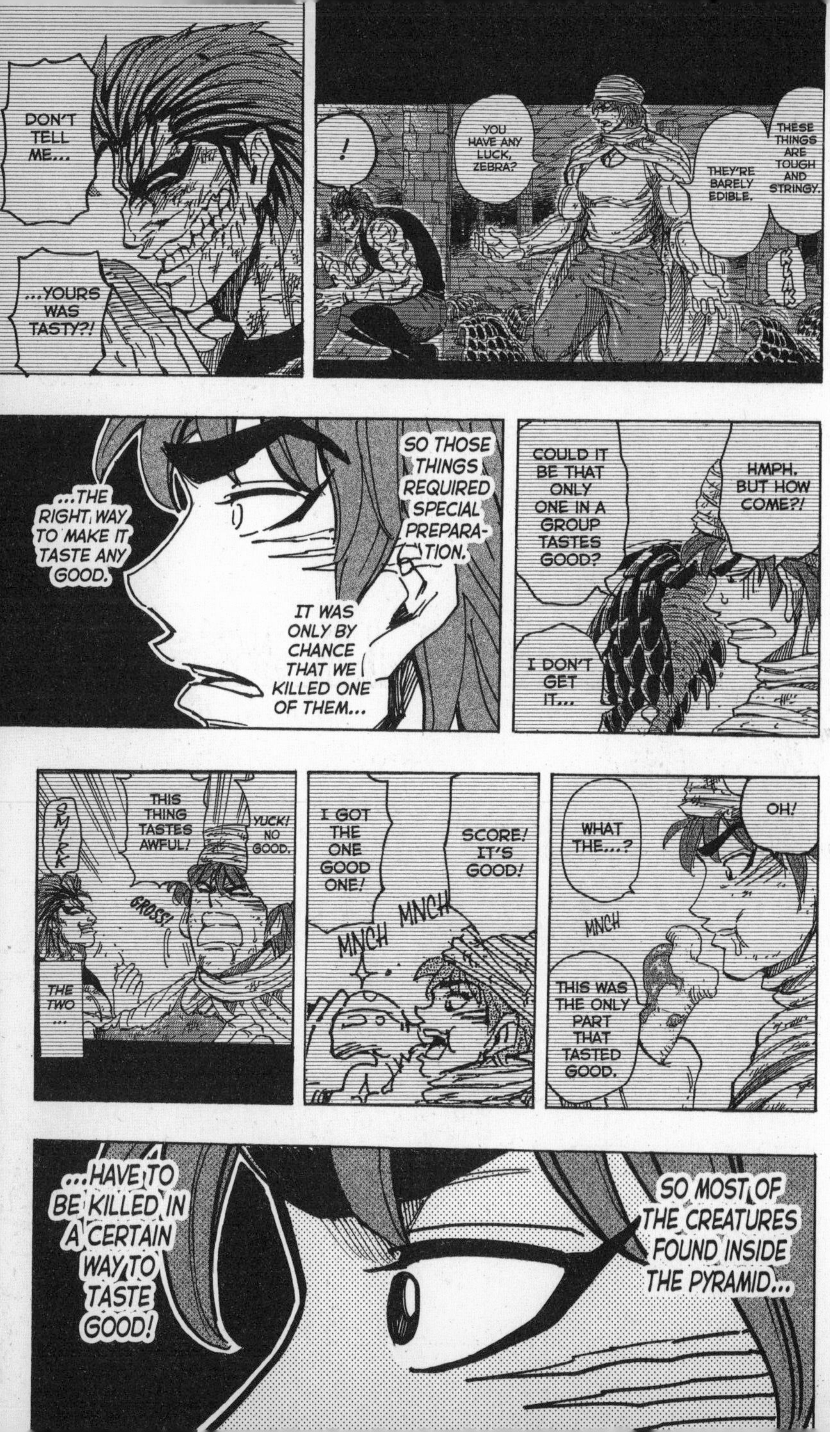
THESE THINGS ARE TOUGH AND STRINGY.
THEY'RE BARELY EDIBLE.
YOU HAVE ANY LUCK, ZEBRA?
!
DON'T TELL ME...
...YOURS WAS TASTY?!
HMPH. BUT HOW COME?!
COULD IT BE THAT ONLY ONE IN A GROUP TASTES GOOD?
I DON'T GET IT...
SO THOSE THINGS REQUIRED SPECIAL PREPARATION.
...THE RIGHT WAY TO MAKE IT TASTE ANY GOOD.
IT WAS ONLY BY CHANCE THAT WE KILLED ONE OF THEM...
OH!
WHAT THE...?
MNCH
THIS WAS THE ONLY PART THAT TASTED GOOD.
SCORE! IT'S GOOD!
I GOT THE ONE GOOD ONE!
MNCH MNCH
YUCK! NO GOOD.
THIS THING TASTES AWFUL!
SMIRK
GROSS!
THE TWO...
SO MOST OF THE CREATURES FOUND INSIDE THE PYRAMID...
...HAVE TO BE KILLED IN A CERTAIN WAY TO TASTE GOOD!

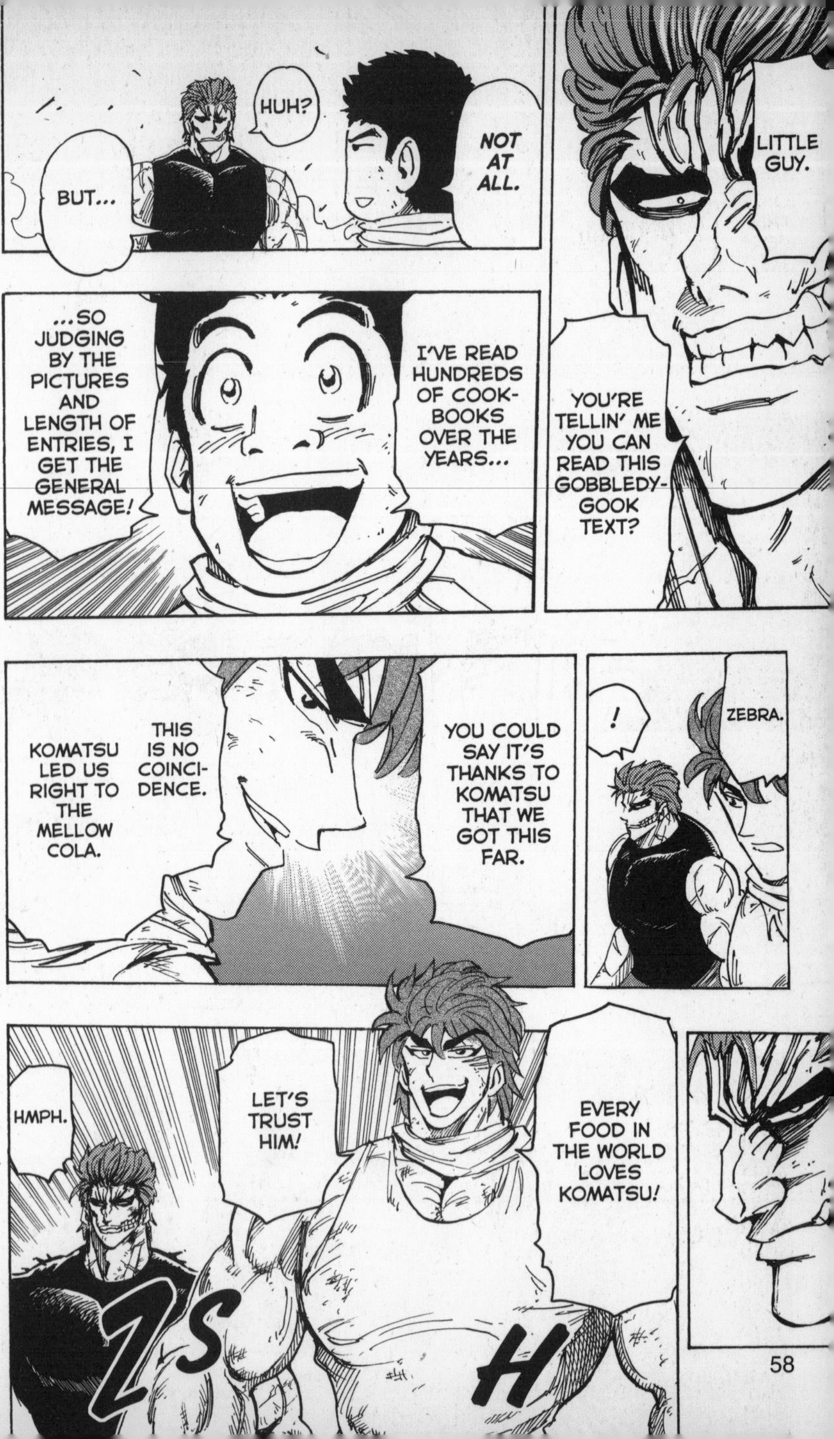

LITTLE GUY.
YOU'RE TELLIN' ME YOU CAN READ THIS GOBBLEDY-GOOK TEXT?
NOT AT ALL.
HUH?
BUT...
I'VE READ HUNDREDS OF COOK-BOOKS OVER THE YEARS...
...SO JUDGING BY THE PICTURES AND LENGTH OF ENTRIES, I GET THE GENERAL MESSAGE!
ZEBRA.
!
YOU COULD SAY IT'S THANKS TO KOMATSU THAT WE GOT THIS FAR.
THIS IS NO COINCI-DENCE.
KOMATSU LED US RIGHT TO THE MELLOW COLA.
EVERY FOOD IN THE WORLD LOVES KOMATSU!
LET'S TRUST HIM!
HMPH.
ZSH

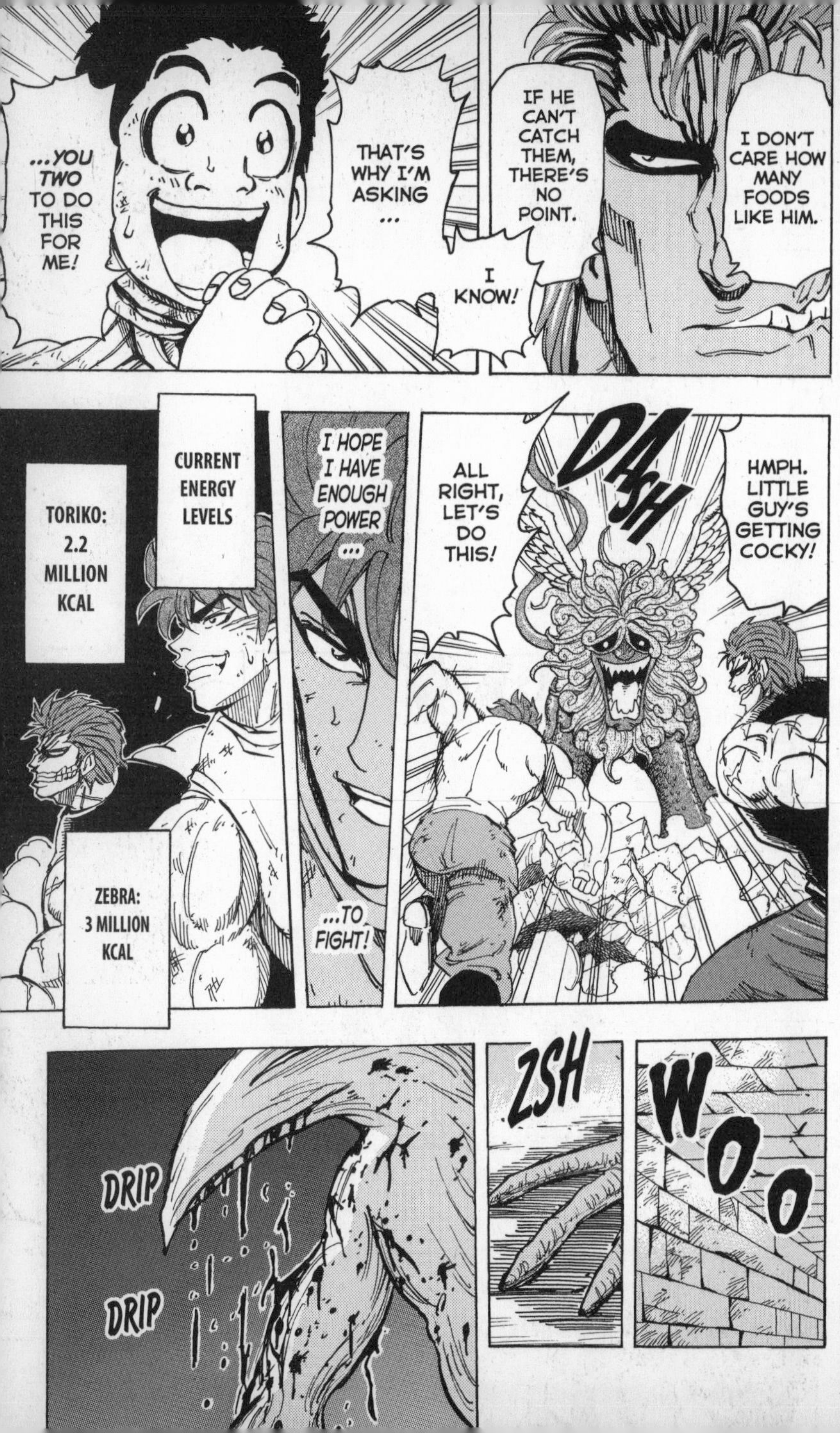
I DON'T CARE HOW MANY FOODS LIKE HIM.
IF HE CAN'T CATCH THEM, THERE'S NO POINT.
I KNOW!
THAT'S WHY I'M ASKING ...
...YOU TWO TO DO THIS FOR ME!
HMPH. LITTLE GUY'S GETTING COCKY!
DASH
ALL RIGHT, LET'S DO THIS!
I HOPE I HAVE ENOUGH POWER ...
...TO FIGHT!
CURRENT ENERGY LEVELS
TORIKO: 2.2 MILLION KCAL
ZEBRA: 3 MILLION KCAL
WOOO
ZSH
DRIP
DRIP

TORIKO

GOURMET CHECKLIST

Vol. 158
ASHURA TIGER
(MAMMAL)

CAPTURE LEVEL: UNKNOWN
HABITAT: GOURMET WORLD
LENGTH: 70 METERS
HEIGHT: 30 METERS
WEIGHT: 720 TONS
PRICE: UNKNOWN

SCALE

A THREE-FACED TIGER THAT LIVES IN THE GOURMET WORLD'S UNDERGROUND FOREST, 20,000 METERS BELOW SEA LEVEL. DETAILS REGARDING ITS BEHAVIOR, CAPTURE LEVEL, AND MORE ARE A COMPLETE MYSTERY. IT IS SAID THAT CURRENTLY NO MORE THAN TWENTY PEOPLE IN THE HUMAN WORLD CAN HOLD THEIR OWN AGAINST THE CREATURES OF THE GOURMET WORLD.

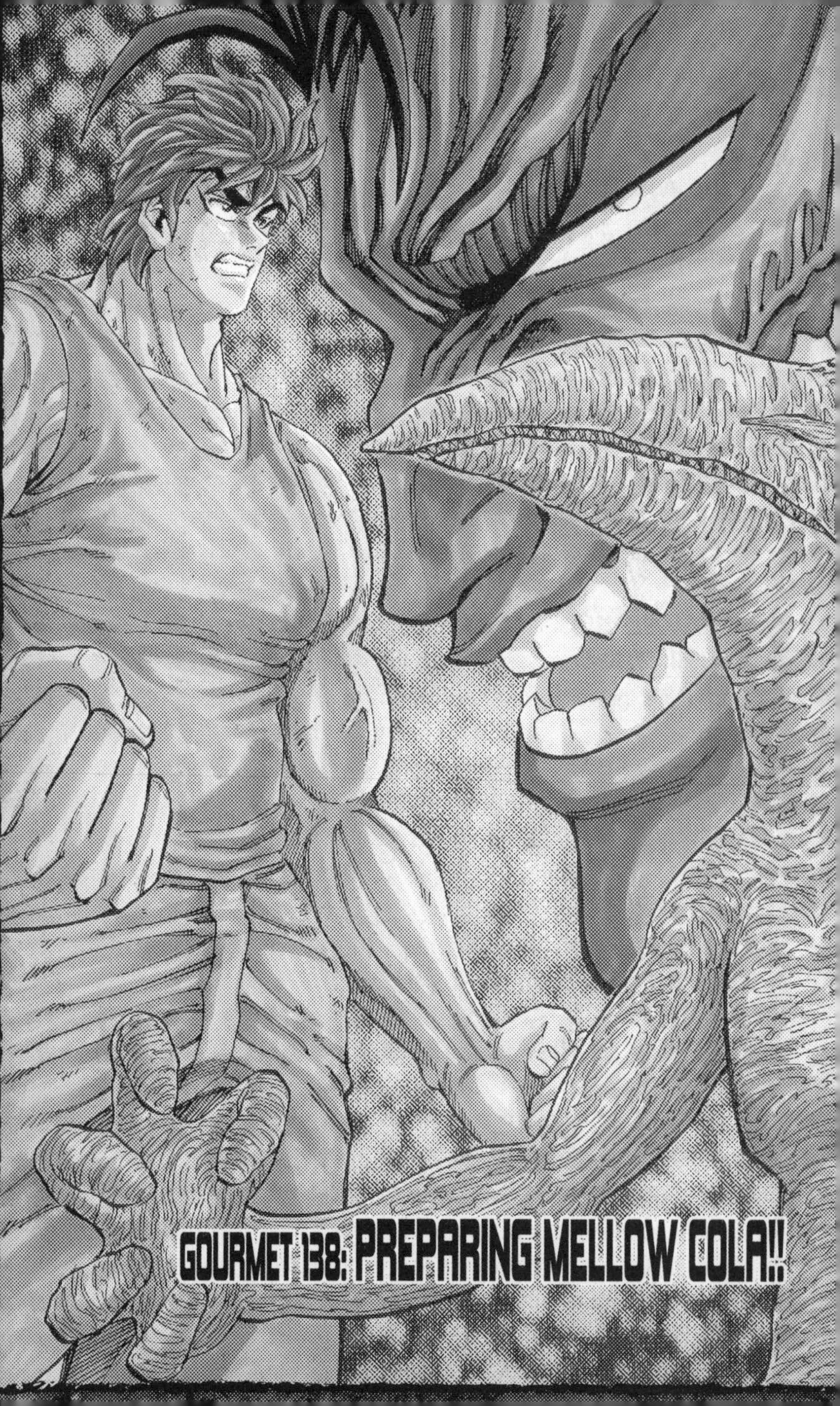
GOURMET 138: PREPARING MELLOW COLA!!

TORIKO

GOURMET CHECKLIST

Vol. 159

KING RENTRA
(MAMMAL)

CAPTURE LEVEL: UNKNOWN

HABITAT: GOURMET WORLD

LENGTH: ---

HEIGHT: 58 METERS

WEIGHT: 850 TONS

PRICE: UNKNOWN

SCALE

LIKE THE ASHURA TIGER, THIS GIANT SILVERBACK GORILLA LIVES IN THE GOURMET WORLD'S UNDERGROUND FOREST, 20,000 METERS BELOW SEA LEVEL. DETAILS REGARDING ITS BEHAVIOR, CAPTURE LEVEL, AND MORE ARE A COMPLETE MYSTERY. IT BOASTS SUCH TOUGHNESS THAT EVEN AFTER TAKING ONE OF TORIKO'S 15-FOLD SPIKED PUNCHES, IT SHOWED NO OBVIOUS SIGN OF DAMAGE.

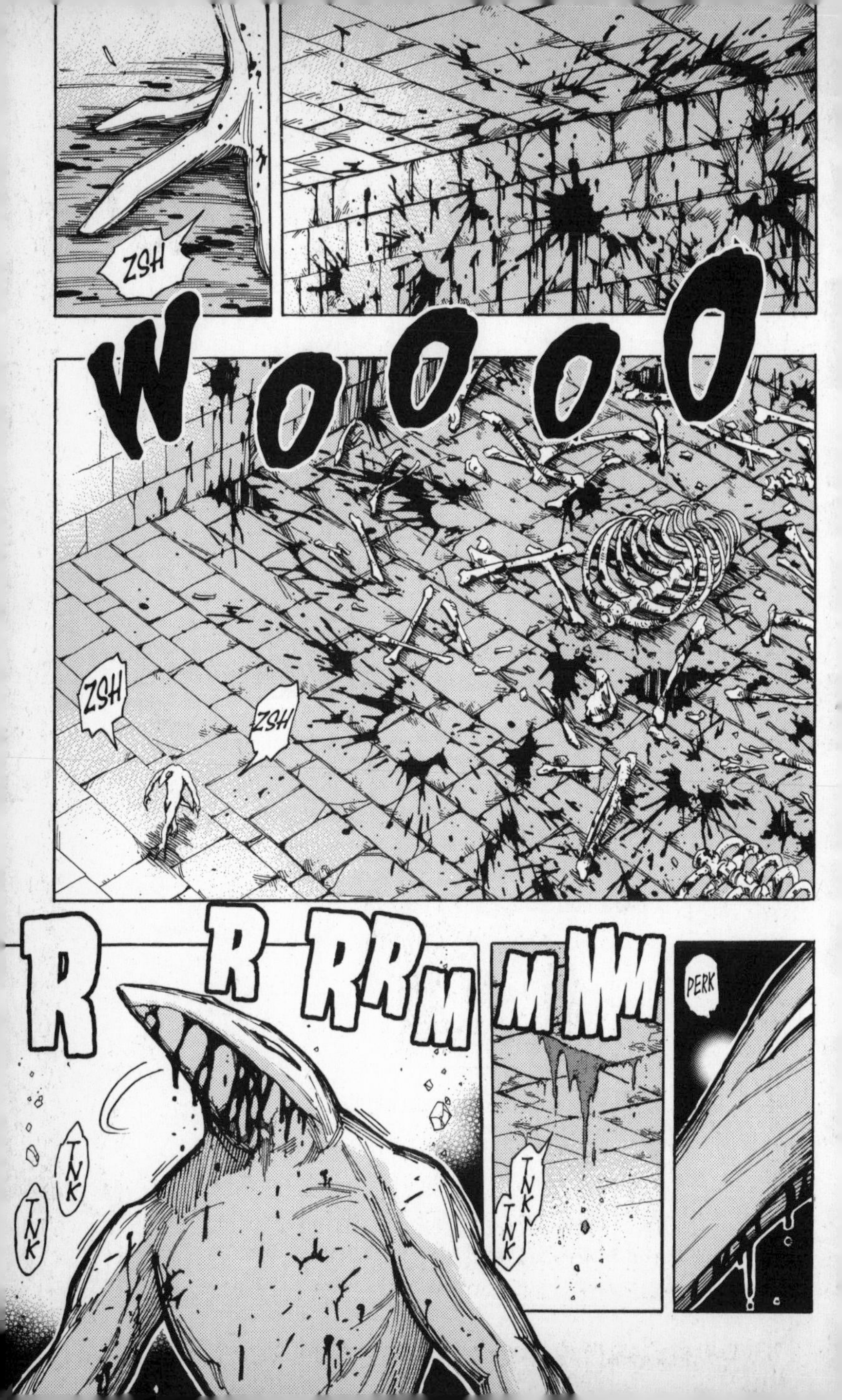

ZSH
WOOOOO
ZSH
ZSH
PERK
TNK TNK
R R RRM MMMM
TNK
TNK

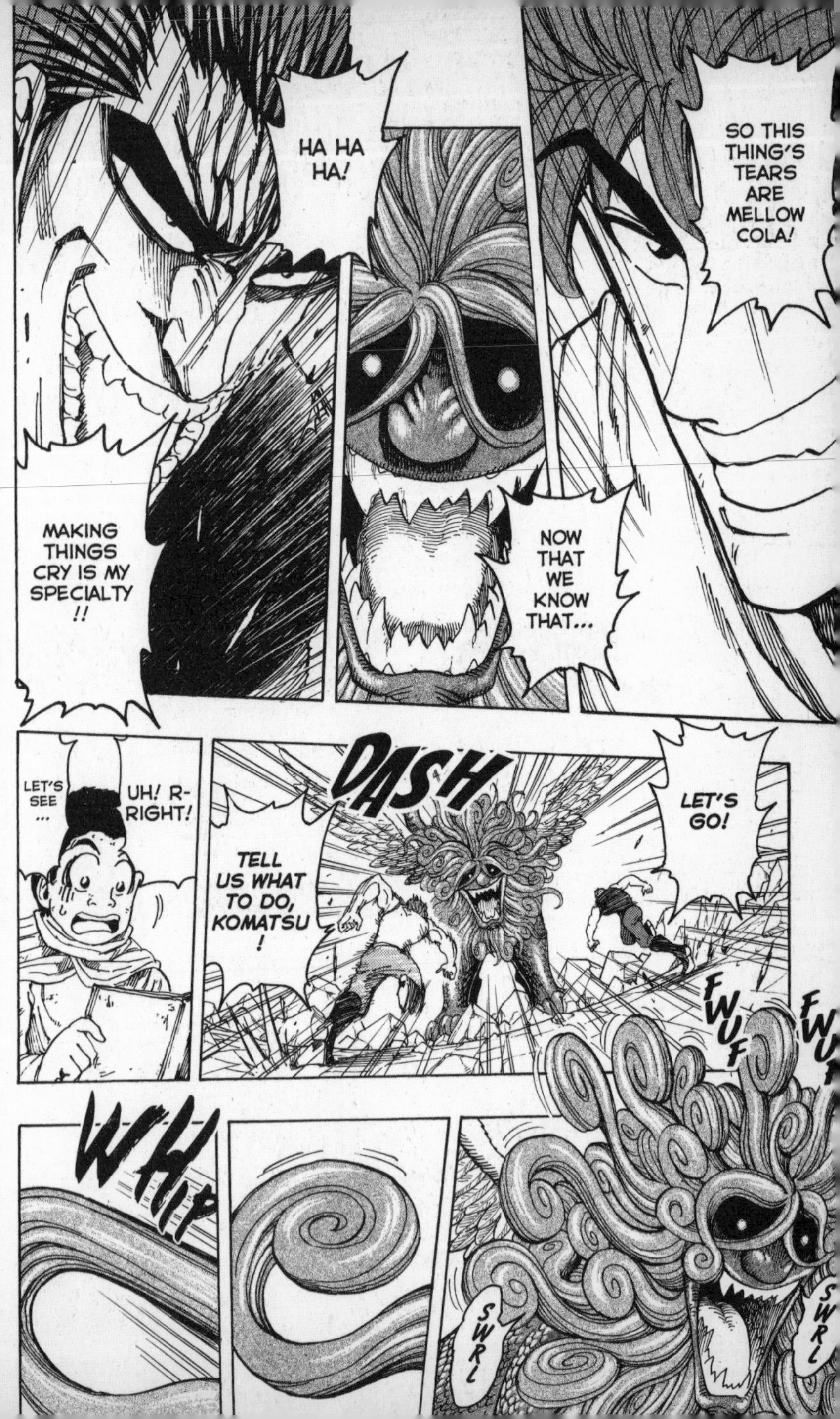
SO THIS THING'S TEARS ARE MELLOW COLA!
NOW THAT WE KNOW THAT...
HA HA HA!
MAKING THINGS CRY IS MY SPECIALTY!!
LET'S GO!
DASH
TELL US WHAT TO DO, KOMATSU!
UH! R-RIGHT!
LET'S SEE...
FWUF
FWUF
SWRL
SWRL
WHIP

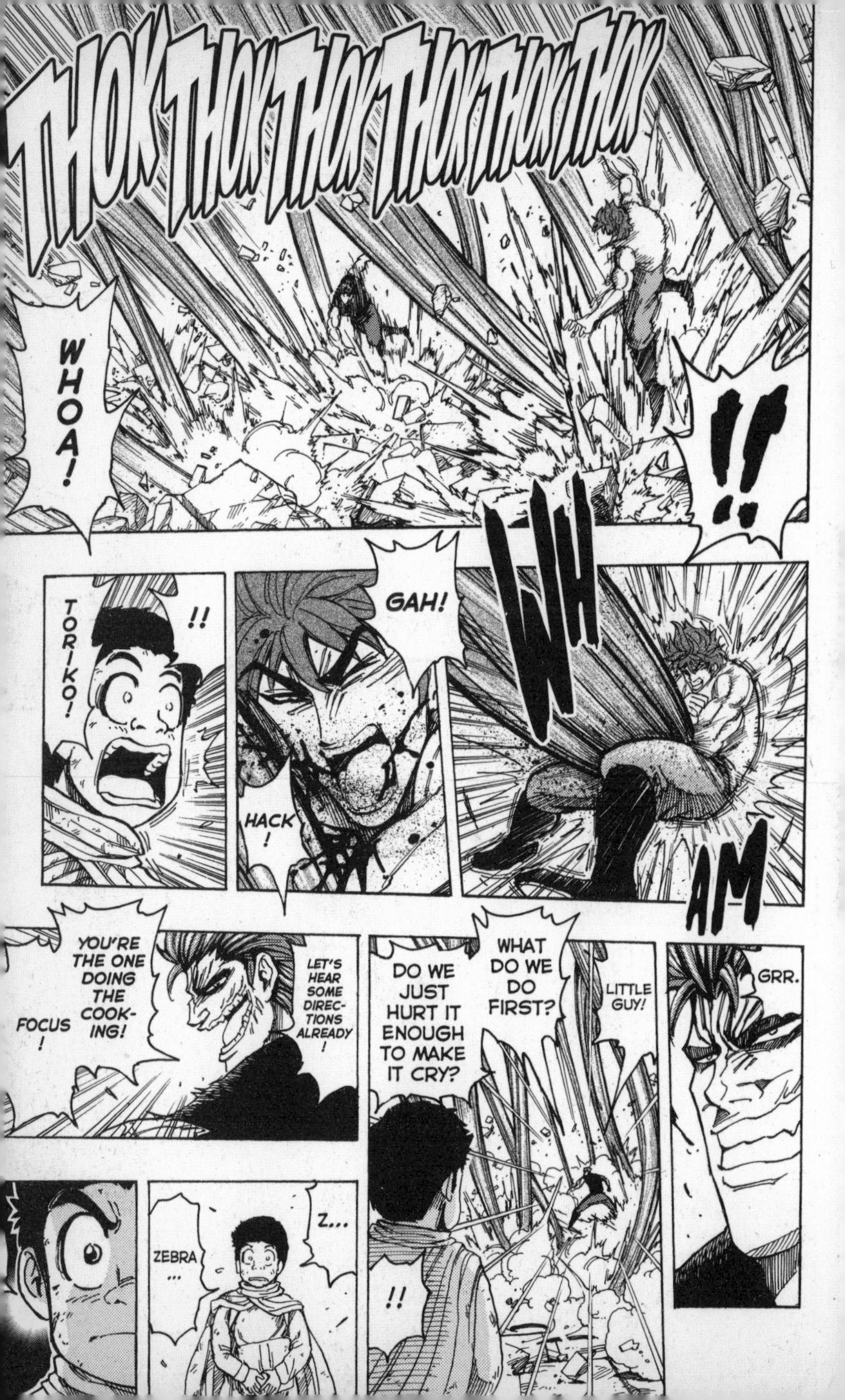
THOK THOK THOK THOK THOK THOK
!!
WHOA!
WHAM
GAH!
HACK!
!!
TORIKO!
GRR.
LITTLE GUY!
WHAT DO WE DO FIRST?
DO WE JUST HURT IT ENOUGH TO MAKE IT CRY?
!!
LET'S HEAR SOME DIRECTIONS ALREADY!
YOU'RE THE ONE DOING THE COOKING!
FOCUS!
Z...
ZEBRA...

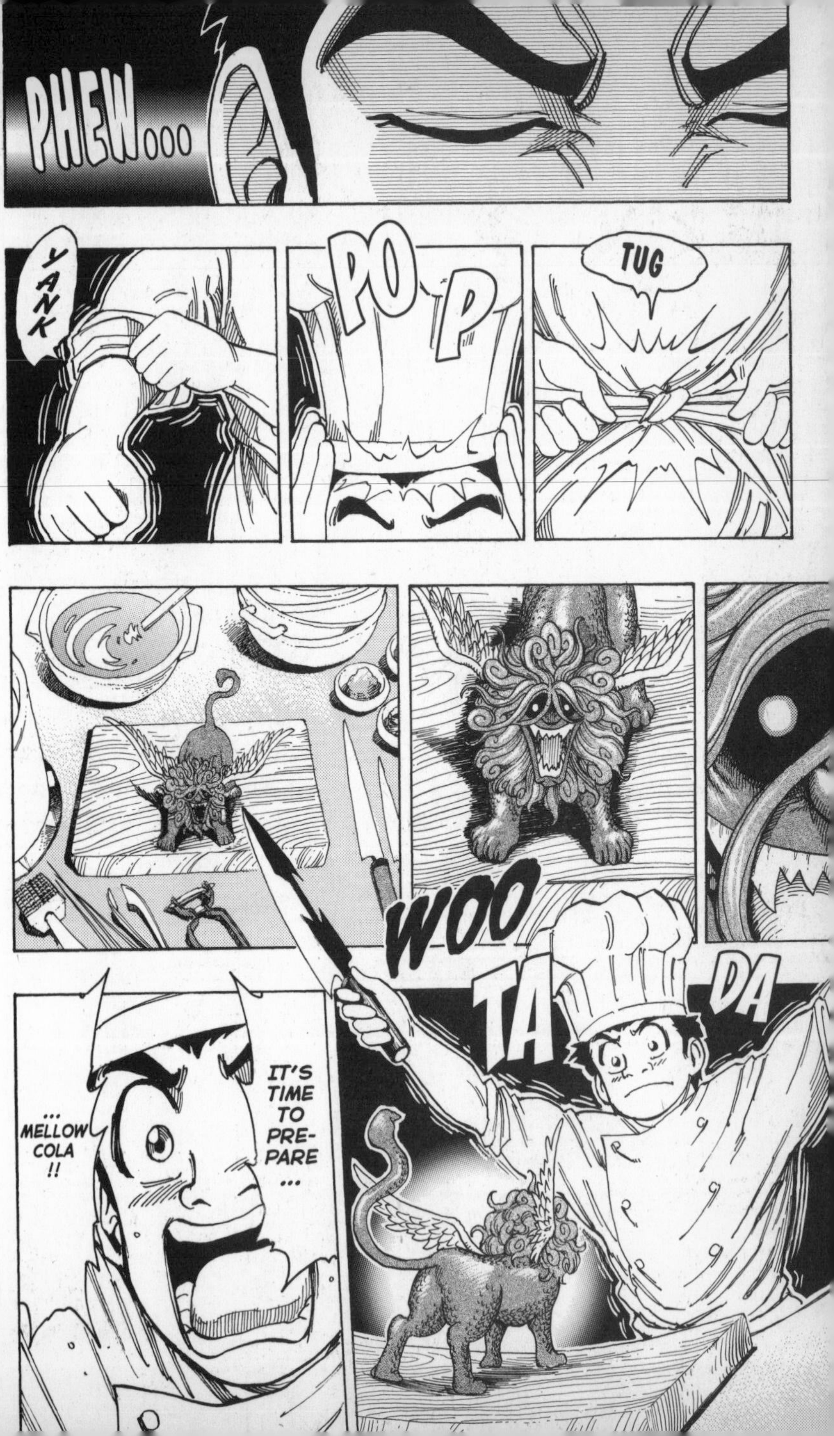
PHEW...
TUG
POP
YANK
WOO TA DA
IT'S TIME TO PREPARE...
...MELLOW COLA!!

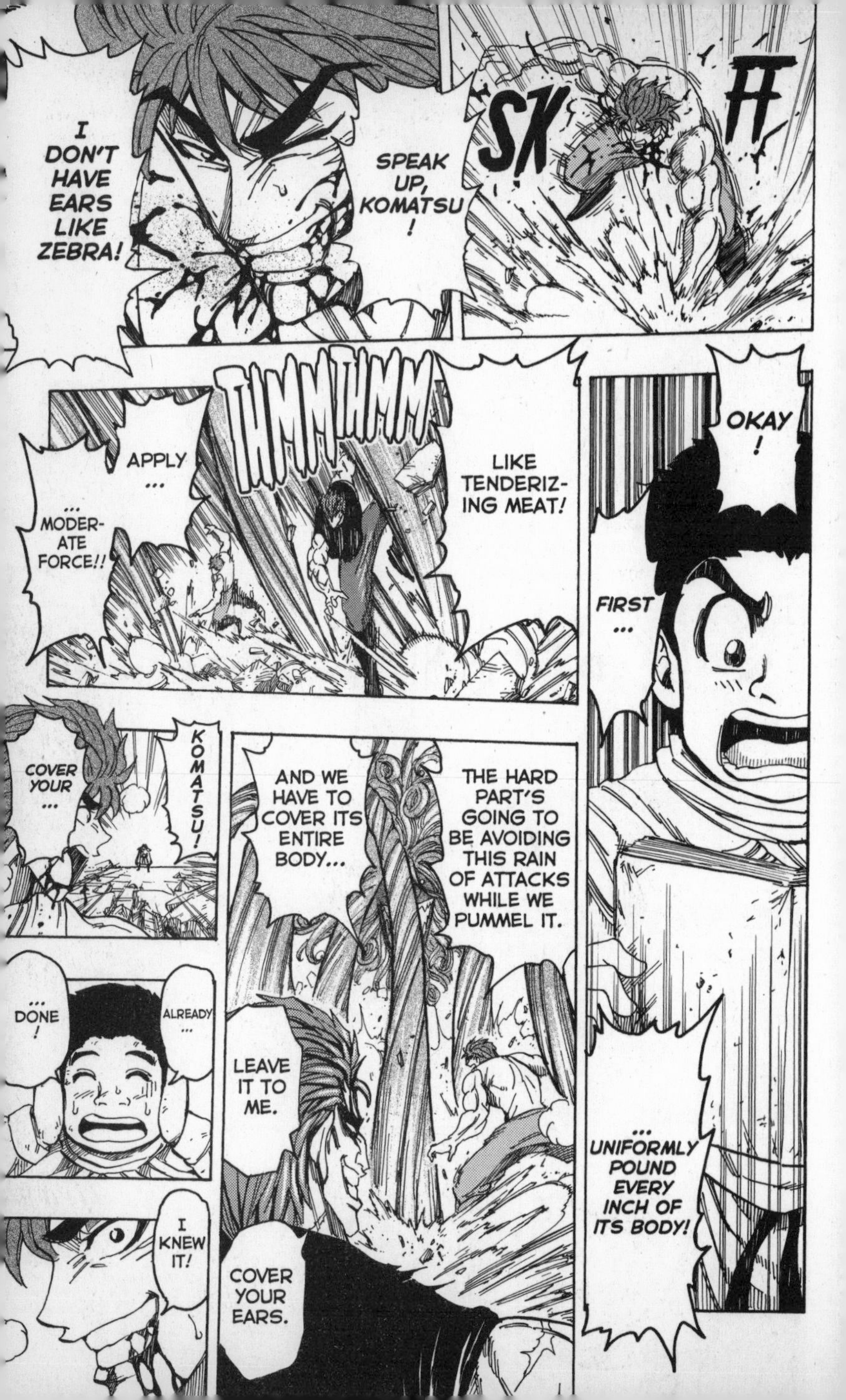
SK
FF
SPEAK UP, KOMATSU!
I DON'T HAVE EARS LIKE ZEBRA!
OKAY!
FIRST...
...UNIFORMLY POUND EVERY INCH OF ITS BODY!
THMM THMM
LIKE TENDERIZING MEAT!
APPLY...
...MODERATE FORCE!!
THE HARD PART'S GOING TO BE AVOIDING THIS RAIN OF ATTACKS WHILE WE PUMMEL IT.
AND WE HAVE TO COVER ITS ENTIRE BODY...
LEAVE IT TO ME.
COVER YOUR EARS.
KOMATSU!
COVER YOUR...
ALREADY...
...DONE!
I KNEW IT!

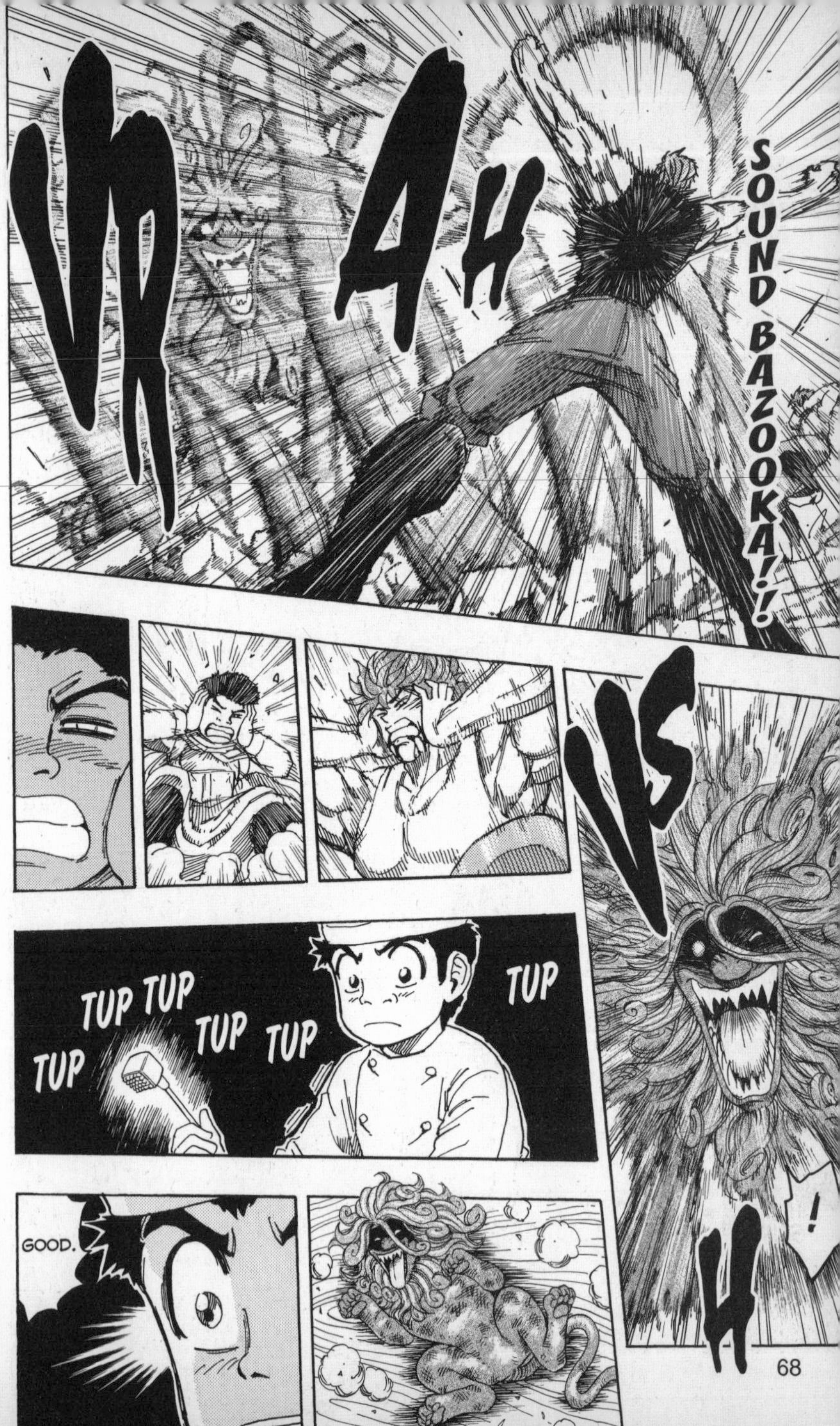
SOUND BAZOOKA!!
TUP
TUP
TUP
TUP
TUP
TUP
!
GOOD.

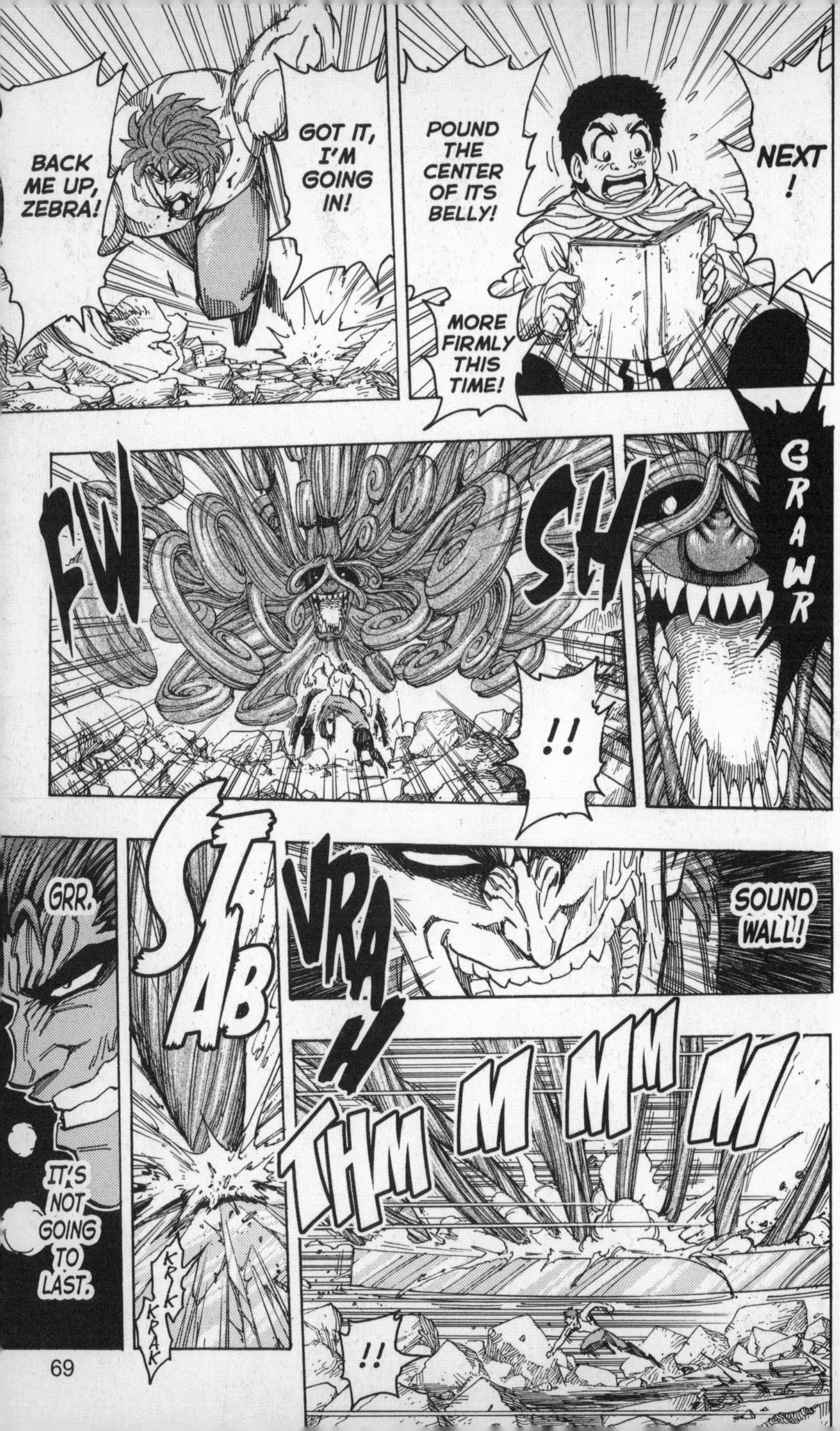
NEXT!
POUND THE CENTER OF ITS BELLY!
MORE FIRMLY THIS TIME!
GOT IT, I'M GOING IN!
BACK ME UP, ZEBRA!
GRAWR
!!
FWSH
SOUND WALL!
VRAHH
STAB
GRR.
IT'S NOT GOING TO LAST.
KRIK KRAK
THMMMMMM
!!

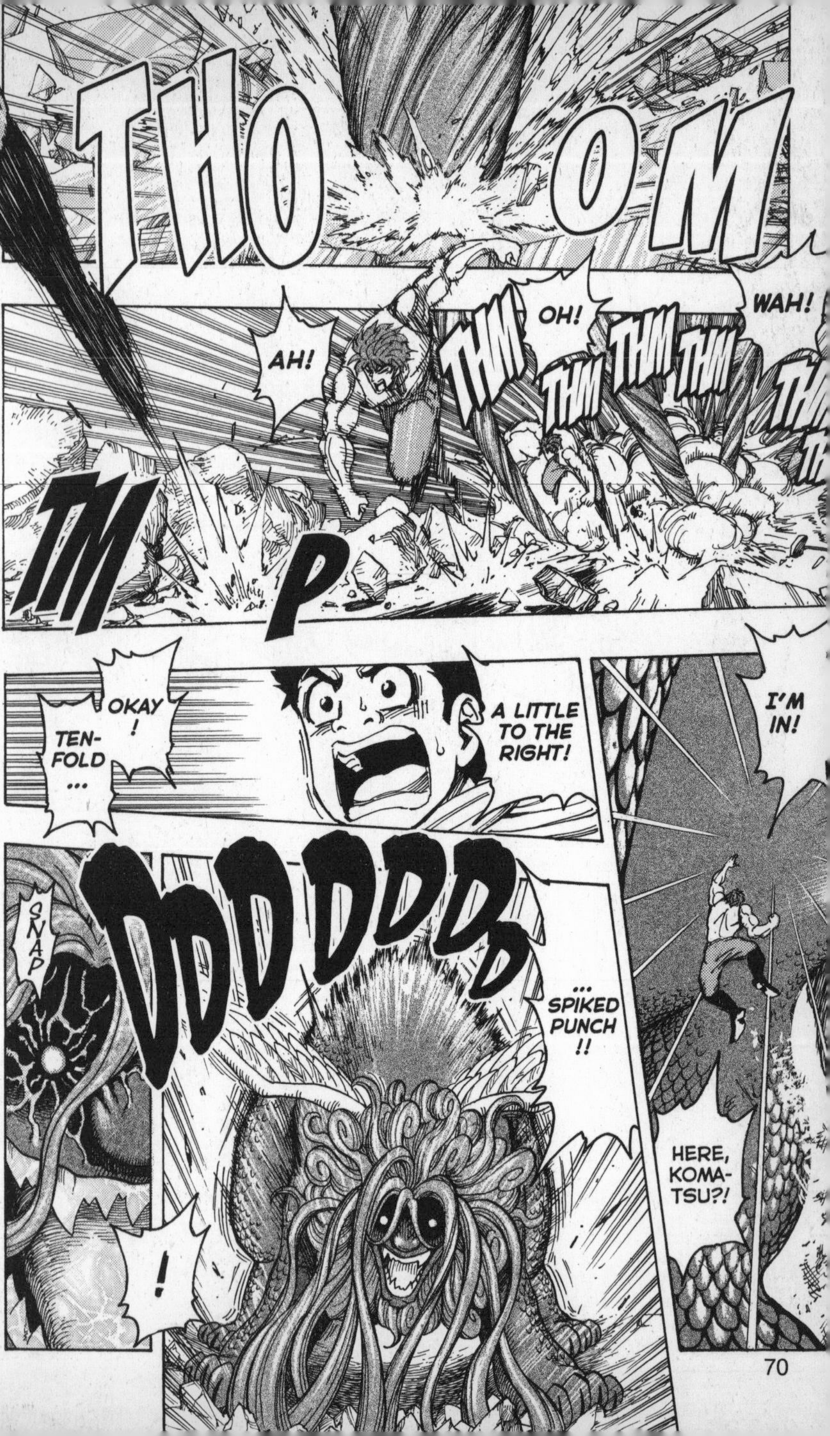
THOOM
WAH!
OH!
THM THM THM THM THM TH
AH!
TMP
I'M IN!
HERE, KOMATSU?!
A LITTLE TO THE RIGHT!
OKAY!
TEN-FOLD...
DDDDDDD
...SPIKED PUNCH!!
SNAP
!

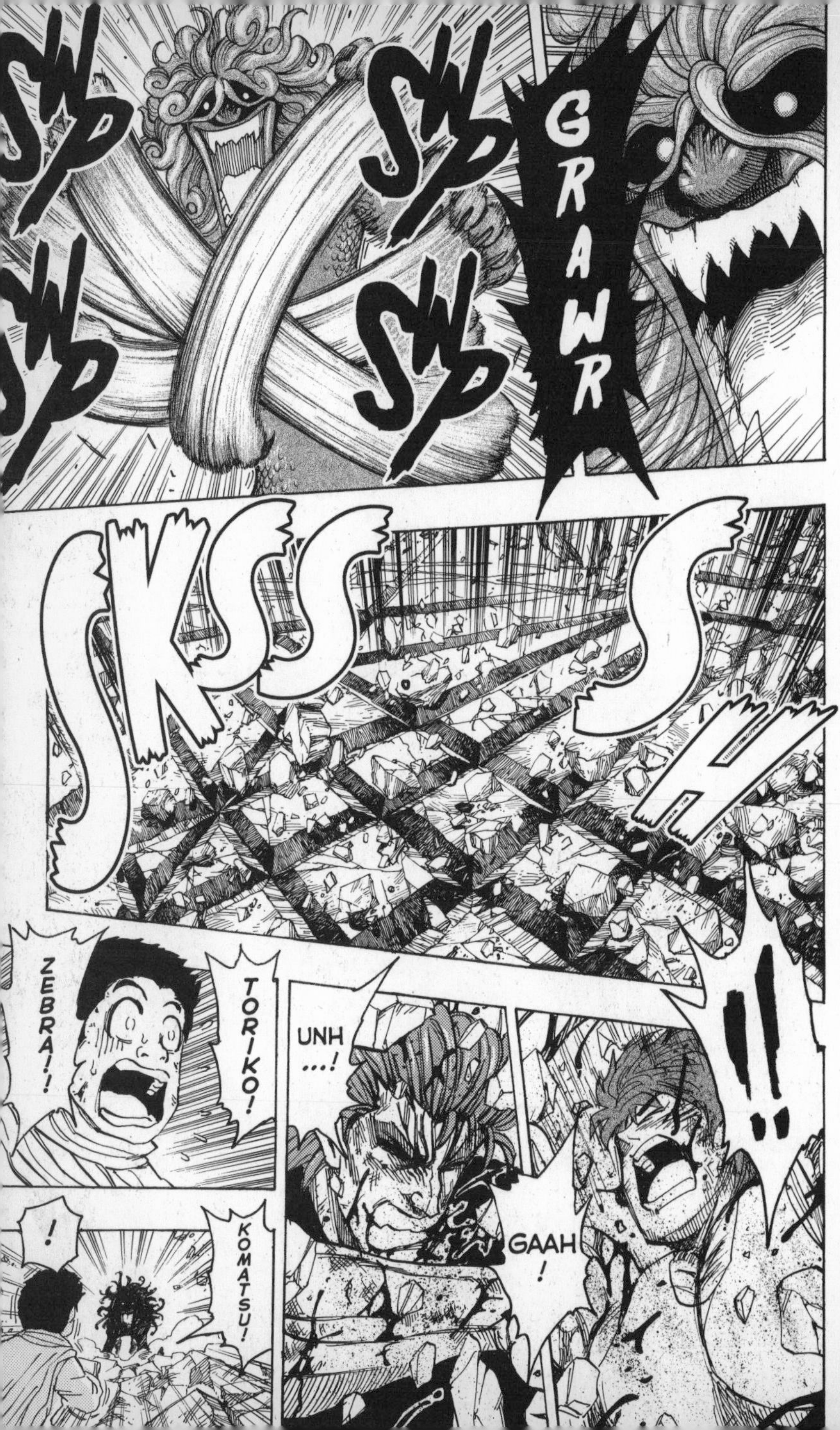
GRAWR
SWSP
SWSP
SWSP
SWSP
SKSSSH
!!
UNH...!
GAAH!
TORIKO!
ZEBRA!!
KOMATSU!
!

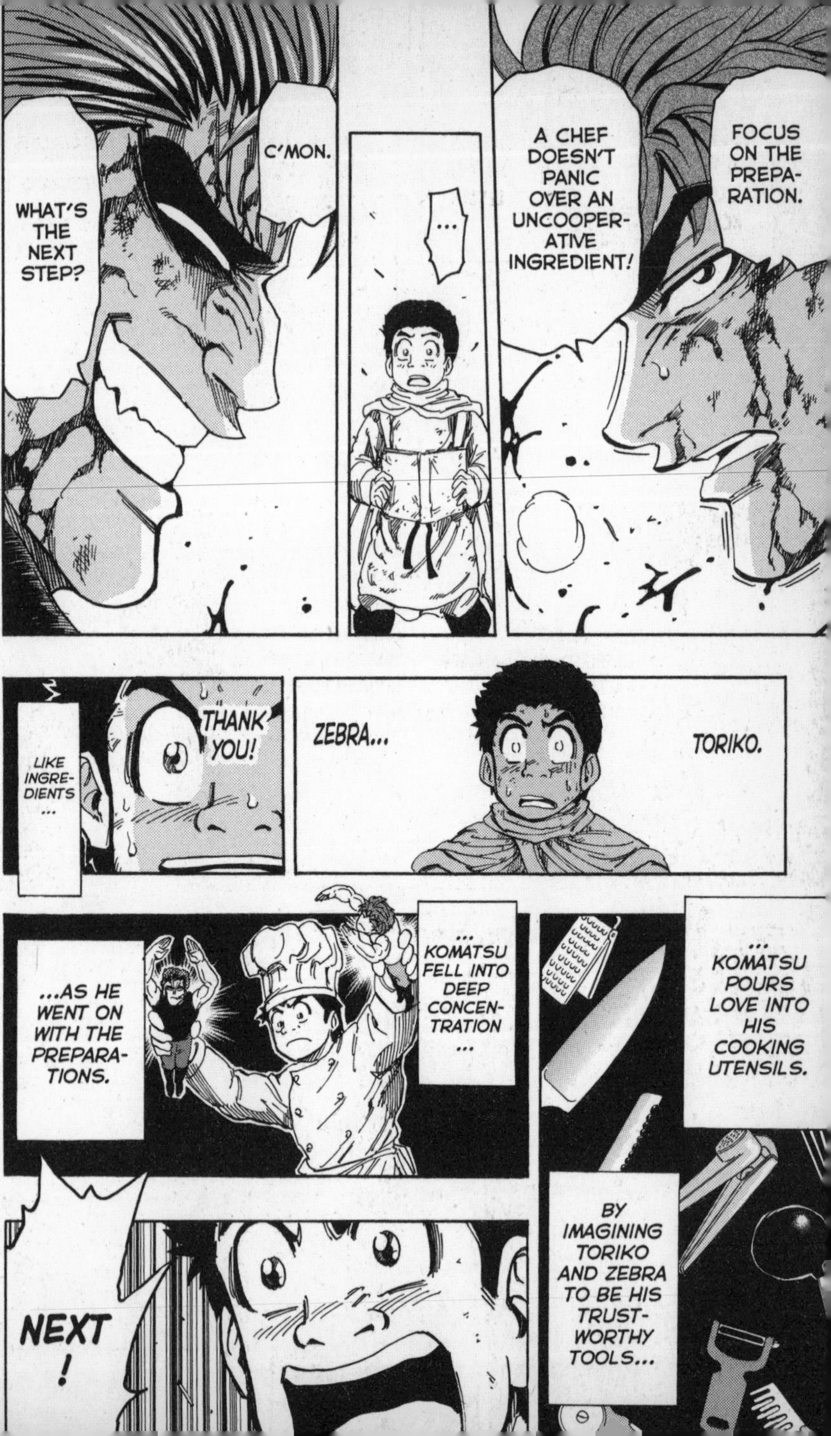
FOCUS ON THE PREPA-RATION.
A CHEF DOESN'T PANIC OVER AN UNCOOPER-ATIVE INGREDIENT!
...
C'MON.
WHAT'S THE NEXT STEP?
TORIKO.
ZEBRA...
THANK YOU!
LIKE INGRE-DIENTS ...
... KOMATSU POURS LOVE INTO HIS COOKING UTENSILS.
BY IMAGINING TORIKO AND ZEBRA TO BE HIS TRUST-WORTHY TOOLS...
... KOMATSU FELL INTO DEEP CONCEN-TRATION ...
...AS HE WENT ON WITH THE PREPARA-TIONS.
NEXT!

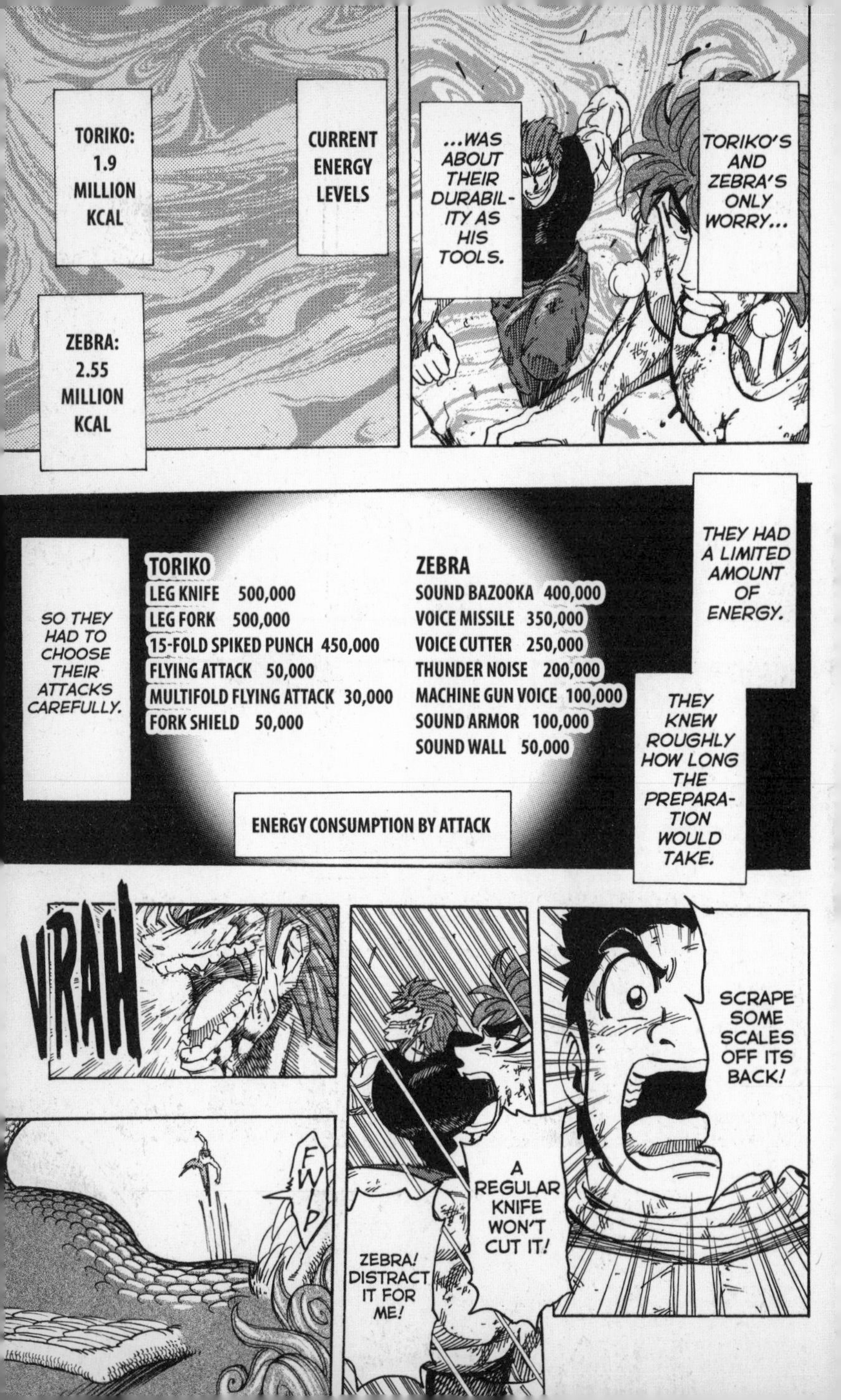
TORIKO'S AND ZEBRA'S ONLY WORRY...
...WAS ABOUT THEIR DURABILITY AS HIS TOOLS.
CURRENT ENERGY LEVELS
TORIKO: 1.9 MILLION KCAL
ZEBRA: 2.55 MILLION KCAL
THEY HAD A LIMITED AMOUNT OF ENERGY.
THEY KNEW ROUGHLY HOW LONG THE PREPARATION WOULD TAKE.
ZEBRA
SOUND BAZOOKA 400,000
VOICE MISSILE 350,000
VOICE CUTTER 250,000
THUNDER NOISE 200,000
MACHINE GUN VOICE 100,000
SOUND ARMOR 100,000
SOUND WALL 50,000
TORIKO
LEG KNIFE 500,000
LEG FORK 500,000
15-FOLD SPIKED PUNCH 450,000
FLYING ATTACK 50,000
MULTIFOLD FLYING ATTACK 30,000
FORK SHIELD 50,000
ENERGY CONSUMPTION BY ATTACK
SO THEY HAD TO CHOOSE THEIR ATTACKS CAREFULLY.
SCRAPE SOME SCALES OFF ITS BACK!
A REGULAR KNIFE WON'T CUT IT!
ZEBRA! DISTRACT IT FOR ME!
VRAH
FWIP

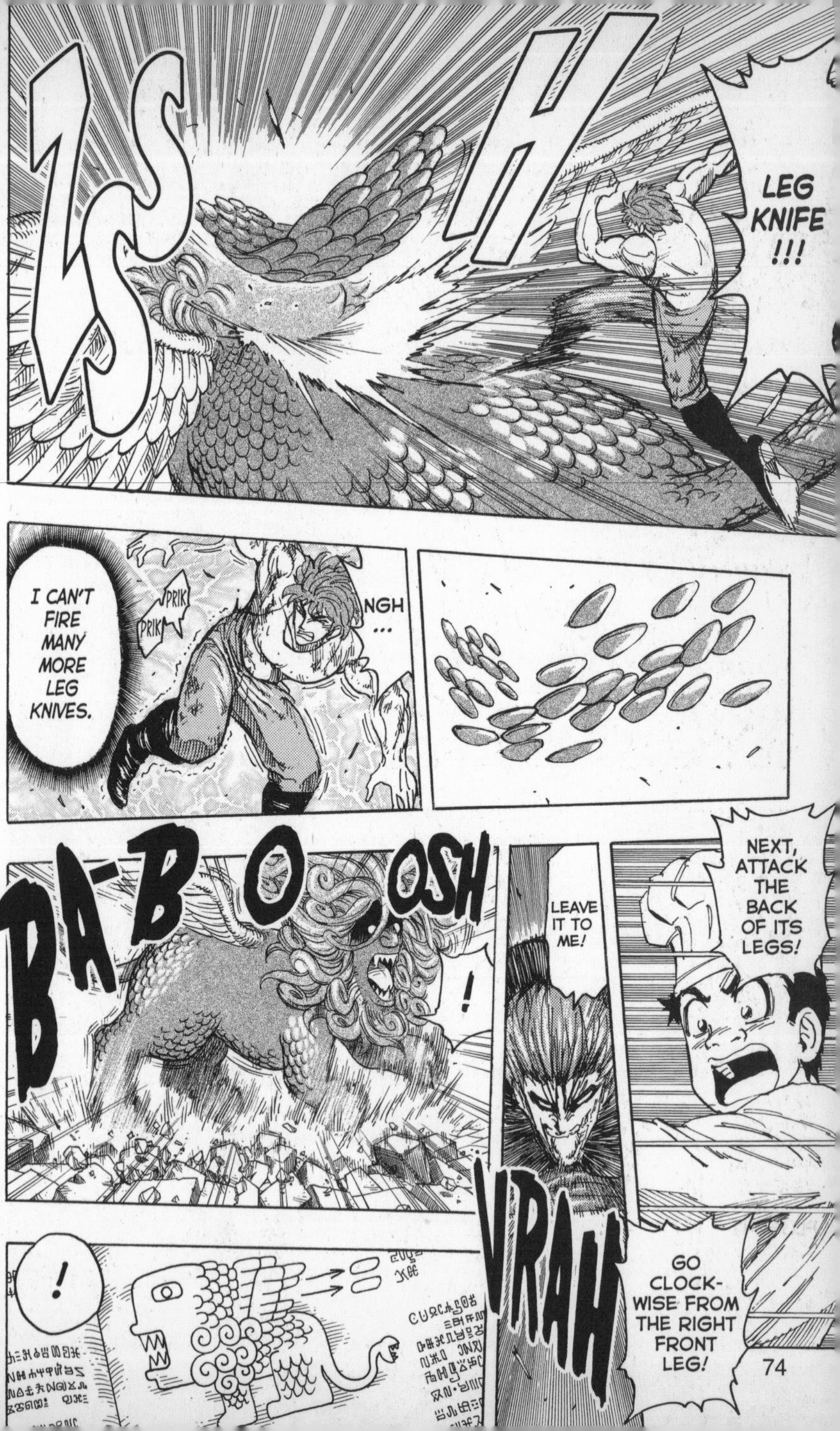
ZSH
LEG KNIFE!!!
NGH...
PRIK
PRIK
I CAN'T FIRE MANY MORE LEG KNIVES.
NEXT, ATTACK THE BACK OF ITS LEGS!
LEAVE IT TO ME!
BA-BOOOSH
!
VRAH
GO CLOCKWISE FROM THE RIGHT FRONT LEG!
!

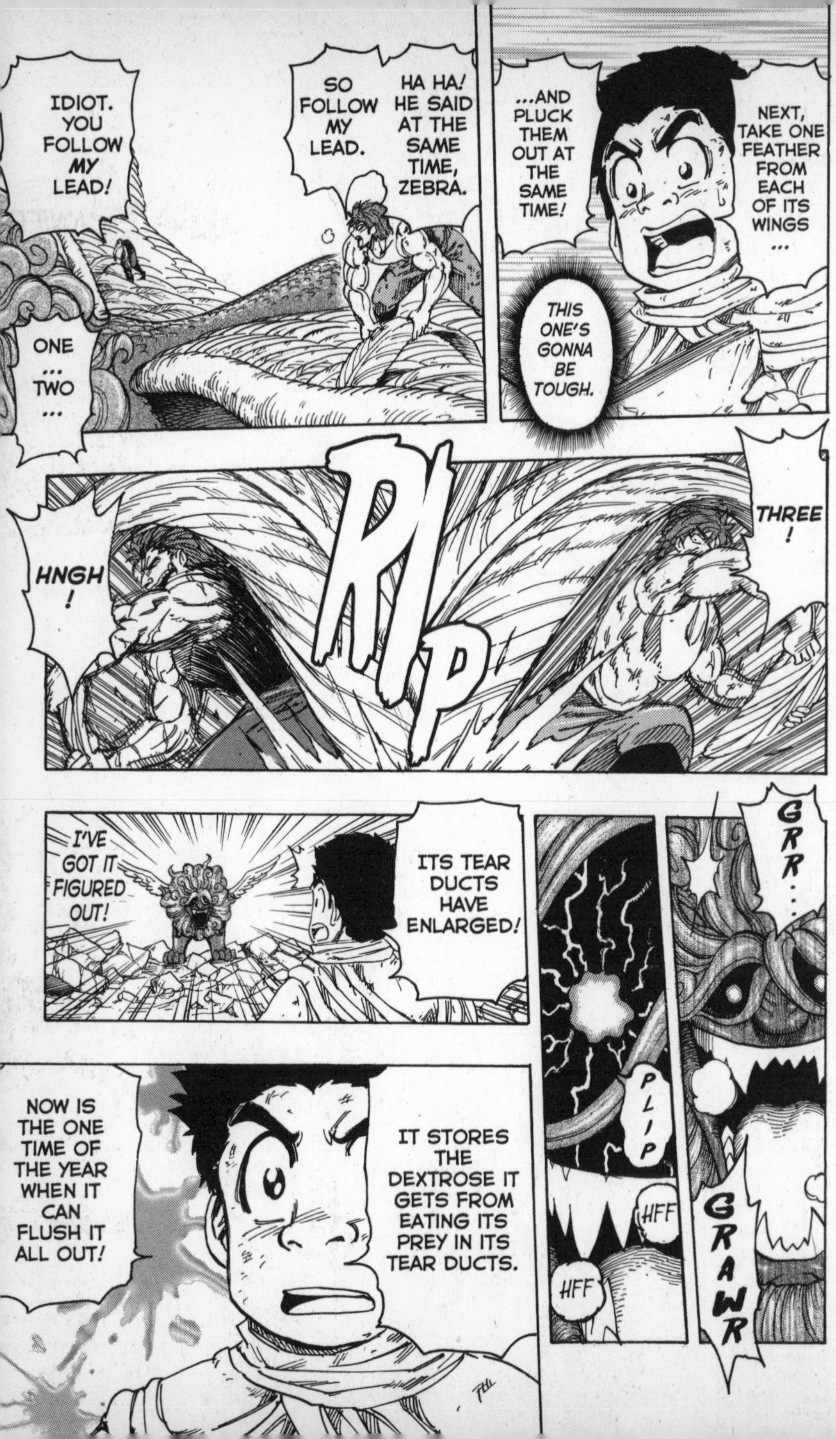
NEXT, TAKE ONE FEATHER FROM EACH OF ITS WINGS ...
...AND PLUCK THEM OUT AT THE SAME TIME!
THIS ONE'S GONNA BE TOUGH.
HA HA! HE SAID AT THE SAME TIME, ZEBRA.
SO FOLLOW MY LEAD.
IDIOT. YOU FOLLOW MY LEAD!
ONE ... TWO ...
THREE!
RIP
HNGH!
GRR...
GRAWR
PLIP
HFF
HFF
ITS TEAR DUCTS HAVE ENLARGED!
I'VE GOT IT FIGURED OUT!
IT STORES THE DEXTROSE IT GETS FROM EATING ITS PREY IN ITS TEAR DUCTS.
NOW IS THE ONE TIME OF THE YEAR WHEN IT CAN FLUSH IT ALL OUT!

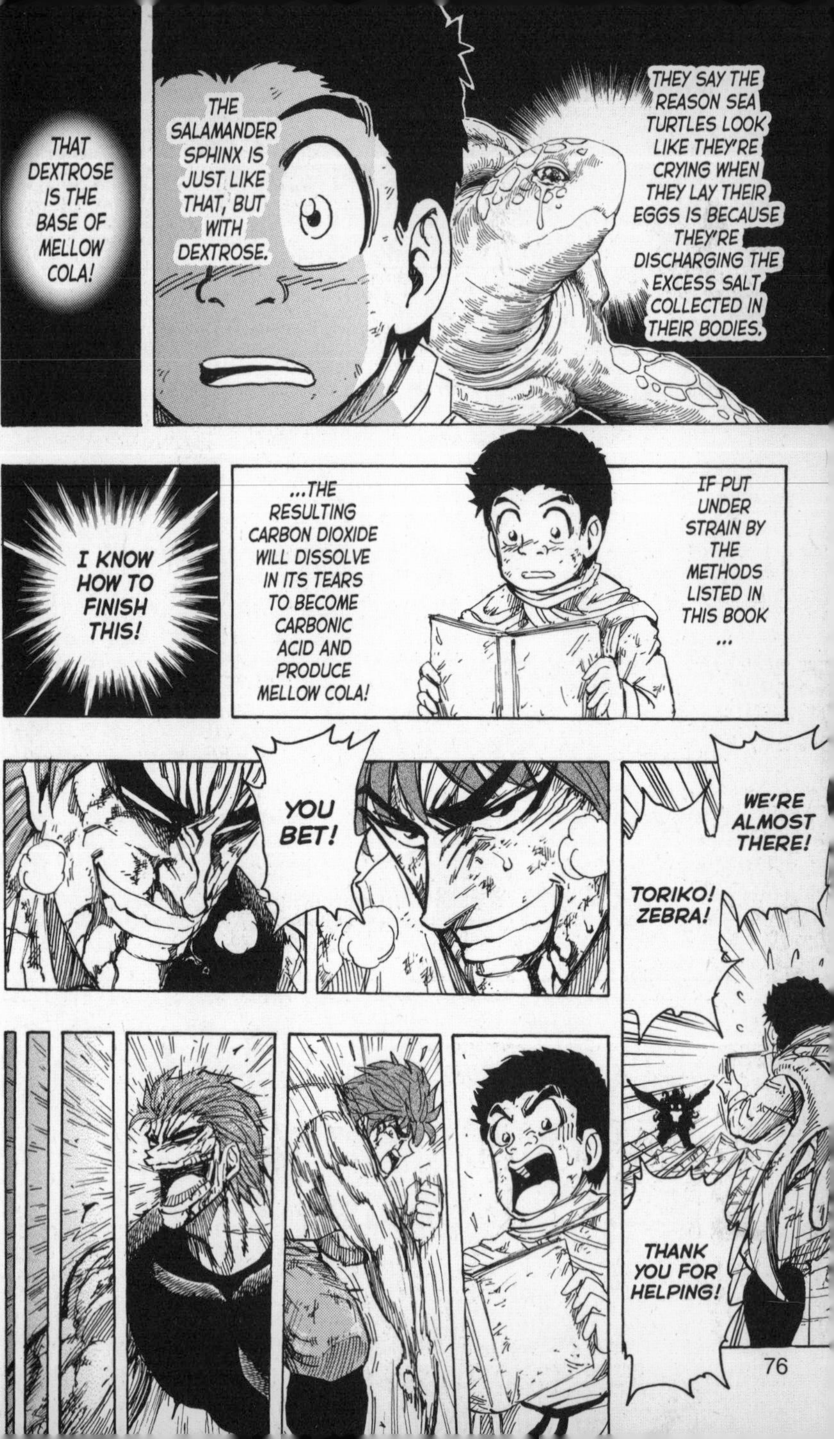
THEY SAY THE REASON SEA TURTLES LOOK LIKE THEY'RE CRYING WHEN THEY LAY THEIR EGGS IS BECAUSE THEY'RE DISCHARGING THE EXCESS SALT COLLECTED IN THEIR BODIES.
THE SALAMANDER SPHINX IS JUST LIKE THAT, BUT WITH DEXTROSE.
THAT DEXTROSE IS THE BASE OF MELLOW COLA!
IF PUT UNDER STRAIN BY THE METHODS LISTED IN THIS BOOK...
...THE RESULTING CARBON DIOXIDE WILL DISSOLVE IN ITS TEARS TO BECOME CARBONIC ACID AND PRODUCE MELLOW COLA!
I KNOW HOW TO FINISH THIS!
WE'RE ALMOST THERE!
TORIKO! ZEBRA!
THANK YOU FOR HELPING!
YOU BET!

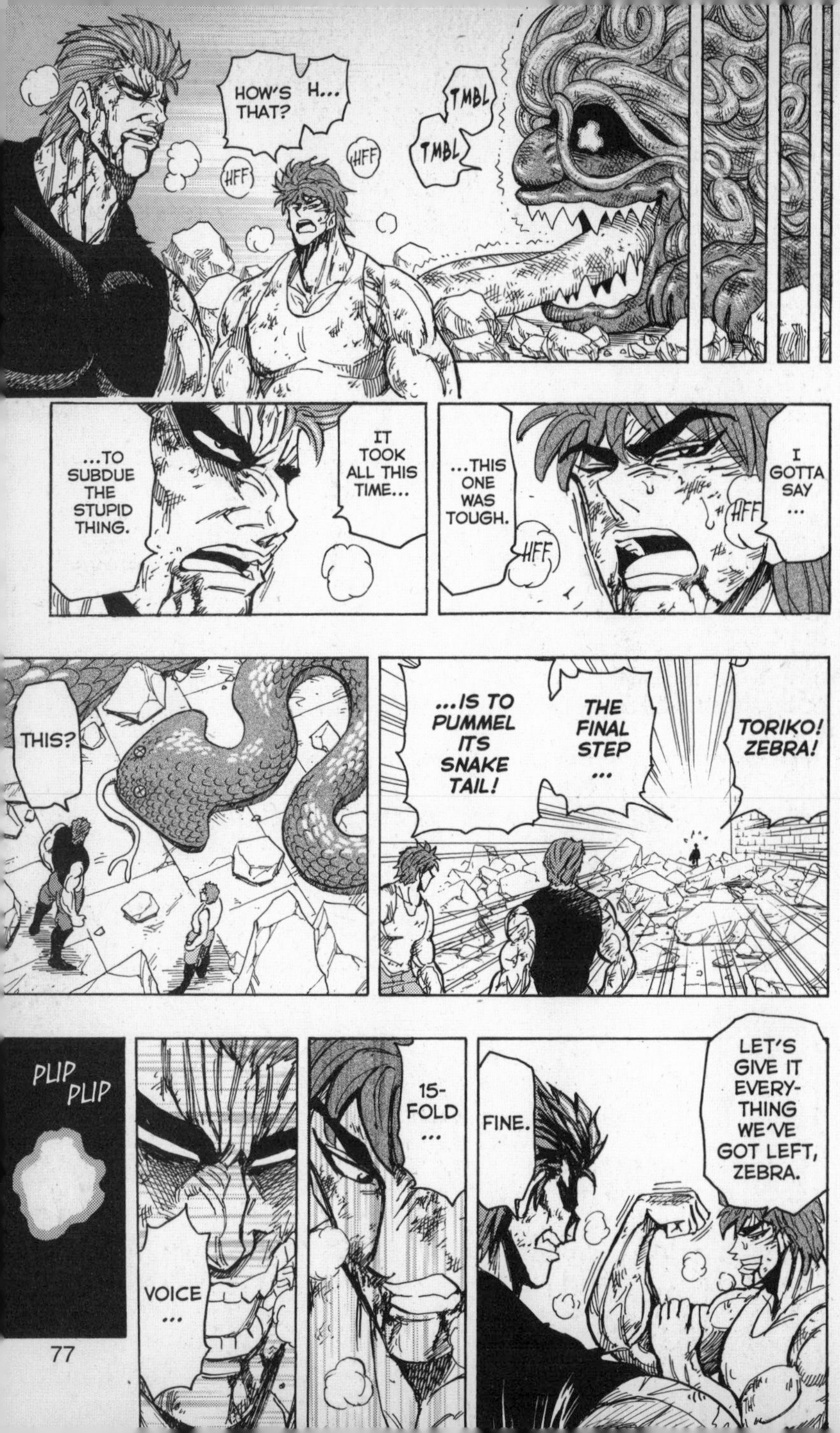
TMBL
TMBL
HFF
HFF
HOW'S THAT? H...
I GOTTA SAY ...
HFF
...THIS ONE WAS TOUGH.
HFF
IT TOOK ALL THIS TIME...
...TO SUBDUE THE STUPID THING.
TORIKO! ZEBRA!
THE FINAL STEP ...
...IS TO PUMMEL ITS SNAKE TAIL!
THIS?
LET'S GIVE IT EVERYTHING WE'VE GOT LEFT, ZEBRA.
FINE.
15-FOLD ...
VOICE ...
PLIP PLIP

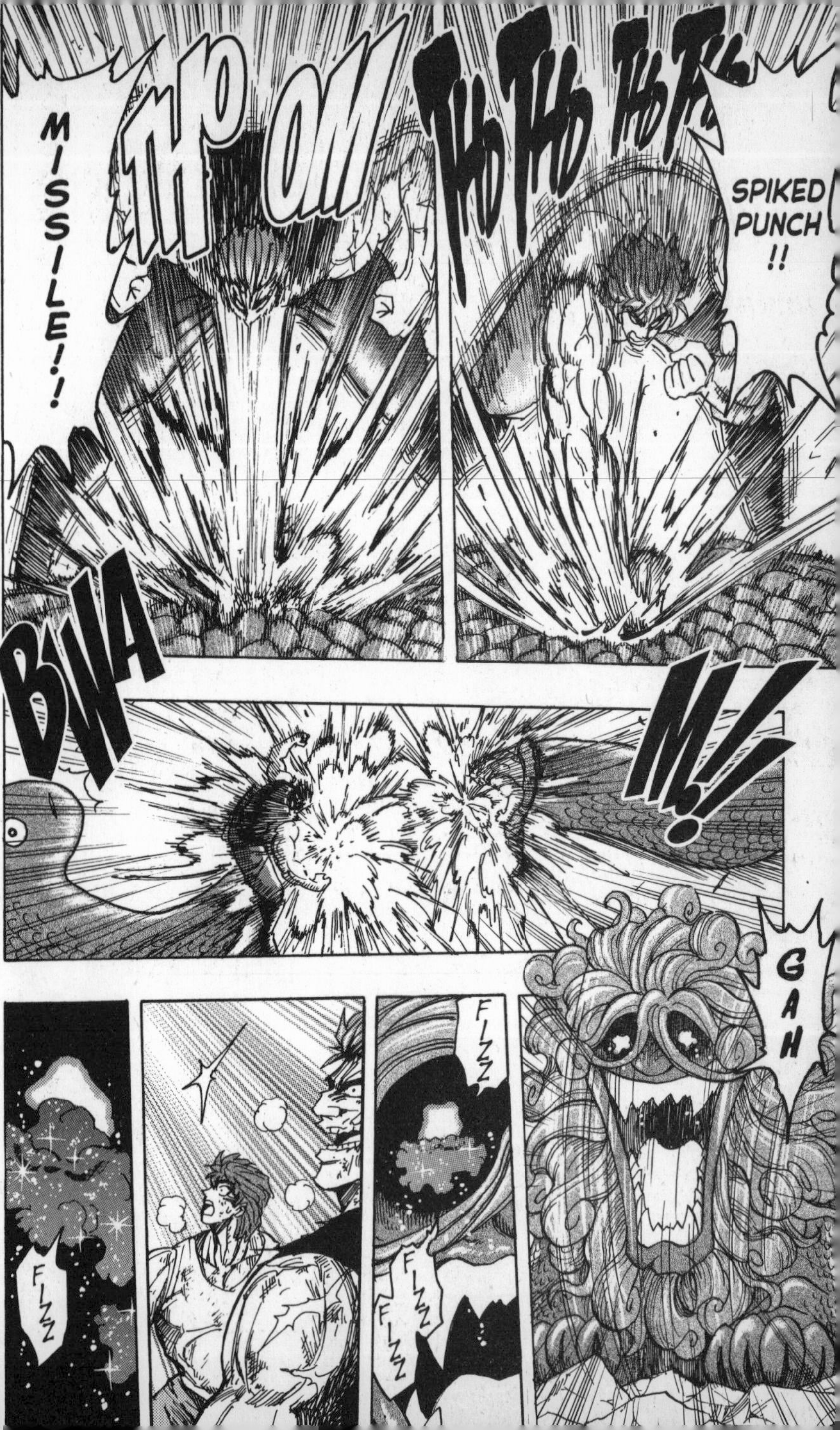
SPIKED PUNCH !!
MISSILE!!!
THOOM
BWAM!!
GAH
FIZZ
FIZZ
FIZZ
FIZZ

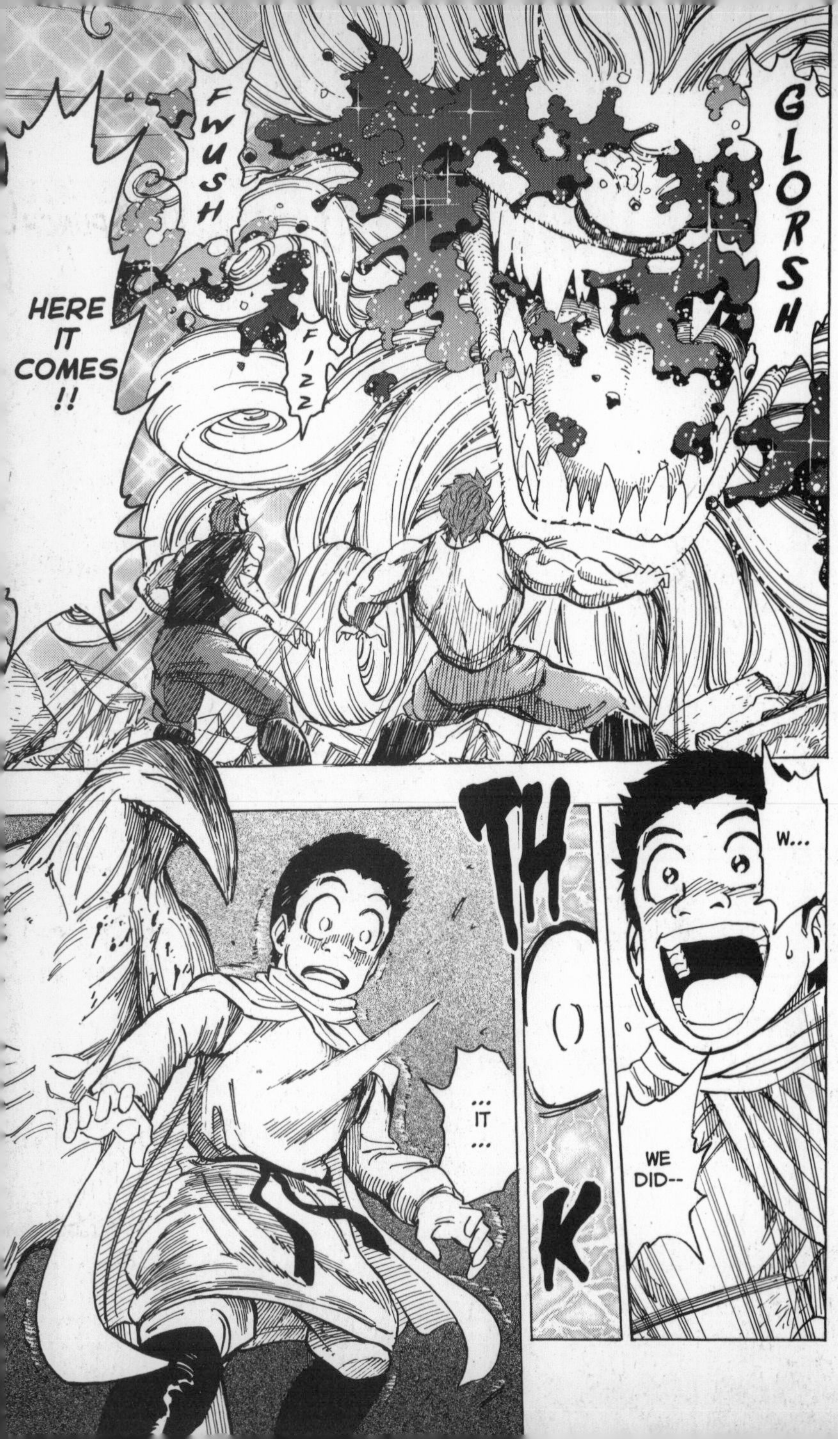
GLORSH
FWUSH
HERE IT COMES!!
FIZZ
W...
WE DID--
THK
...IT...

TORIKO

GOURMET CHECKLIST

Vol. 160

MAMEW
(BIRD)

CAPTURE LEVEL: UNKNOWN

HABITAT: GOURMET WORLD

LENGTH: 5 METERS

HEIGHT: ---

WEIGHT: 4.5 TONS

PRICE: UNKNOWN

SCALE

AS WITH THE PREVIOUS ENTRIES, THIS LARGE BIRD LIVES IN THE GOURMET WORLD'S UNDERGROUND FOREST. DETAILS REGARDING ITS BEHAVIOR, CAPTURE LEVEL, AND MORE ARE A COMPLETE MYSTERY, BUT ACCORDING TO KNOCKING MASTER JIRO (ONE OF THE FEW PEOPLE WHO CAN FREELY PASS BETWEEN THE HUMAN WORLD AND THE GOURMET WORLD) THEY ALWAYS TRAVEL IN FLOCKS AND CALL FOR AN EXCESSIVE AMOUNT OF BACKUP WHEN THREATENED.

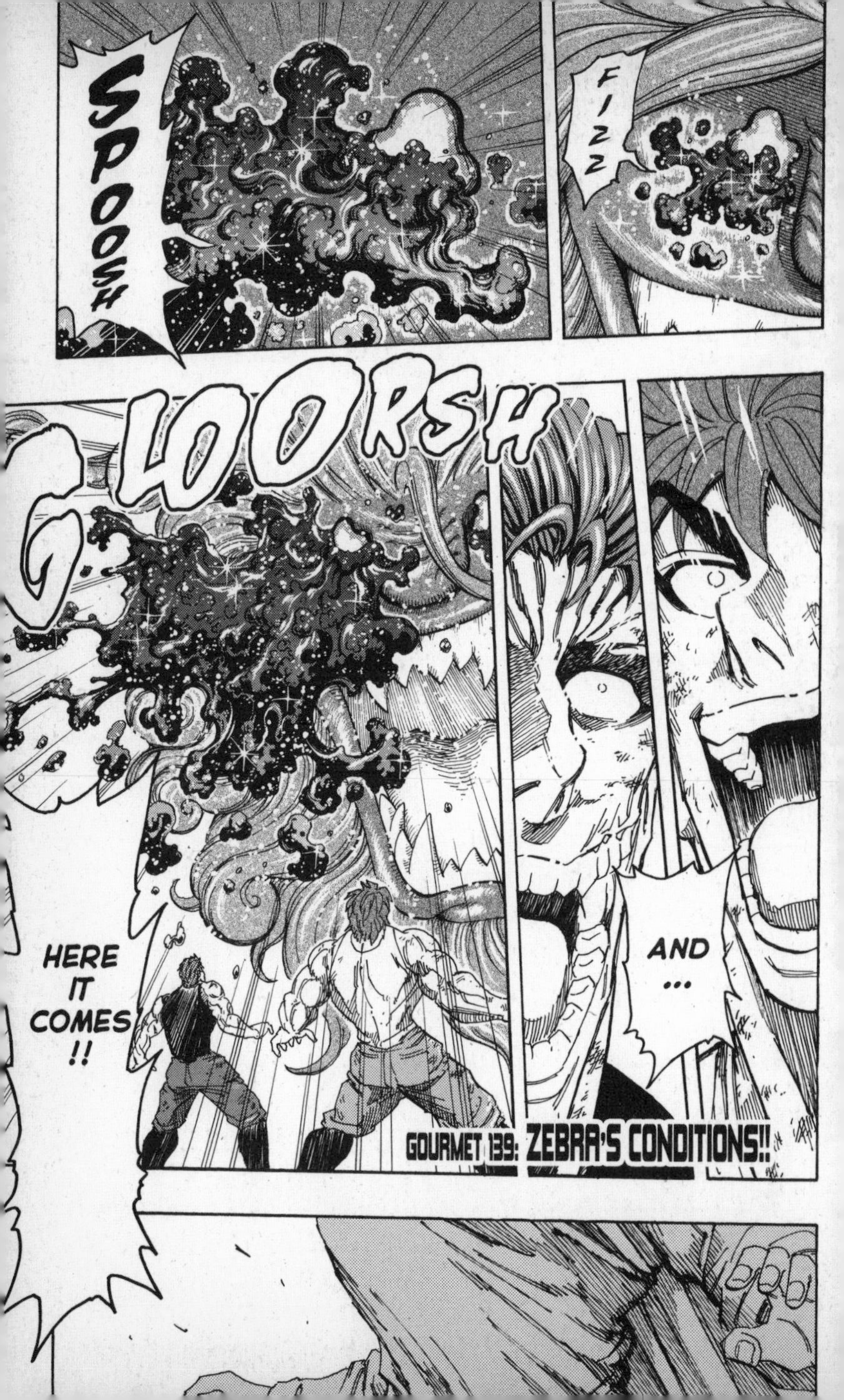
FIZZ
SPOOOSH
AND ...
GLOORSH
HERE IT COMES !!
GOURMET 139: ZEBRA'S CONDITIONS!!

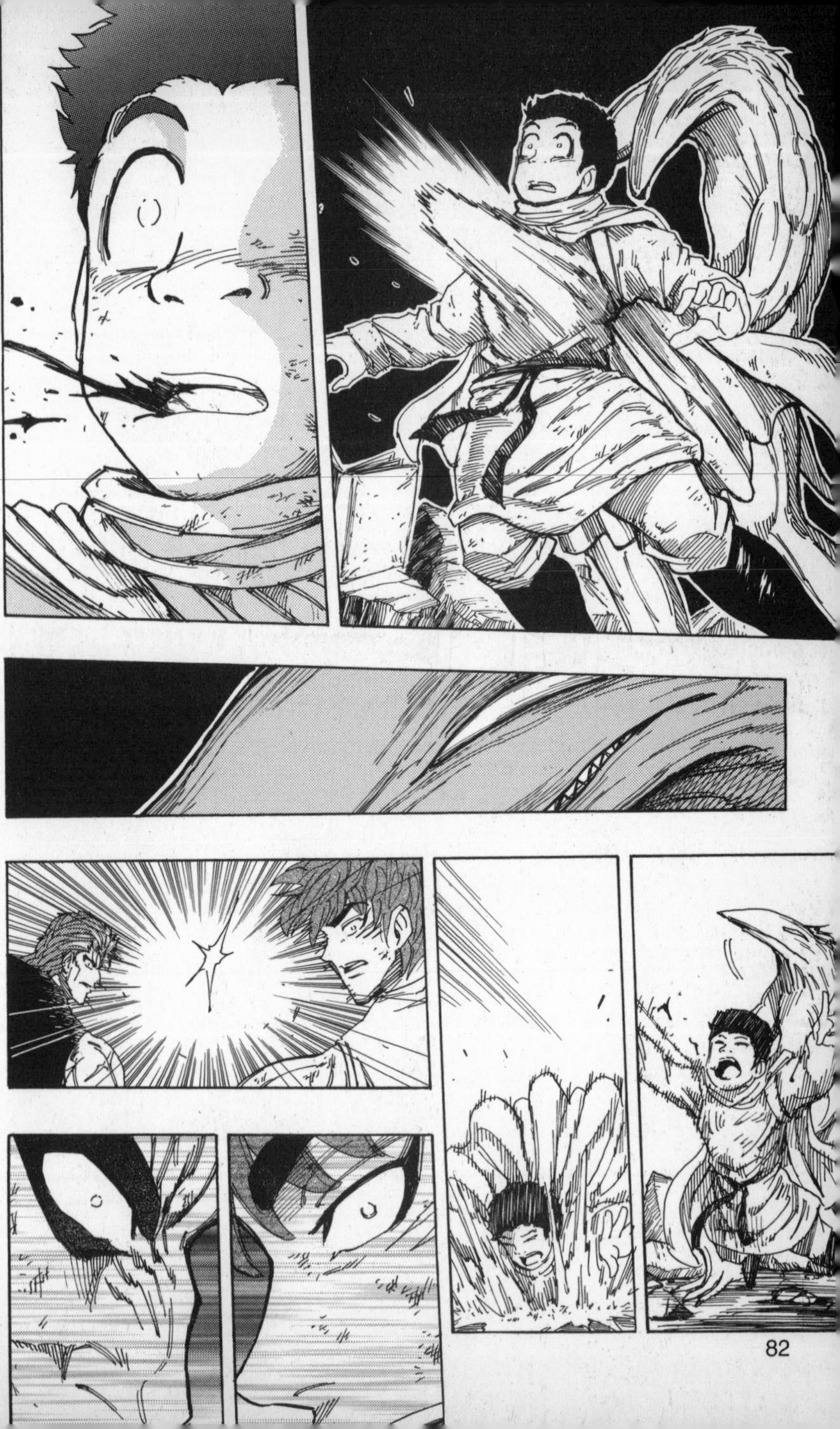

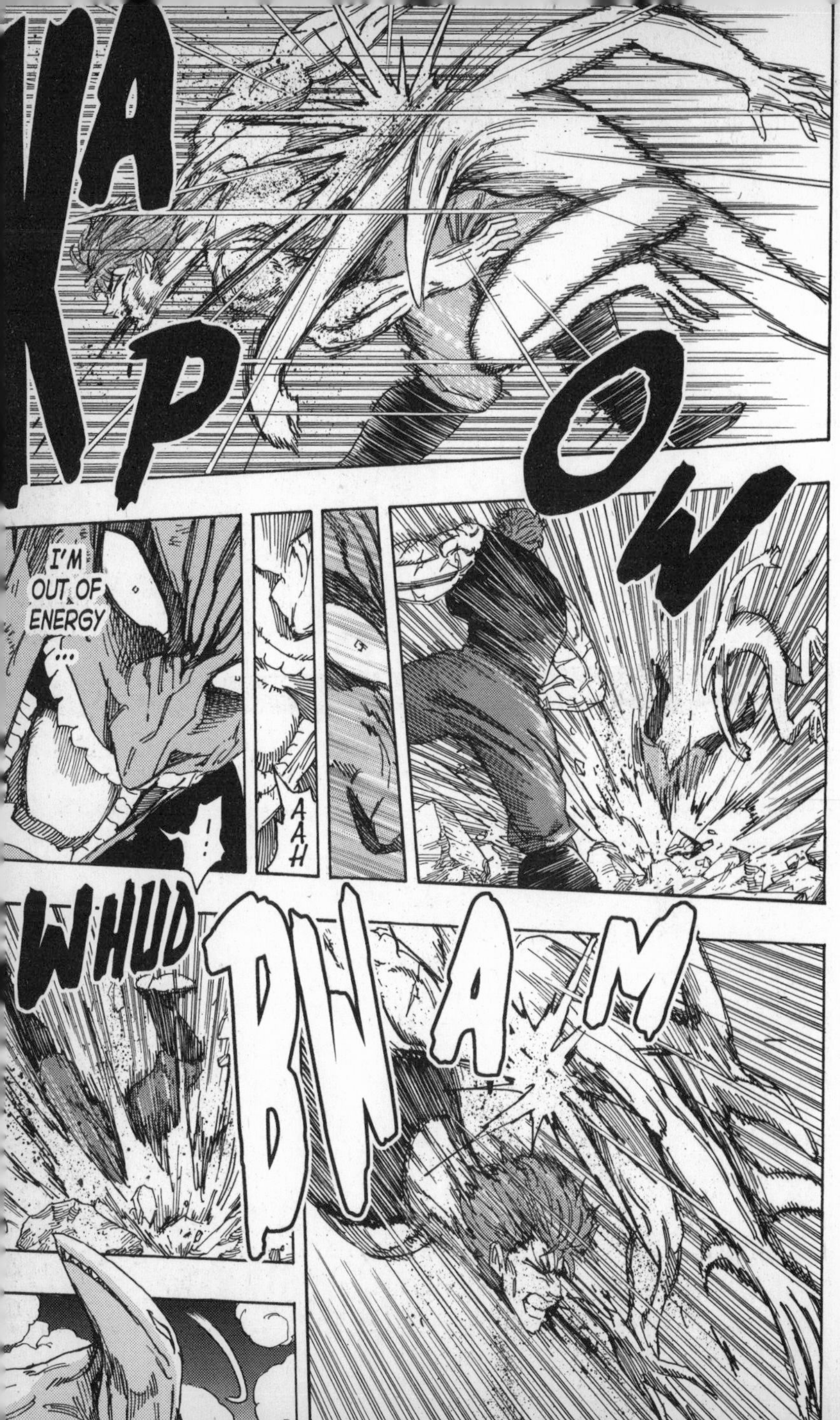
KAPOW
AAAH
I'M OUT OF ENERGY...
!!
BWAM
WHUD

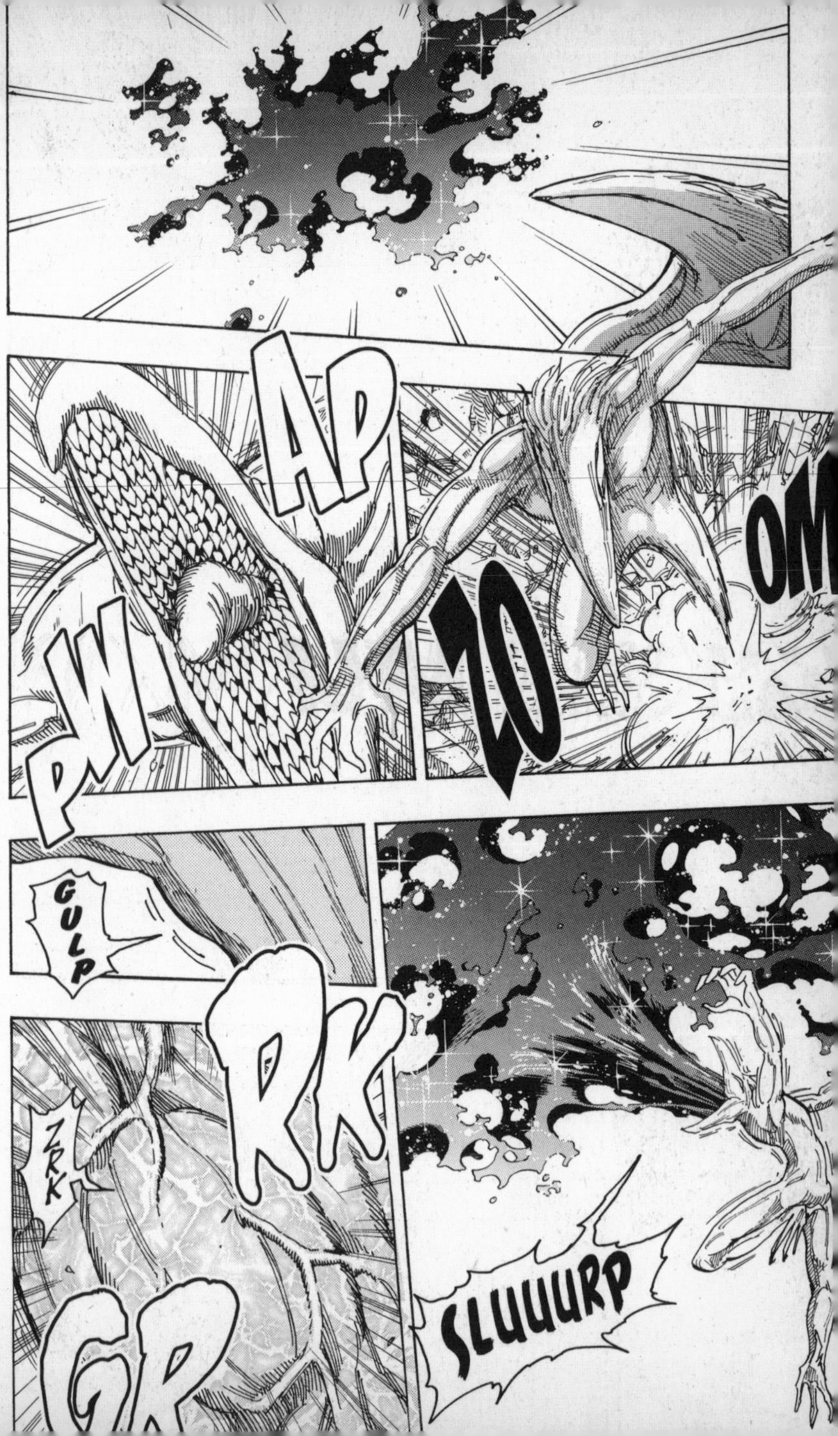
ZOOM
PWAP
SLUUURP
GULP
ZRK
GRRK

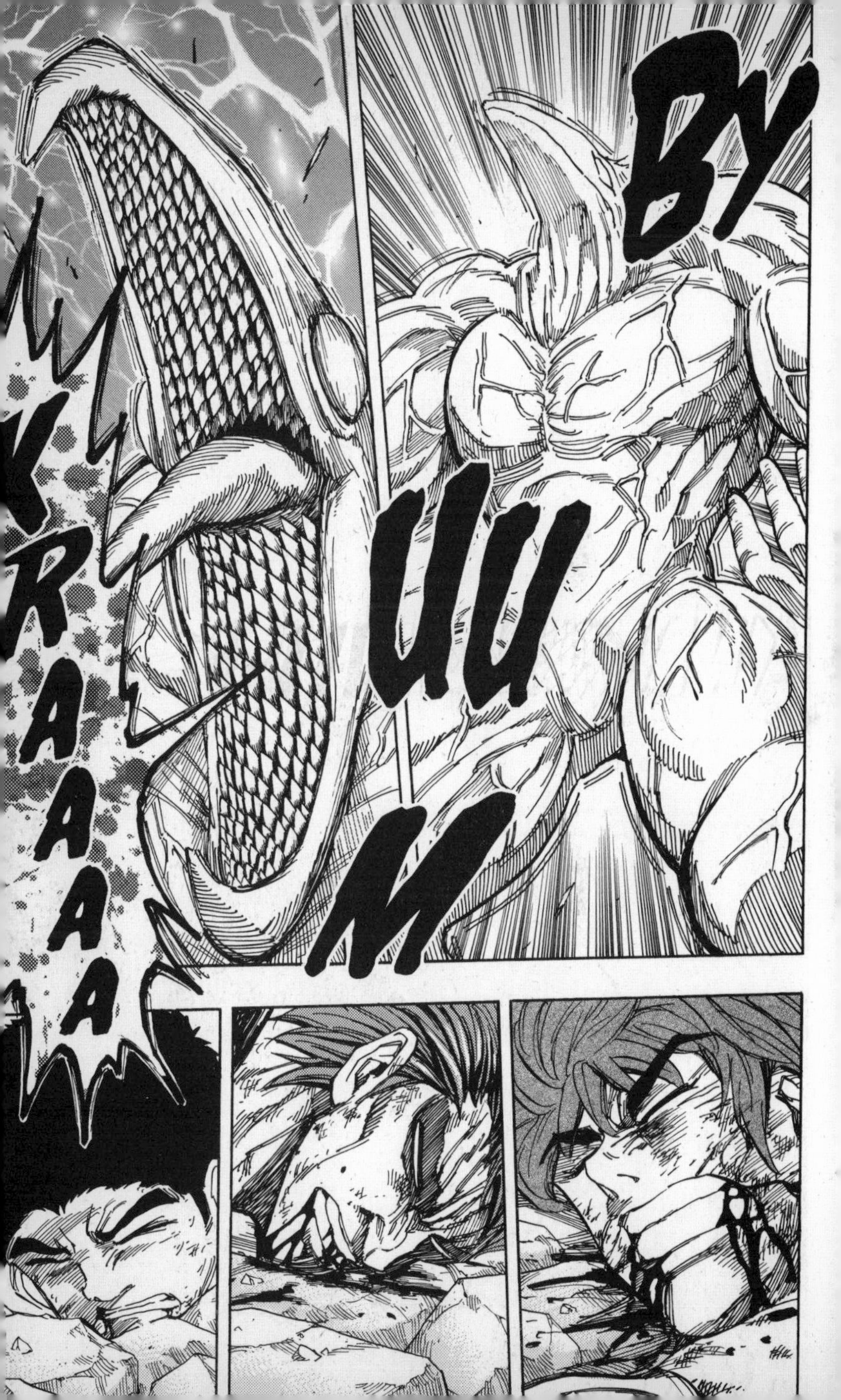
BYUUM
KRAAAA

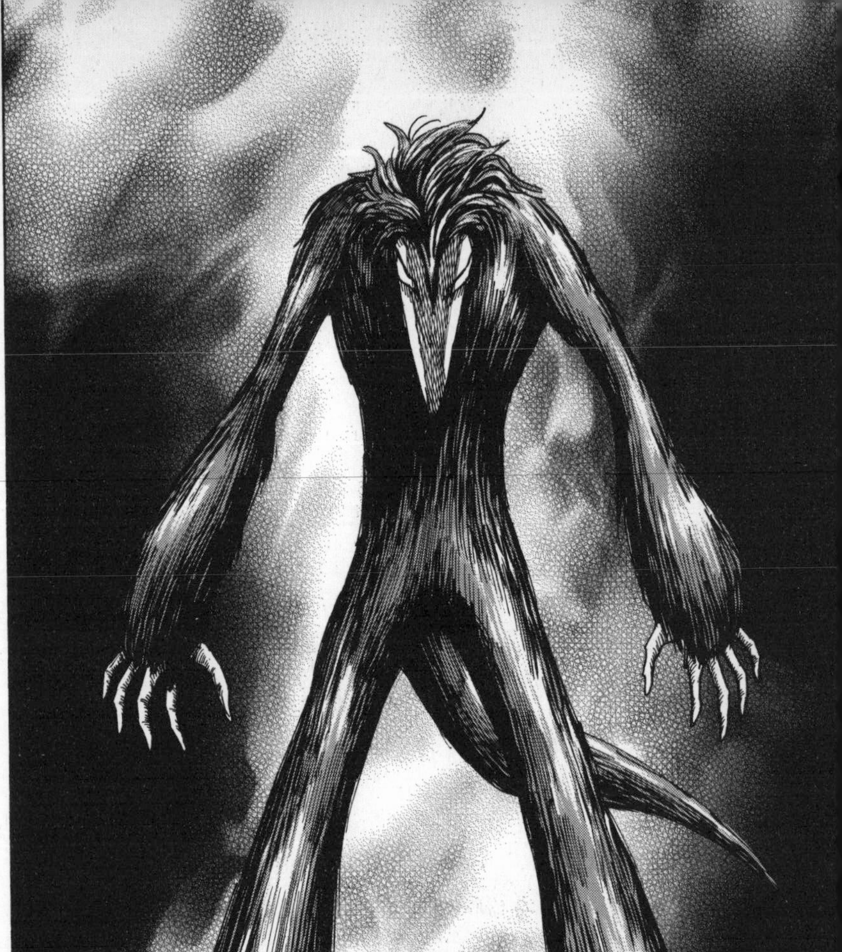
GOURMET 139: ZEBRA'S CONDITIONS!!

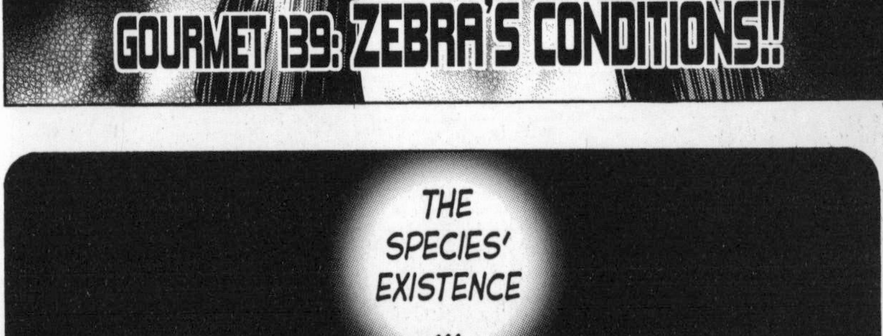
THE SPECIES' EXISTENCE ...

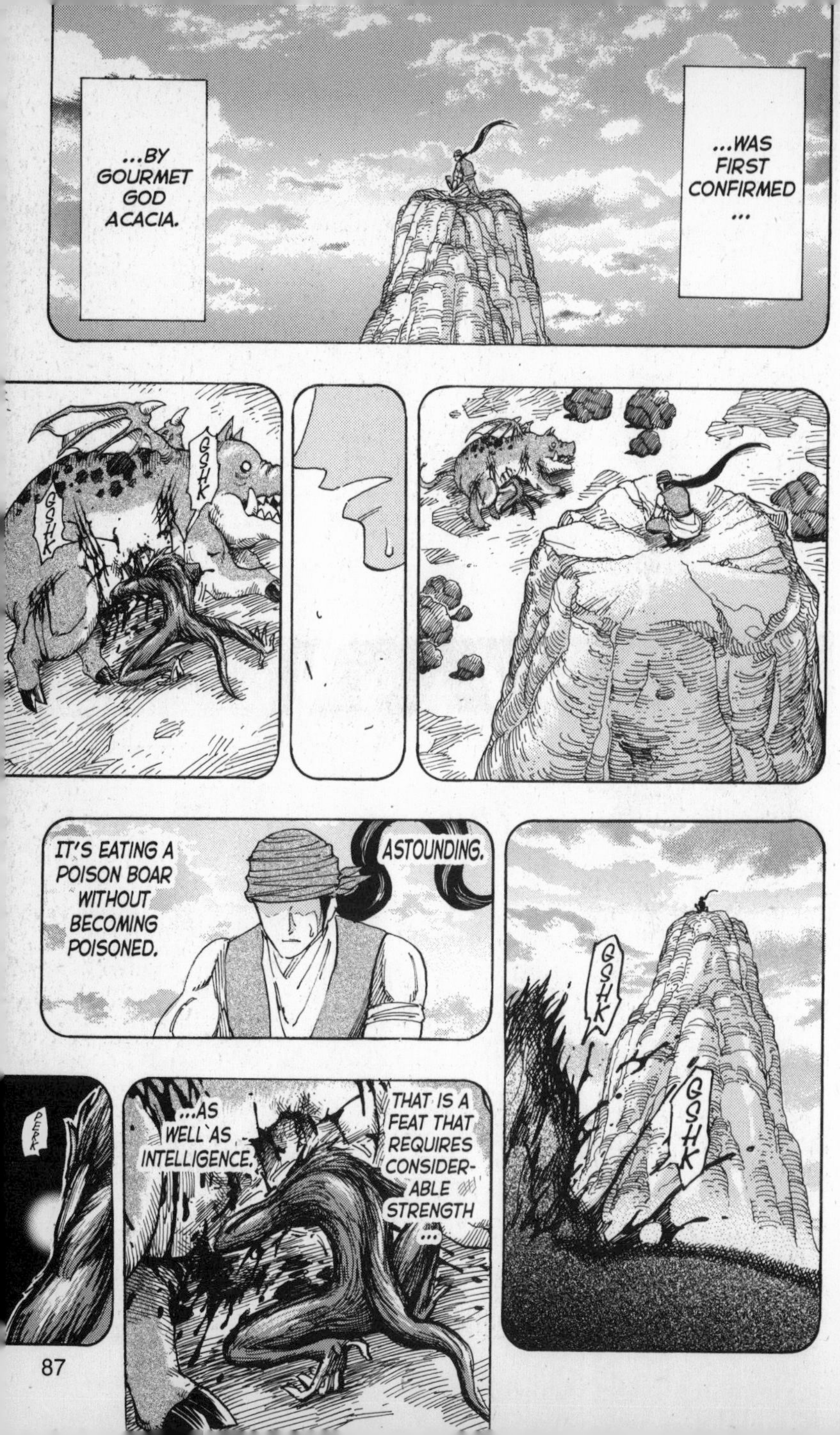

...WAS FIRST CONFIRMED ...
...BY GOURMET GOD ACACIA.
GSHK
GSHK
GSHK
GSHK
ASTOUNDING.
IT'S EATING A POISON BOAR WITHOUT BECOMING POISONED.
THAT IS A FEAT THAT REQUIRES CONSIDER-ABLE STRENGTH ...
...AS WELL AS INTELLIGENCE.

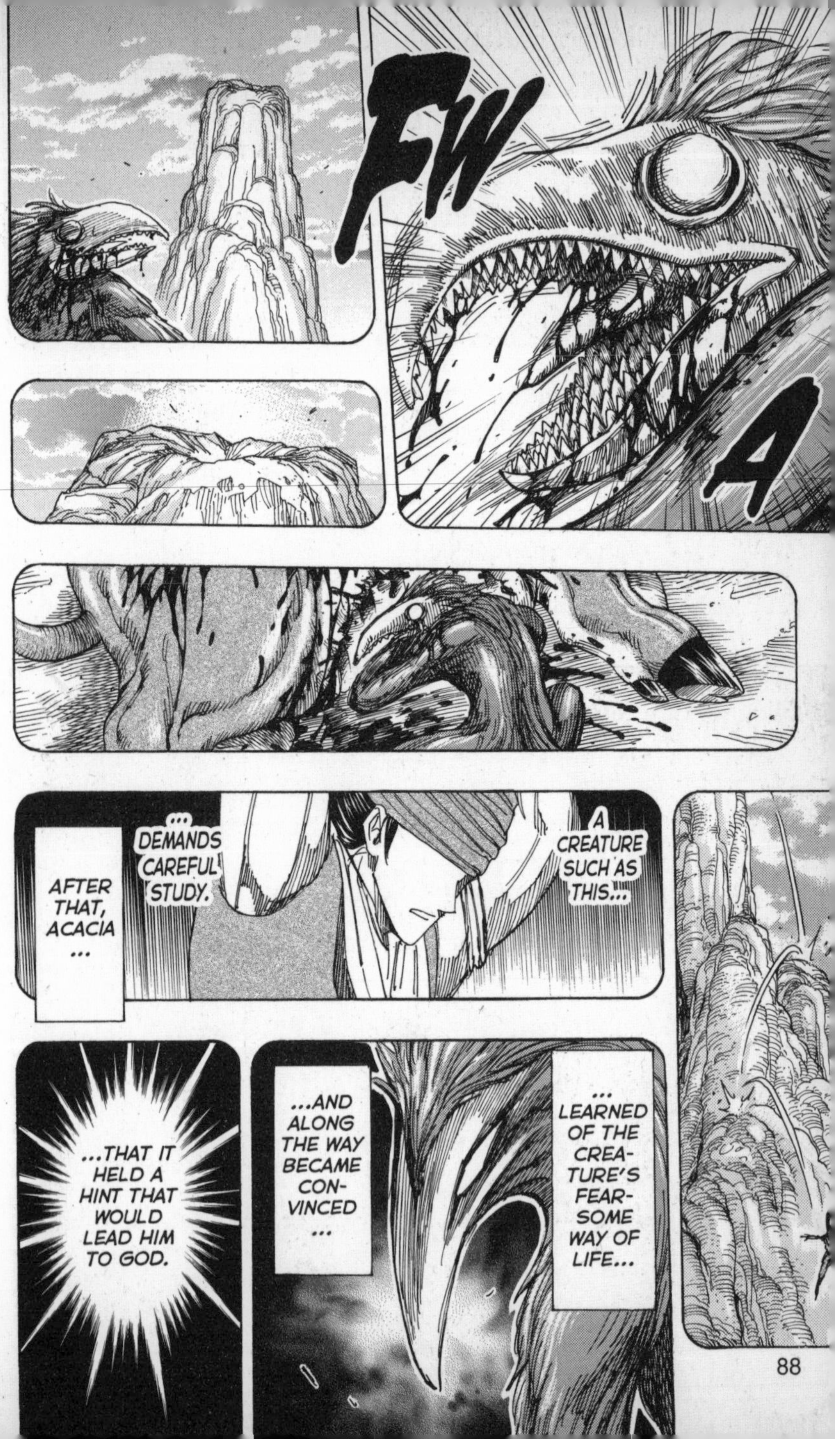

FW
A
A CREATURE SUCH AS THIS...
...DEMANDS CAREFUL STUDY.
AFTER THAT, ACACIA ...
...LEARNED OF THE CREA-TURE'S FEAR-SOME WAY OF LIFE...
...AND ALONG THE WAY BECAME CON-VINCED ...
...THAT IT HELD A HINT THAT WOULD LEAD HIM TO GOD.

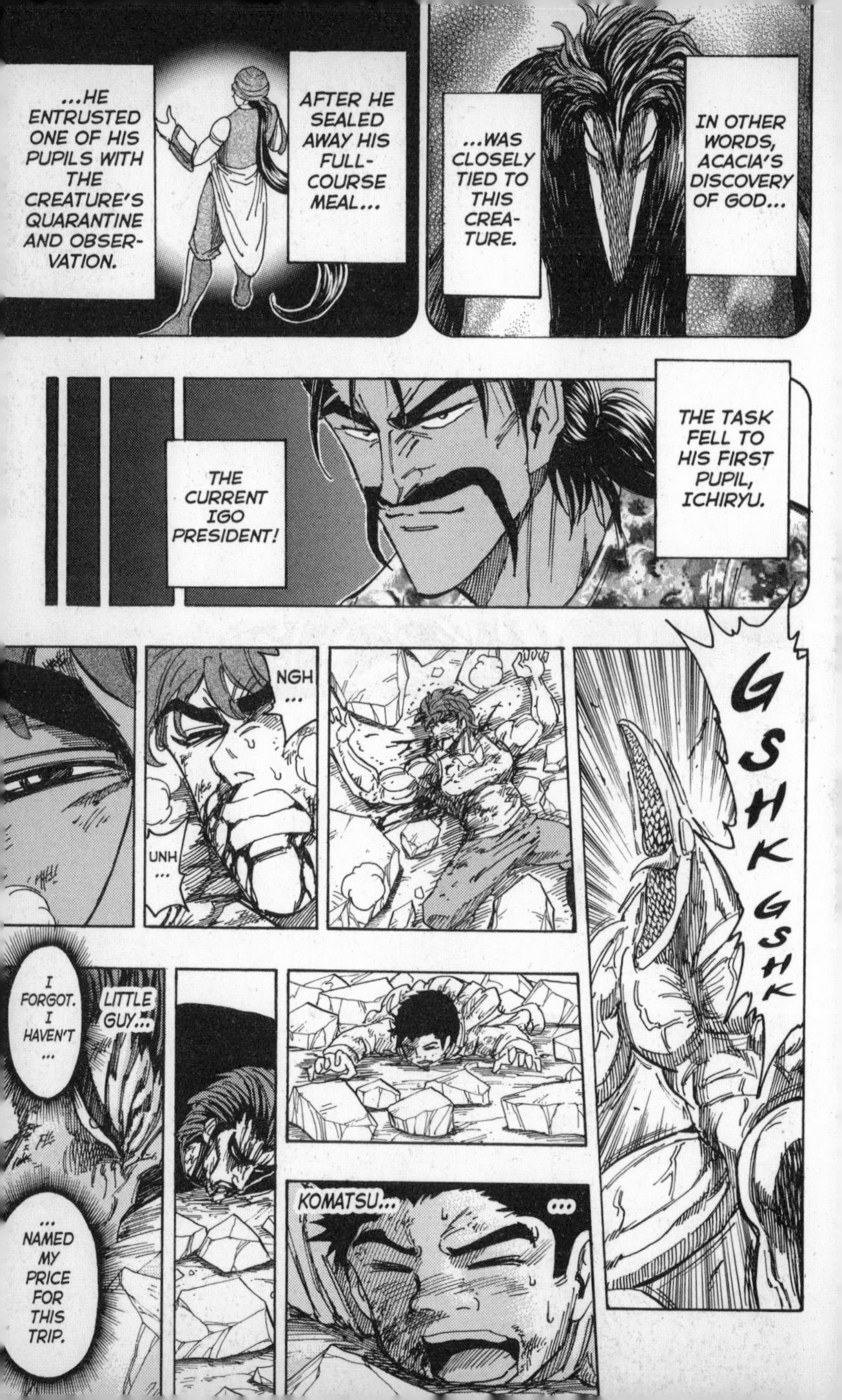
IN OTHER WORDS, ACACIA'S DISCOVERY OF GOD...
...WAS CLOSELY TIED TO THIS CREATURE.
AFTER HE SEALED AWAY HIS FULL-COURSE MEAL...
...HE ENTRUSTED ONE OF HIS PUPILS WITH THE CREATURE'S QUARANTINE AND OBSERVATION.
THE TASK FELL TO HIS FIRST PUPIL, ICHIRYU.
THE CURRENT IGO PRESIDENT!
GSHK
GSHK
NGH...
UNH...
KOMATSU...
...
LITTLE GUY...
I FORGOT. I HAVEN'T...
...NAMED MY PRICE FOR THIS TRIP.

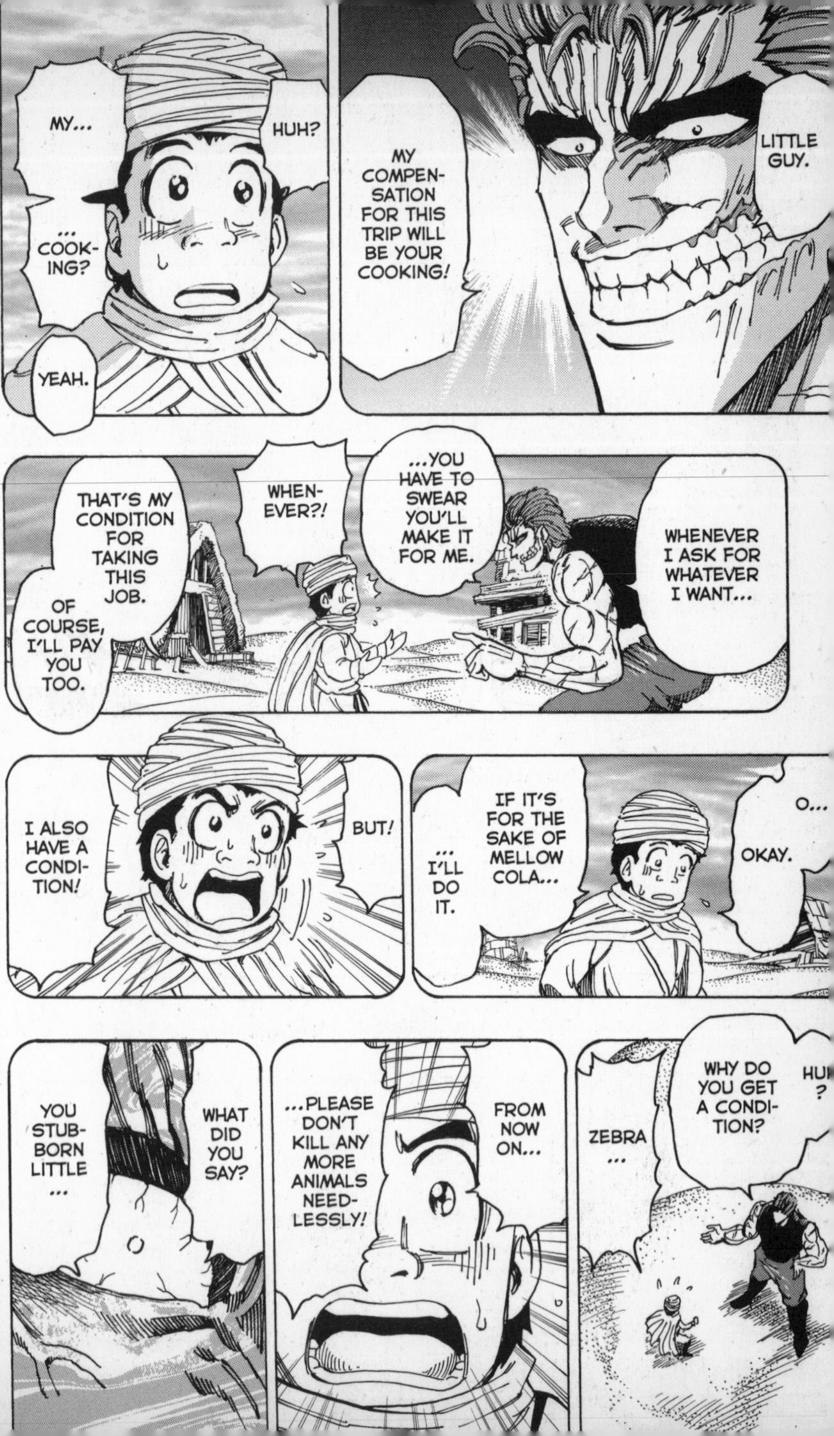
LITTLE GUY.
MY COMPENSATION FOR THIS TRIP WILL BE YOUR COOKING!
HUH?
MY...
...COOKING?
YEAH.
WHENEVER I ASK FOR WHATEVER I WANT...
...YOU HAVE TO SWEAR YOU'LL MAKE IT FOR ME.
WHENEVER?!
THAT'S MY CONDITION FOR TAKING THIS JOB.
OF COURSE, I'LL PAY YOU TOO.
O... OKAY.
IF IT'S FOR THE SAKE OF MELLOW COLA...
...I'LL DO IT.
BUT!
I ALSO HAVE A CONDITION!
HU ?
WHY DO YOU GET A CONDITION?
ZEBRA...
FROM NOW ON...
...PLEASE DON'T KILL ANY MORE ANIMALS NEEDLESSLY!
WHAT DID YOU SAY?
YOU STUBBORN LITTLE...

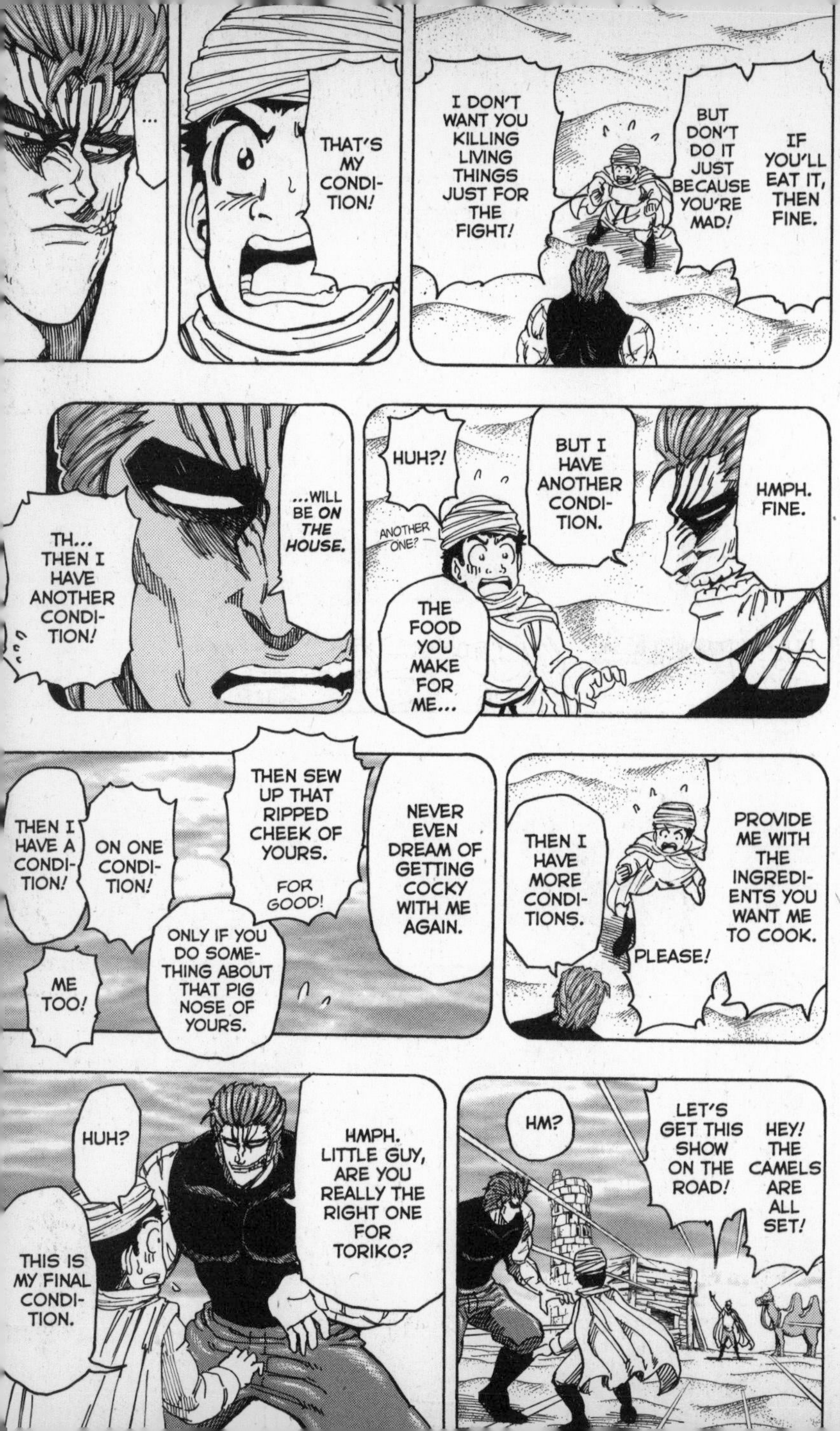

IF YOU'LL EAT IT, THEN FINE.
BUT DON'T DO IT JUST BECAUSE YOU'RE MAD!
I DON'T WANT YOU KILLING LIVING THINGS JUST FOR THE FIGHT!
THAT'S MY CONDITION!
...
HMPH. FINE.
BUT I HAVE ANOTHER CONDITION.
HUH?!
ANOTHER ONE?
THE FOOD YOU MAKE FOR ME...
...WILL BE ON THE HOUSE.
TH... THEN I HAVE ANOTHER CONDITION!
PROVIDE ME WITH THE INGREDIENTS YOU WANT ME TO COOK.
THEN I HAVE MORE CONDITIONS.
PLEASE!
NEVER EVEN DREAM OF GETTING COCKY WITH ME AGAIN.
THEN SEW UP THAT RIPPED CHEEK OF YOURS.
FOR GOOD!
ON ONE CONDITION!
THEN I HAVE A CONDITION!
ONLY IF YOU DO SOMETHING ABOUT THAT PIG NOSE OF YOURS.
ME TOO!
HEY! THE CAMELS ARE ALL SET!
LET'S GET THIS SHOW ON THE ROAD!
HM?
HMPH. LITTLE GUY, ARE YOU REALLY THE RIGHT ONE FOR TORIKO?
HUH?
THIS IS MY FINAL CONDITION.

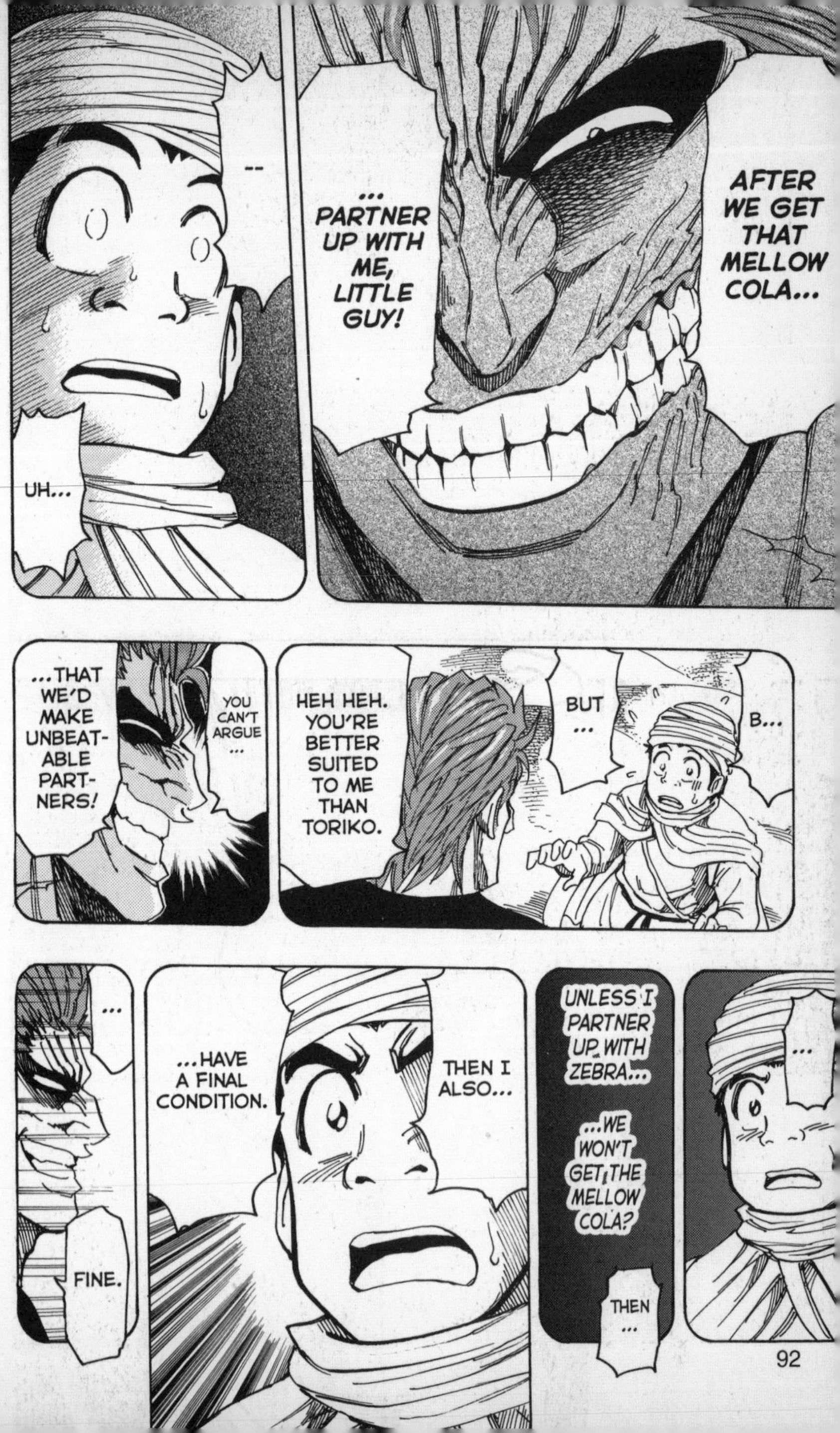
AFTER WE GET THAT MELLOW COLA...
... PARTNER UP WITH ME, LITTLE GUY!
--
UH...
B...
BUT ...
HEH HEH. YOU'RE BETTER SUITED TO ME THAN TORIKO.
YOU CAN'T ARGUE ...
...THAT WE'D MAKE UNBEAT-ABLE PART-NERS!
...
UNLESS I PARTNER UP WITH ZEBRA...
...WE WON'T GET THE MELLOW COLA?
THEN ...
THEN I ALSO...
...HAVE A FINAL CONDITION.
...
FINE.

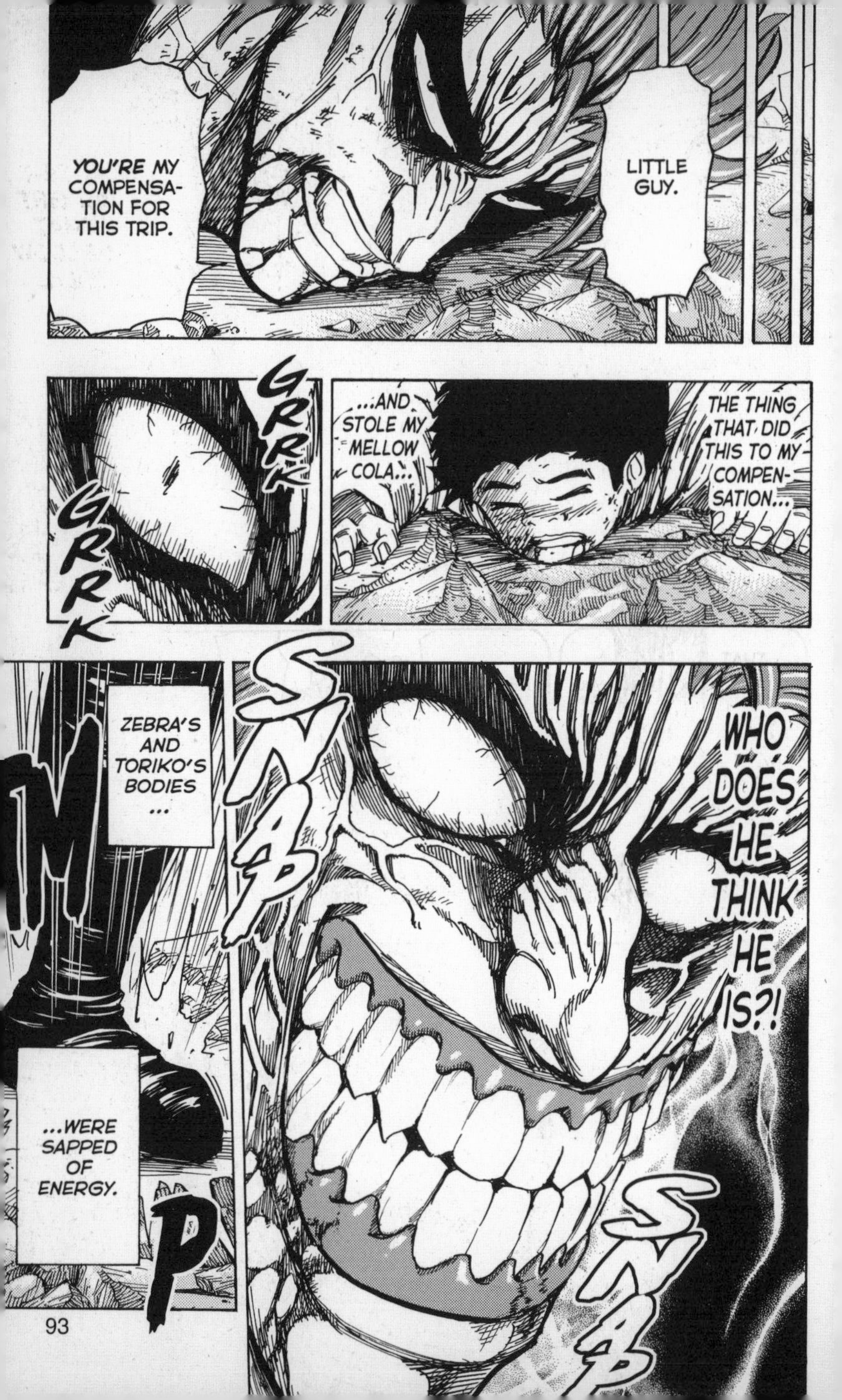
LITTLE GUY.
YOU'RE MY COMPENSATION FOR THIS TRIP.
THE THING THAT DID THIS TO MY COMPENSATION...
...AND STOLE MY MELLOW COLA...
GRRK
GRRK
SNAP
WHO DOES HE THINK HE IS?!
SNAP
ZEBRA'S AND TORIKO'S BODIES...
...WERE SAPPED OF ENERGY.

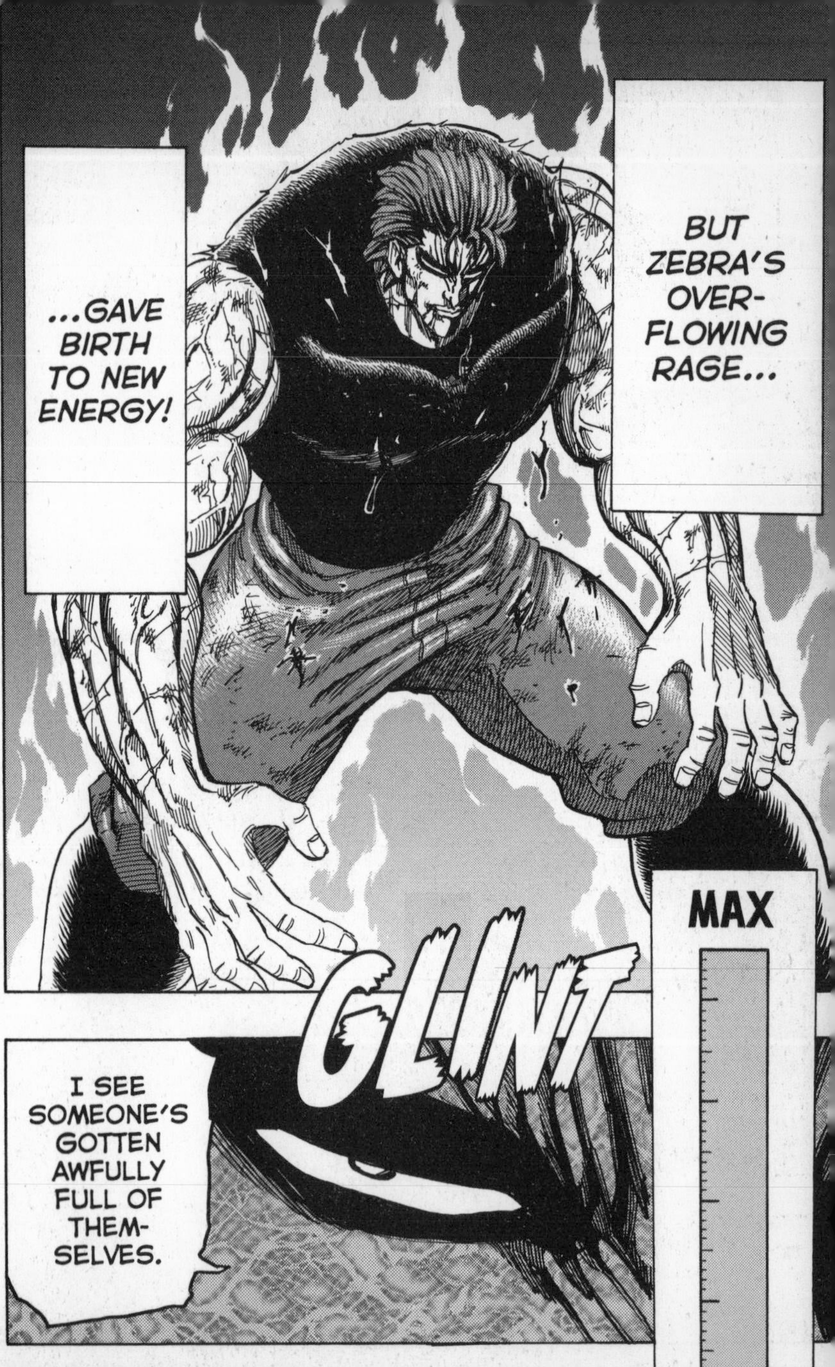
BUT ZEBRA'S OVER-FLOWING RAGE...
...GAVE BIRTH TO NEW ENERGY!
MAX
GLINT
I SEE SOMEONE'S GOTTEN AWFULLY FULL OF THEM-SELVES.

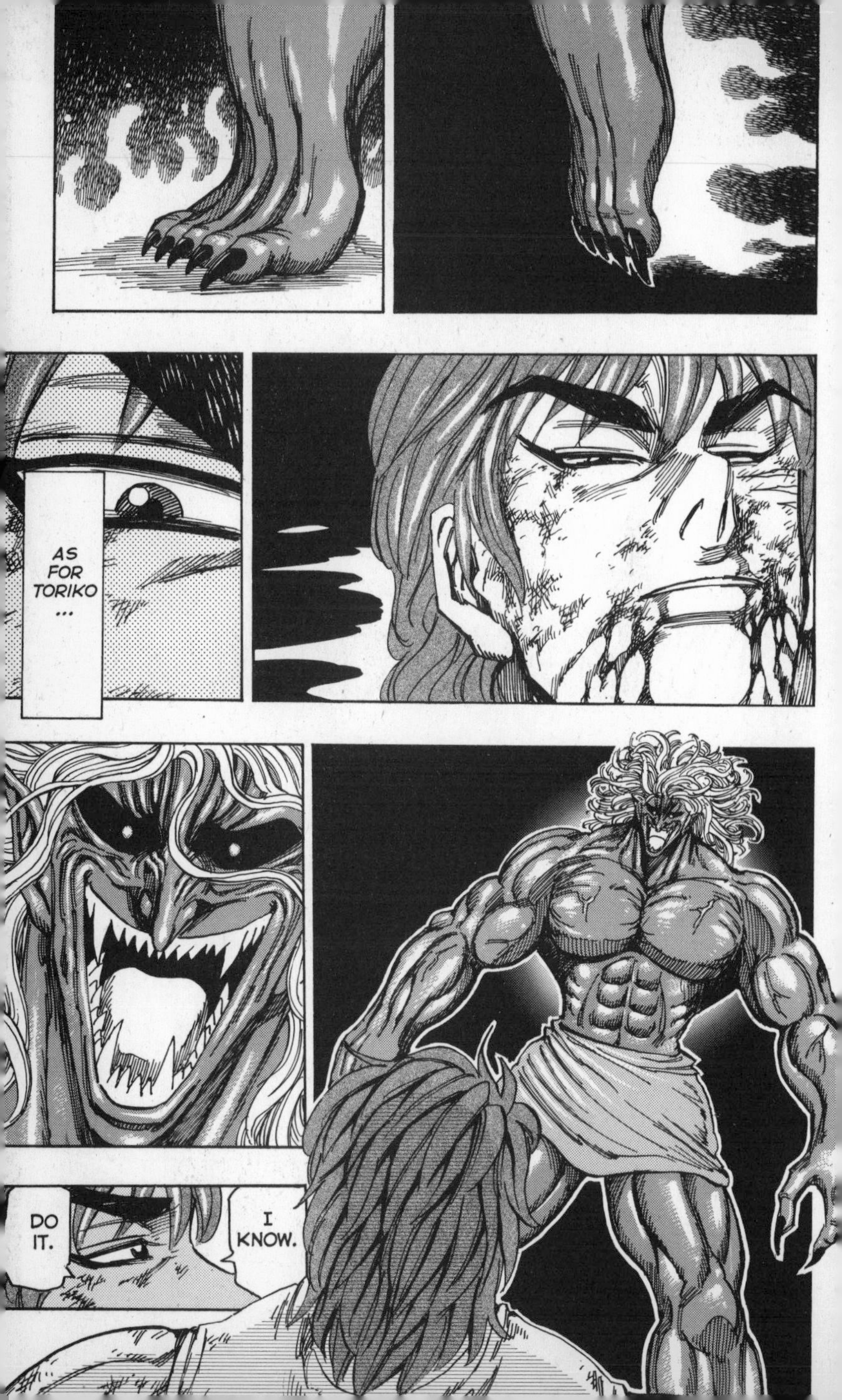
AS FOR TORIKO ...
I KNOW.
DO IT.

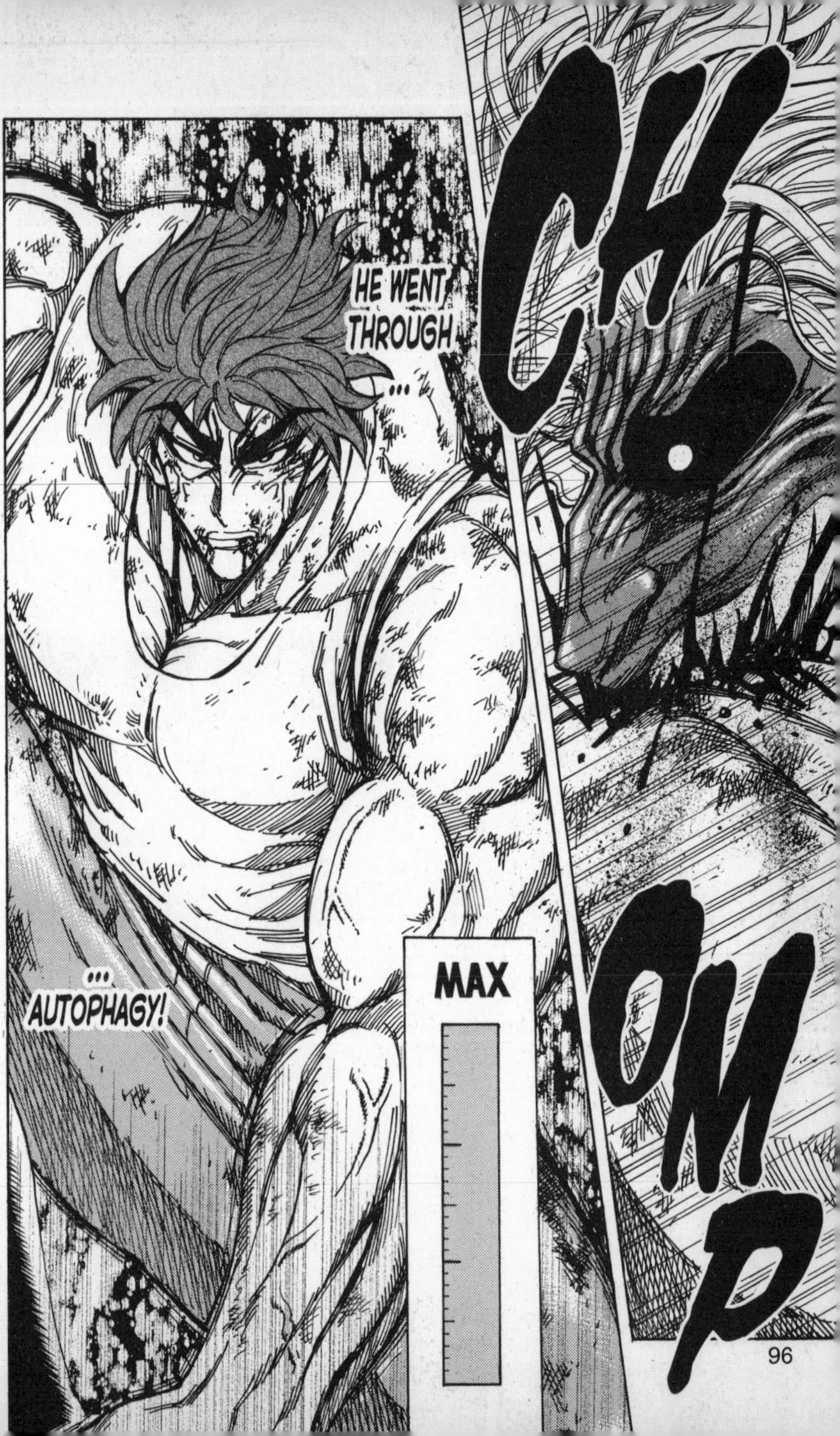
CHOMP
HE WENT THROUGH ...
... AUTOPHAGY!
MAX

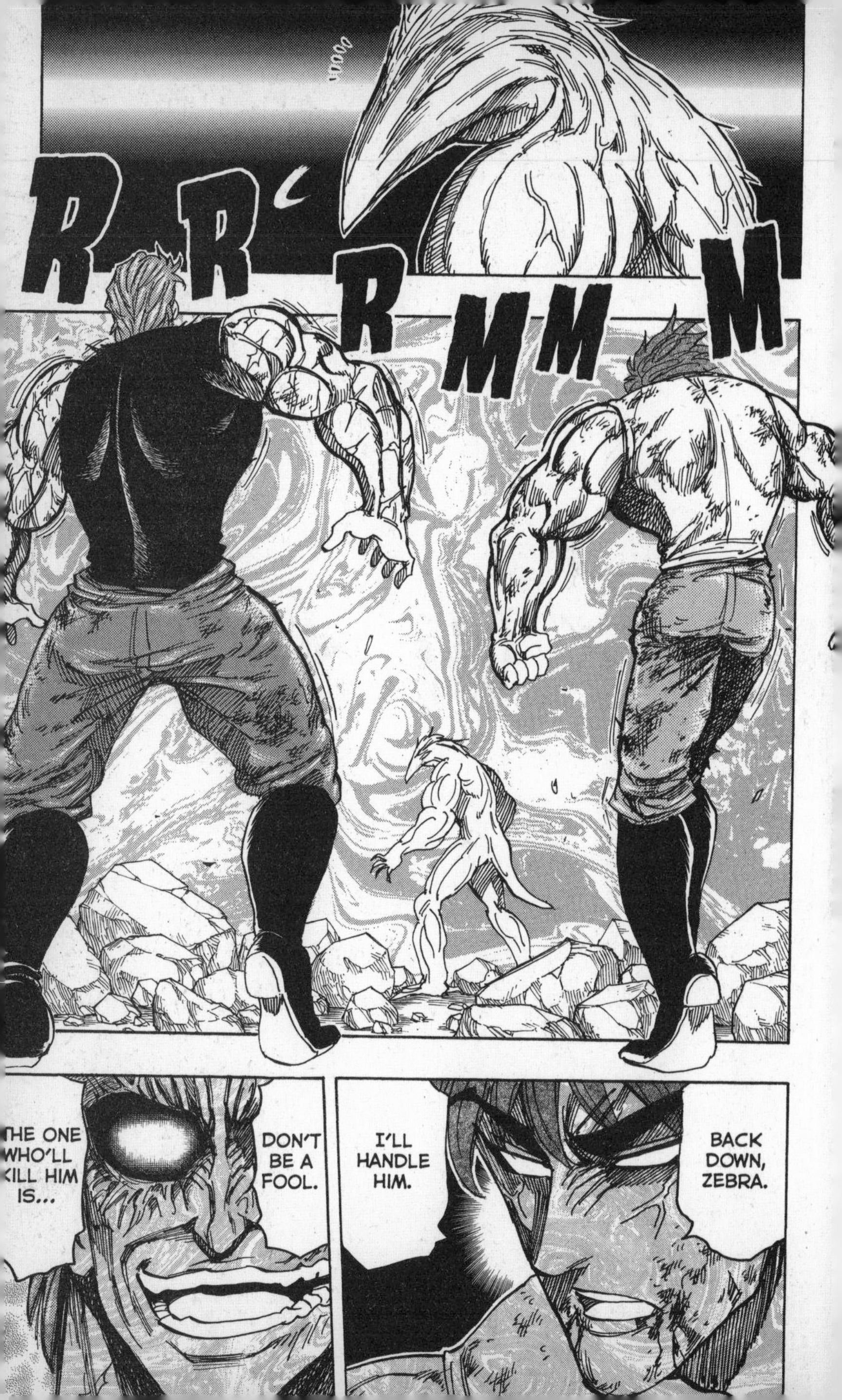
RRRMMM
BACK DOWN, ZEBRA.
I'LL HANDLE HIM.
DON'T BE A FOOL.
THE ONE WHO'LL KILL HIM IS...

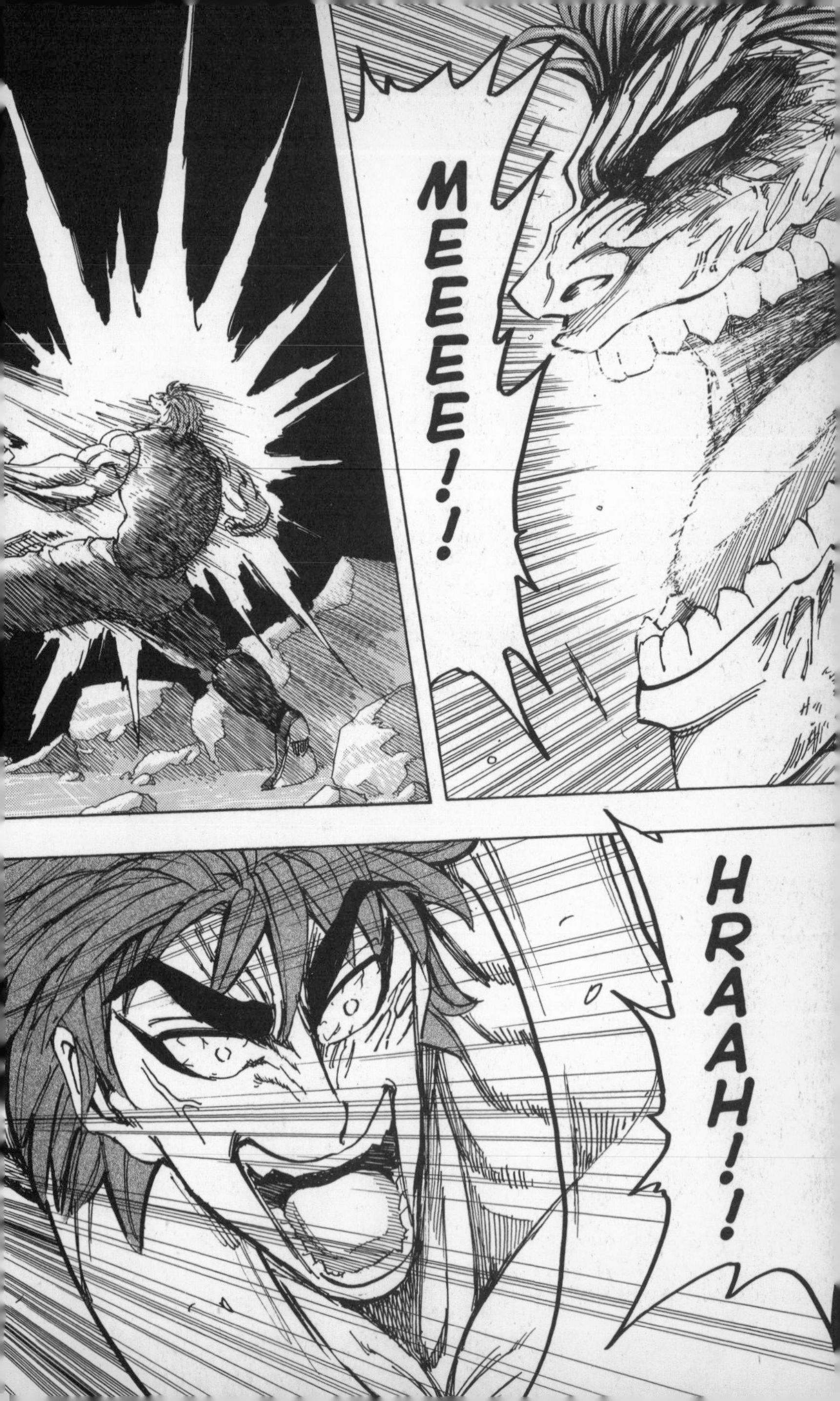
MEEEE!!
HRAAH!!!

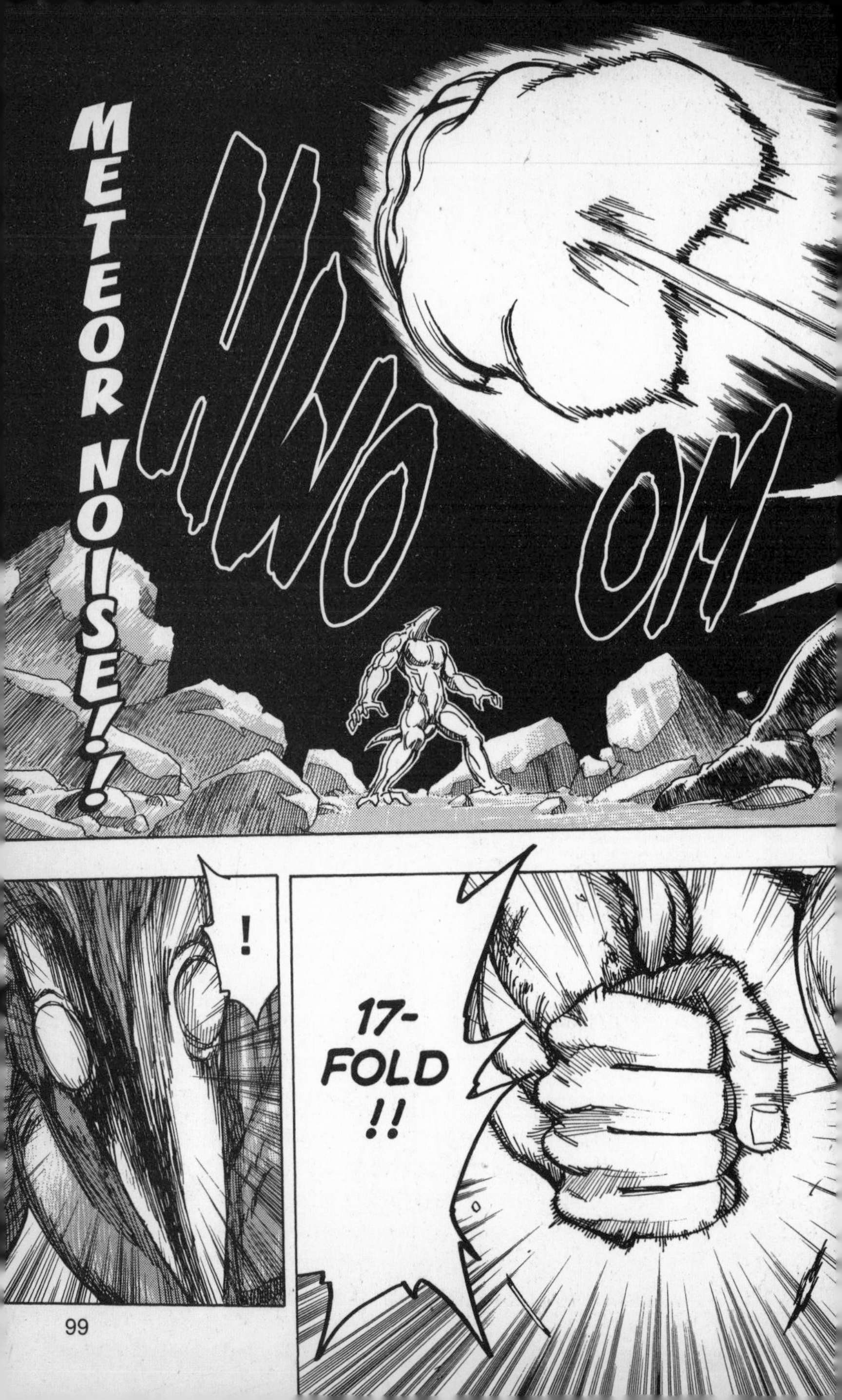
METEOR NOISE!!
17-FOLD !!
!

TORIKO

GOURMET CHECKLIST

Vol. 161

AIR TREE

(PLANT)

CAPTURE LEVEL: UNKNOWN

HABITAT: GOURMET WORLD

LENGTH: ---

HEIGHT: 30 METERS

WEIGHT: ---

PRICE: UNKNOWN

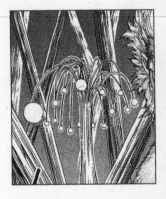

SCALE

AS IN THE PREVIOUS ENTRIES, THIS GIANT PLANT CREATURE LIVES IN THE UNDERGROUND FOREST. DETAILS REGARDING ITS BEHAVIOR, CAPTURE LEVEL, AND MORE ARE A COMPLETE MYSTERY, BUT ACCORDING TO KNOCKING MASTER JIRO ITS FRUITS PRODUCE AIR. BUT BECAUSE THEY PRODUCE OXYGEN, CARBONIC GAS, CARBON MONOXIDE AND OTHER GASES AT RANDOM, SOMETIMES THEY OVERPRODUCE CERTAIN GASES. ITS FRUITS CAN BE EATEN, BUT THEY REQUIRE EXTRA SPECIAL PREPARATION.

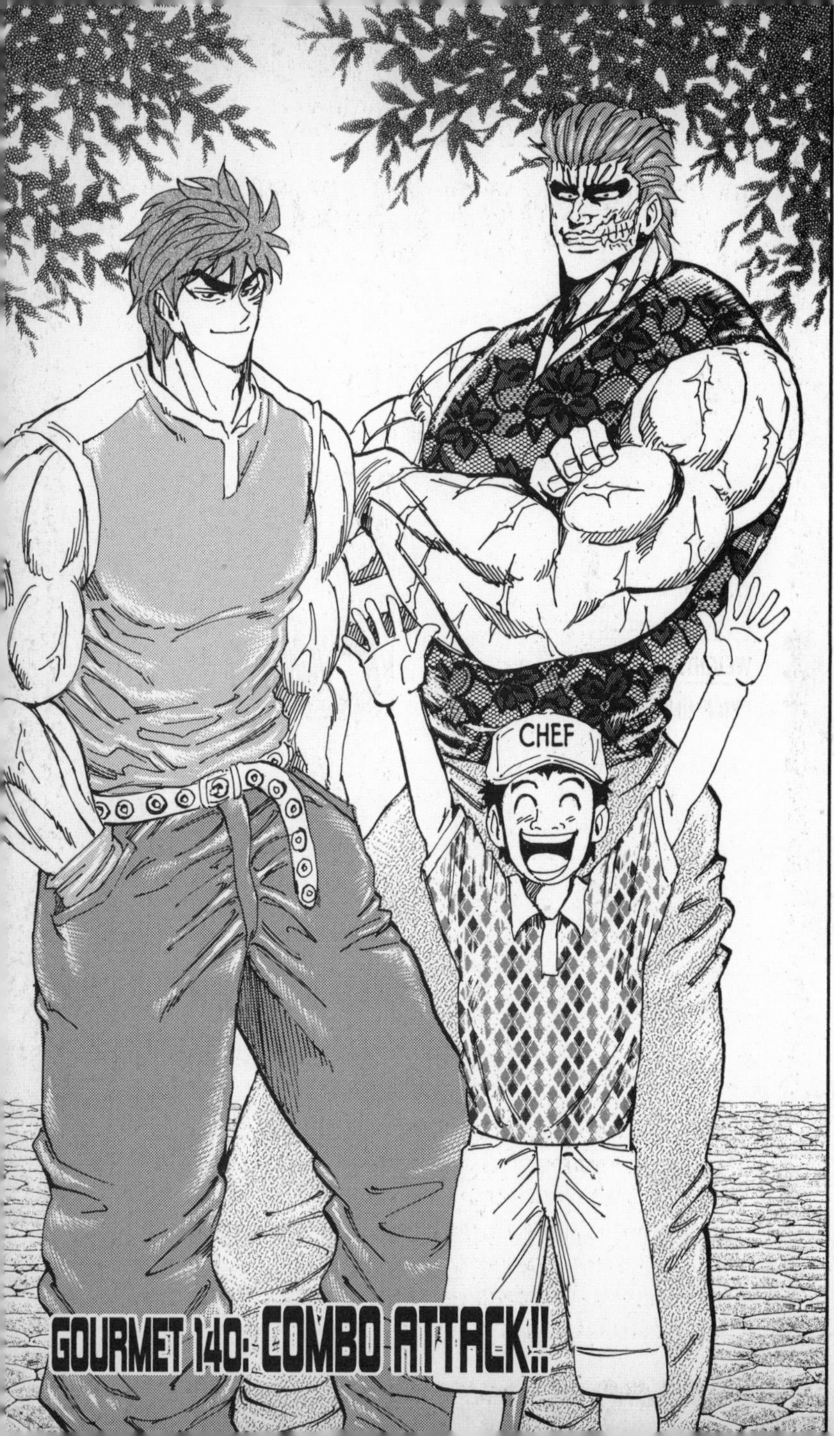
CHEF
GOURMET 140: COMBO ATTACK!!

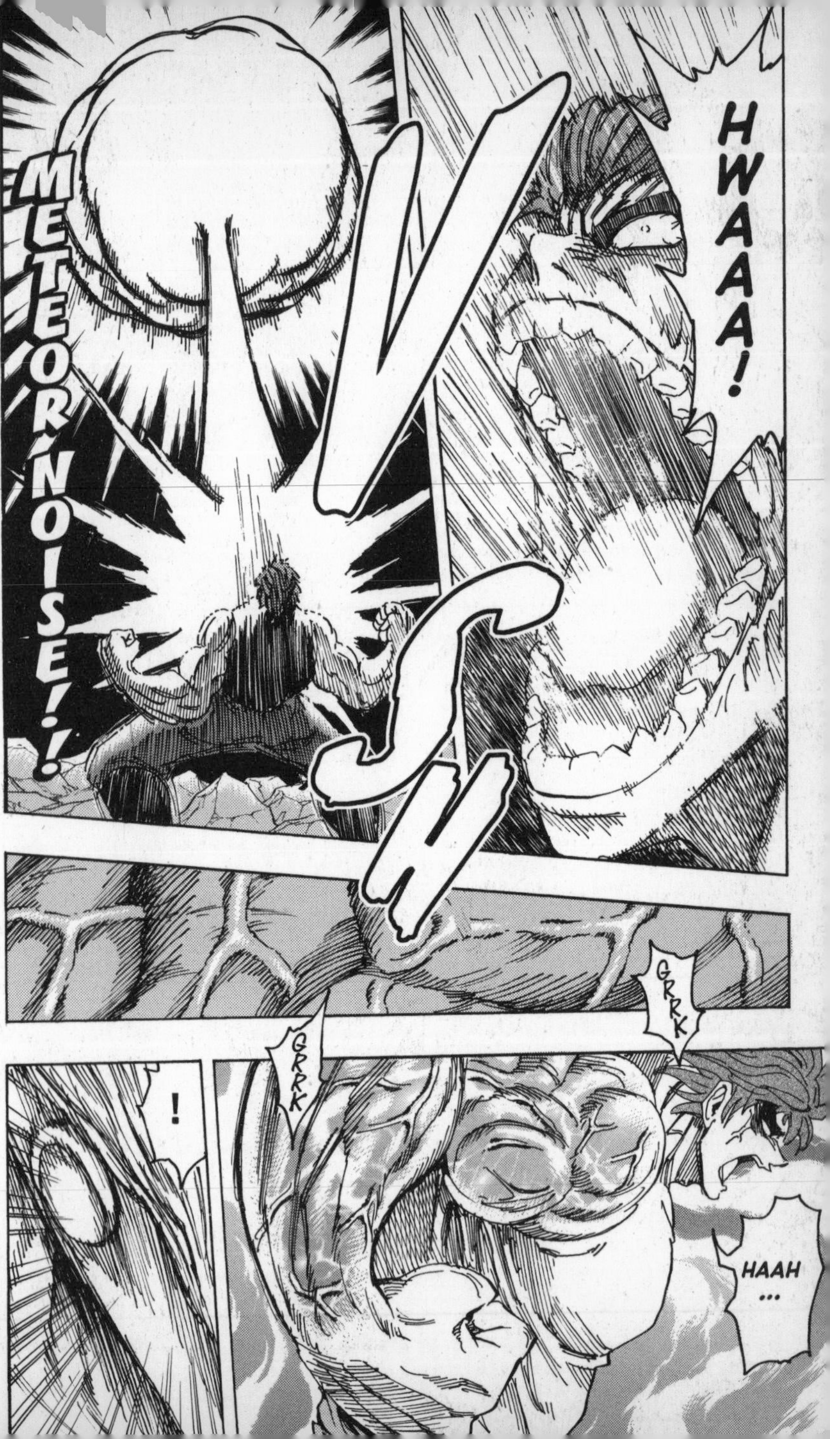
HWAAA!
METEOR NOISE!!!
GRRK
GRRK
HAAH ...
!

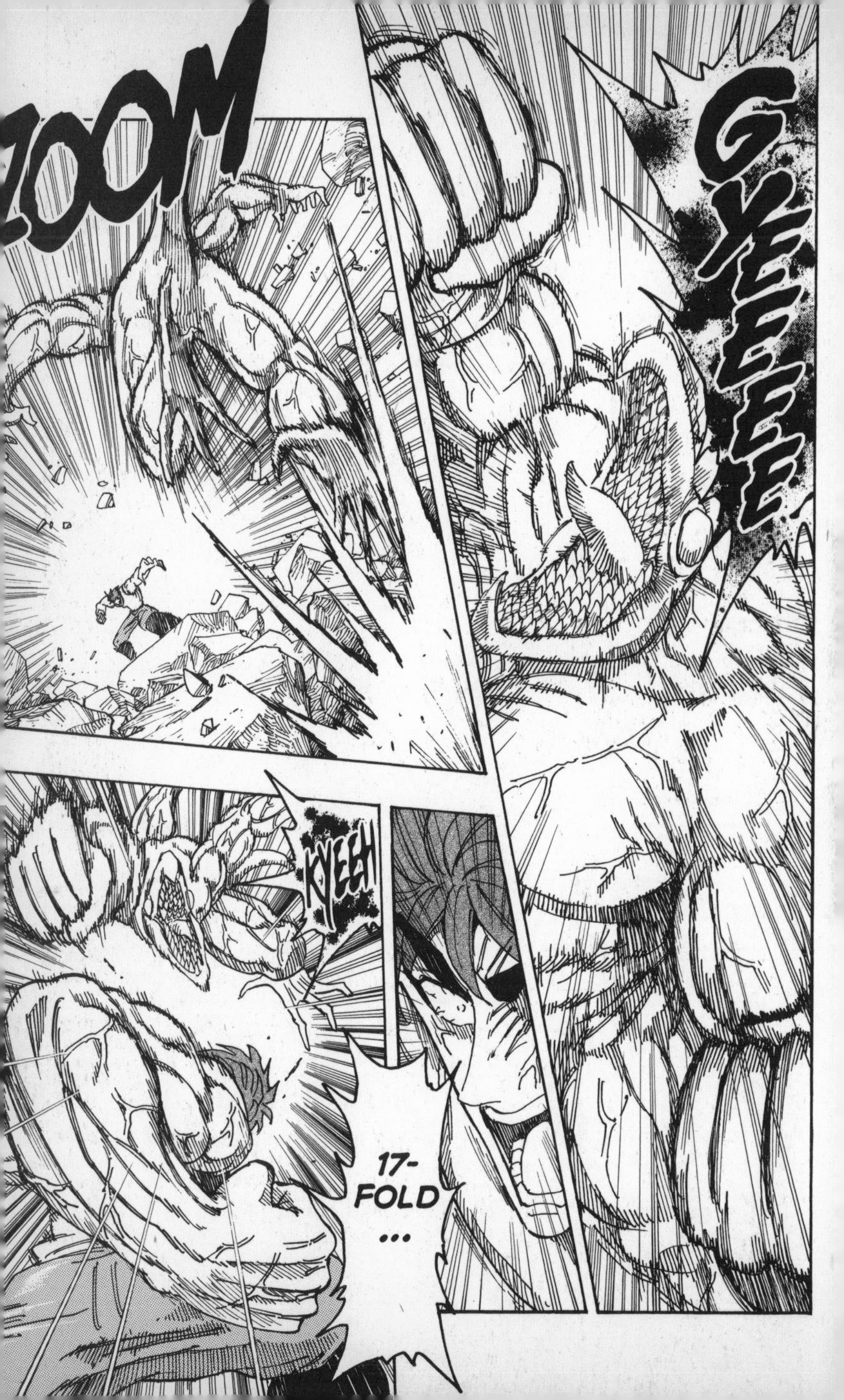
GYEEEEE
ZOOM
17-FOLD
...
KYEEH

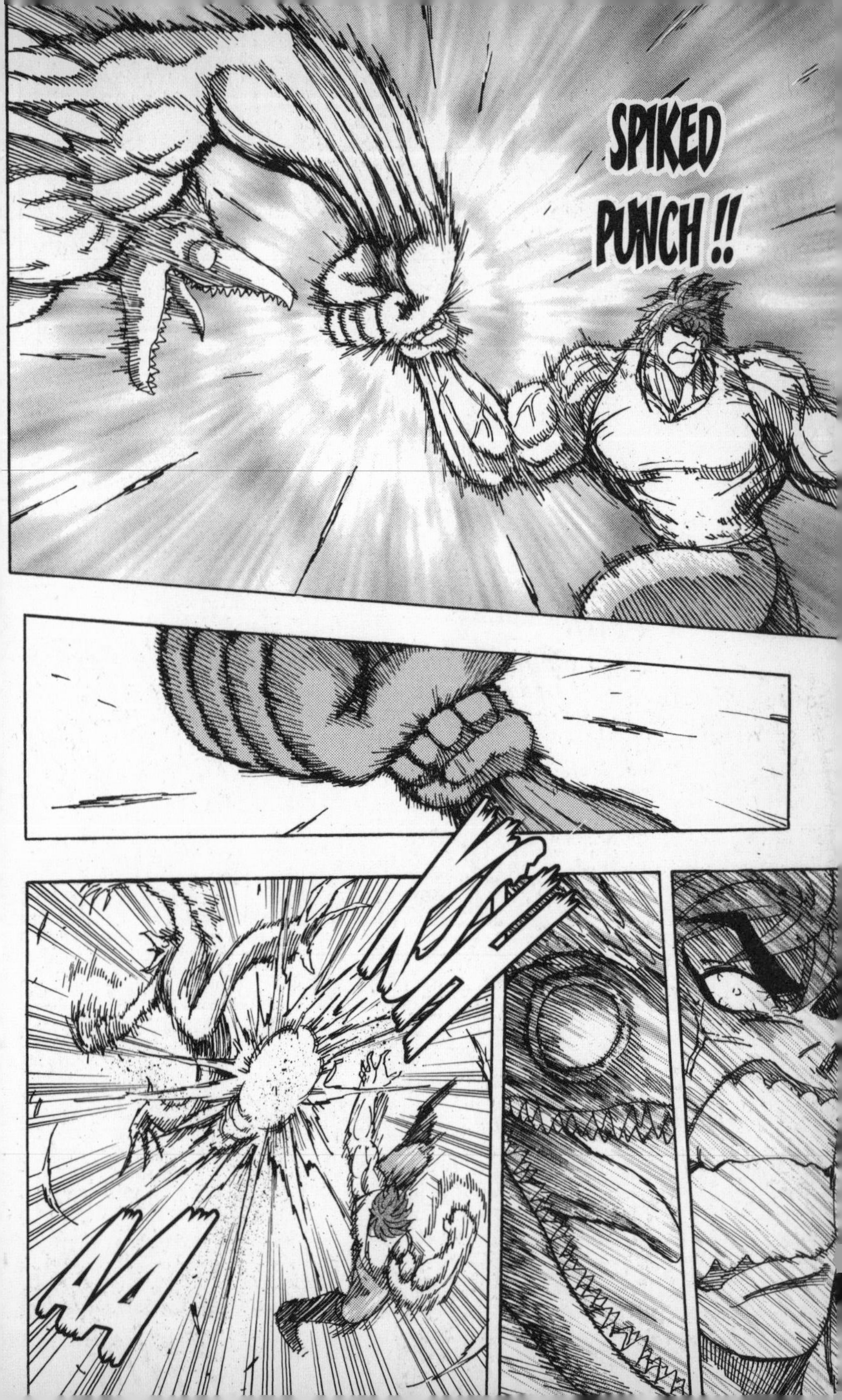
SPIKED PUNCH !!

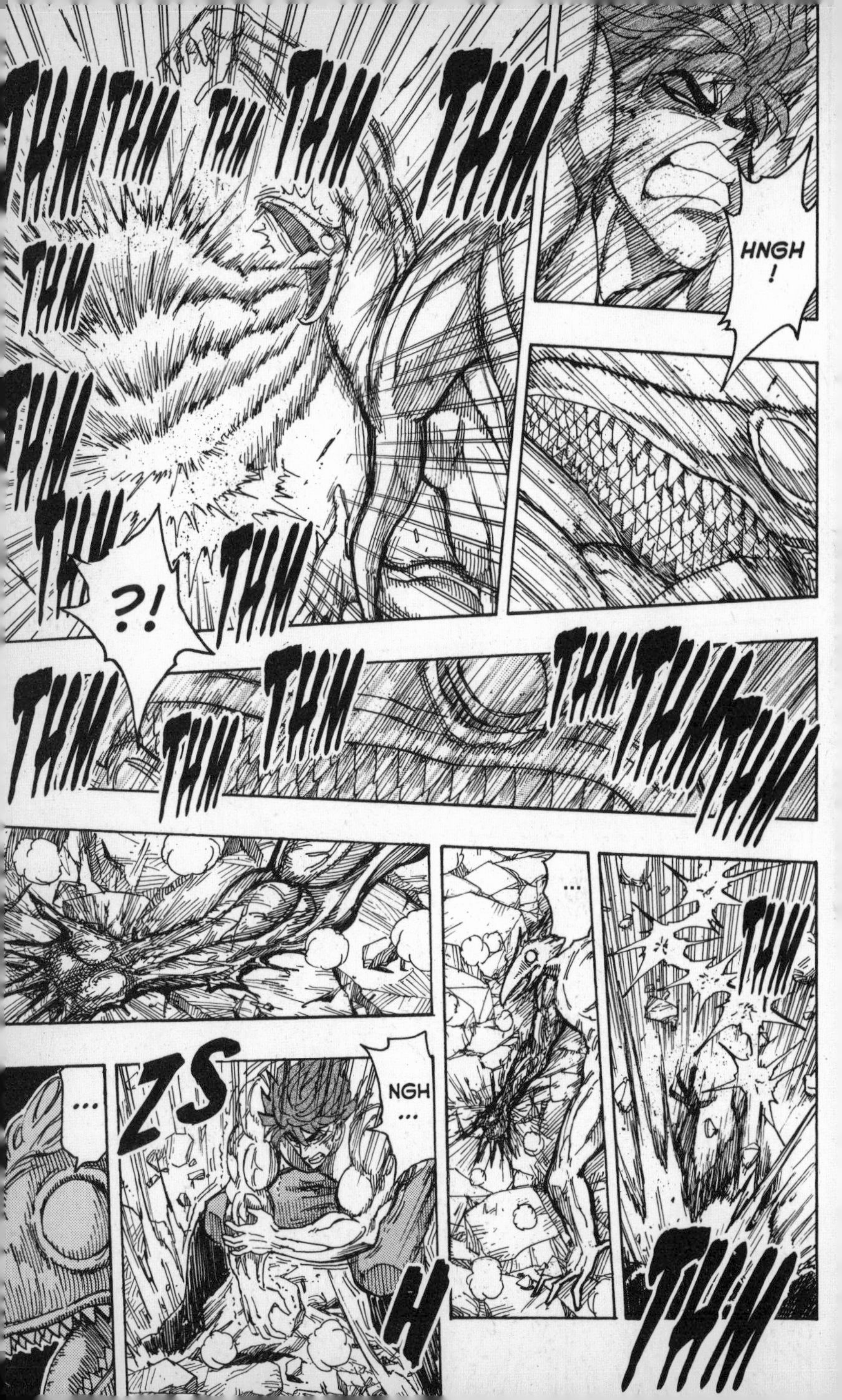

HNGH!
THM THM THM THM
THM
THM
THM
THM
?!
THM THM THM THM
THM THM THM THM THM
THM
...
THM
NGH...
ZS
H
...

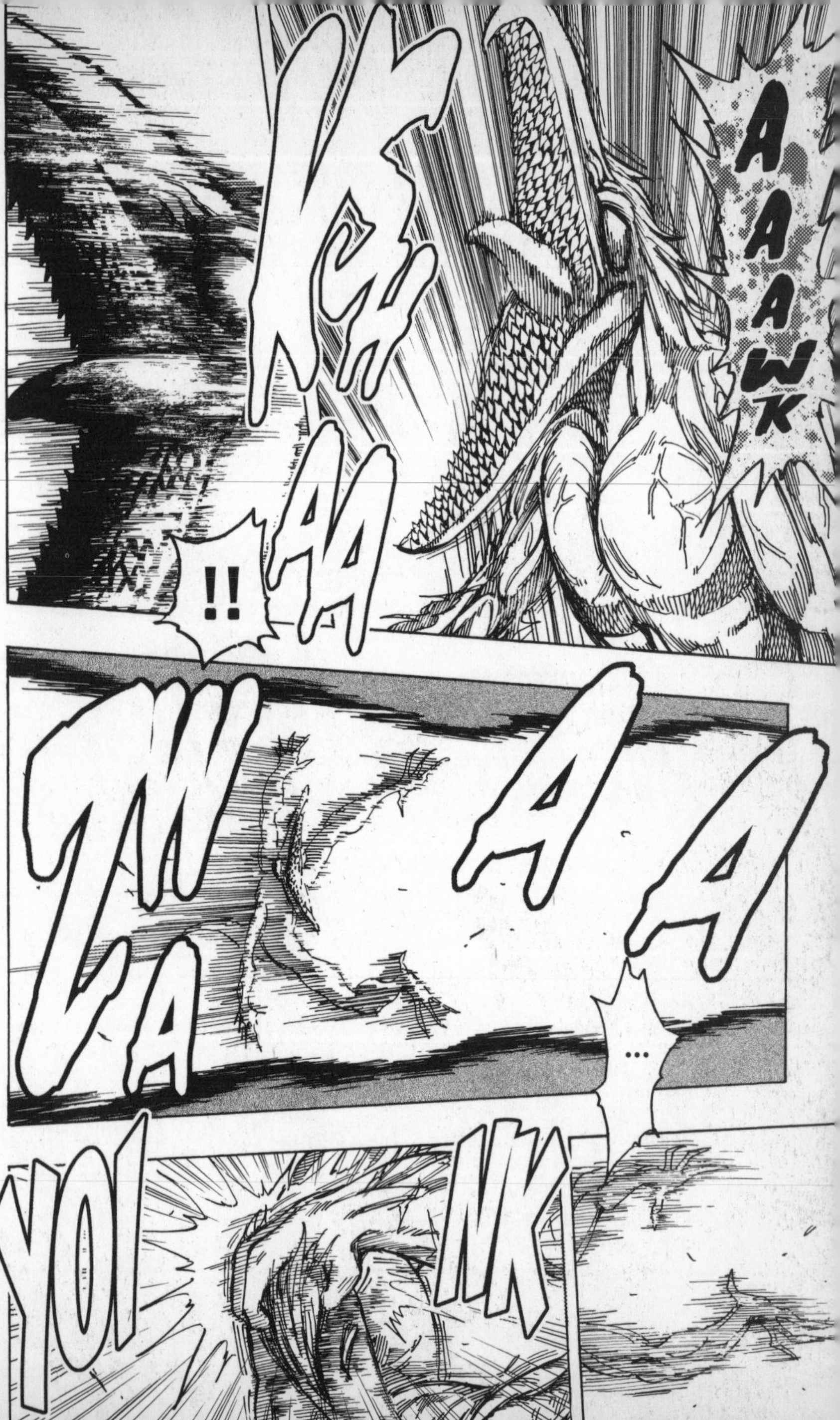
AAAAWK
KCHAA
!!
ZWAAA
...
YOINK

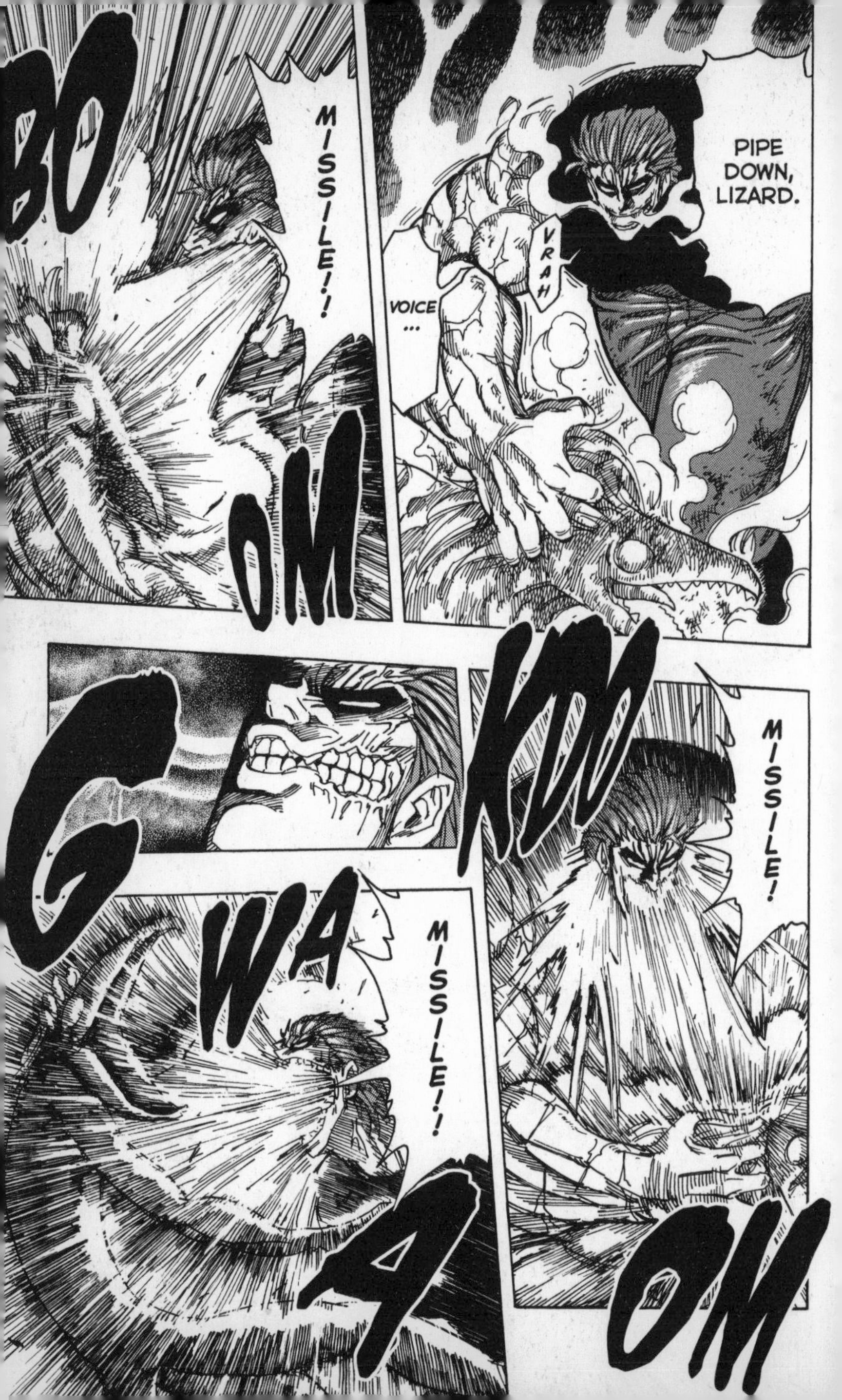
PIPE DOWN, LIZARD.
VRAH
VOICE ...
BO
OM
MISSILE!!
KOO
MISSILE!
OM
G
WA
A
MISSILE!!

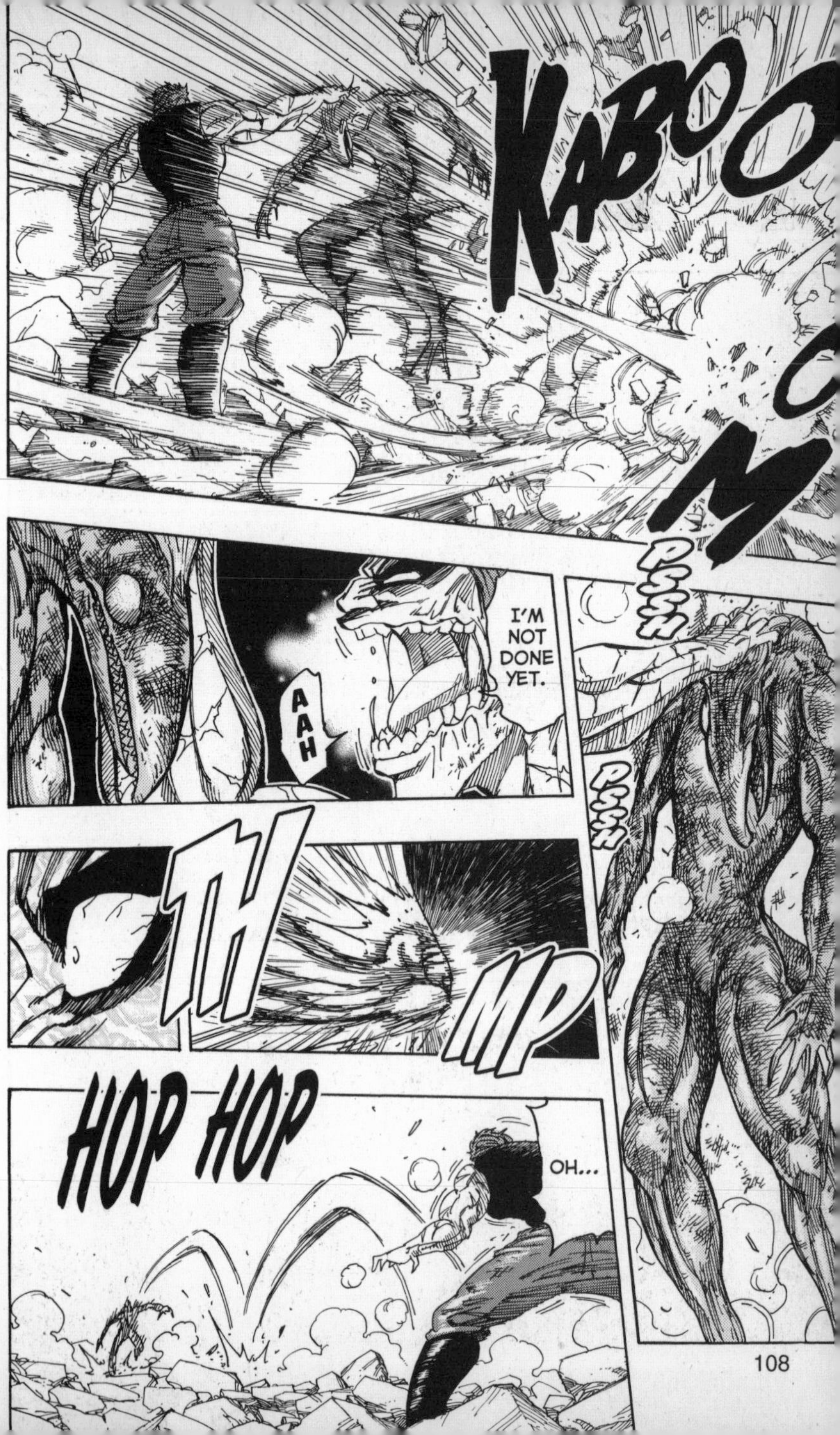
KABOOOM
PSSH
PSSH
I'M NOT DONE YET.
AAH
THMP
HOP HOP
OH...

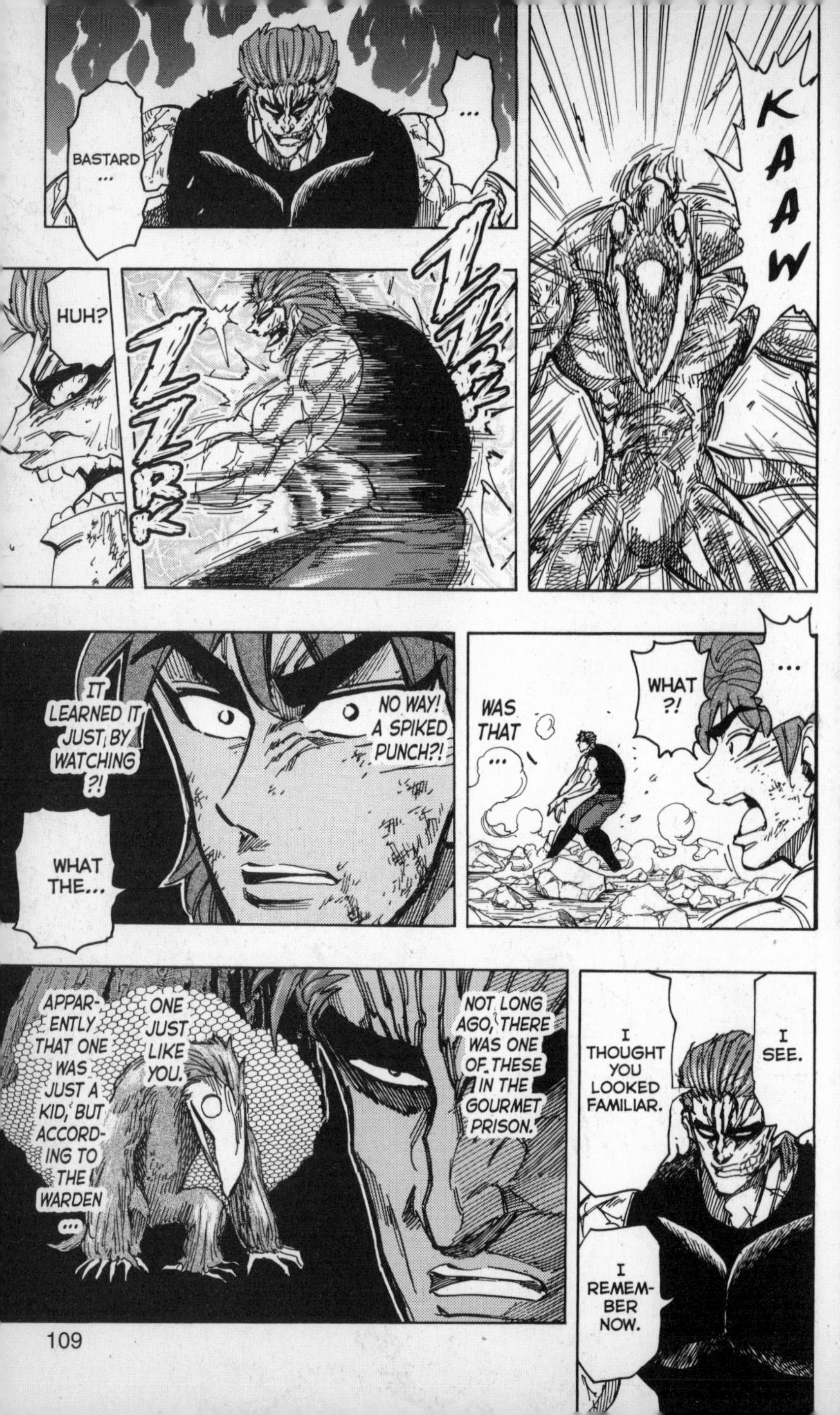
KAAW
...
BASTARD ...
ZZZRK
ZZZRK
HUH?
...
WHAT?!
WAS THAT ...
NO WAY! A SPIKED PUNCH?!
IT LEARNED IT JUST BY WATCHING?!
WHAT THE...
I SEE.
I THOUGHT YOU LOOKED FAMILIAR.
I REMEMBER NOW.
NOT LONG AGO, THERE WAS ONE OF THESE IN THE GOURMET PRISON.
ONE JUST LIKE YOU.
APPARENTLY THAT ONE WAS JUST A KID, BUT ACCORDING TO THE WARDEN ...

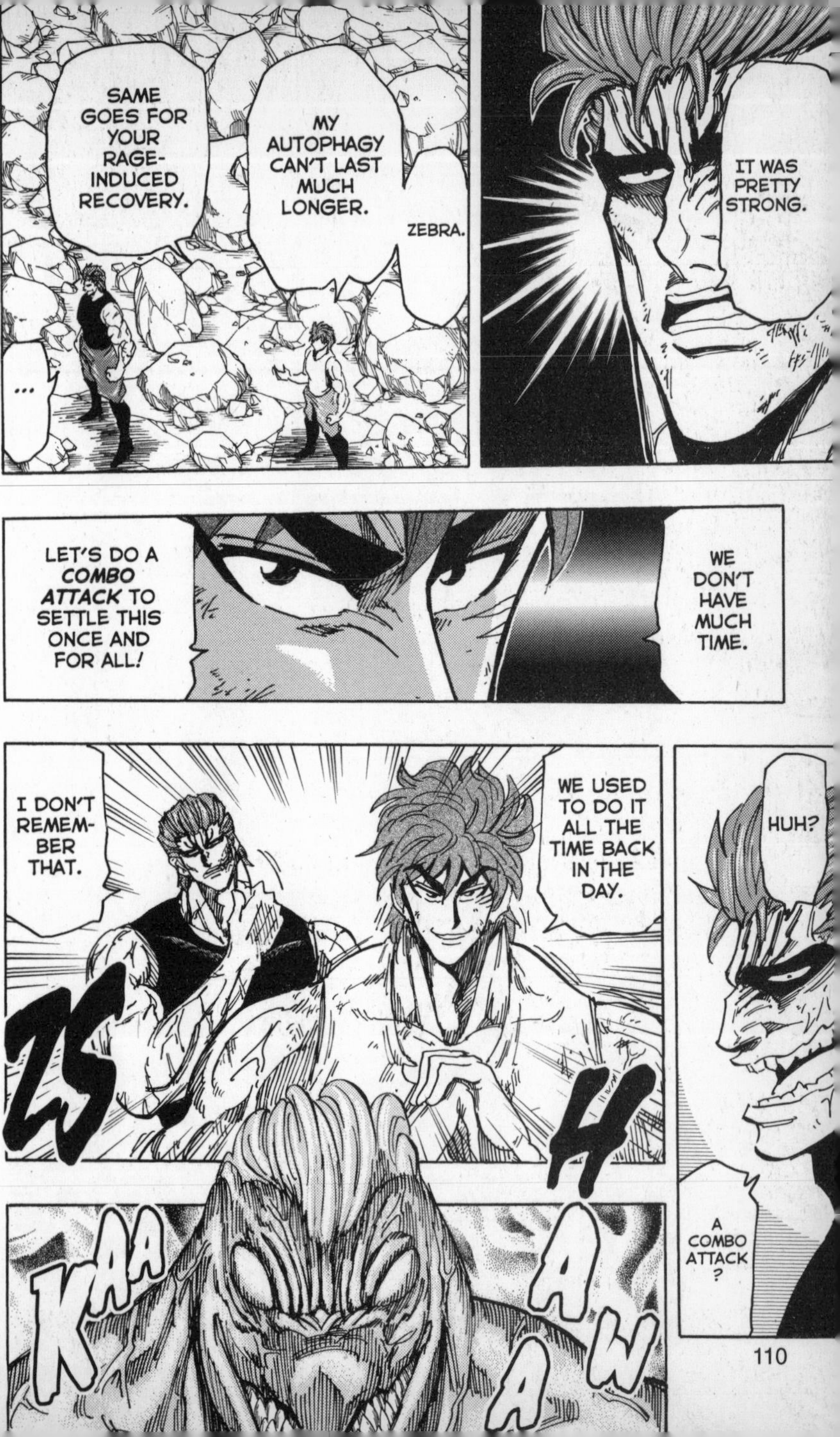

IT WAS PRETTY STRONG.
ZEBRA.
MY AUTOPHAGY CAN'T LAST MUCH LONGER.
SAME GOES FOR YOUR RAGE-INDUCED RECOVERY.
...
WE DON'T HAVE MUCH TIME.
LET'S DO A *COMBO ATTACK* TO SETTLE THIS ONCE AND FOR ALL!
HUH?
A COMBO ATTACK?
WE USED TO DO IT ALL THE TIME BACK IN THE DAY.
I DON'T REMEM-BER THAT.
ZSH
KAAAAAWN

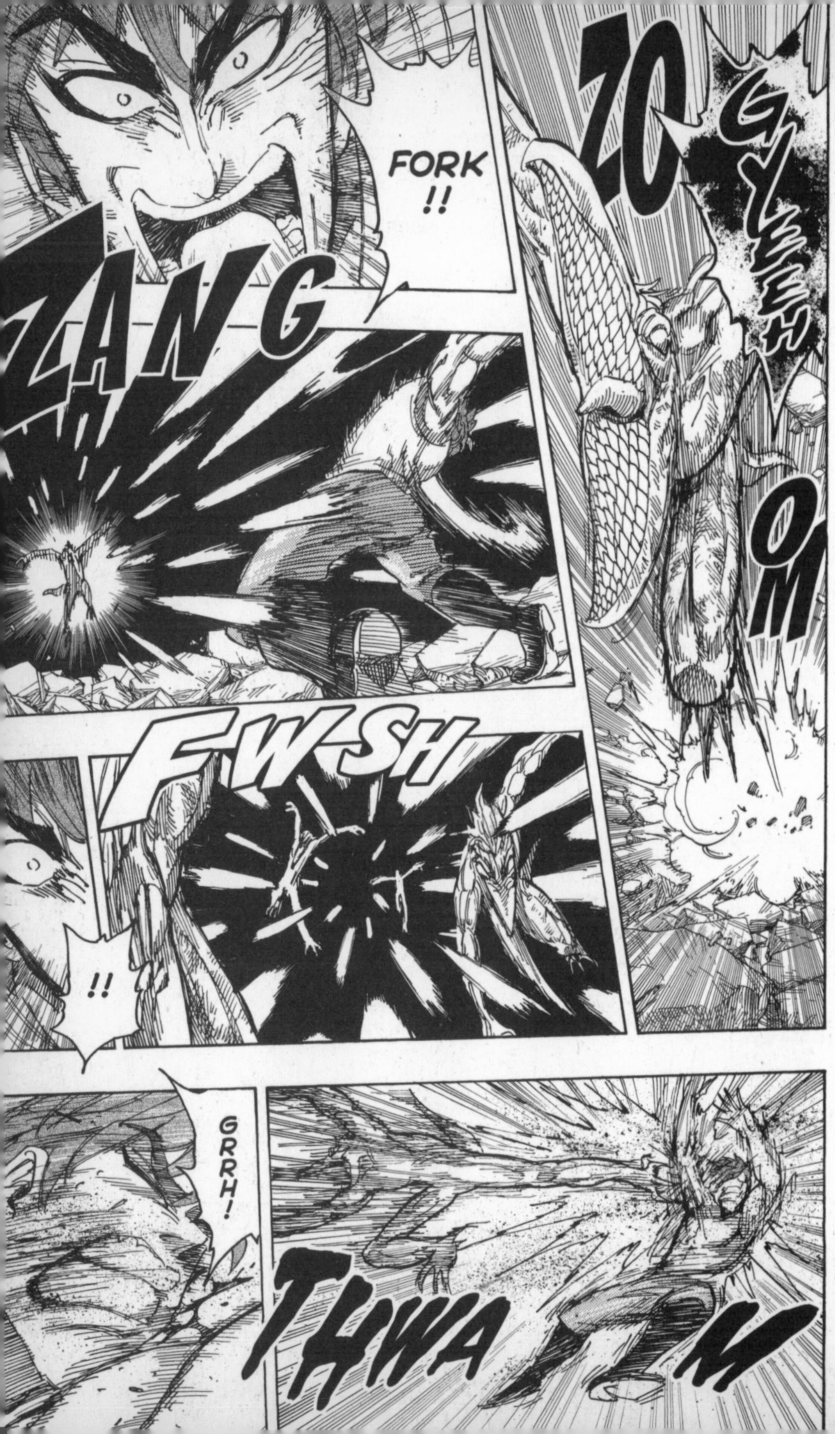
ZO
OM
FORK !!
ZANG
F-W-SH
!!
GRRH!
THWA
M!

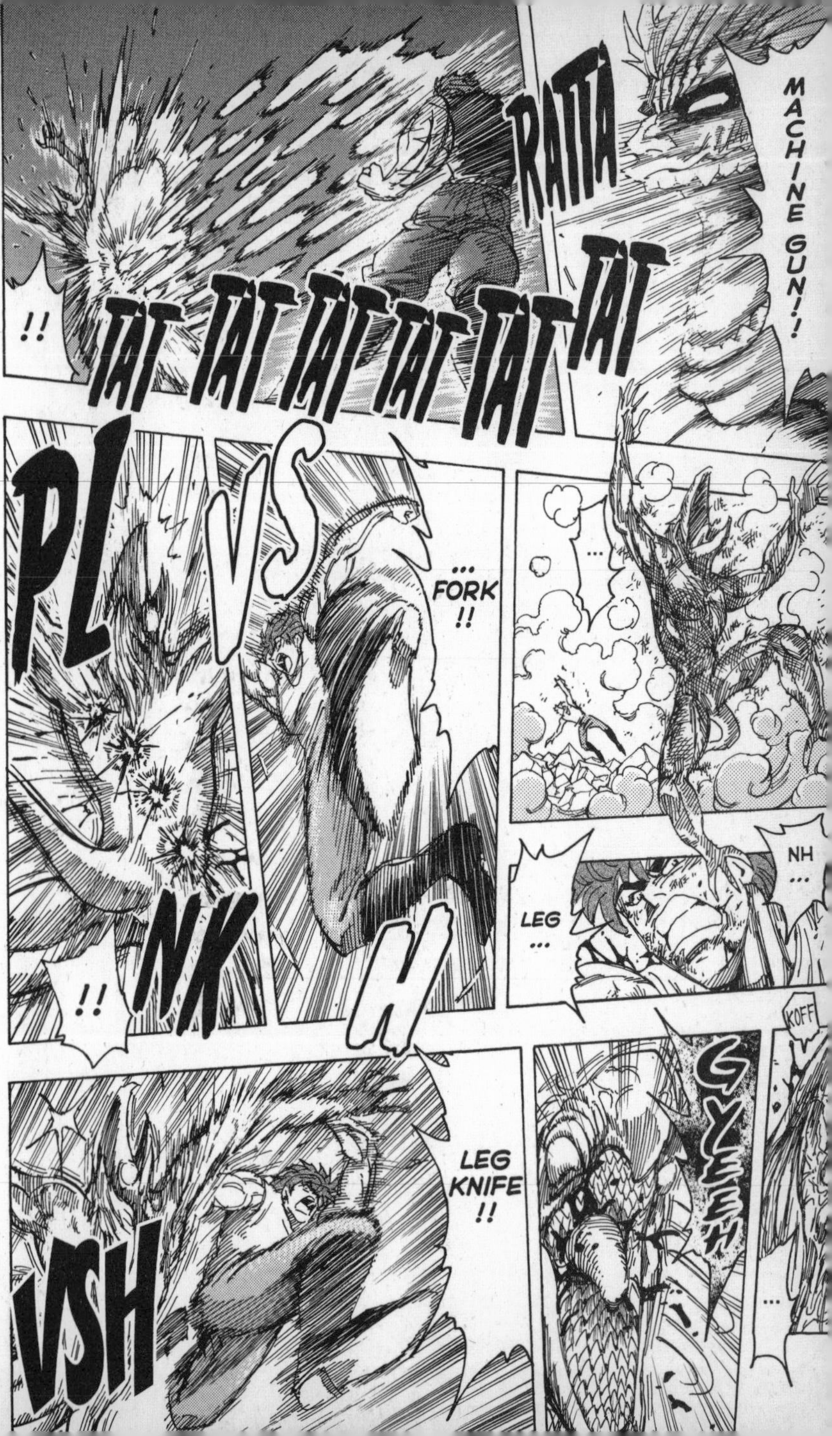
MACHINE GUN!!
RATTA
TAT TAT TAT TAT TAT TAT TAT
!!
...
NH ...
LEG ...
... FORK !!
VS
H
PL
NK
!!
KOFF
...
GYEEH
LEG KNIFE !!
VSH

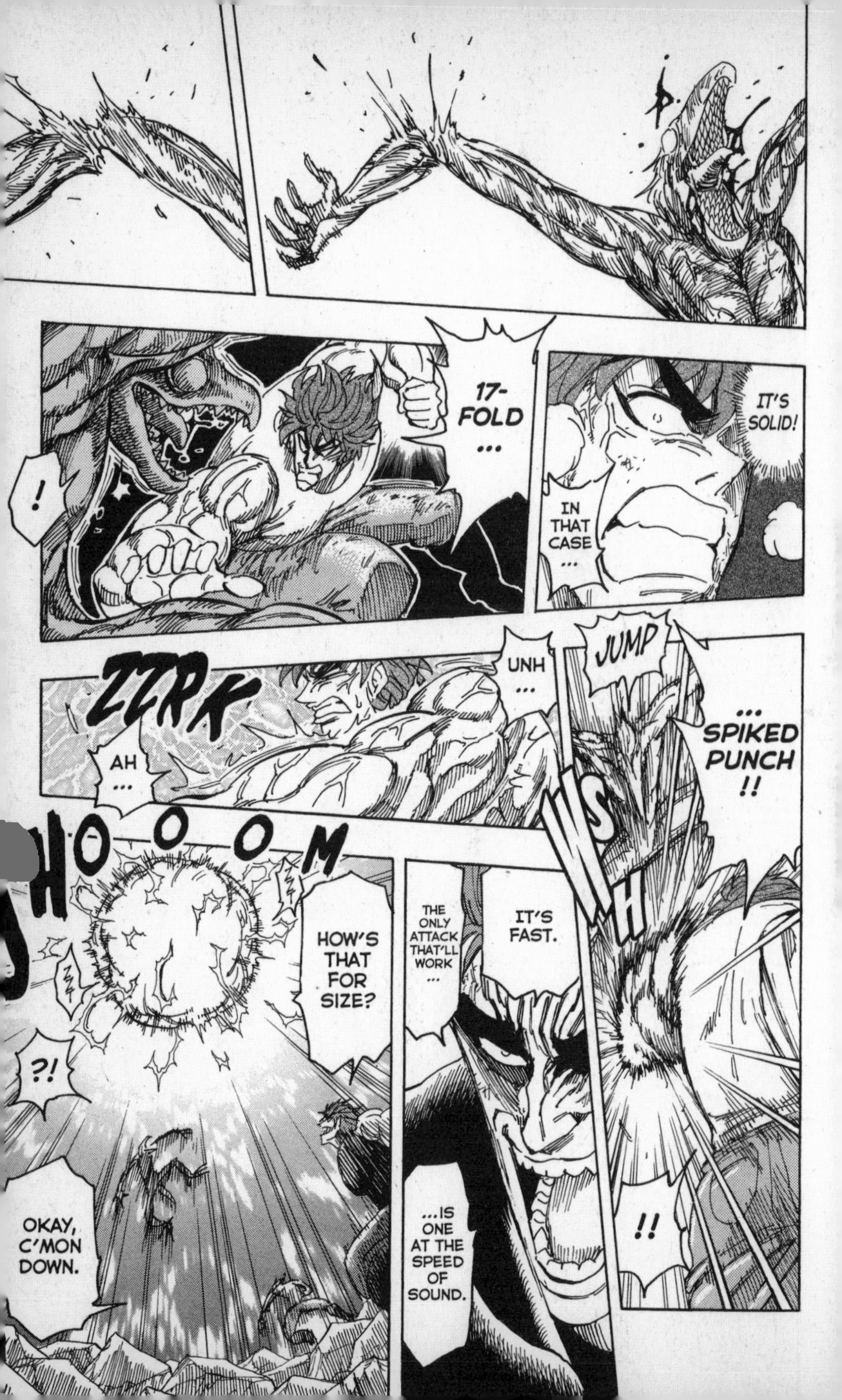
IT'S SOLID!
IN THAT CASE ...
17-FOLD ...
!
JUMP
... SPIKED PUNCH !!
WSH
!!
UNH ...
ZZRK
AH ...
IT'S FAST.
THE ONLY ATTACK THAT'LL WORK ...
...IS ONE AT THE SPEED OF SOUND.
HOOOM
HOW'S THAT FOR SIZE?
?!
OKAY, C'MON DOWN.

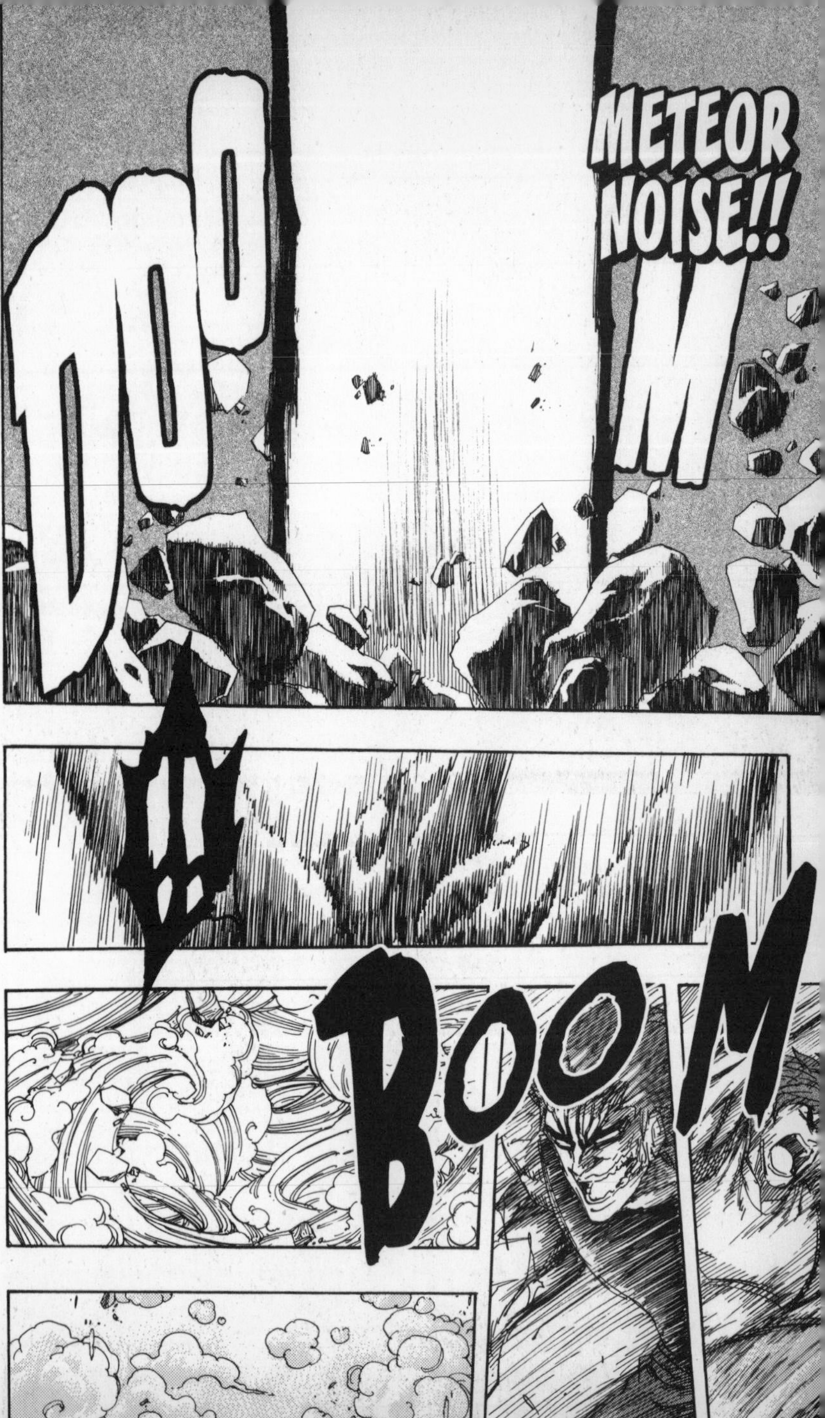
METEOR NOISE!!
DOOM
BOOM

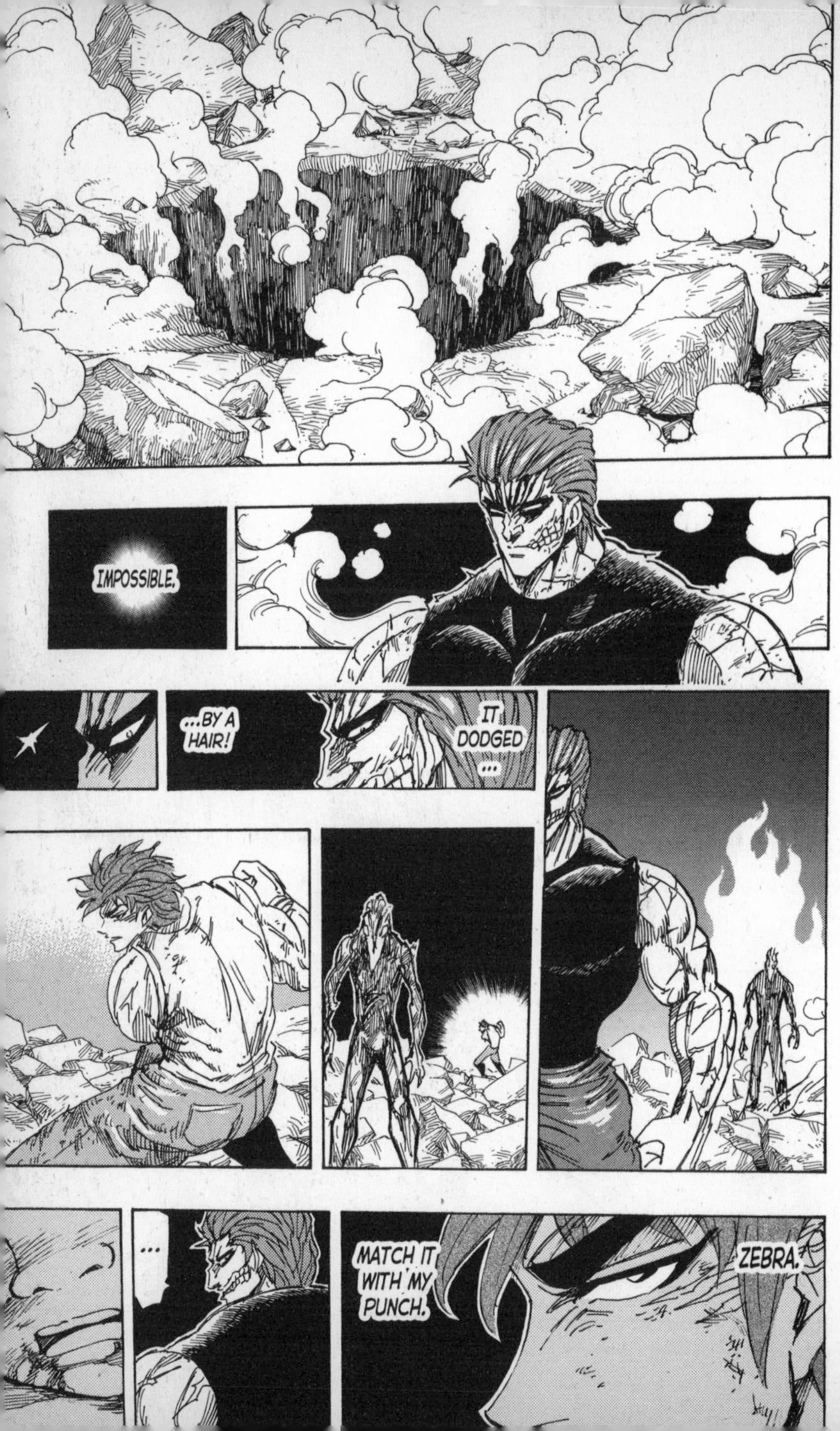
IMPOSSIBLE.
IT DODGED ...
...BY A HAIR!
ZEBRA.
MATCH IT WITH MY PUNCH.
...

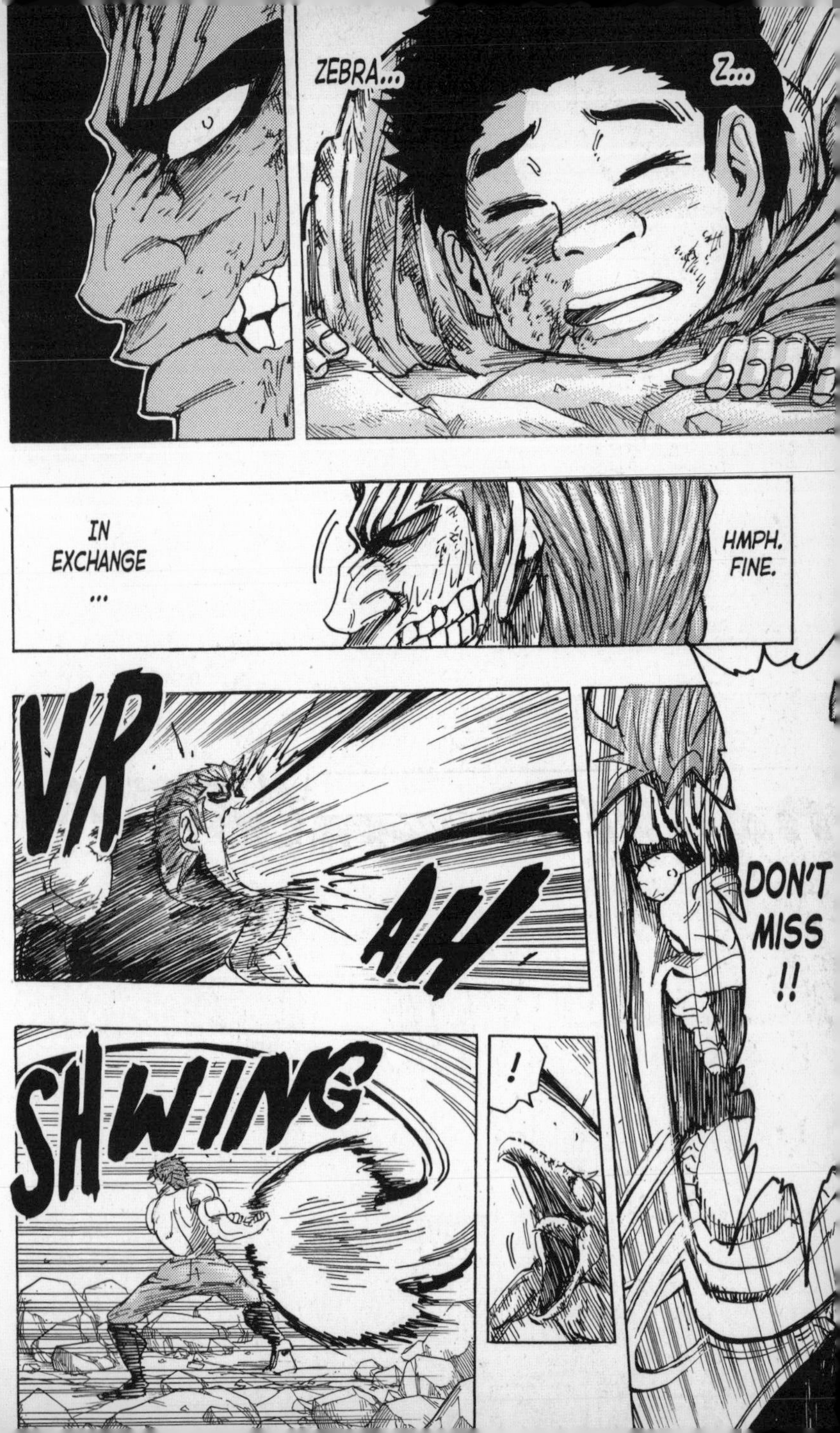
Z...
ZEBRA...
HMPH. FINE.
IN EXCHANGE ...
DON'T MISS !!
VR
AH
!
SHWING

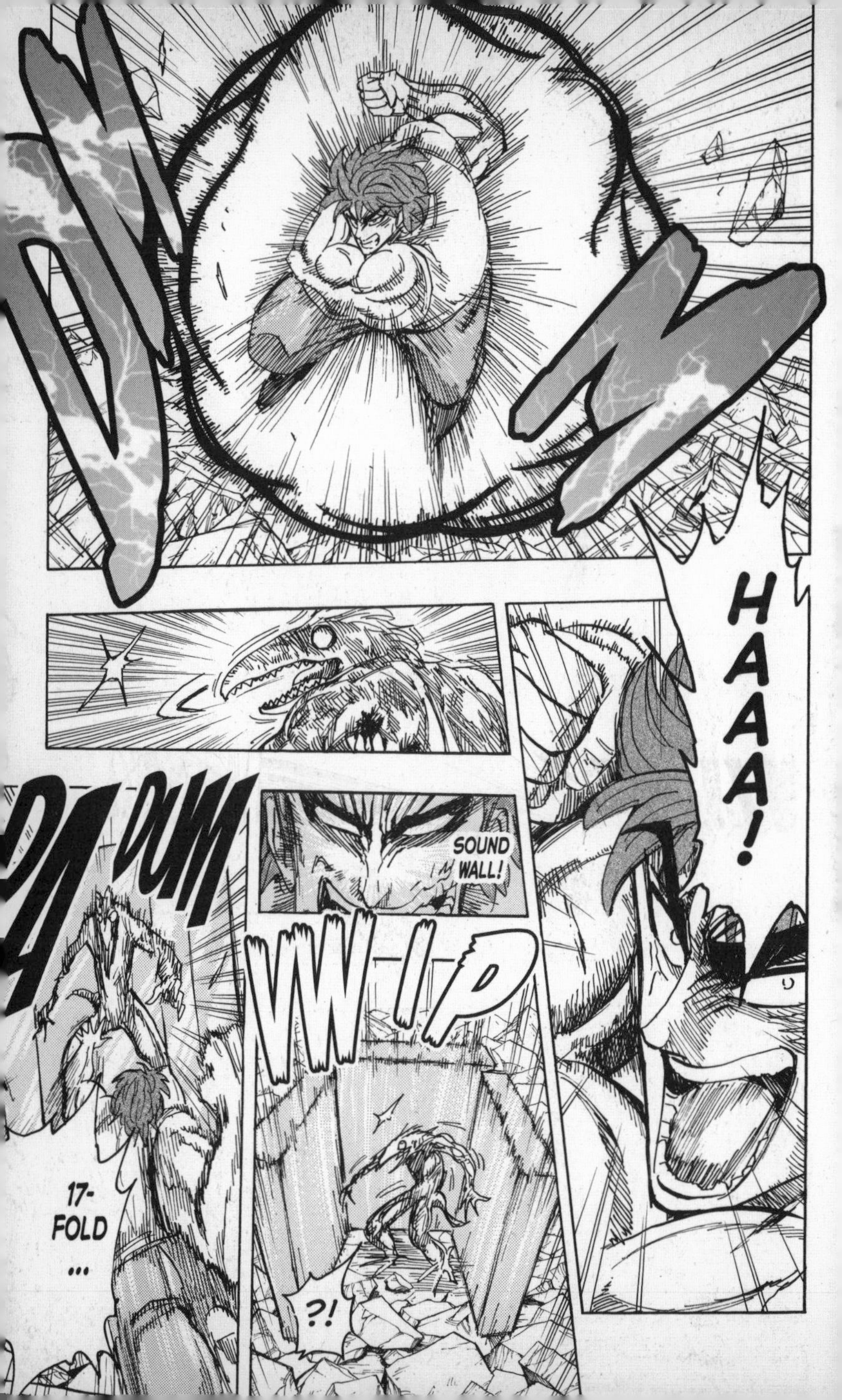
HAAAA!
SOUND WALL!
VWIP
?!
DUM
17-FOLD
...

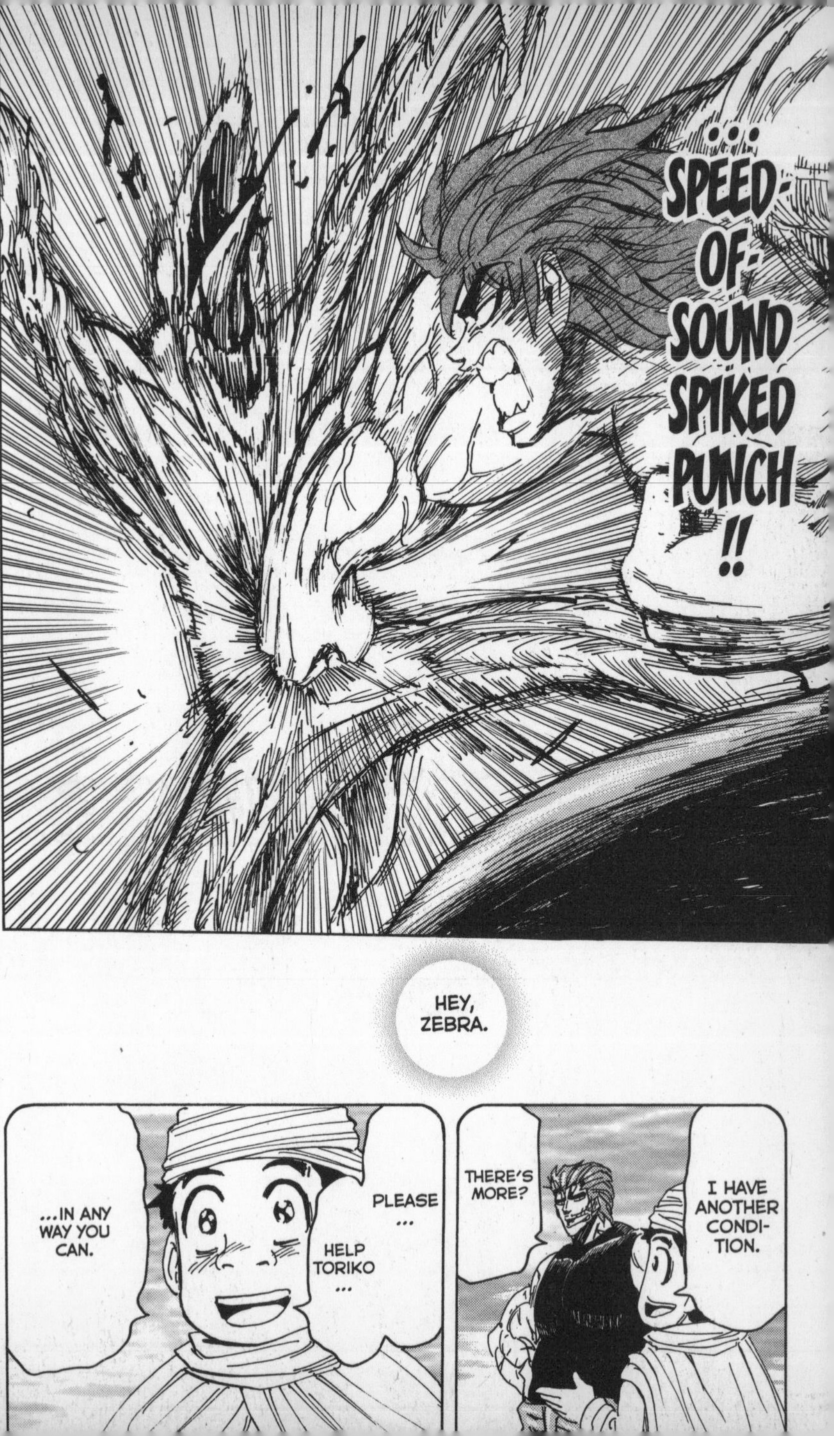

...SPEED-OF-SOUND SPIKED PUNCH!!
HEY, ZEBRA.
I HAVE ANOTHER CONDITION.
THERE'S MORE?
PLEASE...
HELP TORIKO...
...IN ANY WAY YOU CAN.

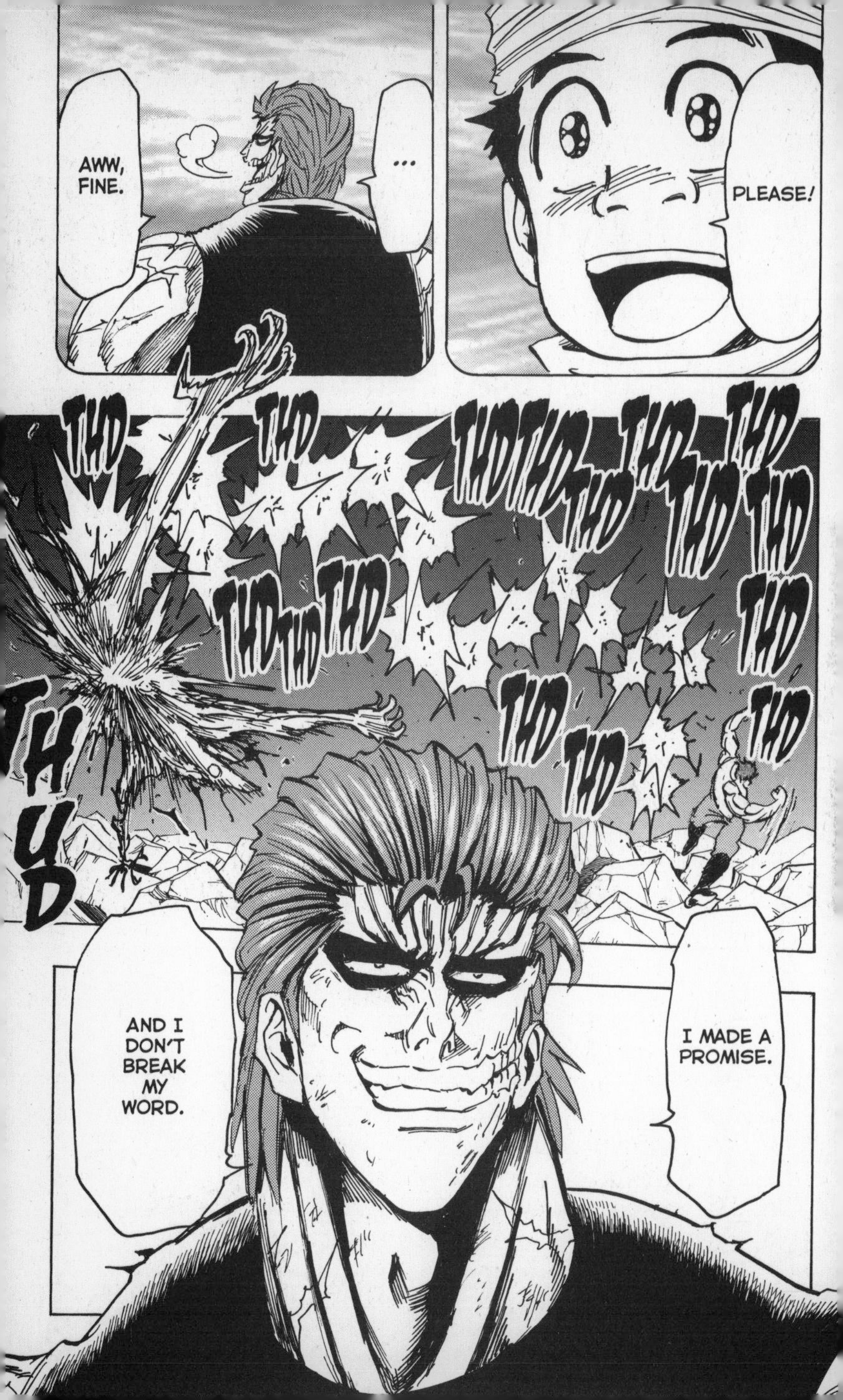
PLEASE!
...
AWW, FINE.
THD THD THD THD
THD THD THD THD
THD THD THD THD
THD THD THD
THD- THD
THUD
I MADE A PROMISE.
AND I DON'T BREAK MY WORD.

TORIKO

GOURMET CHECKLIST

Vol. 162
HEAT PLANET
(UNKNOWN)

CAPTURE LEVEL: UNKNOWN

HABITAT: GOURMET WORLD

LENGTH: 30 METERS

HEIGHT: ---

WEIGHT: ---

PRICE: UNKNOWN

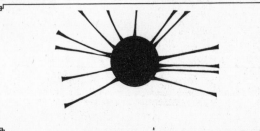

SCALE

A STRANGE PLANT THAT GROWS IN THE GOURMET WORLD'S UNDERGROUND FOREST. DETAILS REGARDING ITS BEHAVIOR, CAPTURE LEVEL, AND MORE ARE A COMPLETE MYSTERY, BUT ACCORDING TO KNOCKING MASTER JIRO, IT POSSESSES ITS OWN GRAVITATIONAL PULL, SO ONE CAN EASILY MOVE AROUND INSIDE OF IT. AT THE SAME TIME, IT EMITS SUCH STRONG HEAT THAT YOU CAN'T COME NEAR IT. THIS ORGANISM IS BIZARRE FOR THE GOURMET WORLD, LET ALONE THE HUMAN WORLD.

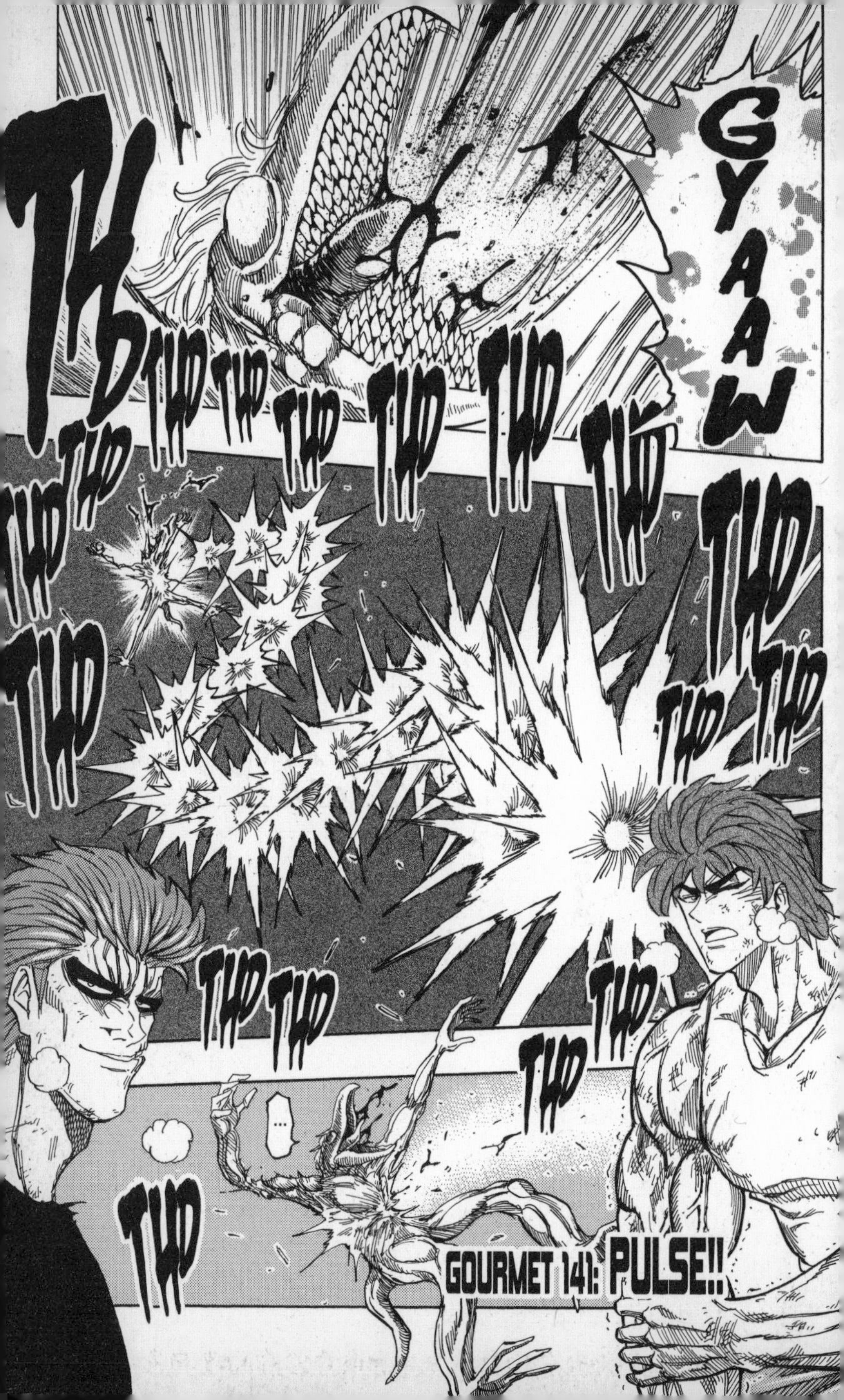
GYAAW
THD THD THD THD THD THD THD THD THD
THD THD THD
THD THD THD
...
THD THD THD THD
THD

GOURMET 141: PULSE!!

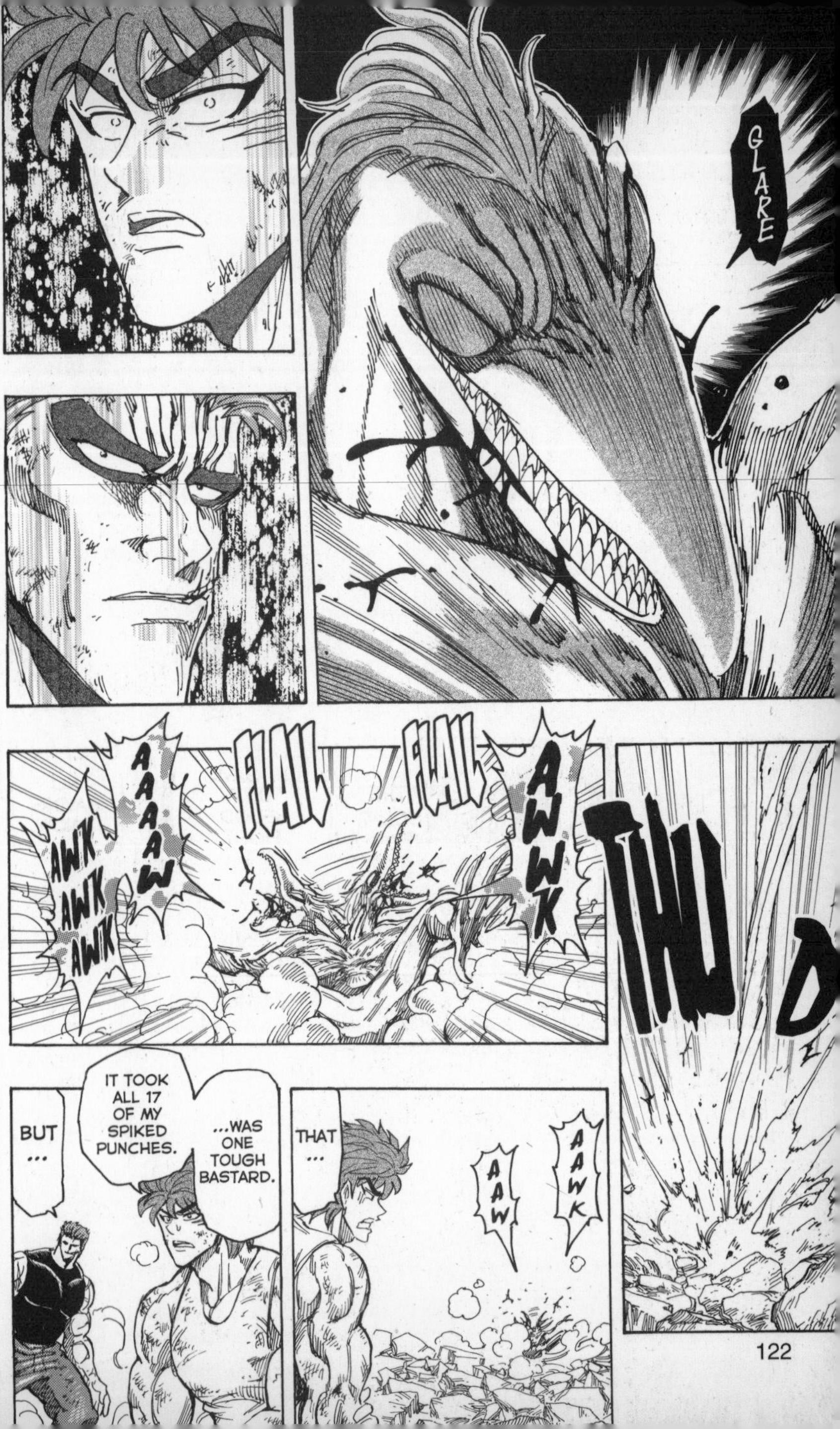
GLARE
THUD
AAWWK
FLAIL
FLAIL
AAAAAW
AWK AWK AWK
AAAWK
AAW
THAT ...
...WAS ONE TOUGH BASTARD.
BUT ...
IT TOOK ALL 17 OF MY SPIKED PUNCHES.

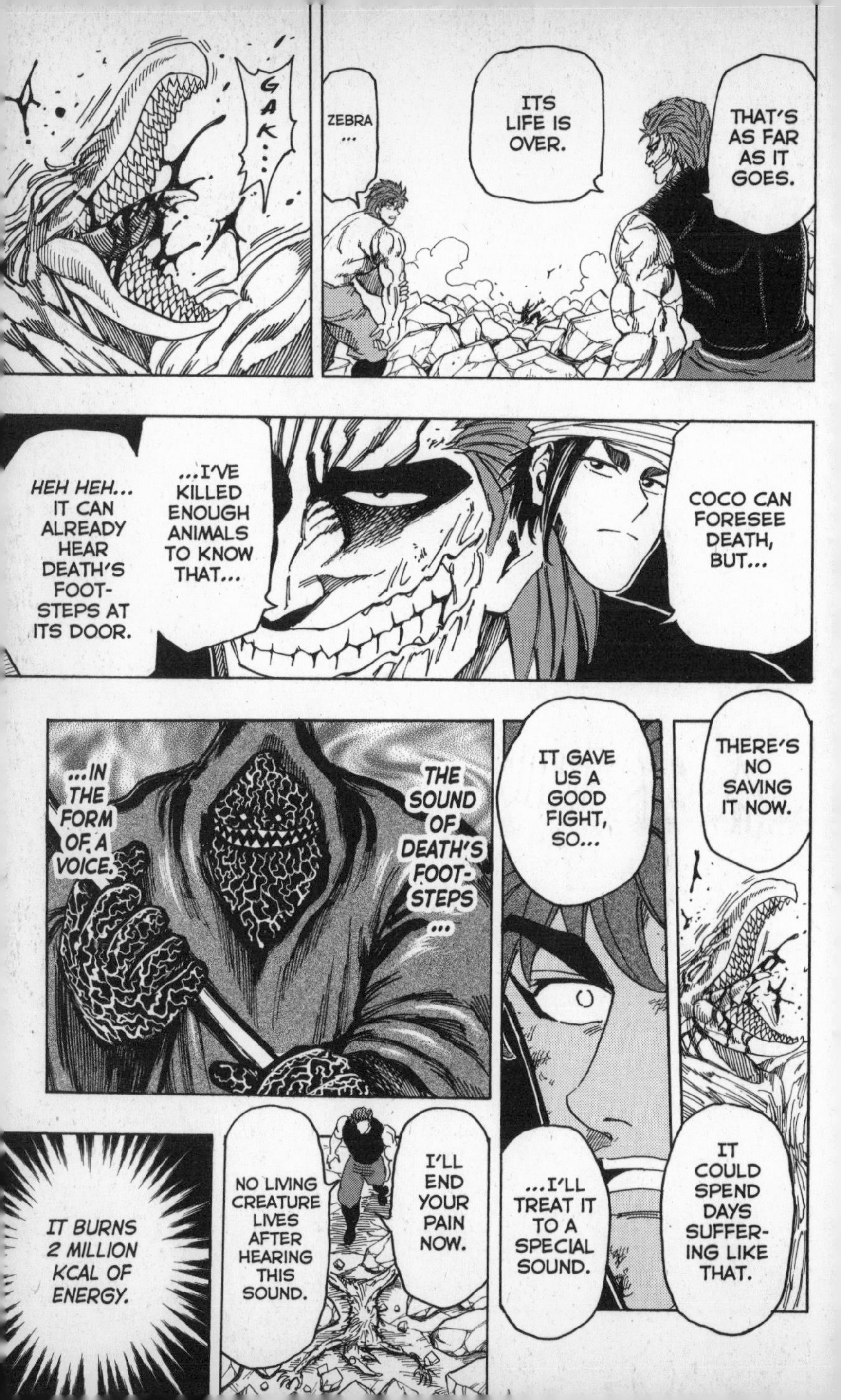
THAT'S AS FAR AS IT GOES.
ITS LIFE IS OVER.
ZEBRA ...
GAK...
COCO CAN FORESEE DEATH, BUT...
...I'VE KILLED ENOUGH ANIMALS TO KNOW THAT...
HEH HEH... IT CAN ALREADY HEAR DEATH'S FOOT-STEPS AT ITS DOOR.
THERE'S NO SAVING IT NOW.
IT COULD SPEND DAYS SUFFER-ING LIKE THAT.
IT GAVE US A GOOD FIGHT, SO...
...I'LL TREAT IT TO A SPECIAL SOUND.
THE SOUND OF DEATH'S FOOT-STEPS ...
...IN THE FORM OF A VOICE.
I'LL END YOUR PAIN NOW.
NO LIVING CREATURE LIVES AFTER HEARING THIS SOUND.
IT BURNS 2 MILLION KCAL OF ENERGY.

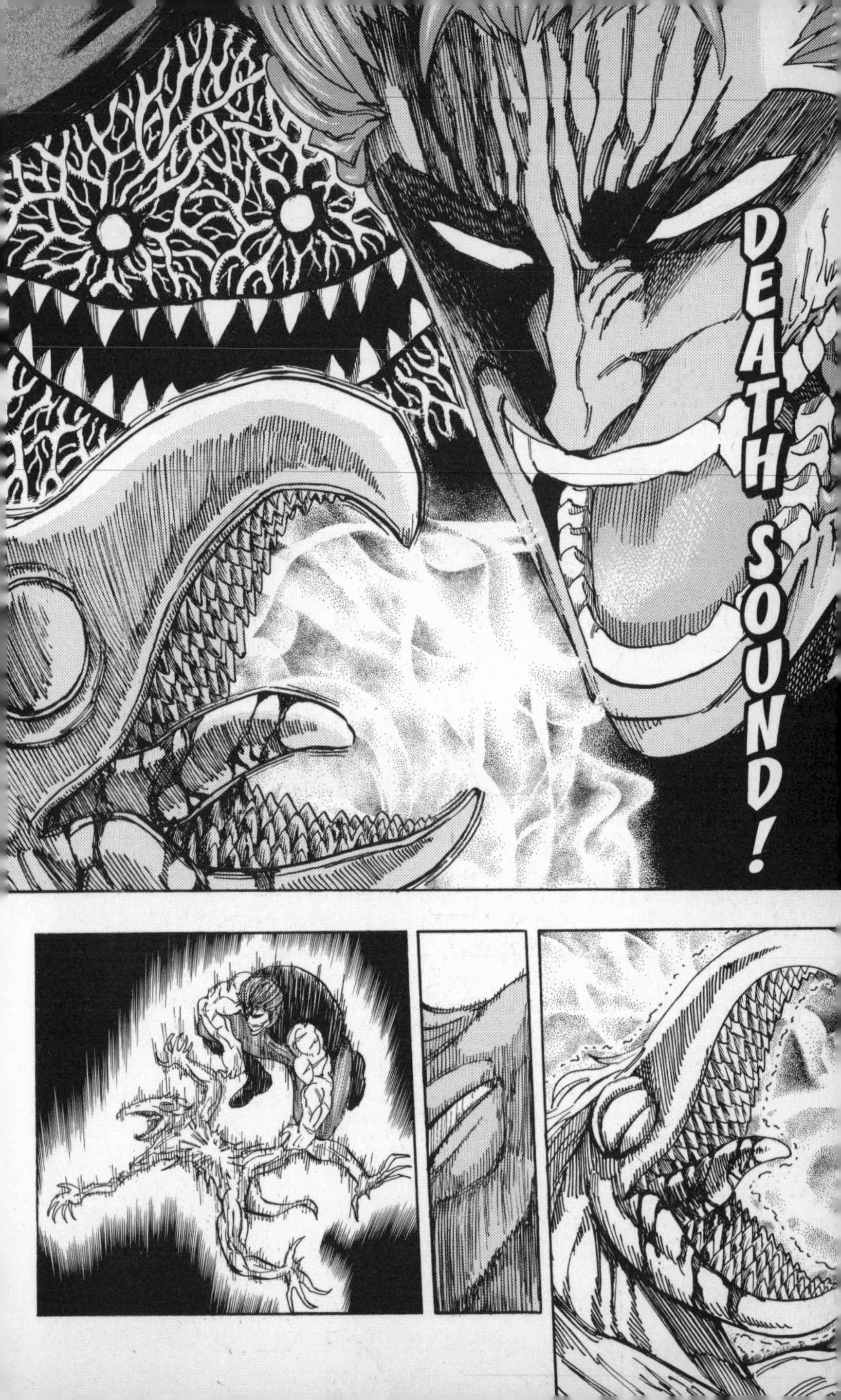
DEATH SOUND!

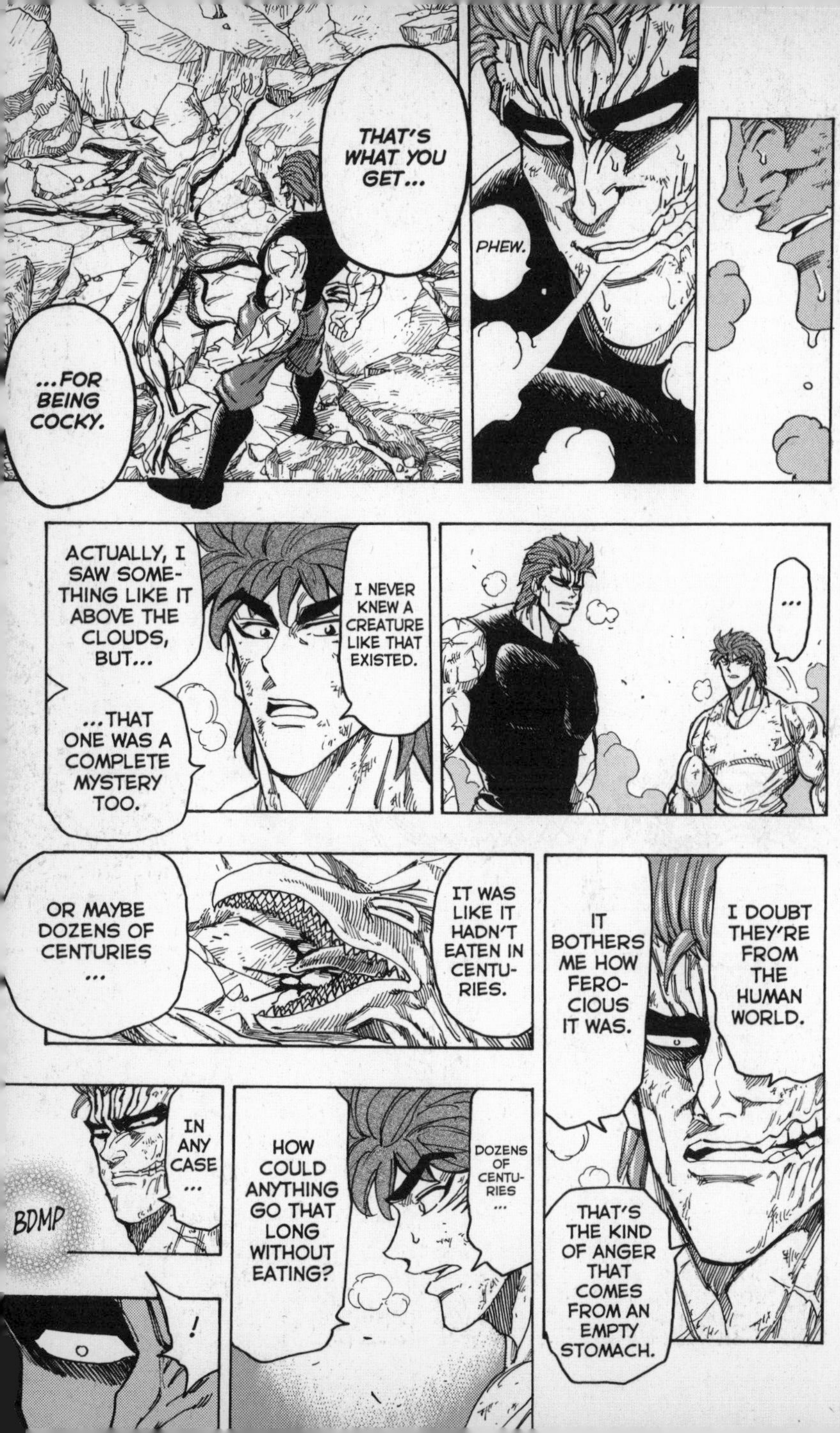
PHEW.
THAT'S WHAT YOU GET...
...FOR BEING COCKY.
...
I NEVER KNEW A CREATURE LIKE THAT EXISTED.
ACTUALLY, I SAW SOME-THING LIKE IT ABOVE THE CLOUDS, BUT...
...THAT ONE WAS A COMPLETE MYSTERY TOO.
I DOUBT THEY'RE FROM THE HUMAN WORLD.
IT BOTHERS ME HOW FERO-CIOUS IT WAS.
THAT'S THE KIND OF ANGER THAT COMES FROM AN EMPTY STOMACH.
IT WAS LIKE IT HADN'T EATEN IN CENTU-RIES.
OR MAYBE DOZENS OF CENTURIES ...
DOZENS OF CENTU-RIES ...
HOW COULD ANYTHING GO THAT LONG WITHOUT EATING?
IN ANY CASE ...
BDMP
!

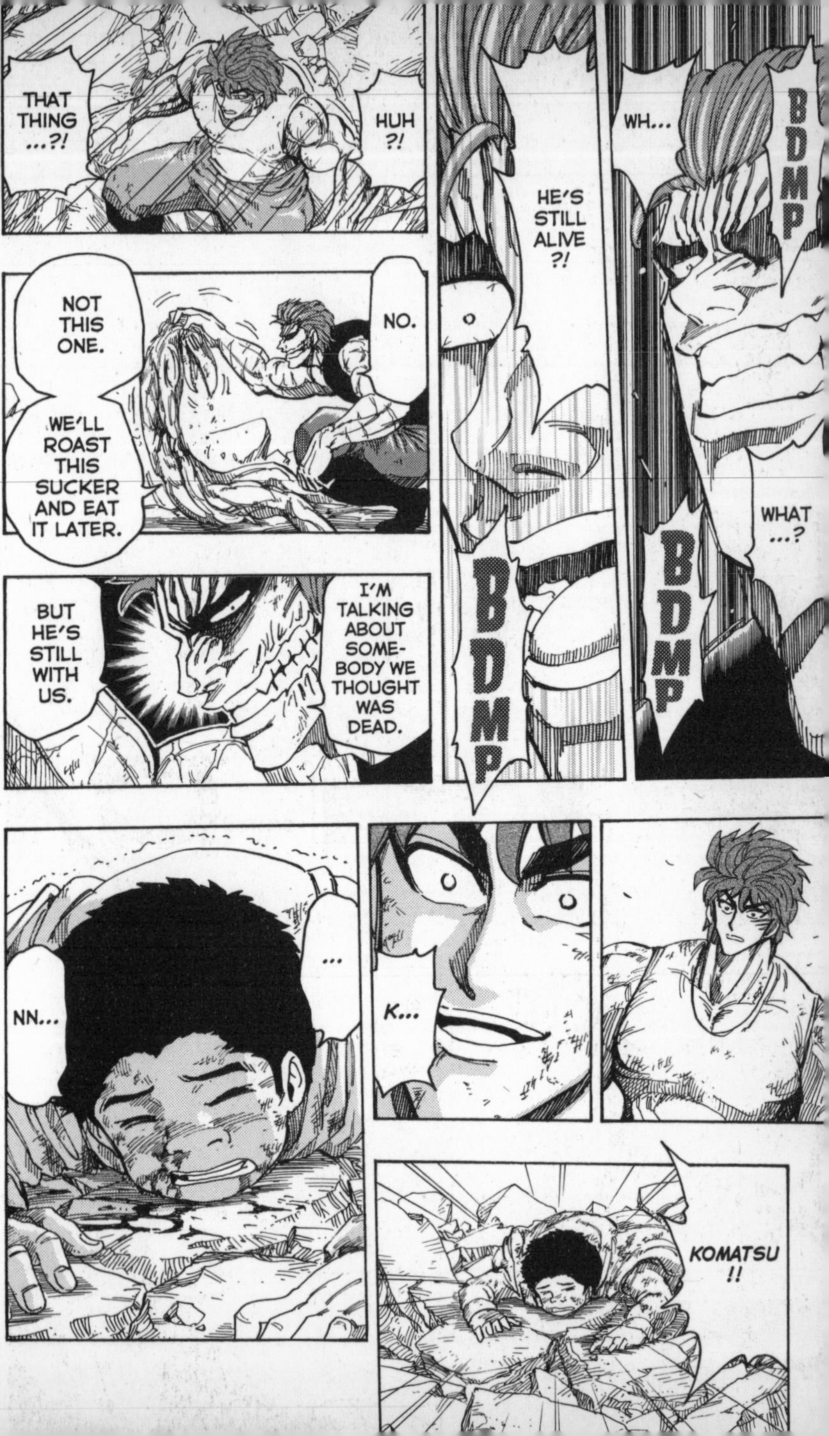
WH...
BDMP
WHAT...?
BDMP
HE'S STILL ALIVE?!
BDMP
HUH?!
THAT THING...?!
NO.
NOT THIS ONE.
WE'LL ROAST THIS SUCKER AND EAT IT LATER.
I'M TALKING ABOUT SOMEBODY WE THOUGHT WAS DEAD.
BUT HE'S STILL WITH US.
K...
KOMATSU!!
...
NN...

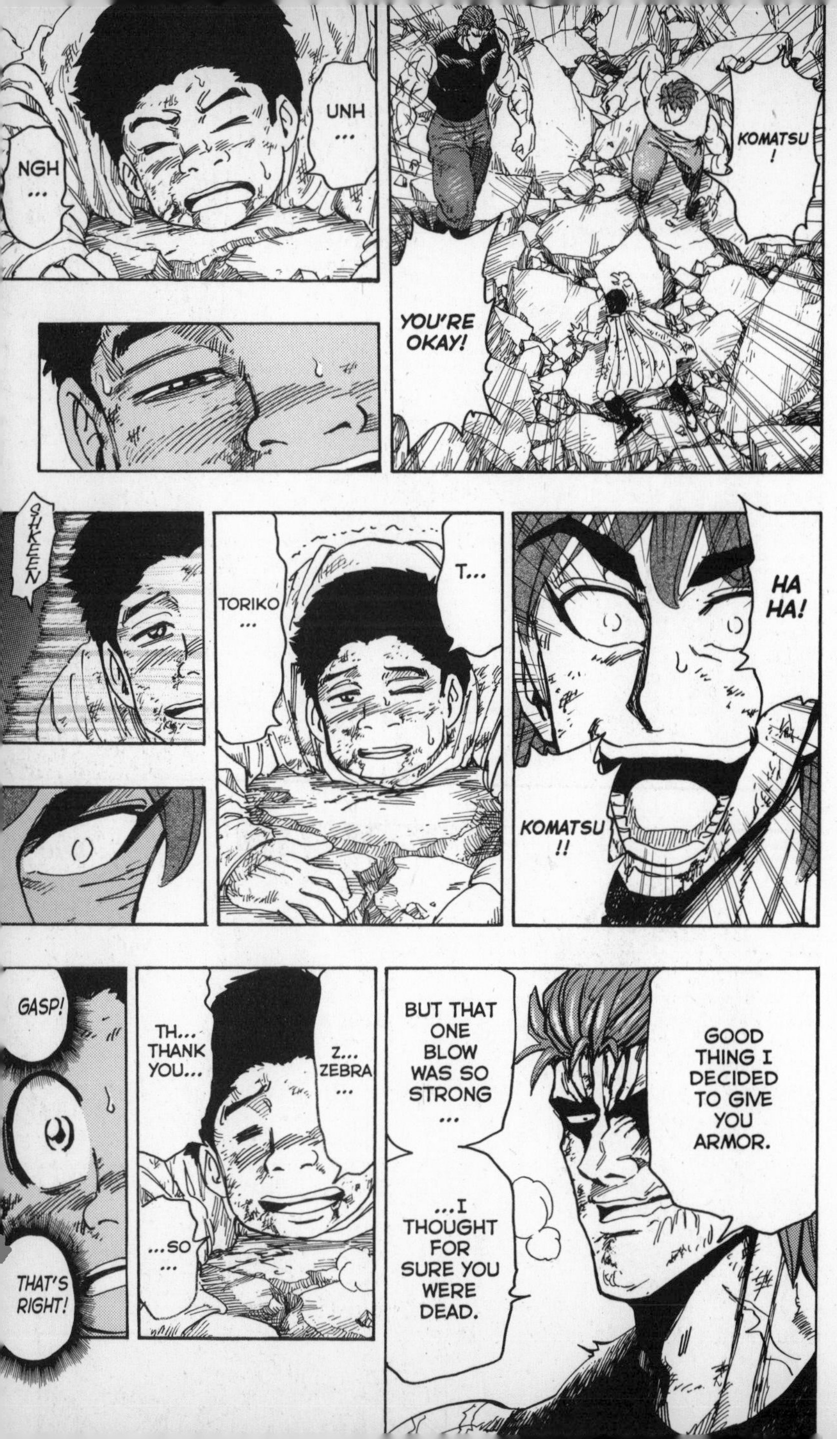
KOMATSU!
YOU'RE OKAY!
UNH...
NGH...
HA HA!
KOMATSU!!
T...
TORIKO...
SHKEEN
GOOD THING I DECIDED TO GIVE YOU ARMOR.
BUT THAT ONE BLOW WAS SO STRONG...
...I THOUGHT FOR SURE YOU WERE DEAD.
Z... ZEBRA...
TH... THANK YOU...
...SO...
GASP!
THAT'S RIGHT!

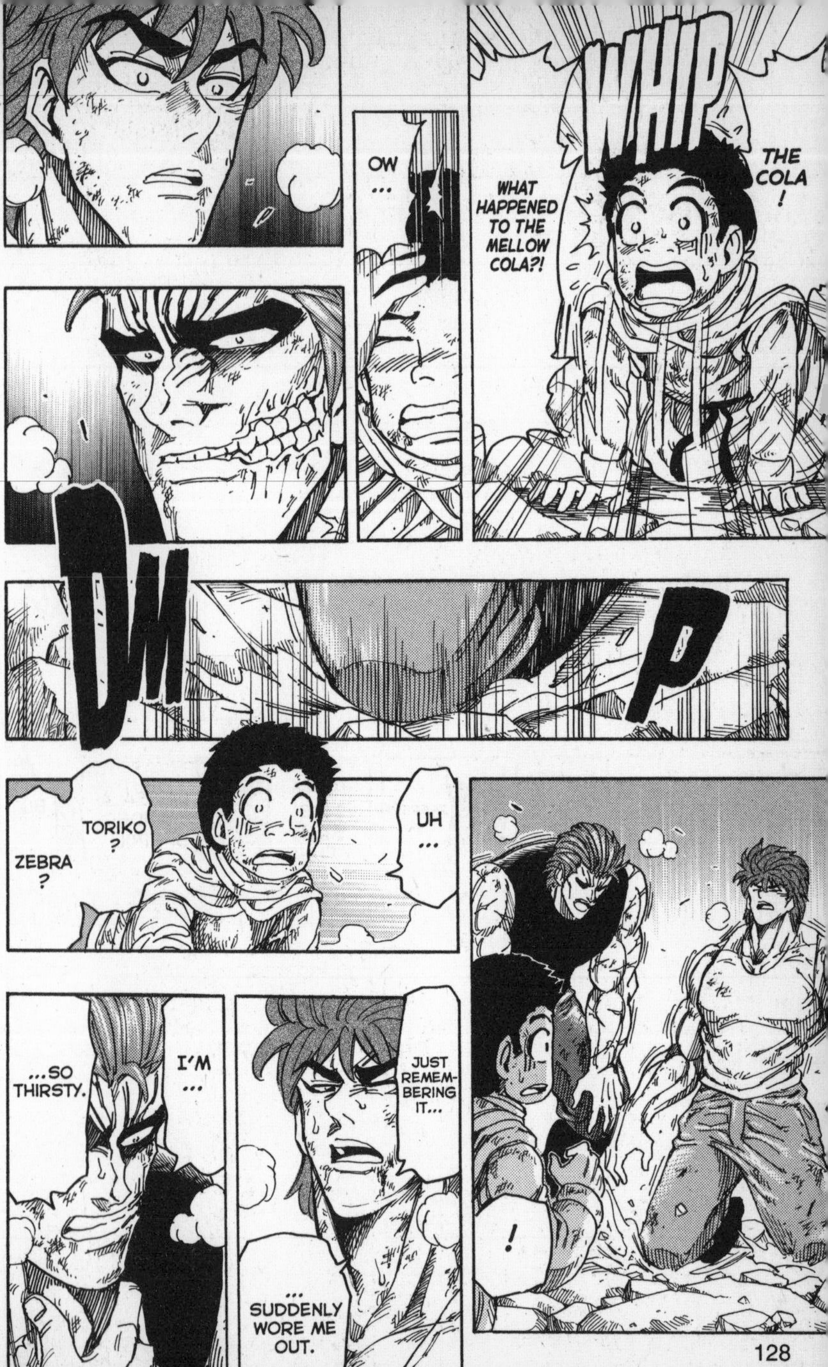
WHIP
THE COLA!
WHAT HAPPENED TO THE MELLOW COLA?!
OW...
DMP
UH...
TORIKO?
ZEBRA?
!
JUST REMEMBERING IT...
...SUDDENLY WORE ME OUT.
I'M...
...SO THIRSTY.

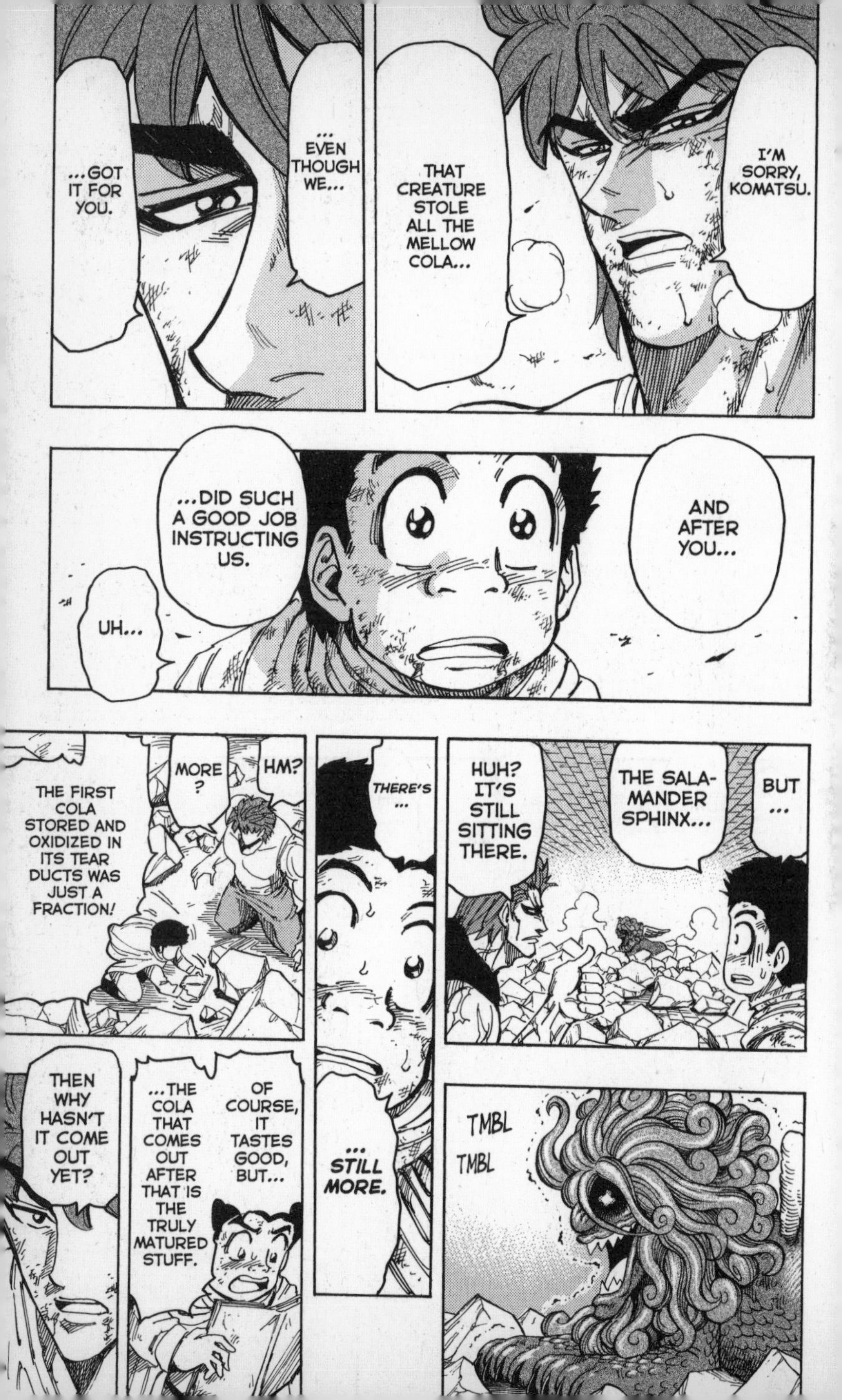
I'M SORRY, KOMATSU.
THAT CREATURE STOLE ALL THE MELLOW COLA...
...EVEN THOUGH WE...
...GOT IT FOR YOU.
AND AFTER YOU...
...DID SUCH A GOOD JOB INSTRUCTING US.
UH...
BUT...
THE SALA-MANDER SPHINX...
HUH? IT'S STILL SITTING THERE.
TMBL
TMBL
THERE'S...
...STILL MORE.
HM?
MORE?
THE FIRST COLA STORED AND OXIDIZED IN ITS TEAR DUCTS WAS JUST A FRACTION!
OF COURSE, IT TASTES GOOD, BUT...
...THE COLA THAT COMES OUT AFTER THAT IS THE TRULY MATURED STUFF.
THEN WHY HASN'T IT COME OUT YET?

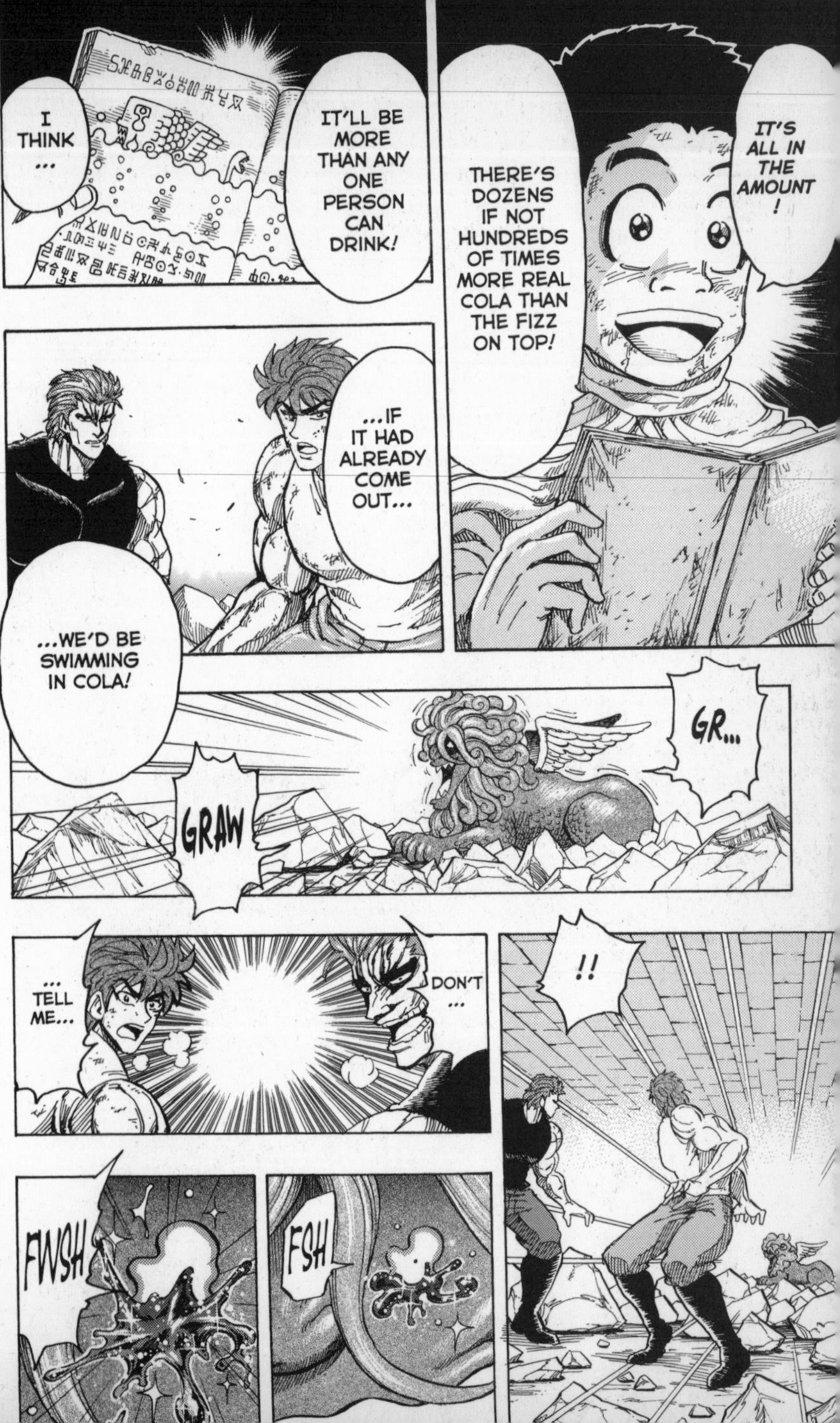

IT'S ALL IN THE AMOUNT!
THERE'S DOZENS IF NOT HUNDREDS OF TIMES MORE REAL COLA THAN THE FIZZ ON TOP!
IT'LL BE MORE THAN ANY ONE PERSON CAN DRINK!
I THINK...
...IF IT HAD ALREADY COME OUT...
...WE'D BE SWIMMING IN COLA!
GR...
GRAW
!!
DON'T...
...TELL ME...
FSH
FWSH

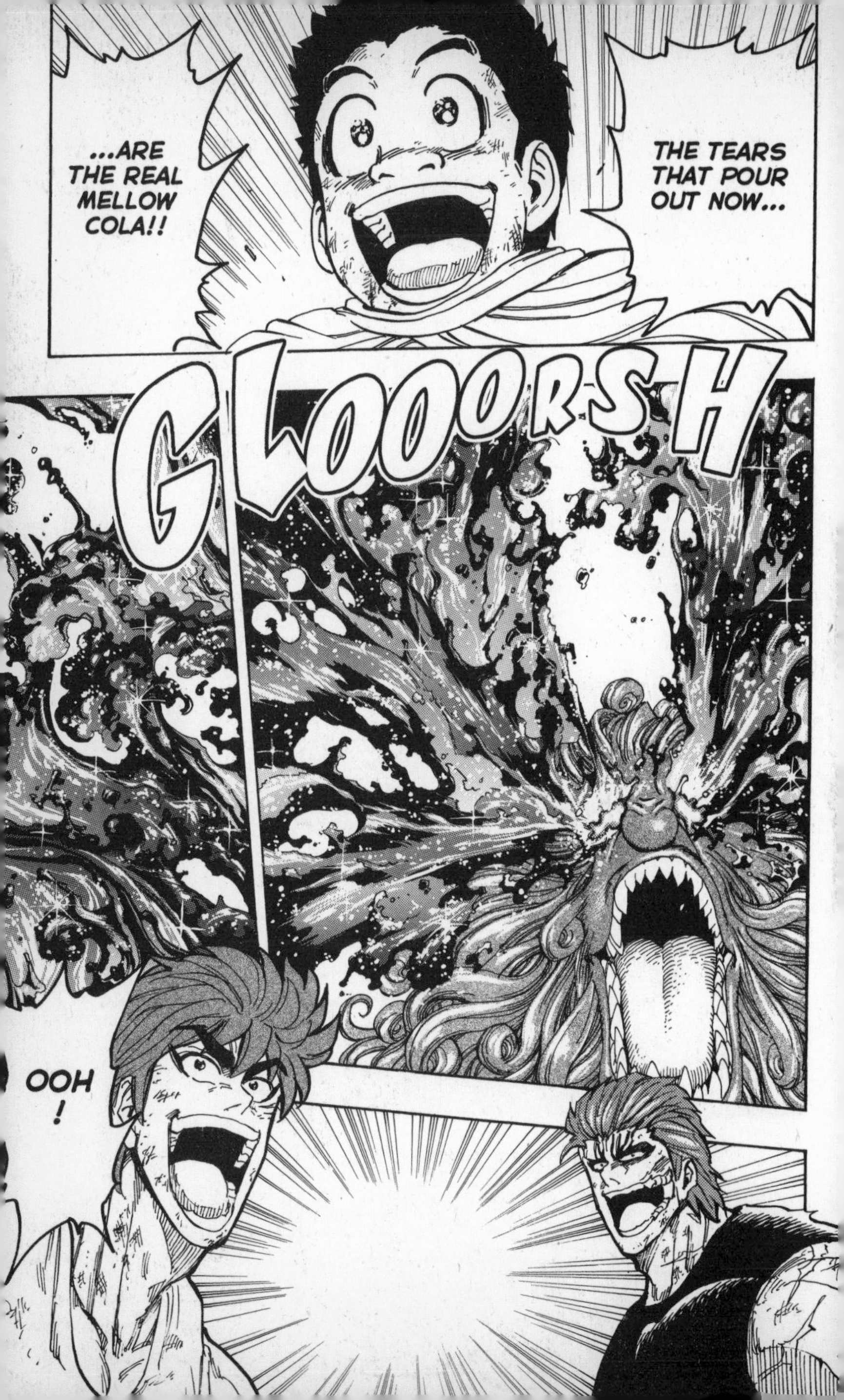
THE TEARS THAT POUR OUT NOW...
...ARE THE REAL MELLOW COLA!!
GLOOORSH
OOH!

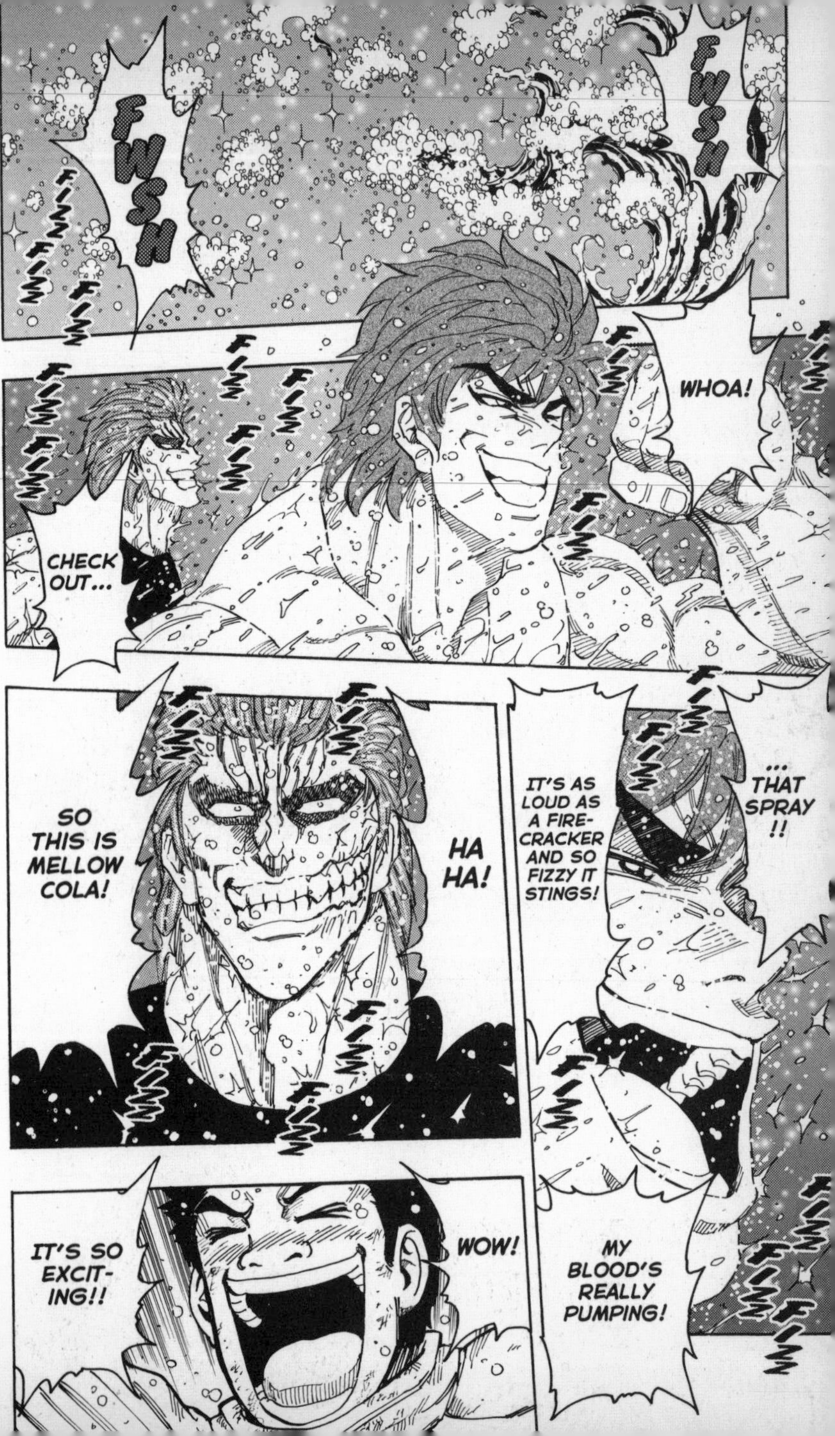
FWSH
FWSH
FIZZ FIZZ FIZZ
FIZZ FIZZ FIZZ
WHOA!
CHECK OUT...
FIZZ FIZZ
...THAT SPRAY!!
IT'S AS LOUD AS A FIRE-CRACKER AND SO FIZZY IT STINGS!
FIZZ FIZZ
HA HA!
SO THIS IS MELLOW COLA!
FIZZ FIZZ FIZZ
MY BLOOD'S REALLY PUMPING!
WOW!
IT'S SO EXCIT-ING!!

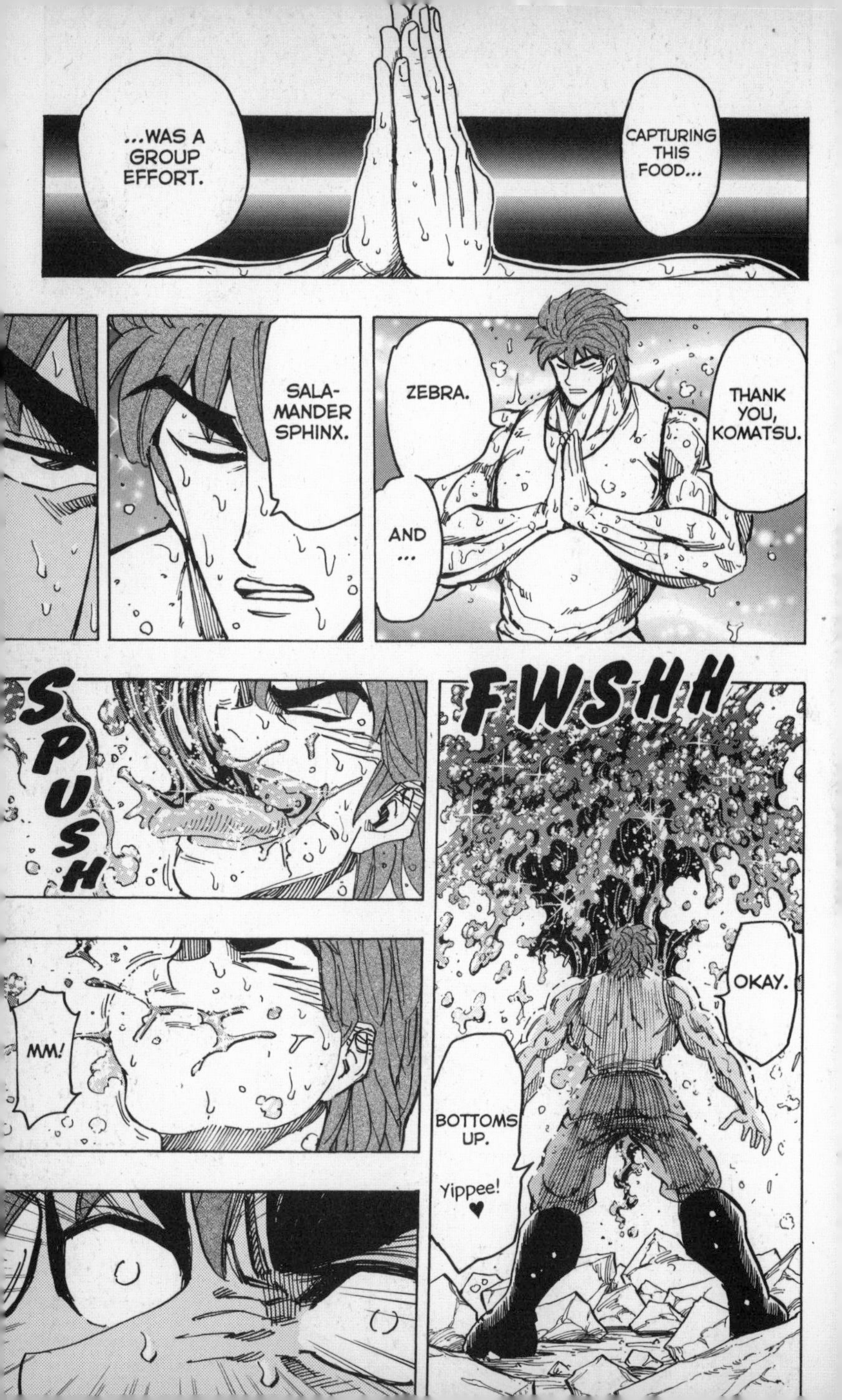
CAPTURING THIS FOOD...
...WAS A GROUP EFFORT.
THANK YOU, KOMATSU.
ZEBRA.
AND ...
SALA-MANDER SPHINX.
FWSHH
OKAY.
BOTTOMS UP.
Yippee! ♥
SPUSH
MM!

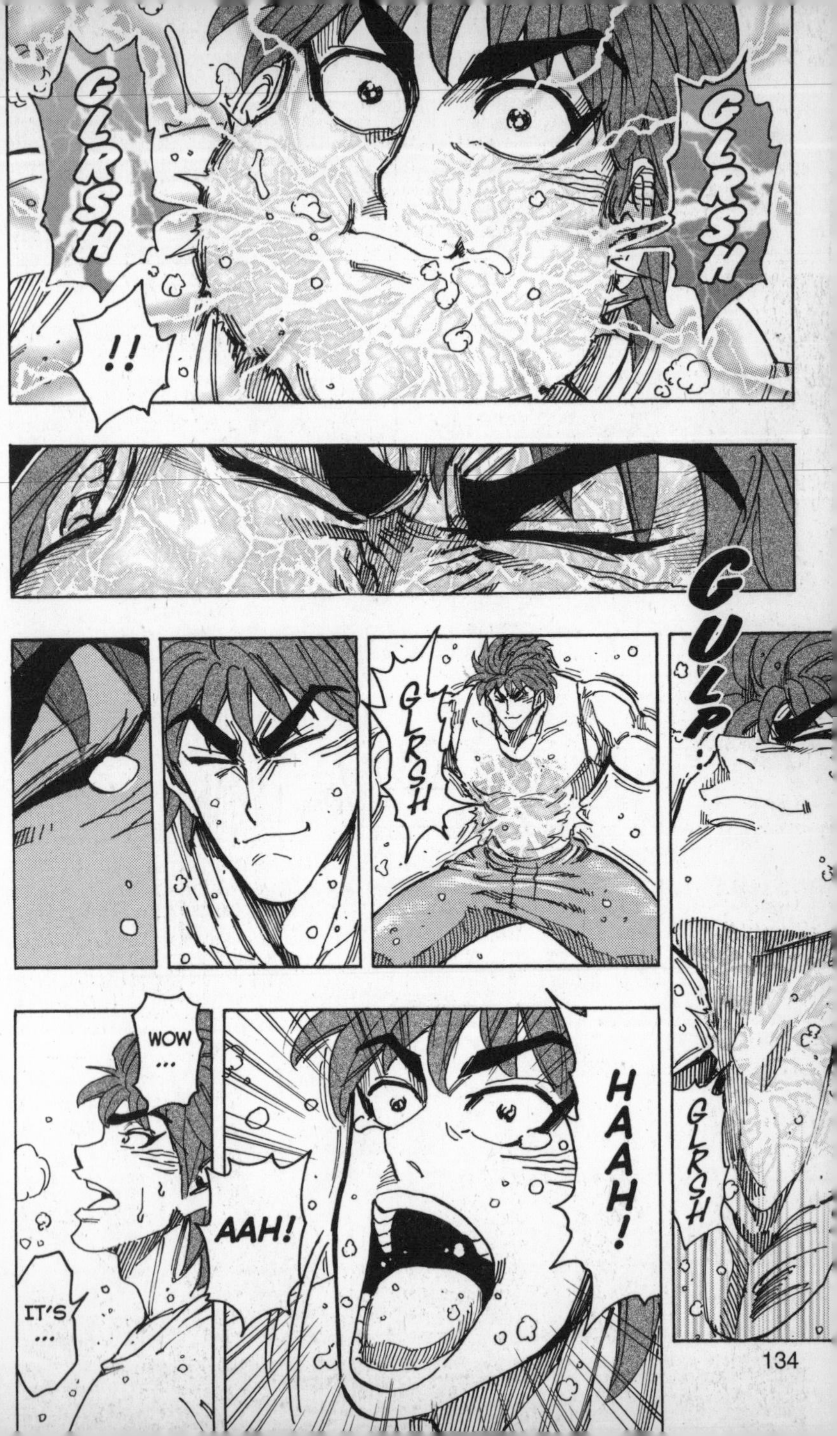
GLRSH
GLRSH
!!
GULP...
GLRSH
GLRSH
HAAAH!
AAH!
WOW ...
IT'S ...

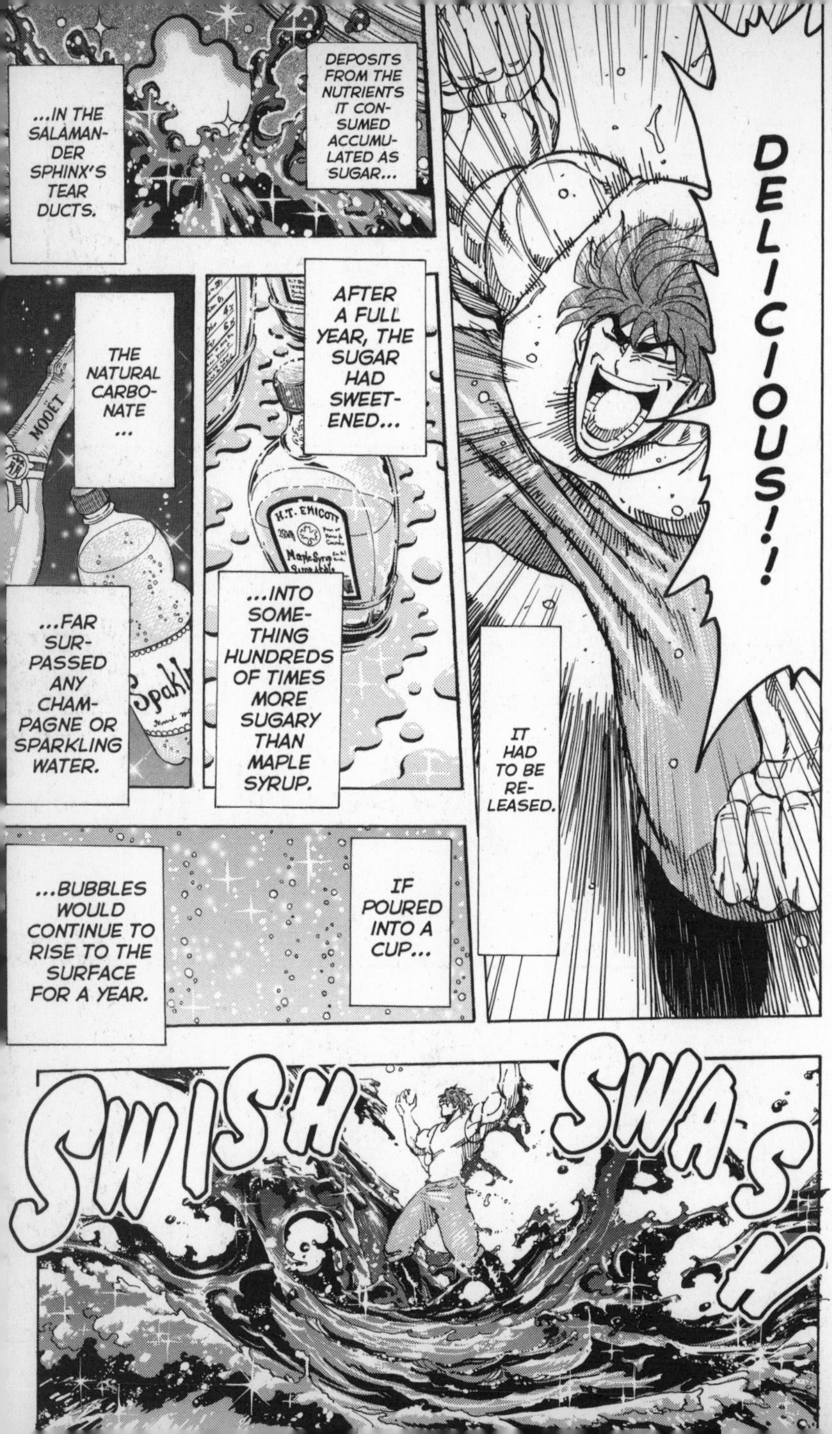
DELICIOUS!!
IT HAD TO BE RELEASED.
DEPOSITS FROM THE NUTRIENTS IT CONSUMED ACCUMULATED AS SUGAR...
...IN THE SALAMANDER SPHINX'S TEAR DUCTS.
AFTER A FULL YEAR, THE SUGAR HAD SWEETENED...
...INTO SOMETHING HUNDREDS OF TIMES MORE SUGARY THAN MAPLE SYRUP.
THE NATURAL CARBONATE...
...FAR SURPASSED ANY CHAMPAGNE OR SPARKLING WATER.
IF POURED INTO A CUP...
...BUBBLES WOULD CONTINUE TO RISE TO THE SURFACE FOR A YEAR.
SWISH SWASH

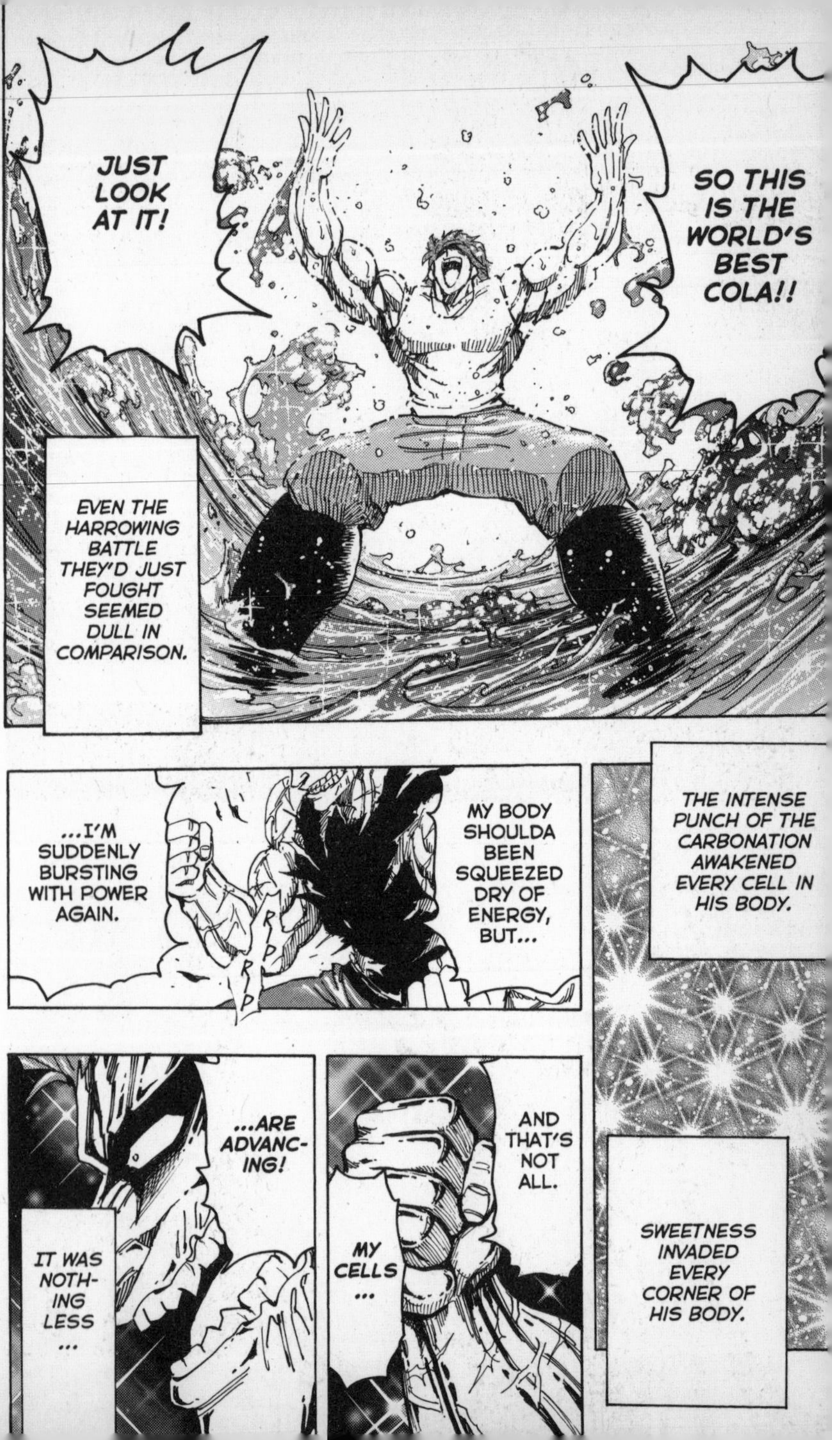
SO THIS IS THE WORLD'S BEST COLA!!
JUST LOOK AT IT!
EVEN THE HARROWING BATTLE THEY'D JUST FOUGHT SEEMED DULL IN COMPARISON.
THE INTENSE PUNCH OF THE CARBONATION AWAKENED EVERY CELL IN HIS BODY.
SWEETNESS INVADED EVERY CORNER OF HIS BODY.
MY BODY SHOULDA BEEN SQUEEZED DRY OF ENERGY, BUT...
...I'M SUDDENLY BURSTING WITH POWER AGAIN.
RIP RIP
AND THAT'S NOT ALL.
MY CELLS...
...ARE ADVANCING!
IT WAS NOTHING LESS...

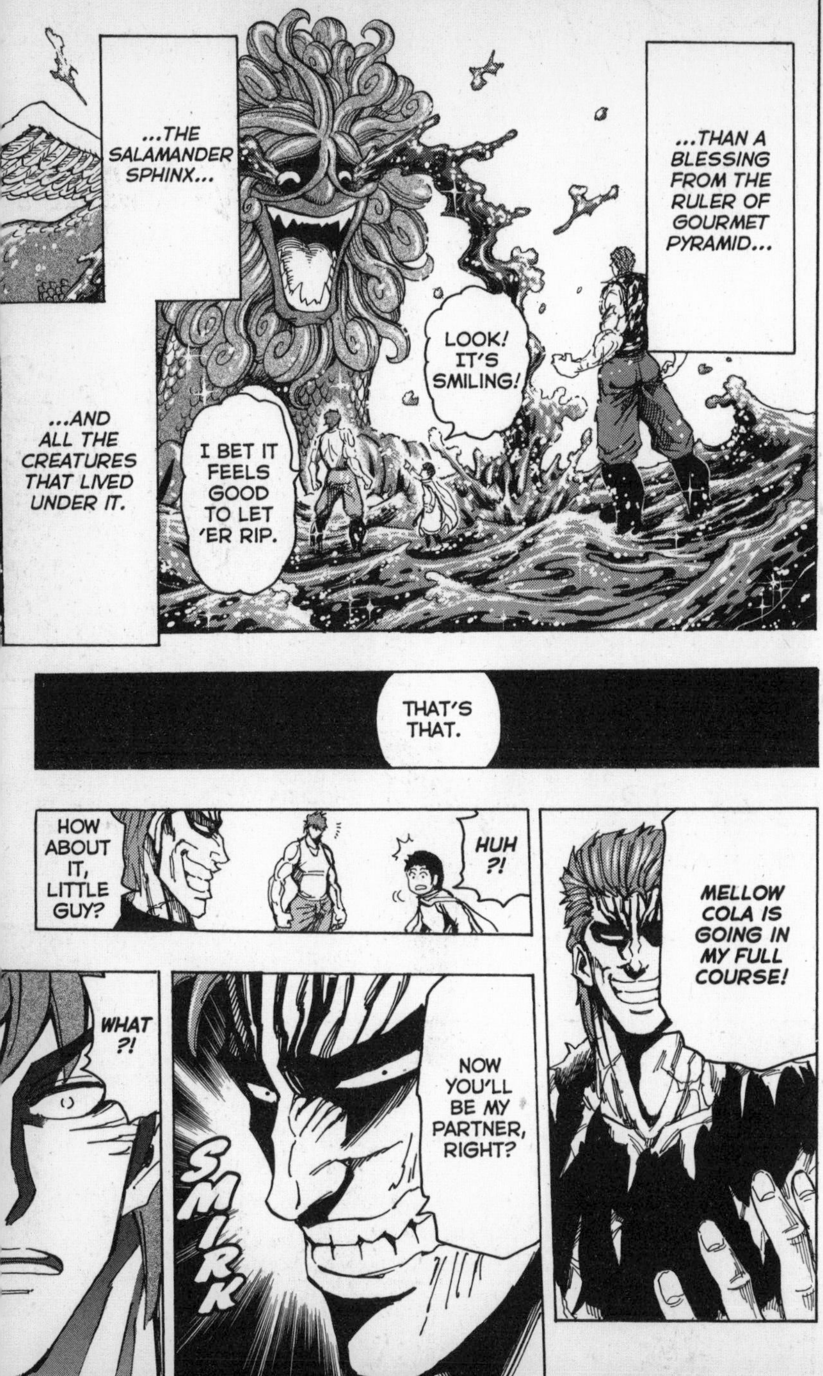
...THAN A BLESSING FROM THE RULER OF GOURMET PYRAMID...
...THE SALAMANDER SPHINX...
LOOK! IT'S SMILING!
...AND ALL THE CREATURES THAT LIVED UNDER IT.
I BET IT FEELS GOOD TO LET 'ER RIP.
THAT'S THAT.
MELLOW COLA IS GOING IN MY FULL COURSE!
HUH?!
HOW ABOUT IT, LITTLE GUY?
NOW YOU'LL BE MY PARTNER, RIGHT?
SMIRK
WHAT?!

TORIKO

GOURMET CHECKLIST

Vol. 163

FALL TREE
(PLANT)

CAPTURE LEVEL: UNKNOWN

HABITAT: GOURMET WORLD

LENGTH: ---

HEIGHT: 40–100 METERS

WEIGHT: ---

PRICE: UNKNOWN

THEN THERE'S THAT FALL TREE YOU GOT STUCK UNDER.

FWSH

SCALE

A GIANT PLANT THAT LIVES IN THE UNDERGROUND FOREST. DETAILS REGARDING ITS BEHAVIOR, CAPTURE LEVEL, AND MORE ARE A COMPLETE MYSTERY, BUT ACCORDING TO KNOCKING MASTER JIRO, WHEN PREY PASSES BENEATH ITS SHADE, THE FALL TREE'S LEAVES FIRE WATER MISSILES, PULVERIZING PREY INTO NUTRIENTS FOR ITS ROOTS. TORIKO BARELY MANAGED TO ESCAPE THIS FEARSOME PLANT.

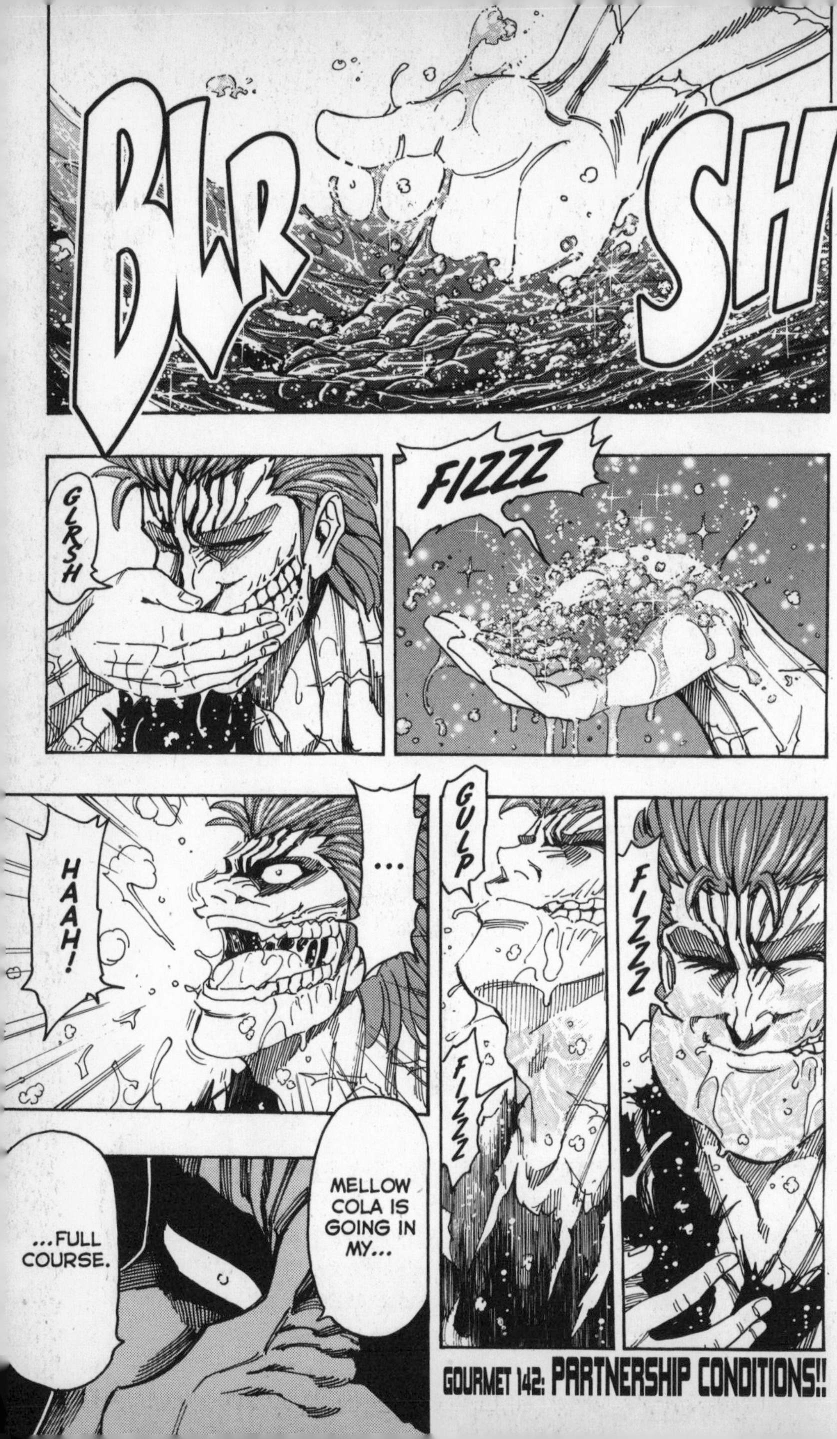
BLRSH
FIZZZ
GLRSH
FIZZZZ
GULP
FIZZZ
...
HAAAH!
MELLOW COLA IS GOING IN MY...
...FULL COURSE.

GOURMET 142: PARTNERSHIP CONDITIONS!!

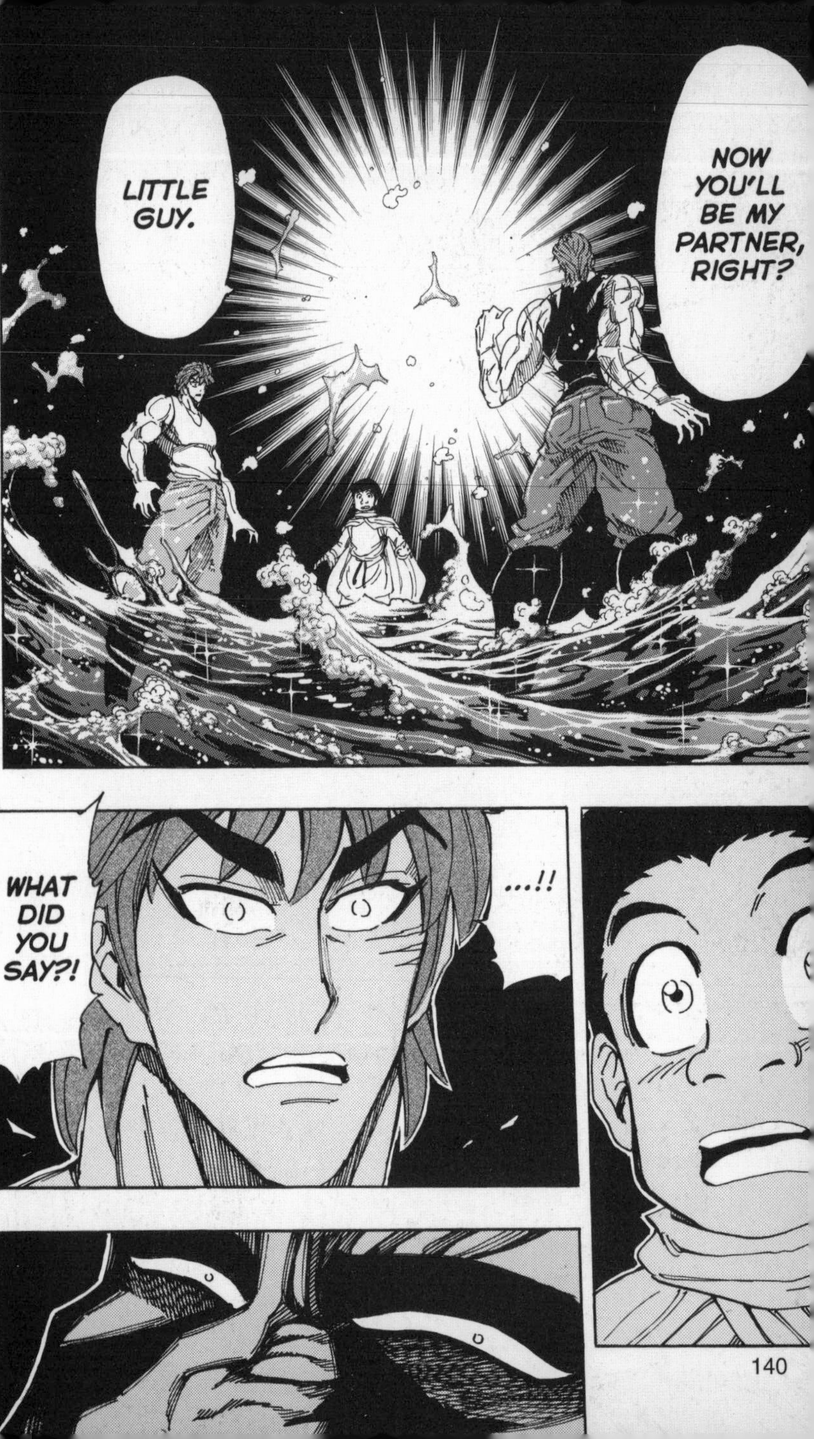
NOW YOU'LL BE MY PARTNER, RIGHT?
LITTLE GUY.
...!!
WHAT DID YOU SAY?!

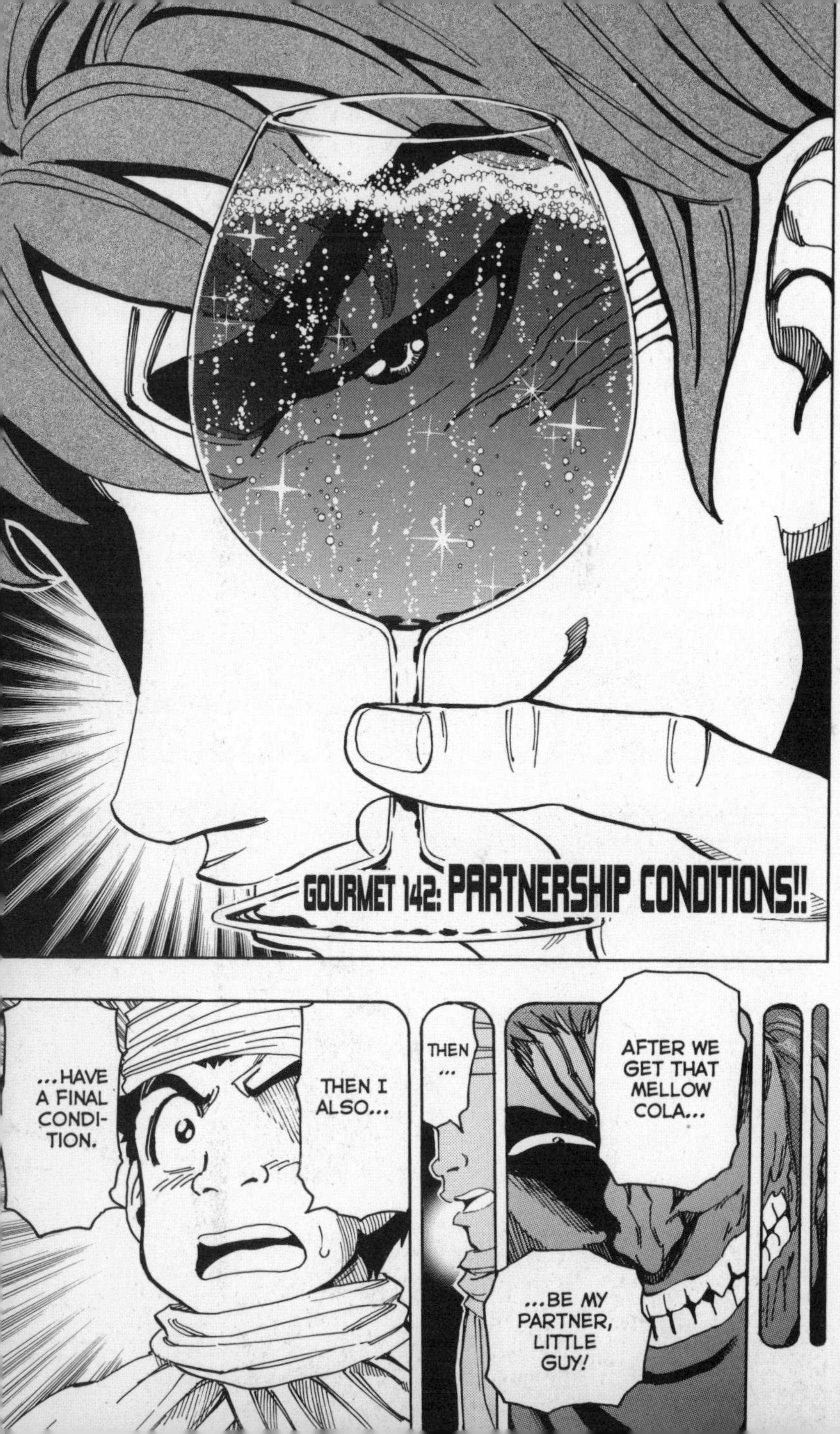
GOURMET 142: PARTNERSHIP CONDITIONS!!
AFTER WE GET THAT MELLOW COLA...
...BE MY PARTNER, LITTLE GUY!
THEN...
THEN I ALSO...
...HAVE A FINAL CONDITION.

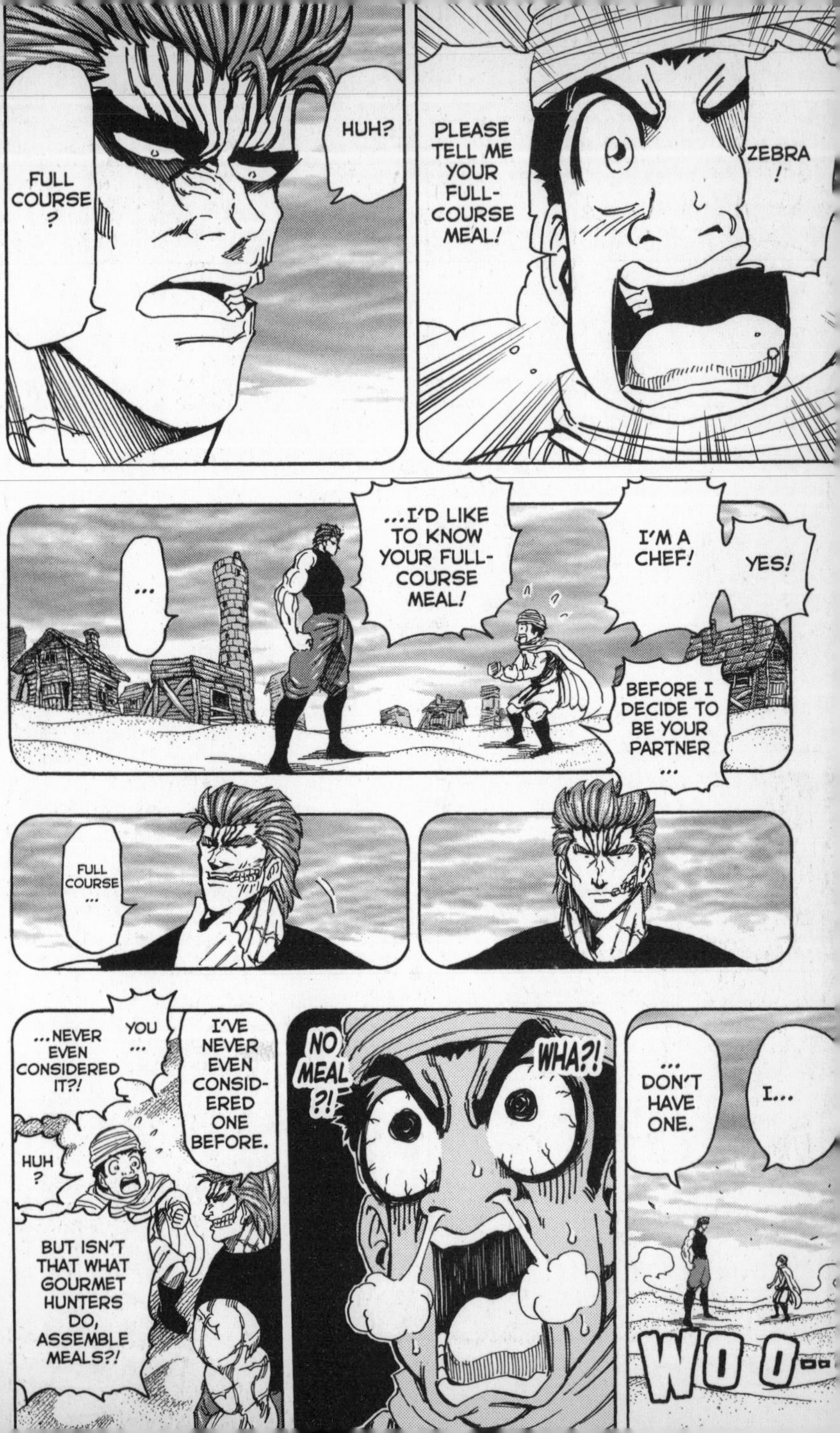
ZEBRA!
PLEASE TELL ME YOUR FULL-COURSE MEAL!
HUH?
FULL COURSE?
YES!
I'M A CHEF!
BEFORE I DECIDE TO BE YOUR PARTNER...
...I'D LIKE TO KNOW YOUR FULL-COURSE MEAL!
...
FULL COURSE...
I...
...DON'T HAVE ONE.
WOO
WHA?!
NO MEAL?!
I'VE NEVER EVEN CONSIDERED ONE BEFORE.
YOU...
...NEVER EVEN CONSIDERED IT?!
HUH?
BUT ISN'T THAT WHAT GOURMET HUNTERS DO, ASSEMBLE MEALS?!

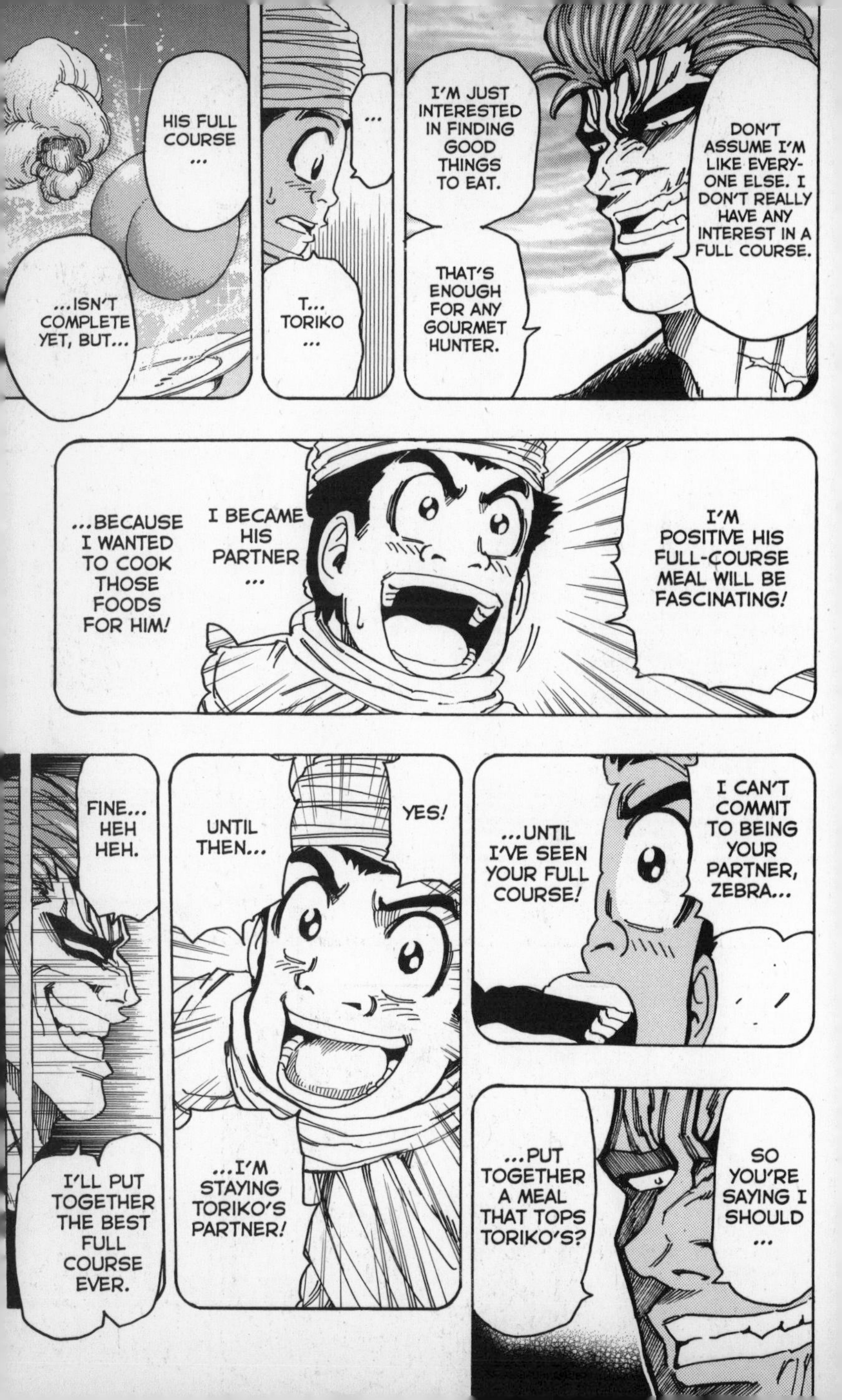
DON'T ASSUME I'M LIKE EVERY-ONE ELSE. I DON'T REALLY HAVE ANY INTEREST IN A FULL COURSE.
I'M JUST INTERESTED IN FINDING GOOD THINGS TO EAT.
THAT'S ENOUGH FOR ANY GOURMET HUNTER.
...
T... TORIKO ...
HIS FULL COURSE ...
...ISN'T COMPLETE YET, BUT...
I'M POSITIVE HIS FULL-COURSE MEAL WILL BE FASCINATING!
I BECAME HIS PARTNER ...
...BECAUSE I WANTED TO COOK THOSE FOODS FOR HIM!
I CAN'T COMMIT TO BEING YOUR PARTNER, ZEBRA...
...UNTIL I'VE SEEN YOUR FULL COURSE!
SO YOU'RE SAYING I SHOULD ...
...PUT TOGETHER A MEAL THAT TOPS TORIKO'S?
YES!
UNTIL THEN...
...I'M STAYING TORIKO'S PARTNER!
FINE... HEH HEH.
I'LL PUT TOGETHER THE BEST FULL COURSE EVER.

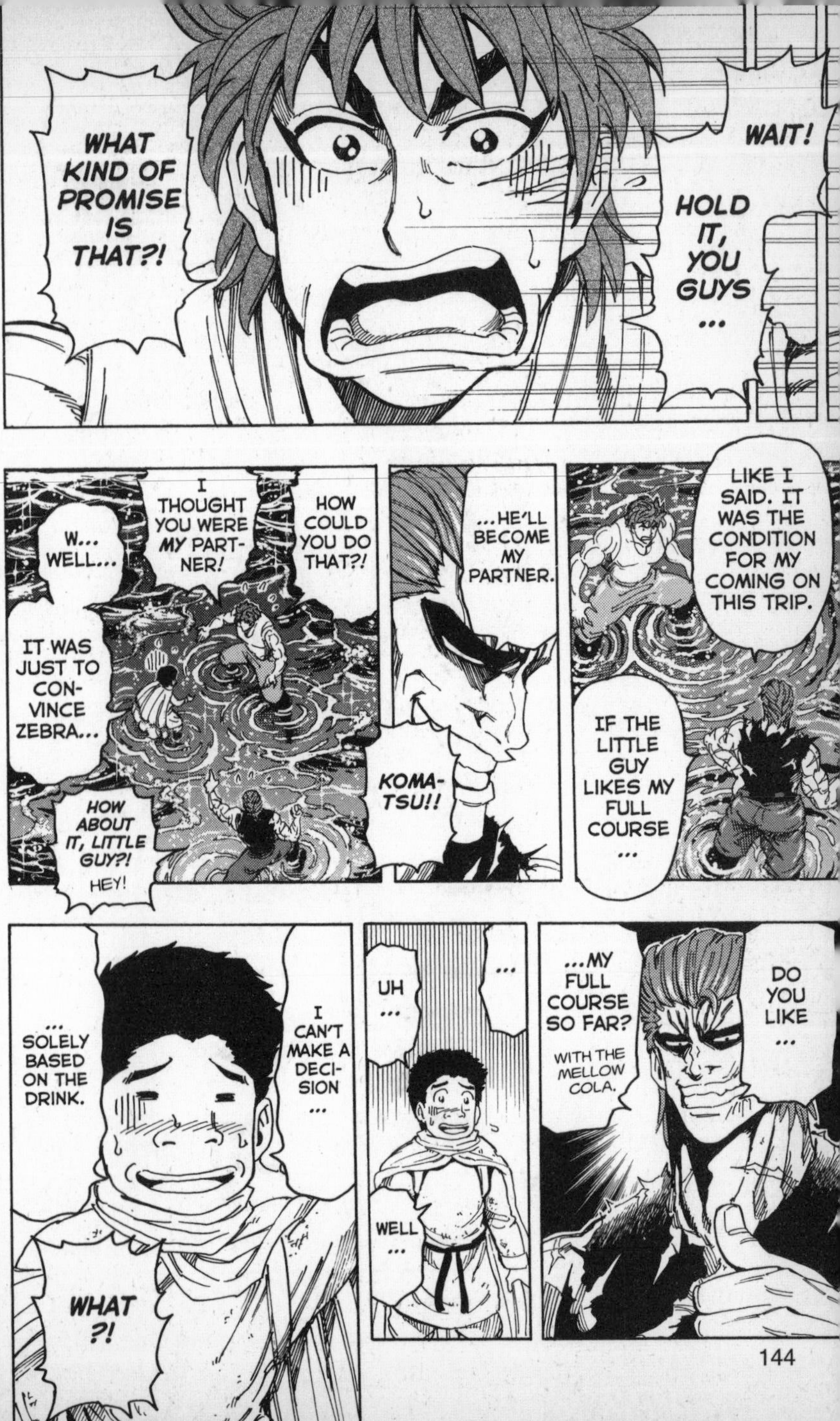
WAIT!
HOLD IT, YOU GUYS...
WHAT KIND OF PROMISE IS THAT?!
LIKE I SAID. IT WAS THE CONDITION FOR MY COMING ON THIS TRIP.
IF THE LITTLE GUY LIKES MY FULL COURSE...
...HE'LL BECOME MY PARTNER.
KOMATSU!!
HOW COULD YOU DO THAT?!
I THOUGHT YOU WERE MY PARTNER!
W... WELL...
IT WAS JUST TO CONVINCE ZEBRA...
HOW ABOUT IT, LITTLE GUY?!
HEY!
DO YOU LIKE...
...MY FULL COURSE SO FAR?
WITH THE MELLOW COLA.
...
UH...
WELL...
I CAN'T MAKE A DECISION...
...SOLELY BASED ON THE DRINK.
WHAT?!

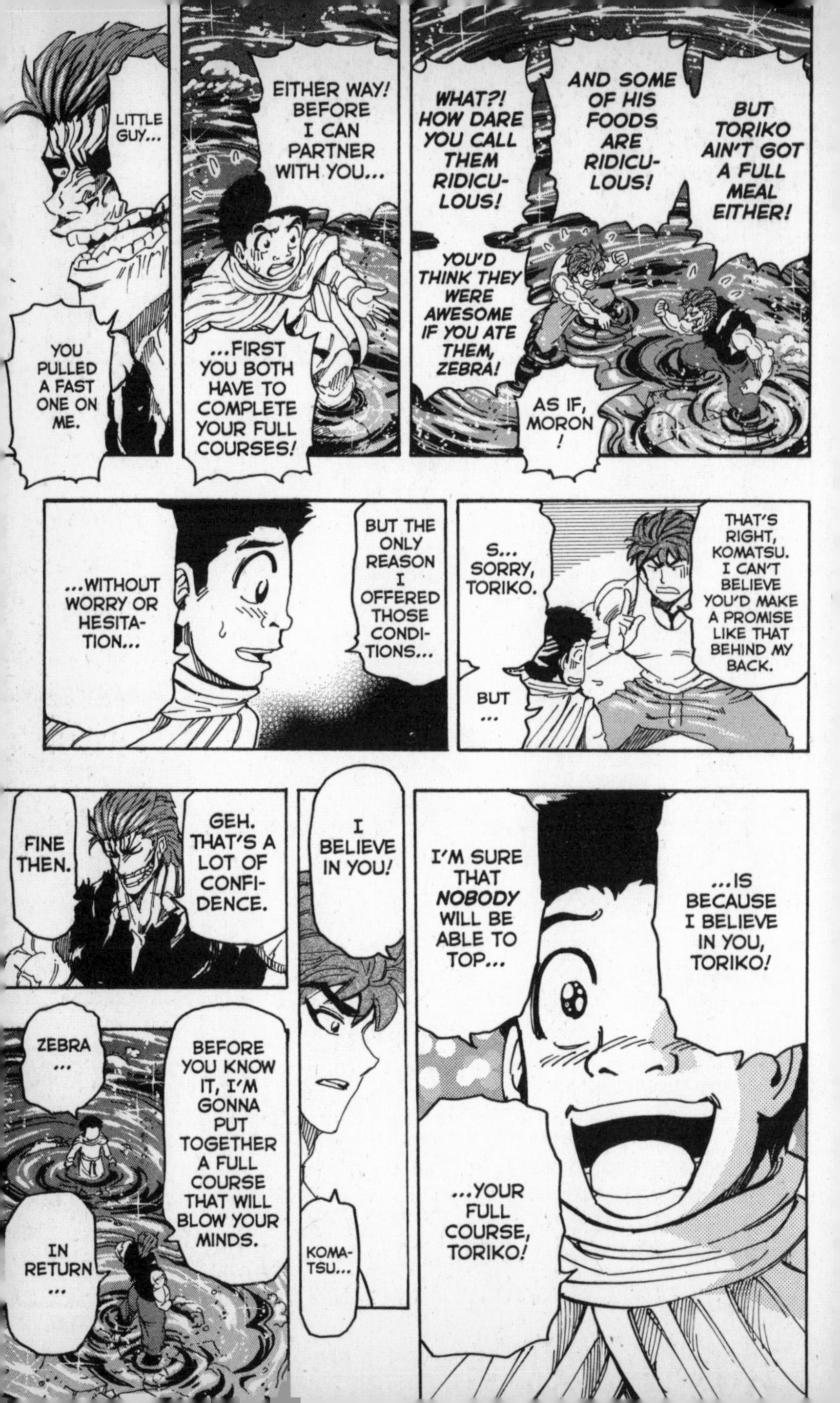
BUT TORIKO AIN'T GOT A FULL MEAL EITHER!
AND SOME OF HIS FOODS ARE RIDICULOUS!
WHAT?! HOW DARE YOU CALL THEM RIDICULOUS!
YOU'D THINK THEY WERE AWESOME IF YOU ATE THEM, ZEBRA!
AS IF, MORON!
EITHER WAY! BEFORE I CAN PARTNER WITH YOU...
...FIRST YOU BOTH HAVE TO COMPLETE YOUR FULL COURSES!
LITTLE GUY...
YOU PULLED A FAST ONE ON ME.
THAT'S RIGHT, KOMATSU. I CAN'T BELIEVE YOU'D MAKE A PROMISE LIKE THAT BEHIND MY BACK.
S... SORRY, TORIKO.
BUT ...
BUT THE ONLY REASON I OFFERED THOSE CONDITIONS...
...WITHOUT WORRY OR HESITATION...
...IS BECAUSE I BELIEVE IN YOU, TORIKO!
I'M SURE THAT NOBODY WILL BE ABLE TO TOP...
...YOUR FULL COURSE, TORIKO!
I BELIEVE IN YOU!
KOMATSU...
GEH. THAT'S A LOT OF CONFIDENCE.
FINE THEN.
BEFORE YOU KNOW IT, I'M GONNA PUT TOGETHER A FULL COURSE THAT WILL BLOW YOUR MINDS.
ZEBRA...
IN RETURN...

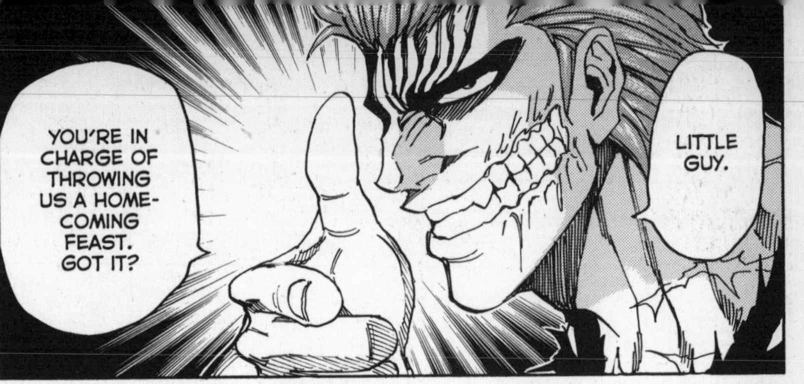
LITTLE GUY.
YOU'RE IN CHARGE OF THROWING US A HOME-COMING FEAST. GOT IT?

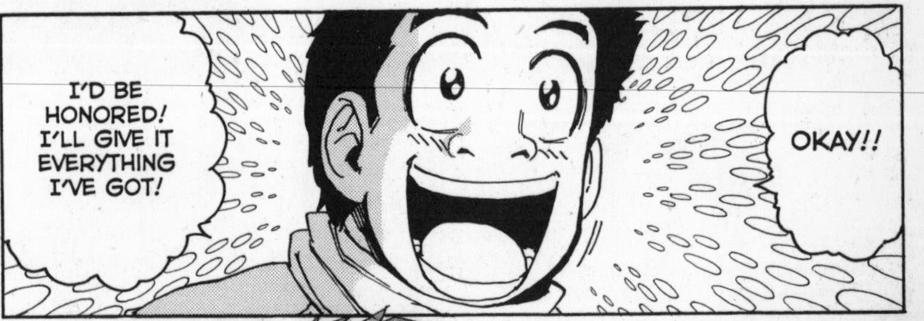
OKAY!!
I'D BE HONORED! I'LL GIVE IT EVERYTHING I'VE GOT!

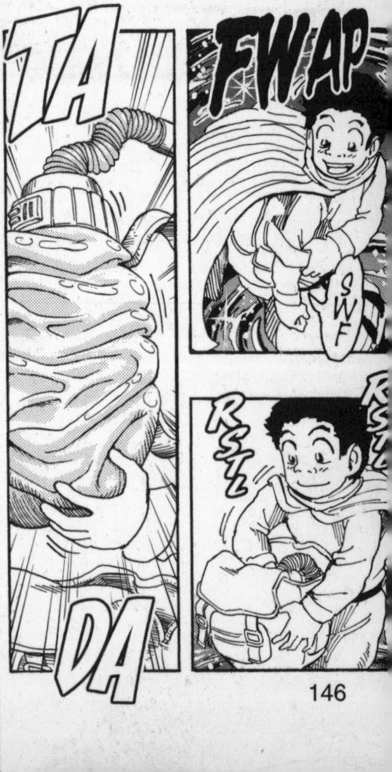
FWAP
SWF
RSL
RSL
TA
DA

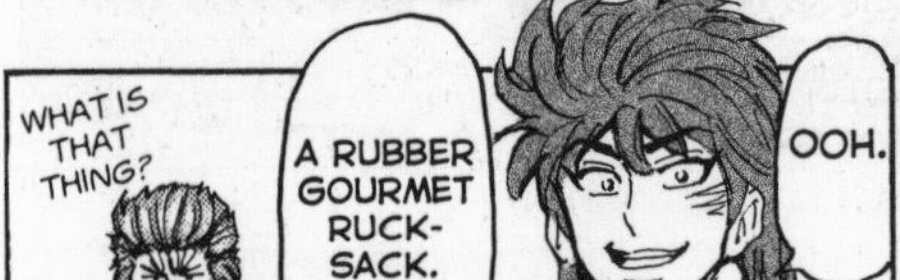
OOH.
A RUBBER GOURMET RUCK-SACK.
WHAT IS THAT THING?

GOURMET RUCKSACK

■ 10,000 LITER VERSION

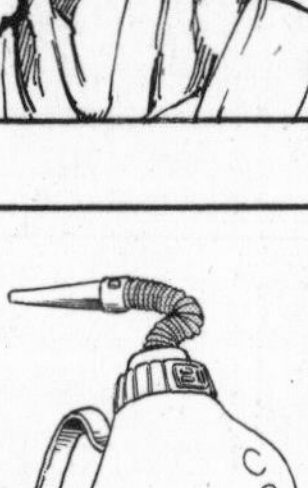

A GOURMET CASE USED FOR TRANSPORTING LIQUID FOODSTUFFS. MADE OF A UNIQUE NATURAL RUBBER MATERIAL, THE CONTAINER STRETCHES TO ACCOMMODATE THE CONTENTS. THE RUBBER IS HIGHLY ELASTIC, BUT WHEN THE MAXIMUM LOAD IS EXCEEDED, IT DAMAGES AND RUPTURES EASILY.

RETAIL PRICE: 450,000 YEN

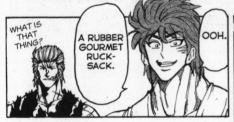

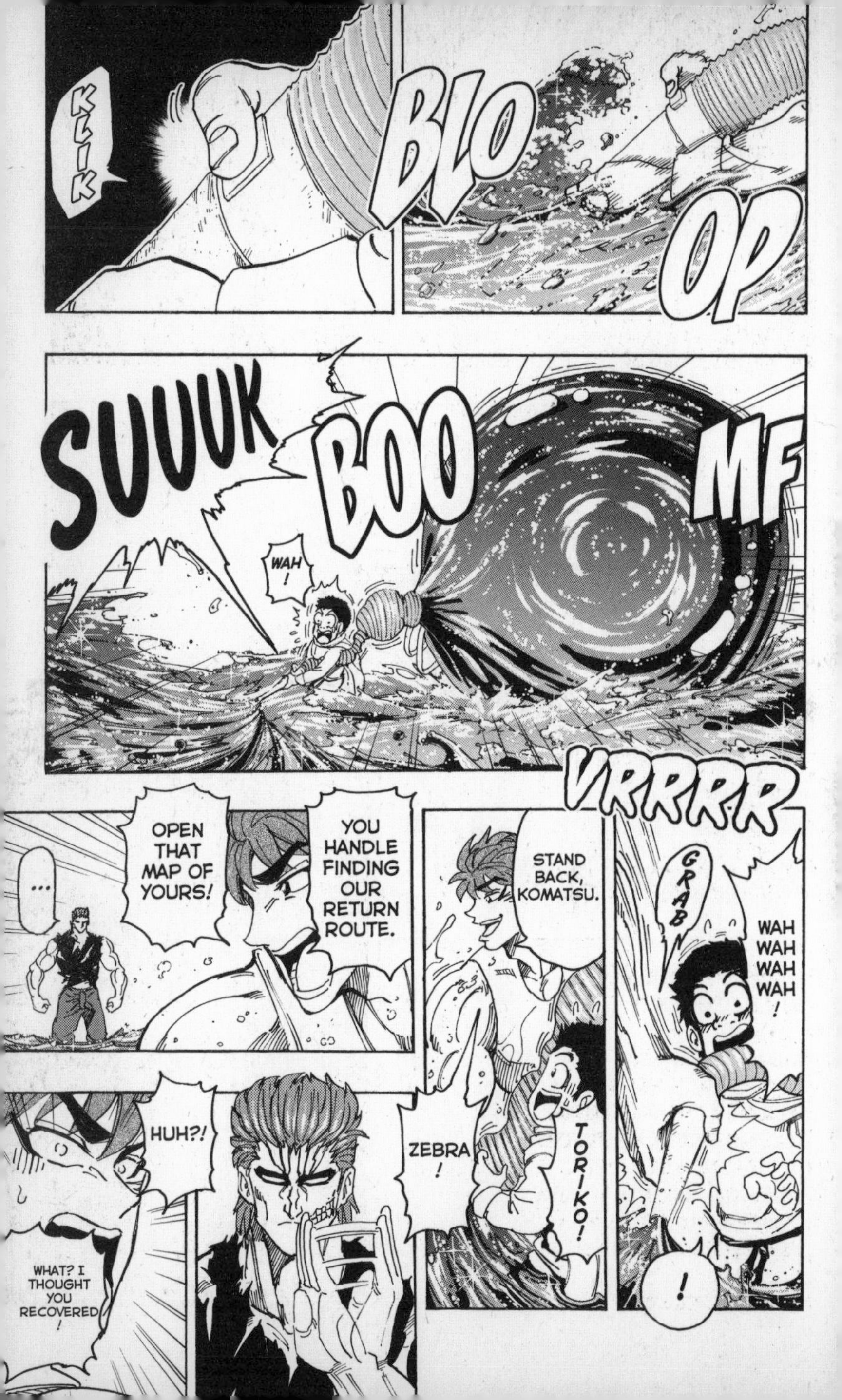

BLO OP
KLIK
SUUUK
BOOMF
WAH!
VRRRR
GRAB
WAH WAH WAH WAH!
!
STAND BACK, KOMATSU.
TORIKO!
YOU HANDLE FINDING OUR RETURN ROUTE.
OPEN THAT MAP OF YOURS!
...
ZEBRA!
HUH?!
WHAT? I THOUGHT YOU RECOVERED!

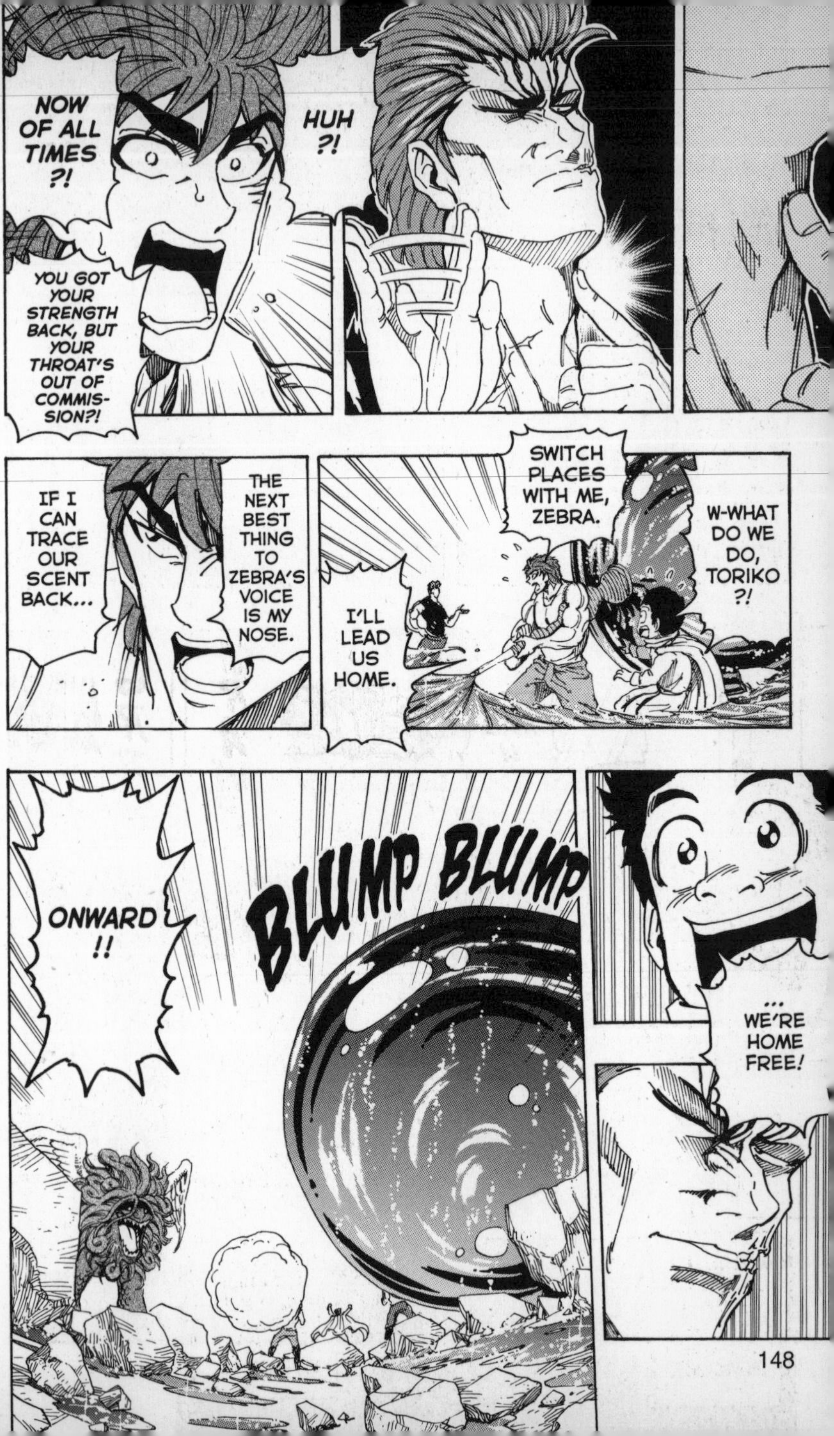
HUH ?!
NOW OF ALL TIMES ?!
YOU GOT YOUR STRENGTH BACK, BUT YOUR THROAT'S OUT OF COMMIS-SION?!
W-WHAT DO WE DO, TORIKO ?!
SWITCH PLACES WITH ME, ZEBRA.
I'LL LEAD US HOME.
THE NEXT BEST THING TO ZEBRA'S VOICE IS MY NOSE.
IF I CAN TRACE OUR SCENT BACK...
... WE'RE HOME FREE!
BLUMP BLUMP
ONWARD !!

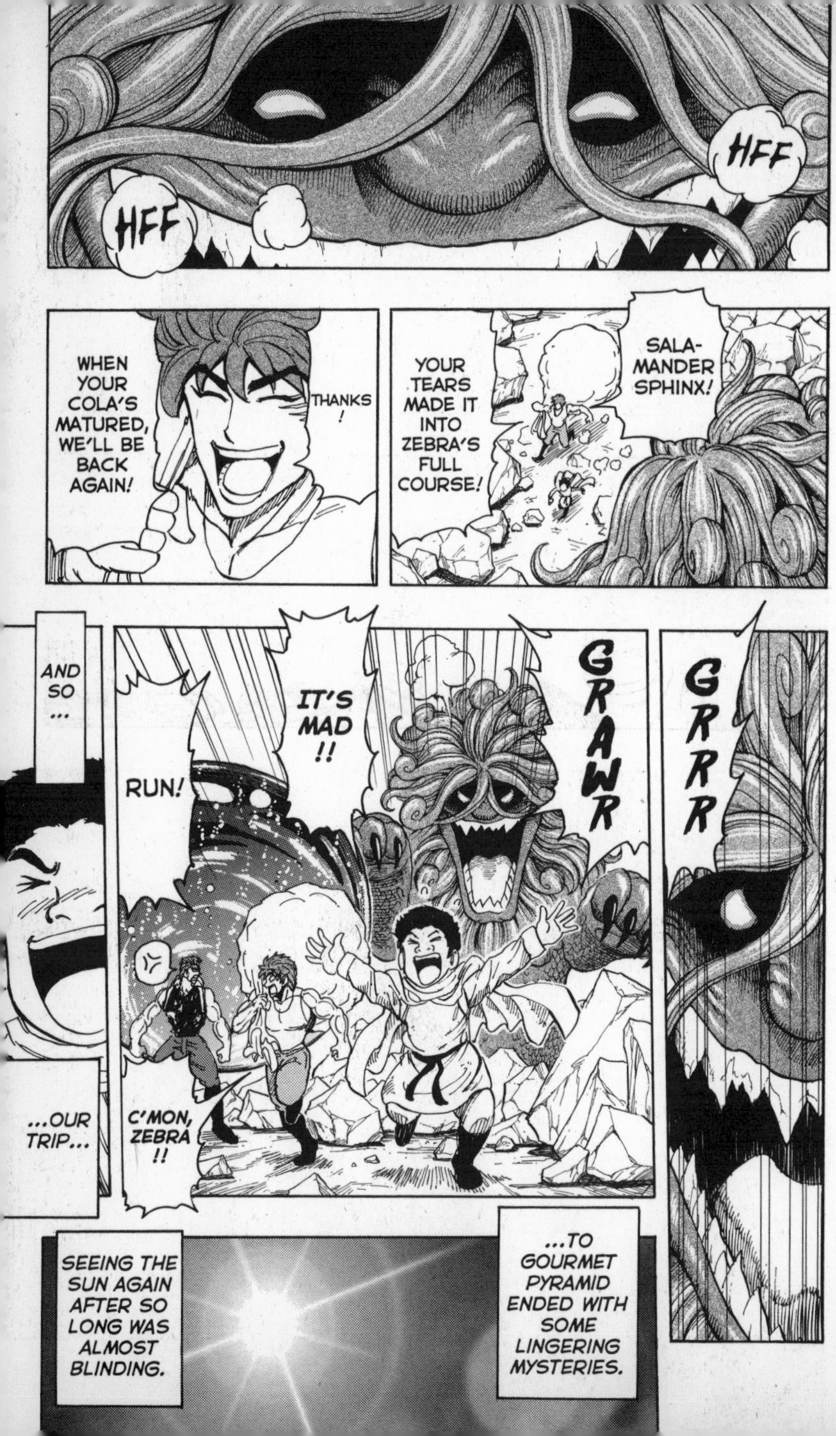
HFF
HFF
SALAMANDER SPHINX!
YOUR TEARS MADE IT INTO ZEBRA'S FULL COURSE!
THANKS!
WHEN YOUR COLA'S MATURED, WE'LL BE BACK AGAIN!
GRRR
GRAWR
IT'S MAD!!
RUN!
C'MON, ZEBRA!!
AND SO...
...OUR TRIP...
...TO GOURMET PYRAMID ENDED WITH SOME LINGERING MYSTERIES.
SEEING THE SUN AGAIN AFTER SO LONG WAS ALMOST BLINDING.

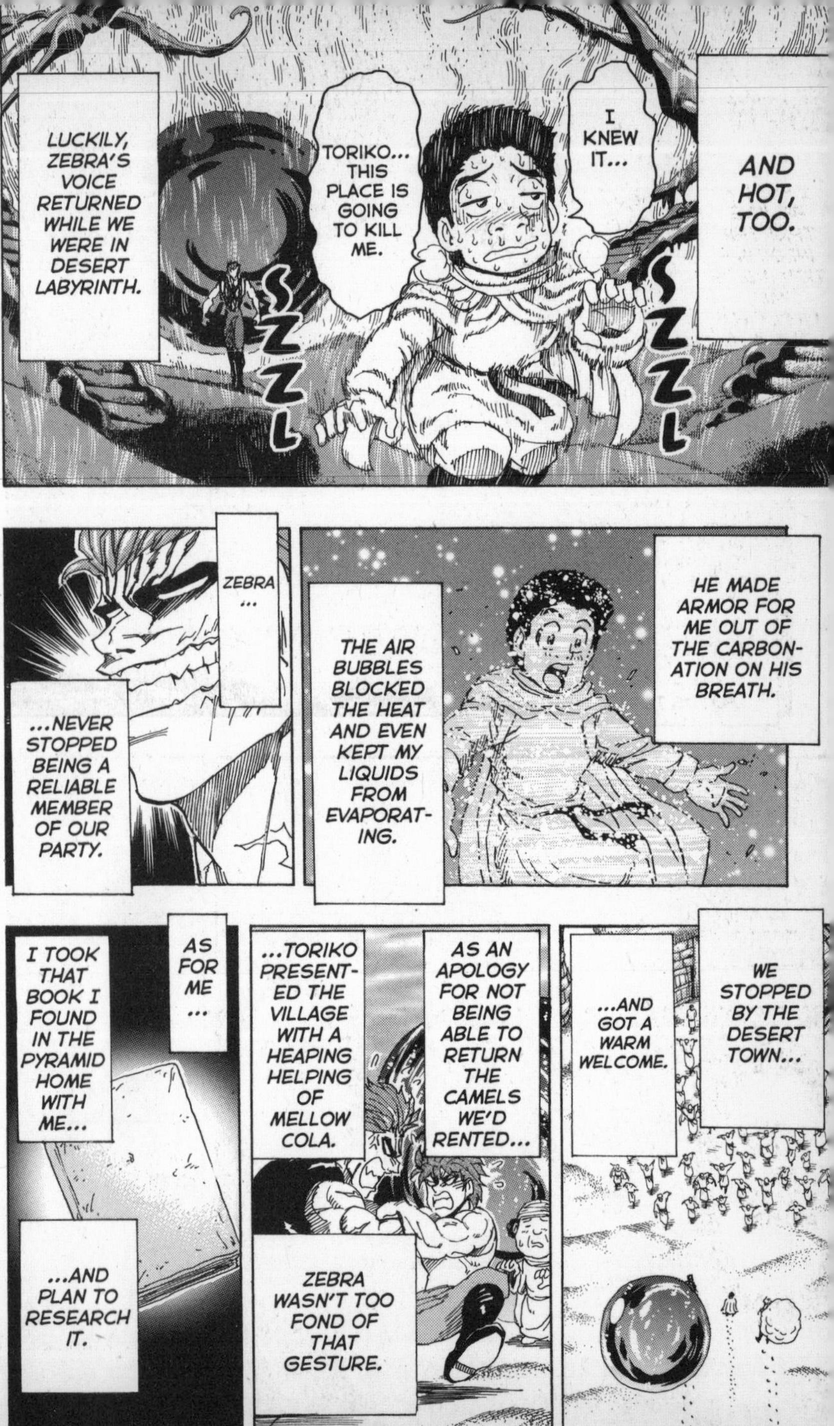
AND HOT, TOO.
I KNEW IT...
TORIKO... THIS PLACE IS GOING TO KILL ME.
LUCKILY, ZEBRA'S VOICE RETURNED WHILE WE WERE IN DESERT LABYRINTH.
SZZL
SZZL
HE MADE ARMOR FOR ME OUT OF THE CARBON-ATION ON HIS BREATH.
THE AIR BUBBLES BLOCKED THE HEAT AND EVEN KEPT MY LIQUIDS FROM EVAPORAT-ING.
ZEBRA...
...NEVER STOPPED BEING A RELIABLE MEMBER OF OUR PARTY.
WE STOPPED BY THE DESERT TOWN...
...AND GOT A WARM WELCOME.
AS AN APOLOGY FOR NOT BEING ABLE TO RETURN THE CAMELS WE'D RENTED...
...TORIKO PRESENT-ED THE VILLAGE WITH A HEAPING HELPING OF MELLOW COLA.
ZEBRA WASN'T TOO FOND OF THAT GESTURE.
AS FOR ME...
I TOOK THAT BOOK I FOUND IN THE PYRAMID HOME WITH ME...
...AND PLAN TO RESEARCH IT.

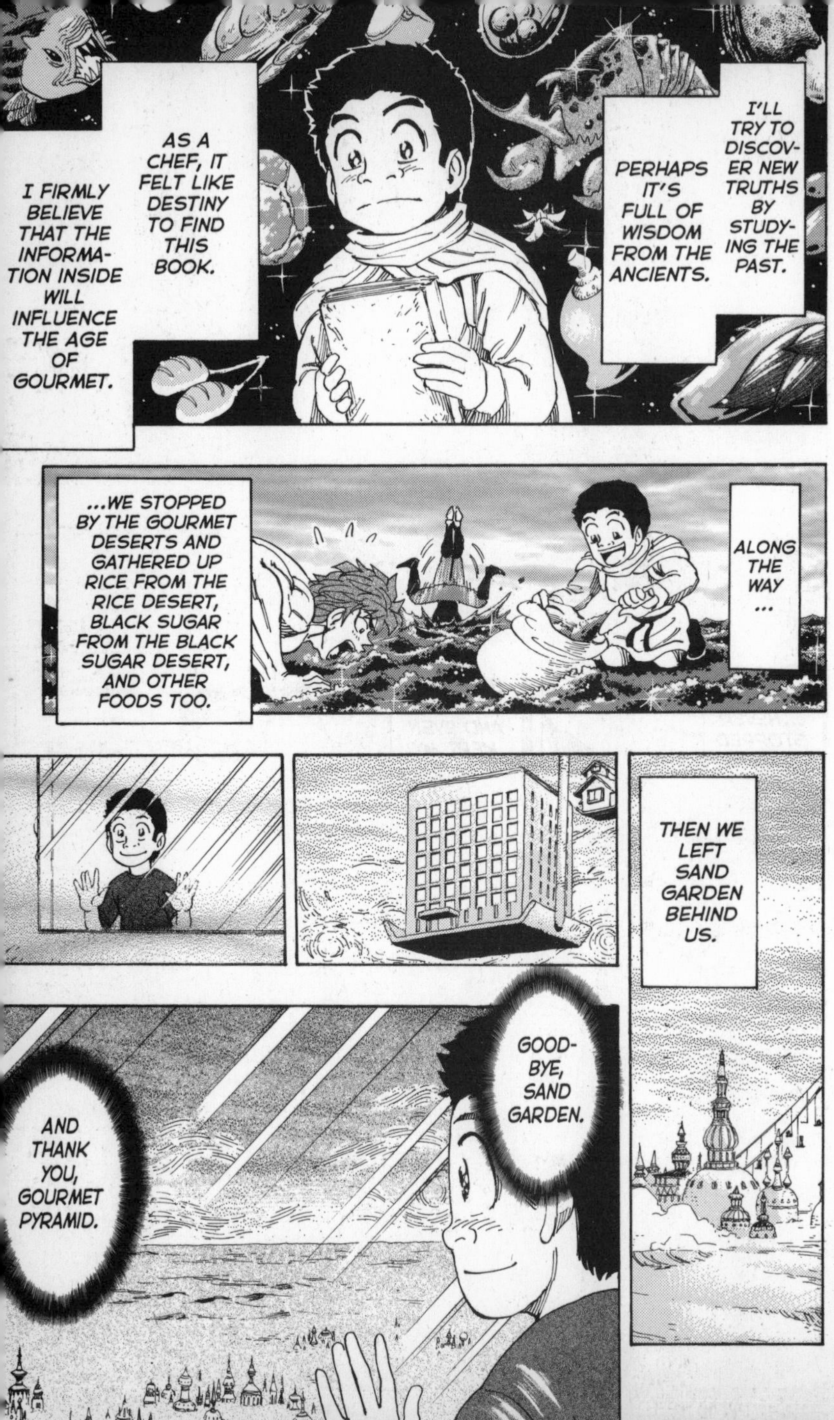
I'LL TRY TO DISCOVER NEW TRUTHS BY STUDYING THE PAST.
PERHAPS IT'S FULL OF WISDOM FROM THE ANCIENTS.
AS A CHEF, IT FELT LIKE DESTINY TO FIND THIS BOOK.
I FIRMLY BELIEVE THAT THE INFORMATION INSIDE WILL INFLUENCE THE AGE OF GOURMET.
ALONG THE WAY...
...WE STOPPED BY THE GOURMET DESERTS AND GATHERED UP RICE FROM THE RICE DESERT, BLACK SUGAR FROM THE BLACK SUGAR DESERT, AND OTHER FOODS TOO.
THEN WE LEFT SAND GARDEN BEHIND US.
GOOD-BYE, SAND GARDEN.
AND THANK YOU, GOURMET PYRAMID.

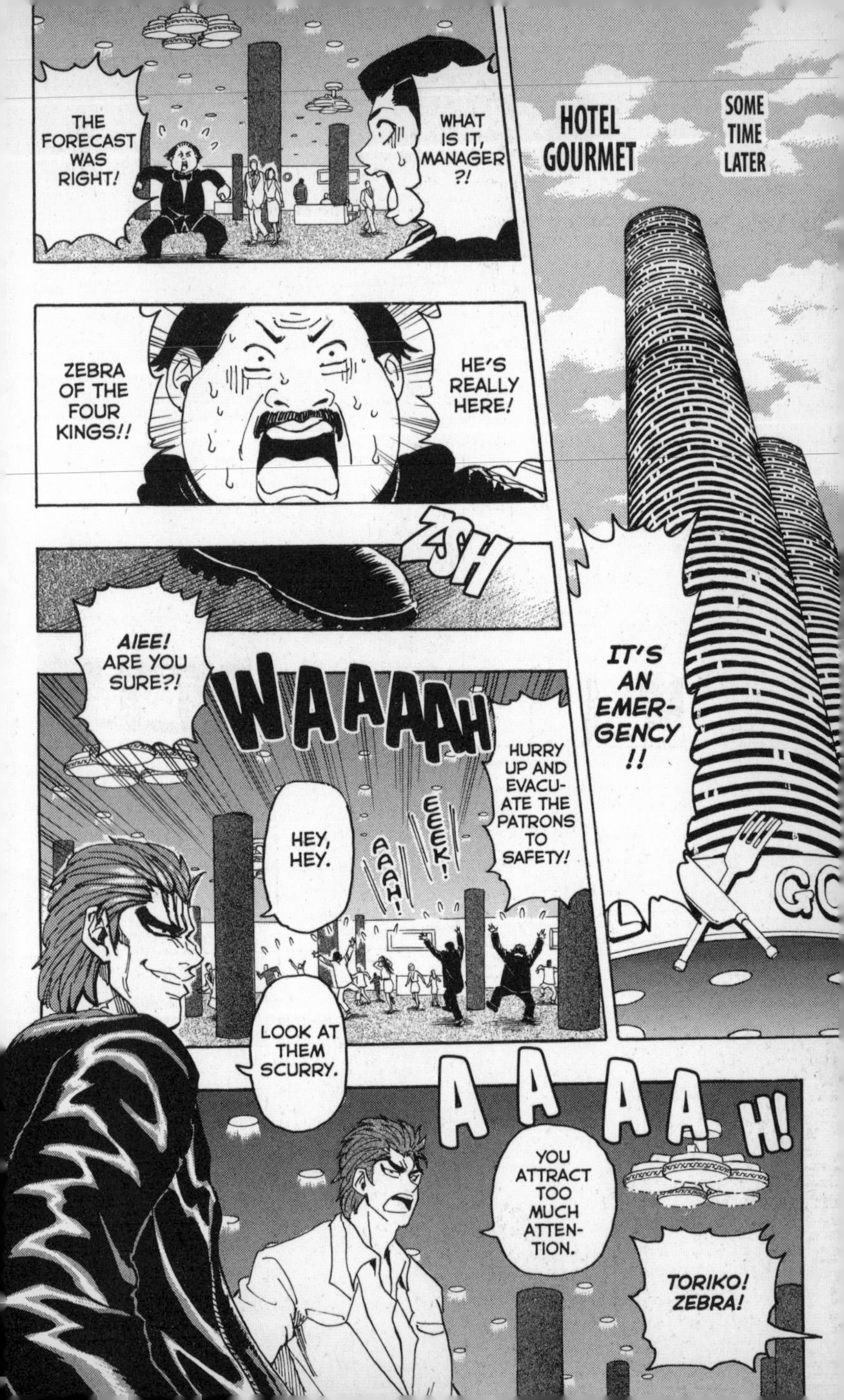
SOME TIME LATER
HOTEL GOURMET
IT'S AN EMERGENCY!!
WHAT IS IT, MANAGER?!
THE FORECAST WAS RIGHT!
HE'S REALLY HERE!
ZEBRA OF THE FOUR KINGS!!
ZSH
AIEE! ARE YOU SURE?!
HURRY UP AND EVACUATE THE PATRONS TO SAFETY!
WAAAAH
EEEK!
AAAH!
HEY, HEY.
LOOK AT THEM SCURRY.
AAAAH!
YOU ATTRACT TOO MUCH ATTENTION.
TORIKO! ZEBRA!

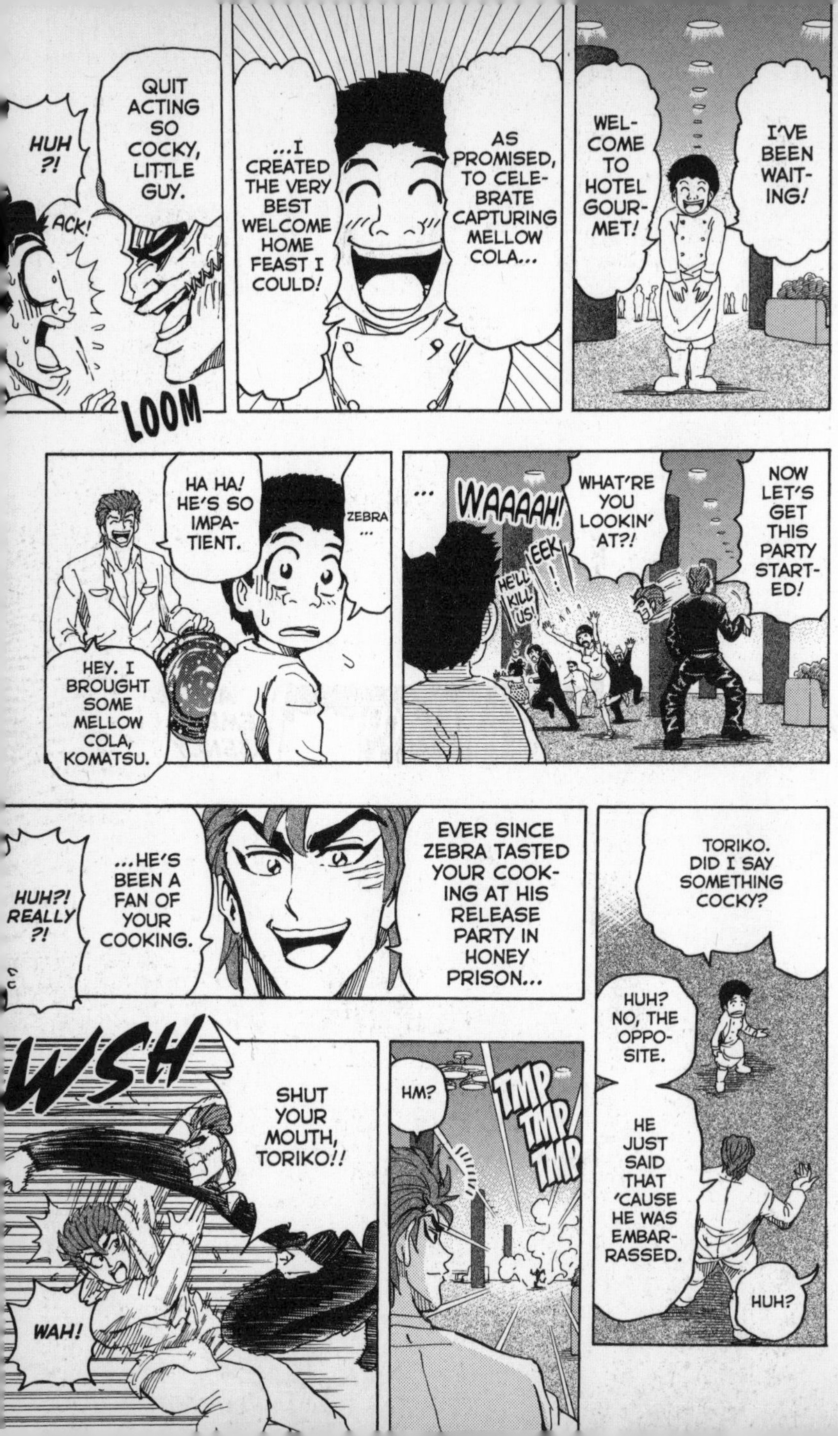
I'VE BEEN WAIT-ING!
WEL-COME TO HOTEL GOUR-MET!
AS PROMISED, TO CELE-BRATE CAPTURING MELLOW COLA...
...I CREATED THE VERY BEST WELCOME HOME FEAST I COULD!
QUIT ACTING SO COCKY, LITTLE GUY.
HUH ?!
ACK!
LOOM
NOW LET'S GET THIS PARTY START-ED!
WHAT'RE YOU LOOKIN' AT?!
WAAAAH!
EEK!
HE'LL KILL US!
...
ZEBRA ...
HA HA! HE'S SO IMPA-TIENT.
HEY. I BROUGHT SOME MELLOW COLA, KOMATSU.
TORIKO. DID I SAY SOMETHING COCKY?
HUH? NO, THE OPPO-SITE.
HE JUST SAID THAT 'CAUSE HE WAS EMBAR-RASSED.
HUH?
EVER SINCE ZEBRA TASTED YOUR COOK-ING AT HIS RELEASE PARTY IN HONEY PRISON...
...HE'S BEEN A FAN OF YOUR COOKING.
HUH?! REALLY ?!
HM?
TMP TMP TMP
WSH
SHUT YOUR MOUTH, TORIKO!!
WAH!

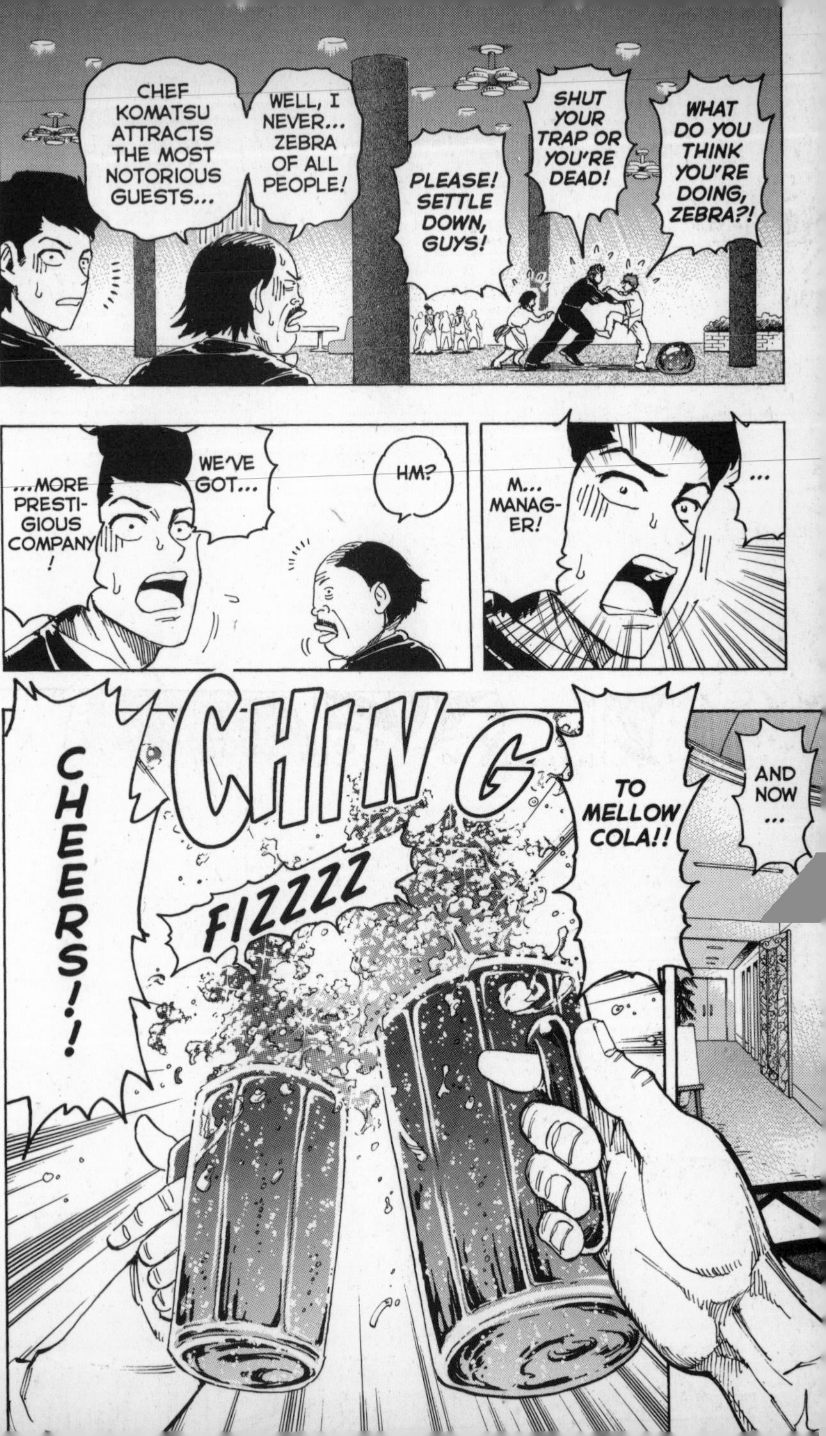
WHAT DO YOU THINK YOU'RE DOING, ZEBRA?!
SHUT YOUR TRAP OR YOU'RE DEAD!
PLEASE! SETTLE DOWN, GUYS!
WELL, I NEVER... ZEBRA OF ALL PEOPLE!
CHEF KOMATSU ATTRACTS THE MOST NOTORIOUS GUESTS...
...
M... MANAG-ER!
HM?
WE'VE GOT...
...MORE PRESTI-GIOUS COMPANY!
AND NOW...
TO MELLOW COLA!!
CHING
FIZZZZZ
CHEERS!!

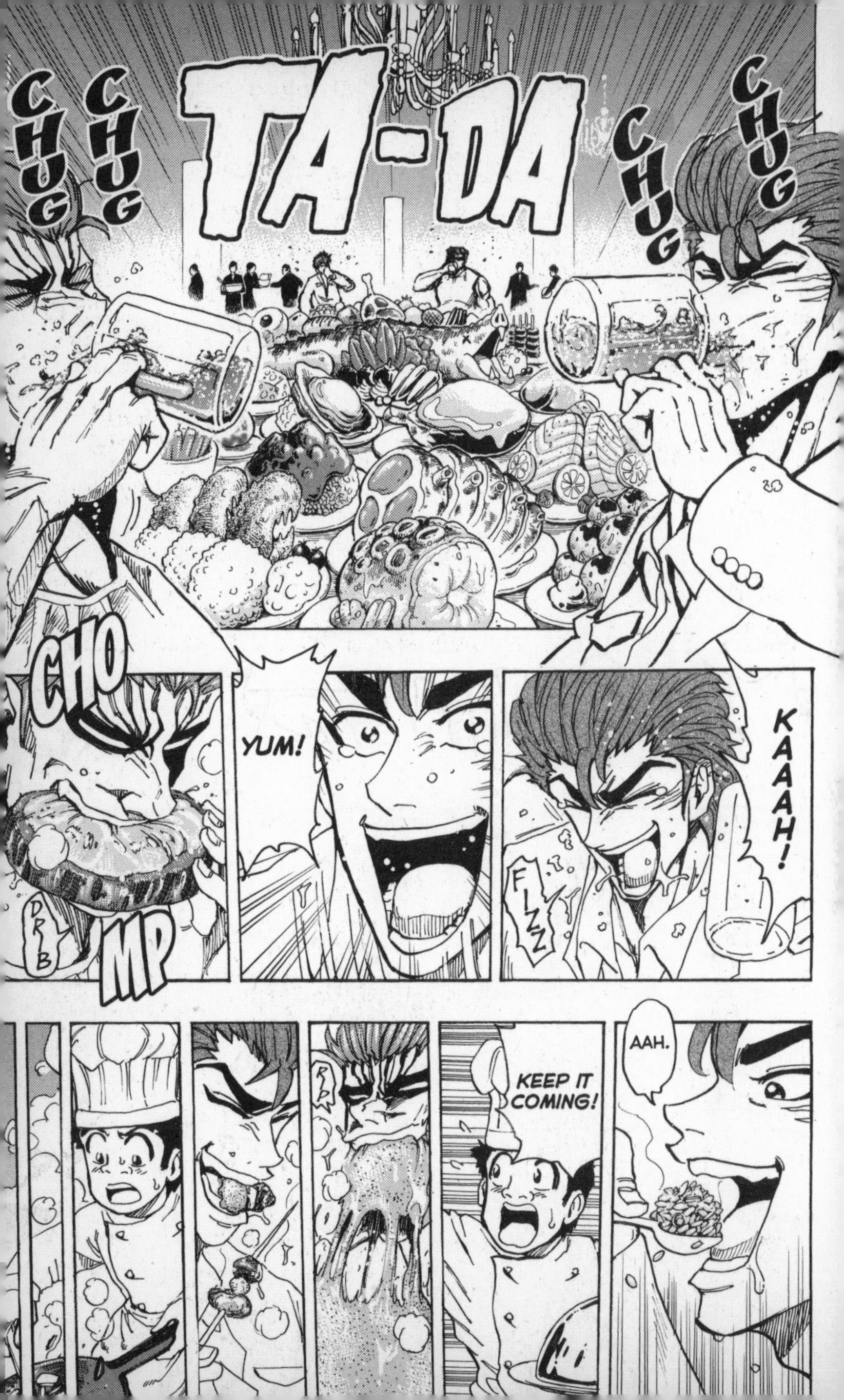
CHUG CHUG
TA-DA
CHUG CHUG
KAAAAH!
FIZZ
YUM!
CHOMP
DRIB
AAH.
KEEP IT COMING!
RIP

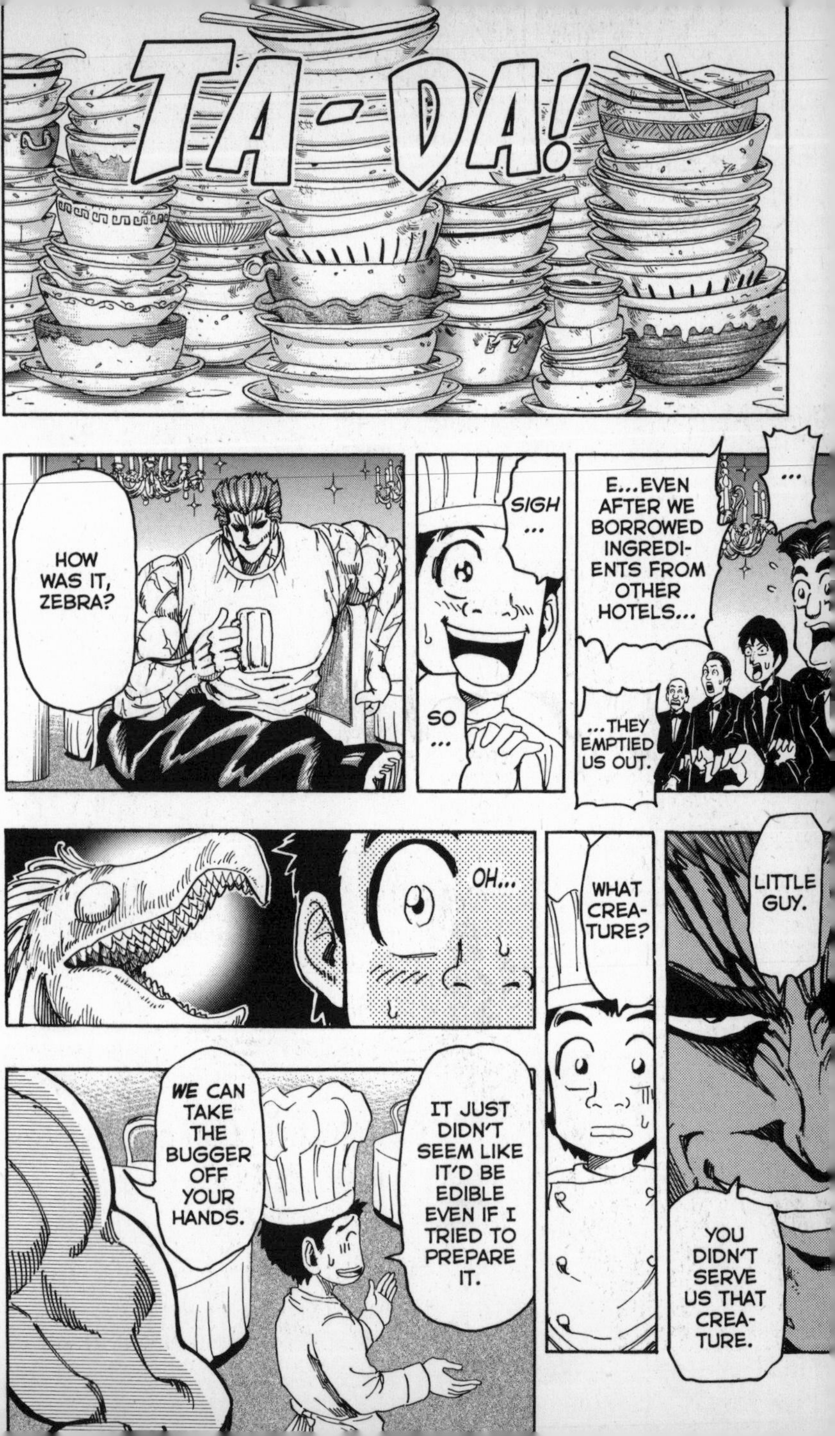
TA-DA!
...
E...EVEN AFTER WE BORROWED INGREDIENTS FROM OTHER HOTELS...
...THEY EMPTIED US OUT.
SIGH ...
SO ...
HOW WAS IT, ZEBRA?
LITTLE GUY.
YOU DIDN'T SERVE US THAT CREATURE.
WHAT CREATURE?
OH...
IT JUST DIDN'T SEEM LIKE IT'D BE EDIBLE EVEN IF I TRIED TO PREPARE IT.
WE CAN TAKE THE BUGGER OFF YOUR HANDS.

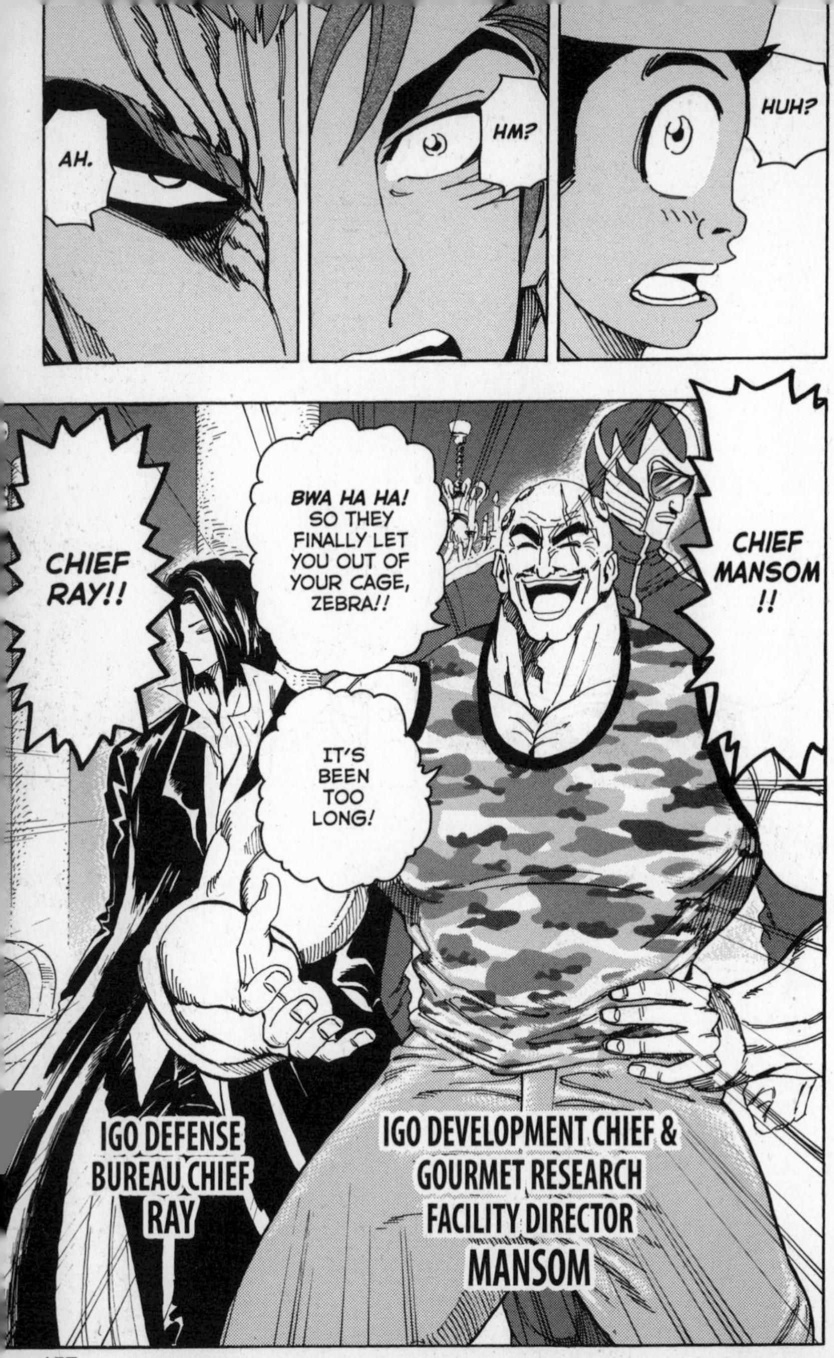
HUH?
HM?
AH.
CHIEF MANSOM!!
BWA HA HA! SO THEY FINALLY LET YOU OUT OF YOUR CAGE, ZEBRA!!
IT'S BEEN TOO LONG!
CHIEF RAY!!
IGO DEVELOPMENT CHIEF & GOURMET RESEARCH FACILITY DIRECTOR MANSOM
IGO DEFENSE BUREAU CHIEF RAY

GOURMET CHECKLIST

Vol. 164

STRAWBERRICE
(FRUIT)

CAPTURE LEVEL: LESS THAN 1

HABITAT: GROWS VIRTUALLY ANYWHERE, AND CAN BE ARTIFICIALLY CULTIVATED

LENGTH: 0.5 CM

HEIGHT: ---

WEIGHT: ---

PRICE: 10 KG / 20,000 YEN

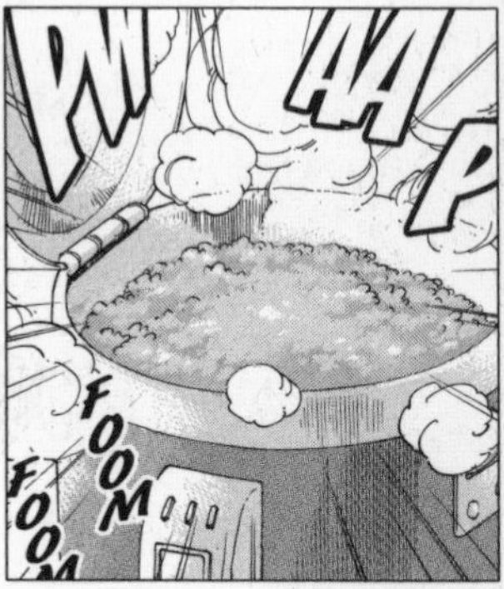
PWAAP
FOOM
FOOM

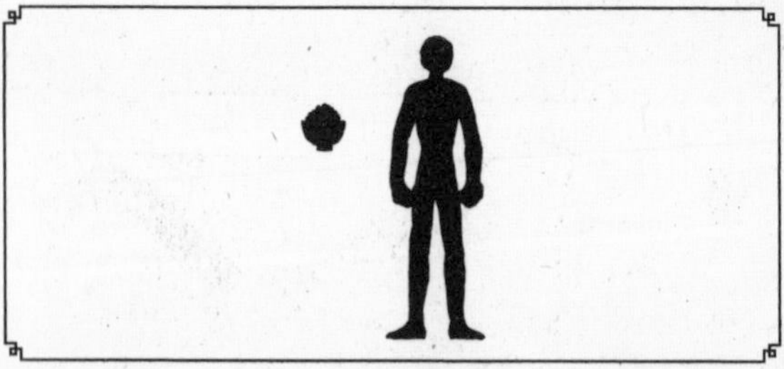

SCALE

EVERY GRAIN OF THIS RICE IS ACTUALLY A TINY STRAWBERRY. ITS MODERATE ACIDITY PUTS IT IN THE SAME CLASS AS THE RICE USED IN HIGH-CLASS SUSHI ESTABLISHMENTS. THE MORE YOU CHEW, THE STRONGER THE STRAWBERRY FLAVOR, MAKING IT A TASTY DELIGHT. STRAWBERRICE IS DELICIOUS AS A DESSERT WITHOUT ANY DRESSING UP, BUT WHEN YOU ADD CHEF KOMATSU'S SECRET INGREDIENTS (SNOT AND SALIVA), THE ADDED SALT COMPLEMENTS THE FLAVOR EVEN MORE...PROBABLY.

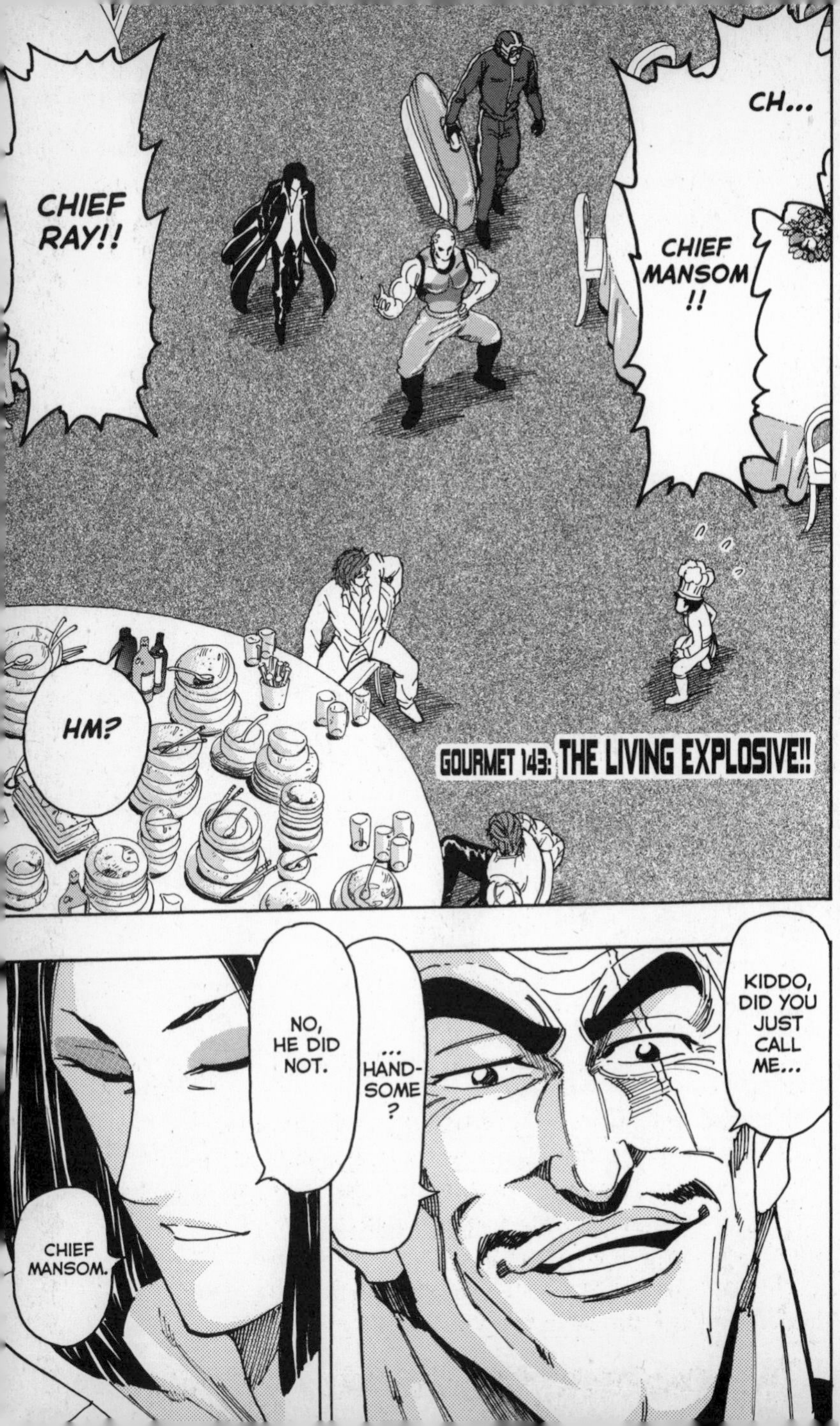
CH...
CHIEF MANSOM !!
CHIEF RAY!!
HM?
GOURMET 143: THE LIVING EXPLOSIVE!!
KIDDO, DID YOU JUST CALL ME...
... HANDSOME ?
NO, HE DID NOT.
CHIEF MANSOM.

GOURMET 143: THE LIVING EXPLOSIVE!!

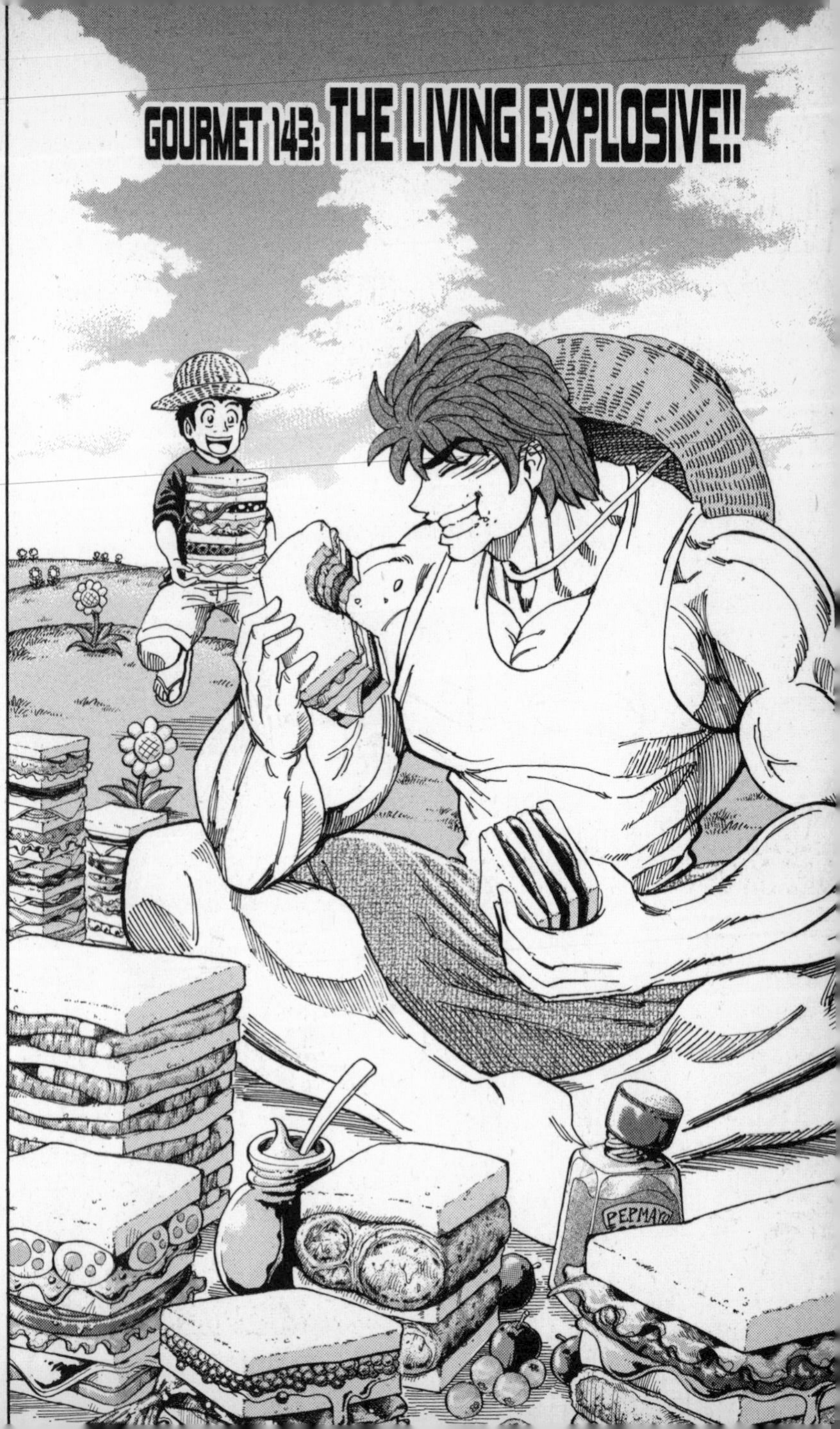
PEPMA

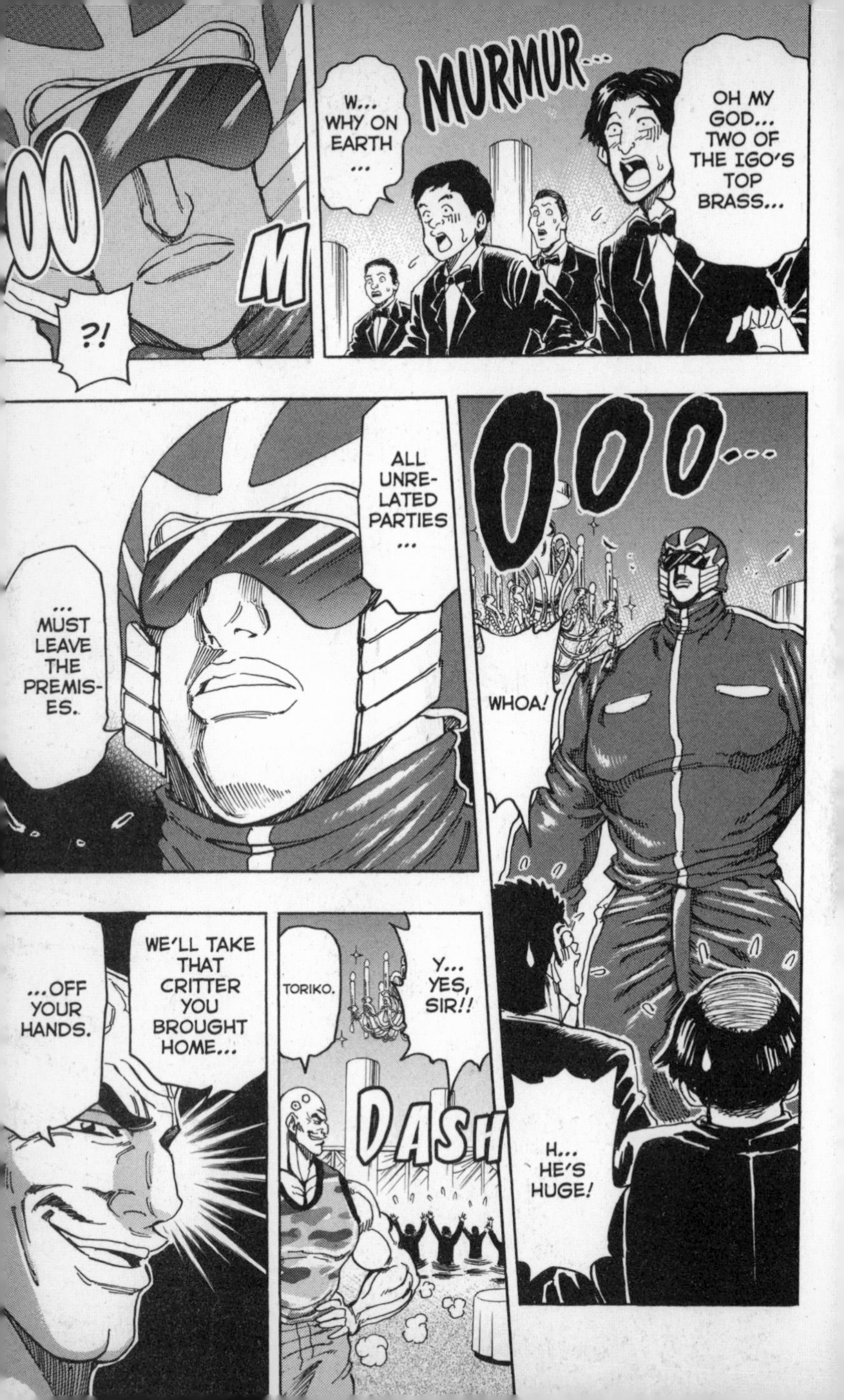
OH MY GOD... TWO OF THE IGO'S TOP BRASS...
MURMUR...
W... WHY ON EARTH...
OOM
?!
OOO...
WHOA!
H... HE'S HUGE!
ALL UNRELATED PARTIES...
...MUST LEAVE THE PREMISES.
Y... YES, SIR!!
TORIKO.
DASH
WE'LL TAKE THAT CRITTER YOU BROUGHT HOME...
...OFF YOUR HANDS.

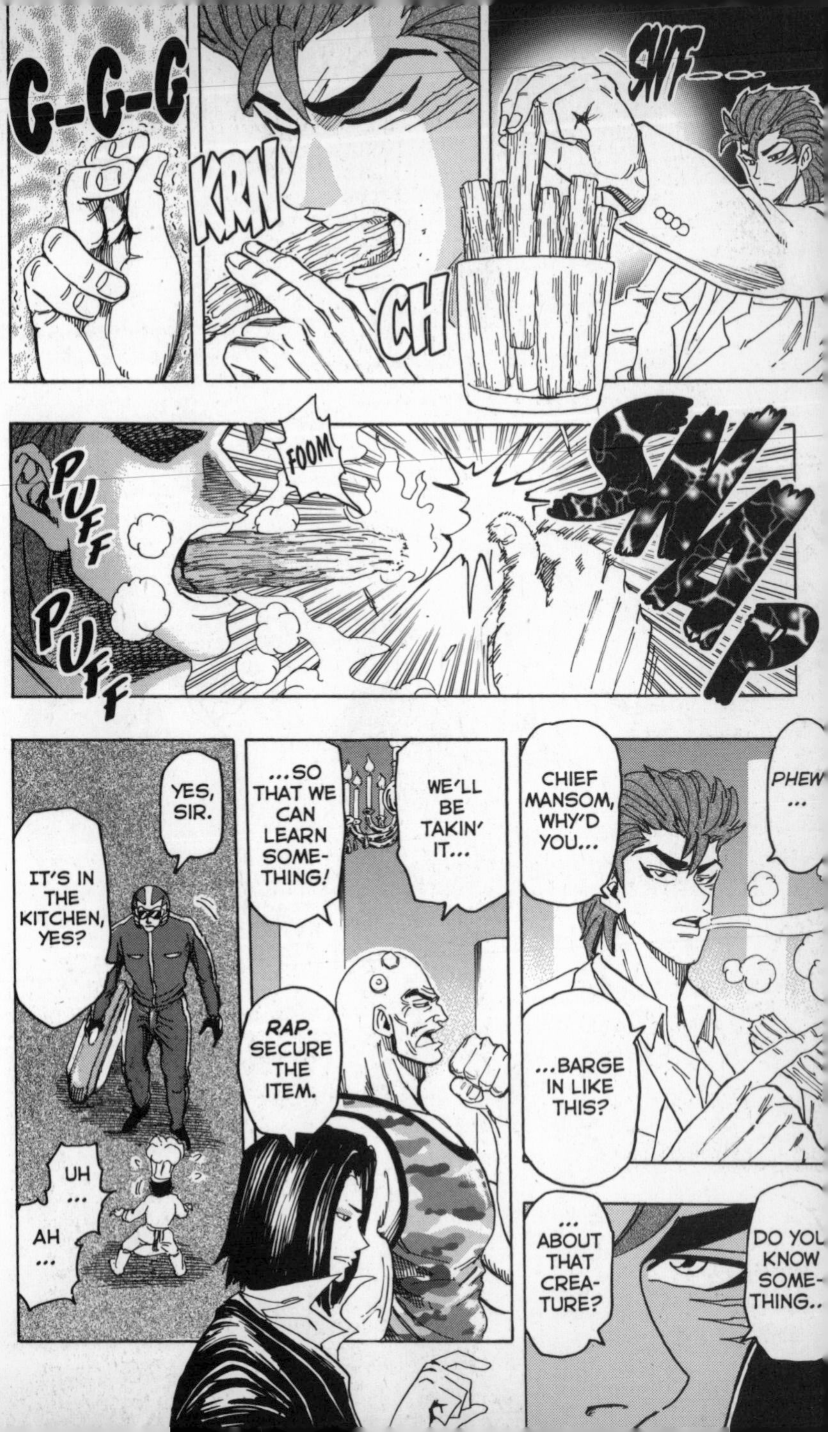
SHF...
KRN
CH
G-G-G
SNAP
FOOM
PUFF
PUFF
PHEW...
CHIEF MANSOM, WHY'D YOU...
...BARGE IN LIKE THIS?
DO YOU KNOW SOMETHING...
...ABOUT THAT CREATURE?
WE'LL BE TAKIN' IT...
...SO THAT WE CAN LEARN SOMETHING!
RAP. SECURE THE ITEM.
YES, SIR.
IT'S IN THE KITCHEN, YES?
UH...
AH...

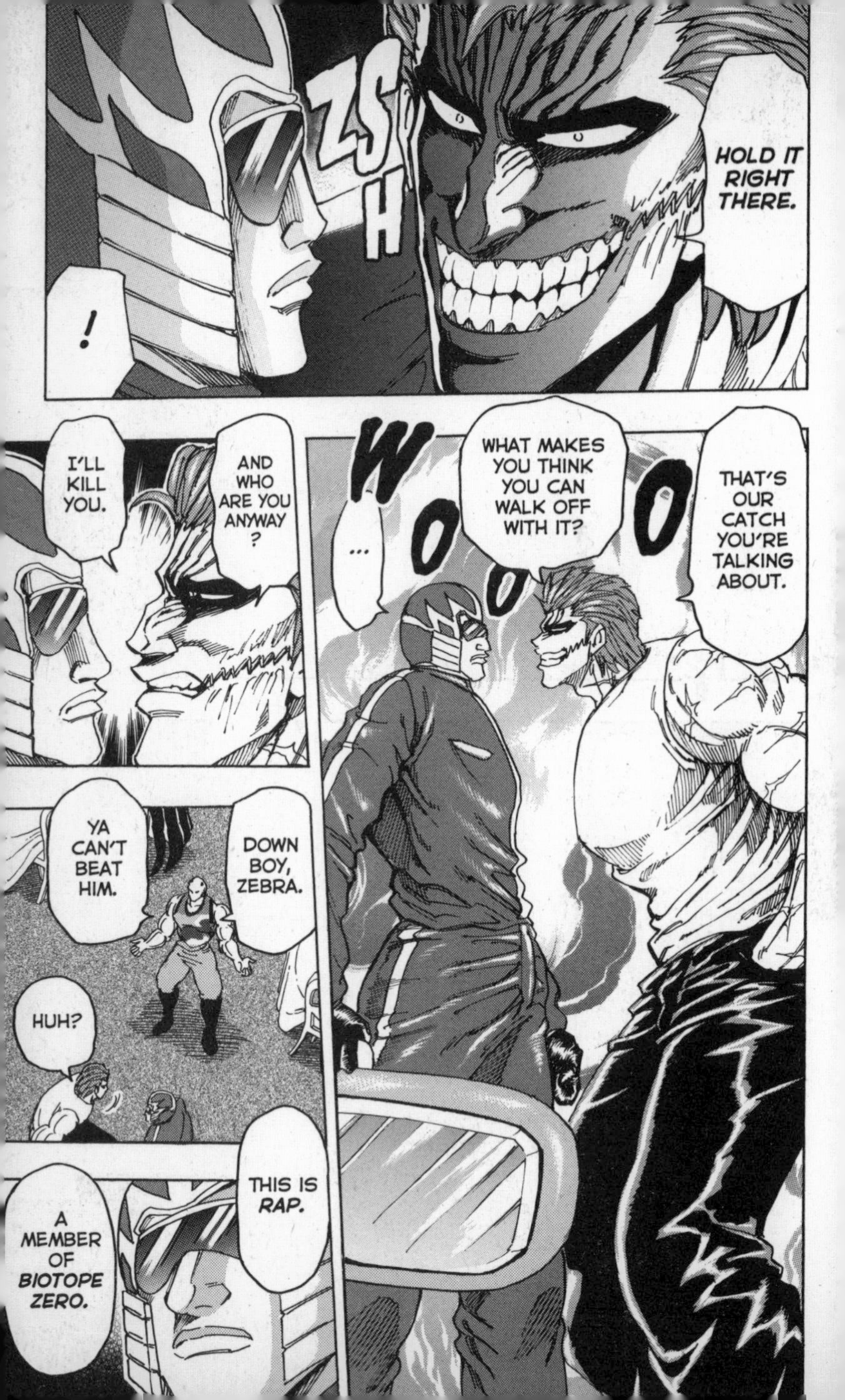
HOLD IT RIGHT THERE.
ZSH
!
THAT'S OUR CATCH YOU'RE TALKING ABOUT.
WHAT MAKES YOU THINK YOU CAN WALK OFF WITH IT?
WOOOO
...
AND WHO ARE YOU ANYWAY?
I'LL KILL YOU.
DOWN BOY, ZEBRA.
YA CAN'T BEAT HIM.
HUH?
THIS IS *RAP.*
A MEMBER OF *BIOTOPE ZERO.*

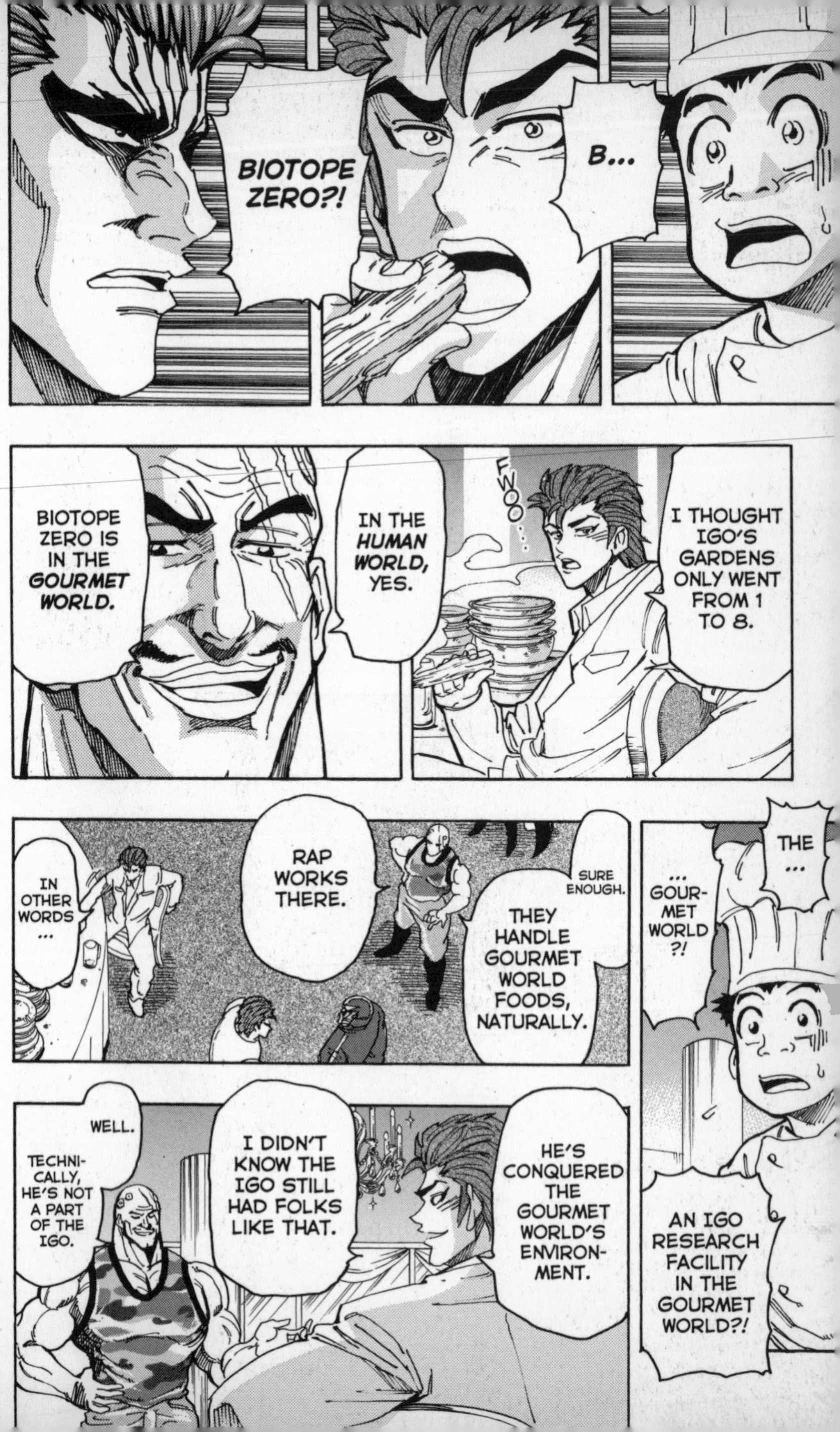
B...
BIOTOPE ZERO?!
I THOUGHT IGO'S GARDENS ONLY WENT FROM 1 TO 8.
FWOO...
IN THE *HUMAN WORLD,* YES.
BIOTOPE ZERO IS IN THE *GOURMET WORLD.*
THE...
...GOURMET WORLD?!
AN IGO RESEARCH FACILITY IN THE GOURMET WORLD?!
SURE ENOUGH.
THEY HANDLE GOURMET WORLD FOODS, NATURALLY.
RAP WORKS THERE.
IN OTHER WORDS...
HE'S CONQUERED THE GOURMET WORLD'S ENVIRONMENT.
I DIDN'T KNOW THE IGO STILL HAD FOLKS LIKE THAT.
WELL.
TECHNICALLY, HE'S NOT A PART OF THE IGO.

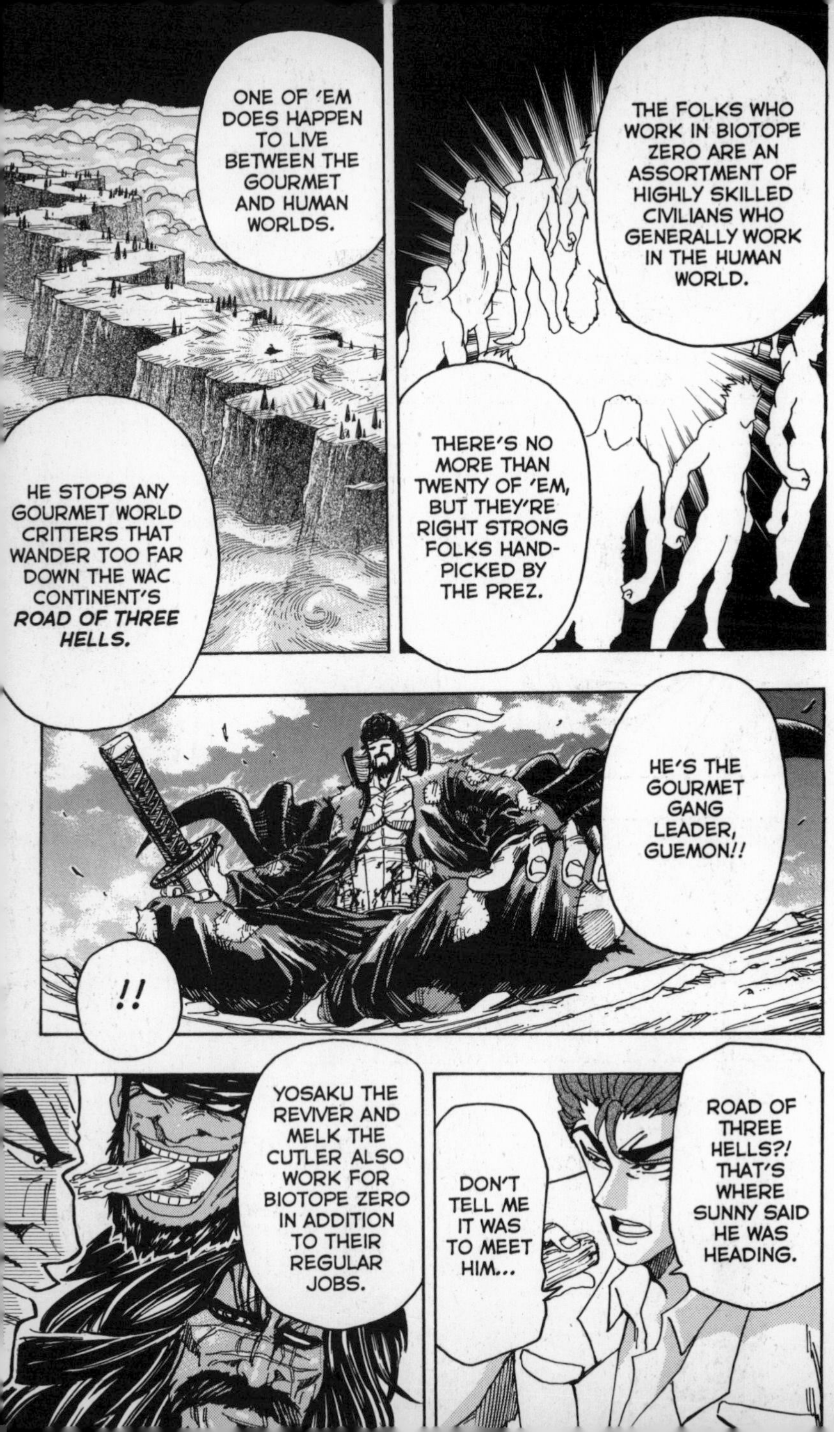
THE FOLKS WHO WORK IN BIOTOPE ZERO ARE AN ASSORTMENT OF HIGHLY SKILLED CIVILIANS WHO GENERALLY WORK IN THE HUMAN WORLD.
THERE'S NO MORE THAN TWENTY OF 'EM, BUT THEY'RE RIGHT STRONG FOLKS HAND-PICKED BY THE PREZ.
ONE OF 'EM DOES HAPPEN TO LIVE BETWEEN THE GOURMET AND HUMAN WORLDS.
HE STOPS ANY GOURMET WORLD CRITTERS THAT WANDER TOO FAR DOWN THE WAC CONTINENT'S *ROAD OF THREE HELLS.*
HE'S THE GOURMET GANG LEADER, GUEMON!!
!!
ROAD OF THREE HELLS?! THAT'S WHERE SUNNY SAID HE WAS HEADING.
DON'T TELL ME IT WAS TO MEET HIM...
YOSAKU THE REVIVER AND MELK THE CUTLER ALSO WORK FOR BIOTOPE ZERO IN ADDITION TO THEIR REGULAR JOBS.

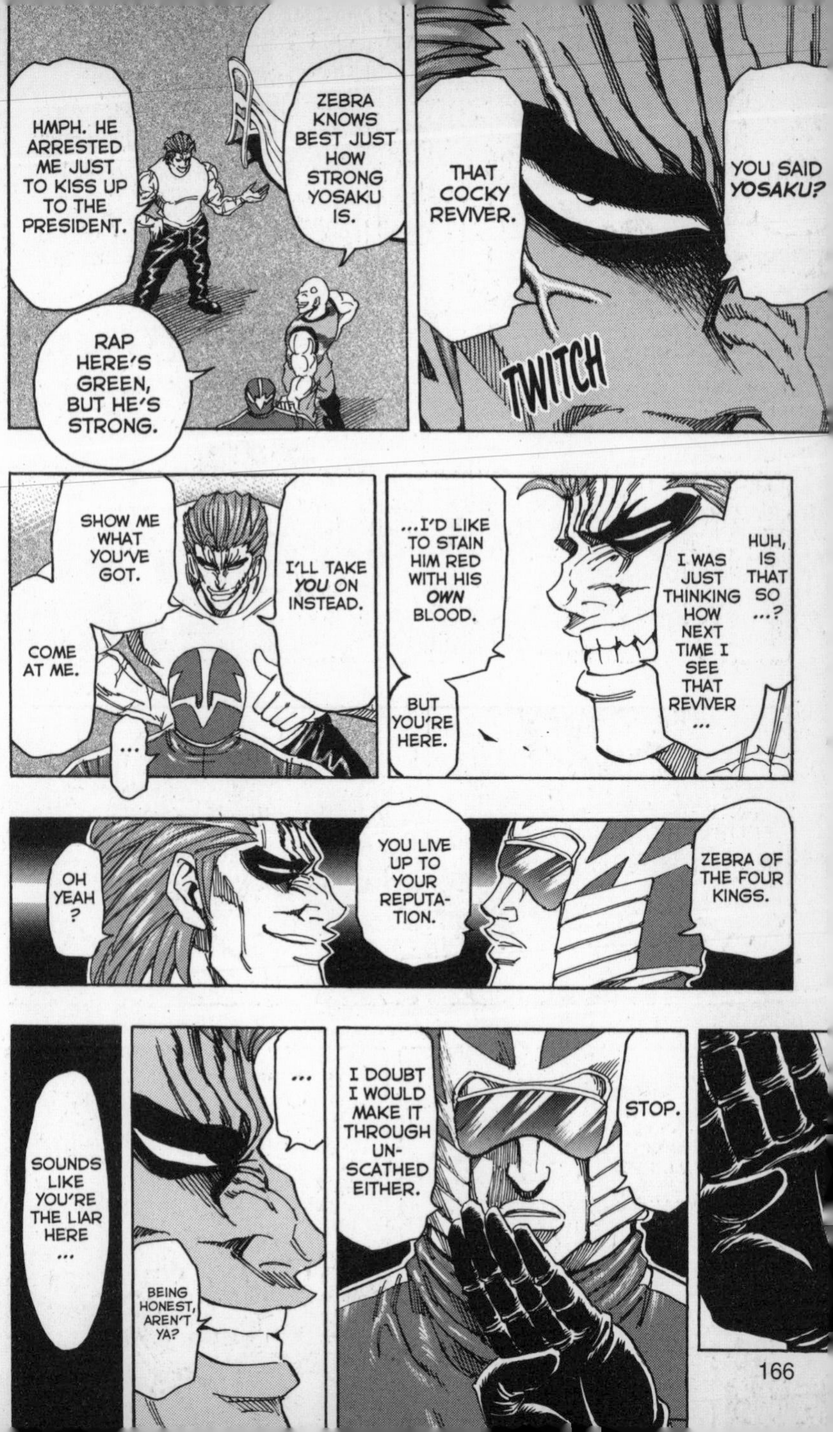
YOU SAID *YOSAKU?*
THAT COCKY REVIVER.
TWITCH
ZEBRA KNOWS BEST JUST HOW STRONG YOSAKU IS.
HMPH. HE ARRESTED ME JUST TO KISS UP TO THE PRESIDENT.
RAP HERE'S GREEN, BUT HE'S STRONG.
HUH, IS THAT SO ...?
I WAS JUST THINKING HOW NEXT TIME I SEE THAT REVIVER ...
...I'D LIKE TO STAIN HIM RED WITH HIS *OWN* BLOOD.
BUT YOU'RE HERE.
I'LL TAKE *YOU* ON INSTEAD.
SHOW ME WHAT YOU'VE GOT.
COME AT ME.
...
ZEBRA OF THE FOUR KINGS.
YOU LIVE UP TO YOUR REPUTATION.
OH YEAH?
STOP.
I DOUBT I WOULD MAKE IT THROUGH UNSCATHED EITHER.
...
SOUNDS LIKE YOU'RE THE LIAR HERE ...
BEING HONEST, AREN'T YA?

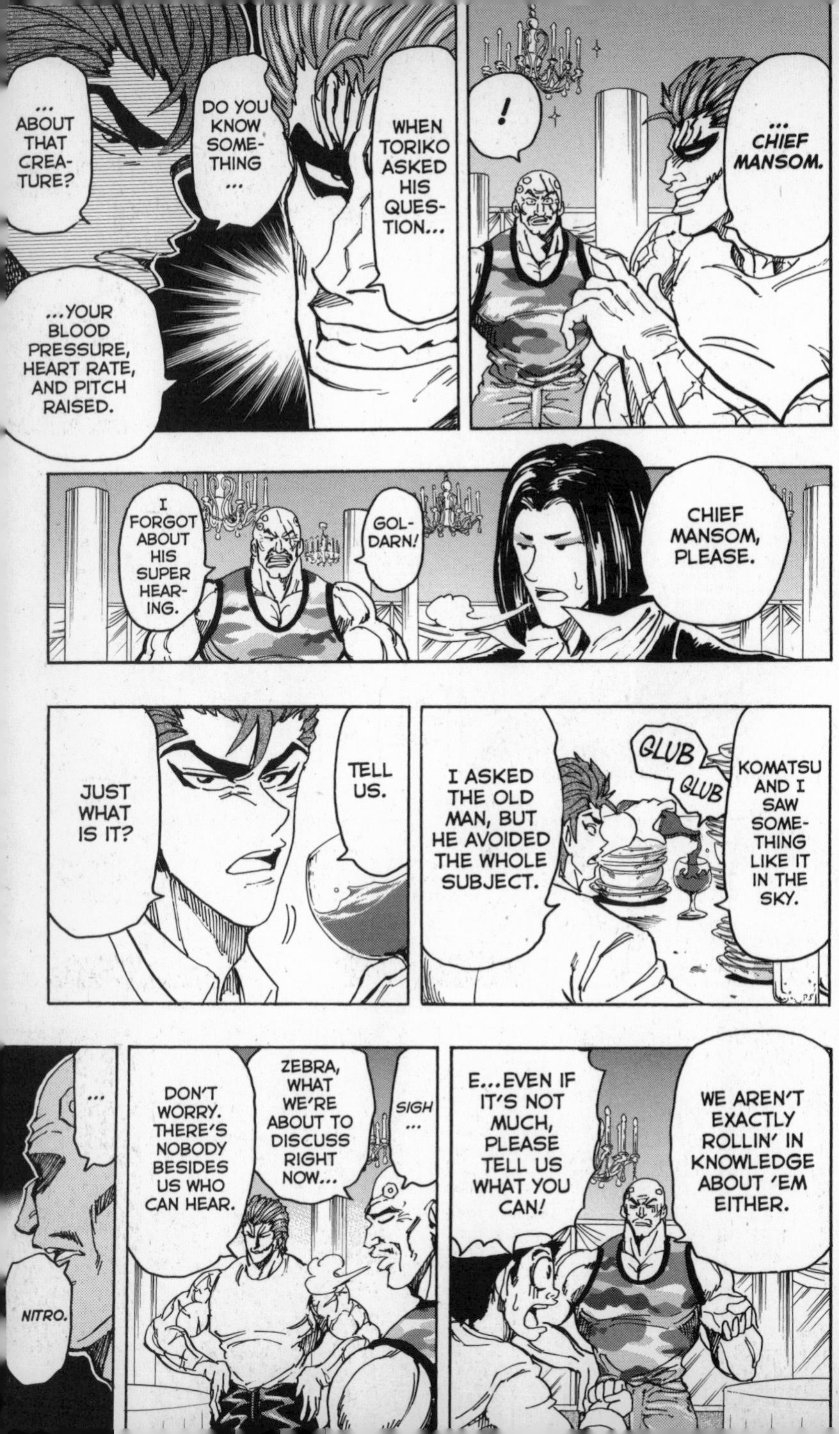
... CHIEF MANSOM.
!
WHEN TORIKO ASKED HIS QUESTION...
DO YOU KNOW SOMETHING ...
... ABOUT THAT CREATURE?
...YOUR BLOOD PRESSURE, HEART RATE, AND PITCH RAISED.
CHIEF MANSOM, PLEASE.
GOL-DARN!
I FORGOT ABOUT HIS SUPER HEARING.
KOMATSU AND I SAW SOMETHING LIKE IT IN THE SKY.
GLUB
GLUB
I ASKED THE OLD MAN, BUT HE AVOIDED THE WHOLE SUBJECT.
TELL US.
JUST WHAT IS IT?
WE AREN'T EXACTLY ROLLIN' IN KNOWLEDGE ABOUT 'EM EITHER.
E...EVEN IF IT'S NOT MUCH, PLEASE TELL US WHAT YOU CAN!
SIGH ...
ZEBRA, WHAT WE'RE ABOUT TO DISCUSS RIGHT NOW...
DON'T WORRY. THERE'S NOBODY BESIDES US WHO CAN HEAR.
...
NITRO.

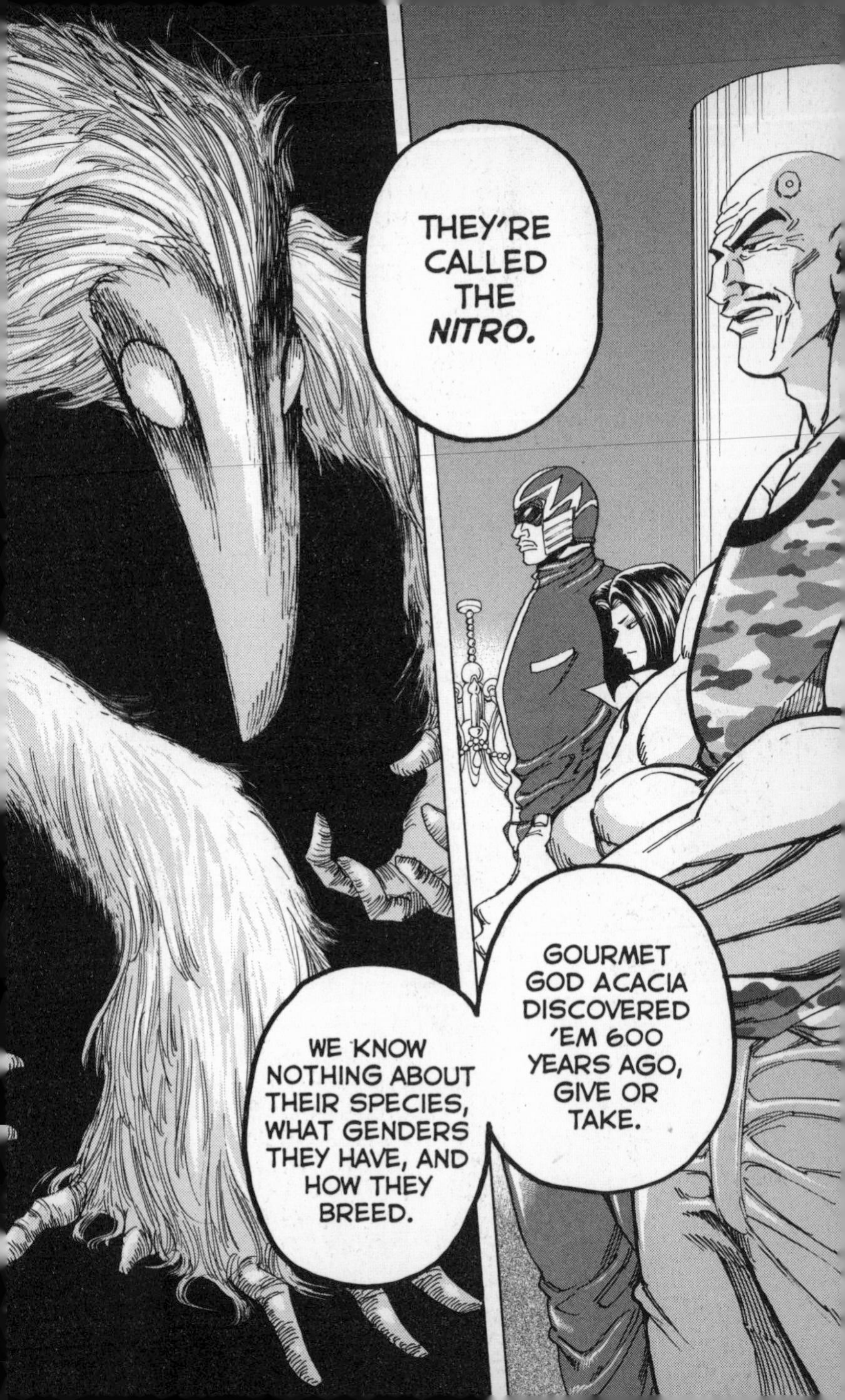
THEY'RE CALLED THE *NITRO.*
GOURMET GOD ACACIA DISCOVERED 'EM 600 YEARS AGO, GIVE OR TAKE.
WE KNOW NOTHING ABOUT THEIR SPECIES, WHAT GENDERS THEY HAVE, AND HOW THEY BREED.

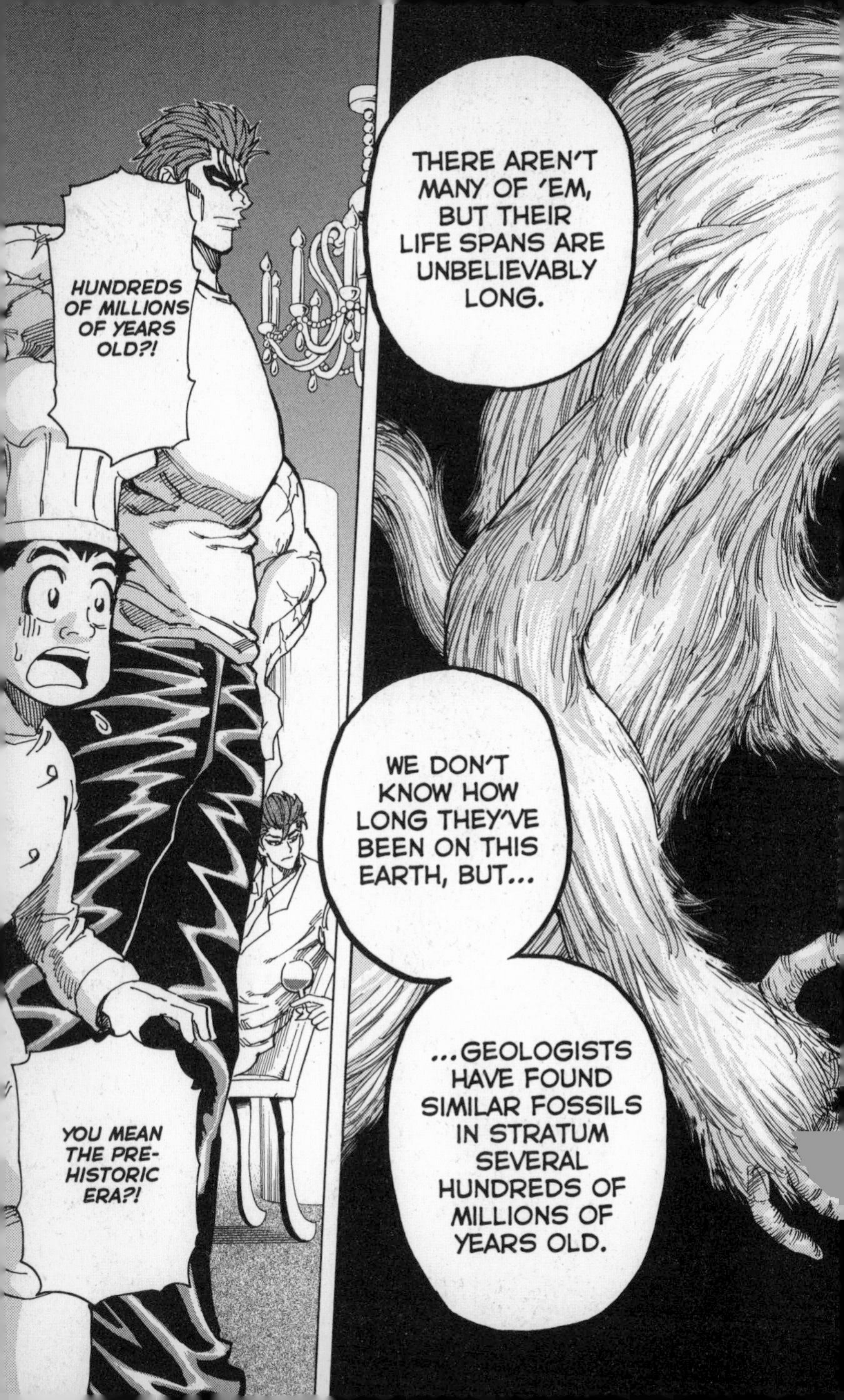
THERE AREN'T MANY OF 'EM, BUT THEIR LIFE SPANS ARE UNBELIEVABLY LONG.
WE DON'T KNOW HOW LONG THEY'VE BEEN ON THIS EARTH, BUT...
...GEOLOGISTS HAVE FOUND SIMILAR FOSSILS IN STRATUM SEVERAL HUNDREDS OF MILLIONS OF YEARS OLD.
HUNDREDS OF MILLIONS OF YEARS OLD?!
YOU MEAN THE PRE-HISTORIC ERA?!

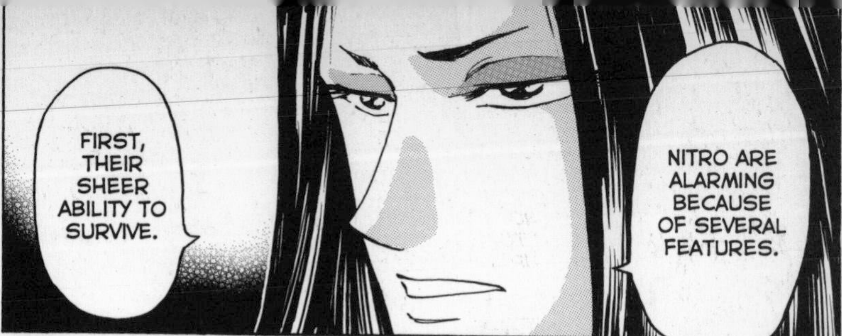
NITRO ARE ALARMING BECAUSE OF SEVERAL FEATURES.
FIRST, THEIR SHEER ABILITY TO SURVIVE.

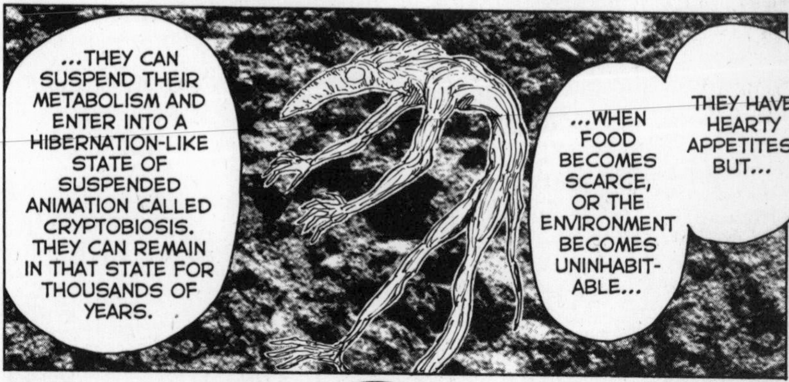
THEY HAVE HEARTY APPETITES, BUT...
...WHEN FOOD BECOMES SCARCE, OR THE ENVIRONMENT BECOMES UNINHABIT-ABLE...
...THEY CAN SUSPEND THEIR METABOLISM AND ENTER INTO A HIBERNATION-LIKE STATE OF SUSPENDED ANIMATION CALLED CRYPTOBIOSIS. THEY CAN REMAIN IN THAT STATE FOR THOUSANDS OF YEARS.

■ REAL LIFE EXAMPLE

THE TARDIGRADE IS AN ACTUAL ORGANISM THAT CAN ENTER A STATE OF SUSPENDED ANIMATION CALLED CRYPTOBIOSIS DURING WHICH IT CAN SURVIVE HEAT OF OVER 150°C, COLD OF ABSOLUTE ZERO, VACUUM, EXTREME DRYNESS, 6,000 PSI PRESSURE, AND EVEN RADIATION.

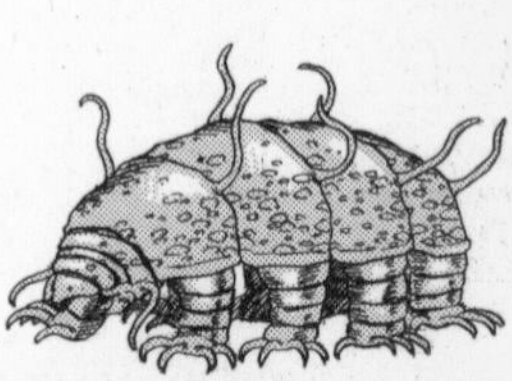

TARDIGRADE

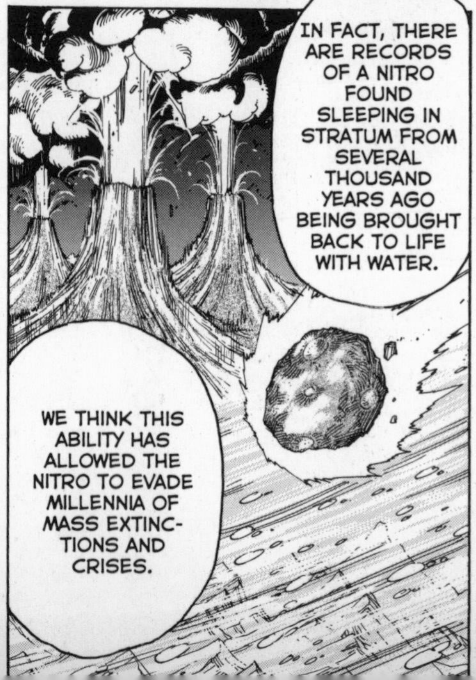
IN FACT, THERE ARE RECORDS OF A NITRO FOUND SLEEPING IN STRATUM FROM SEVERAL THOUSAND YEARS AGO BEING BROUGHT BACK TO LIFE WITH WATER.
WE THINK THIS ABILITY HAS ALLOWED THE NITRO TO EVADE MILLENNIA OF MASS EXTINC-TIONS AND CRISES.

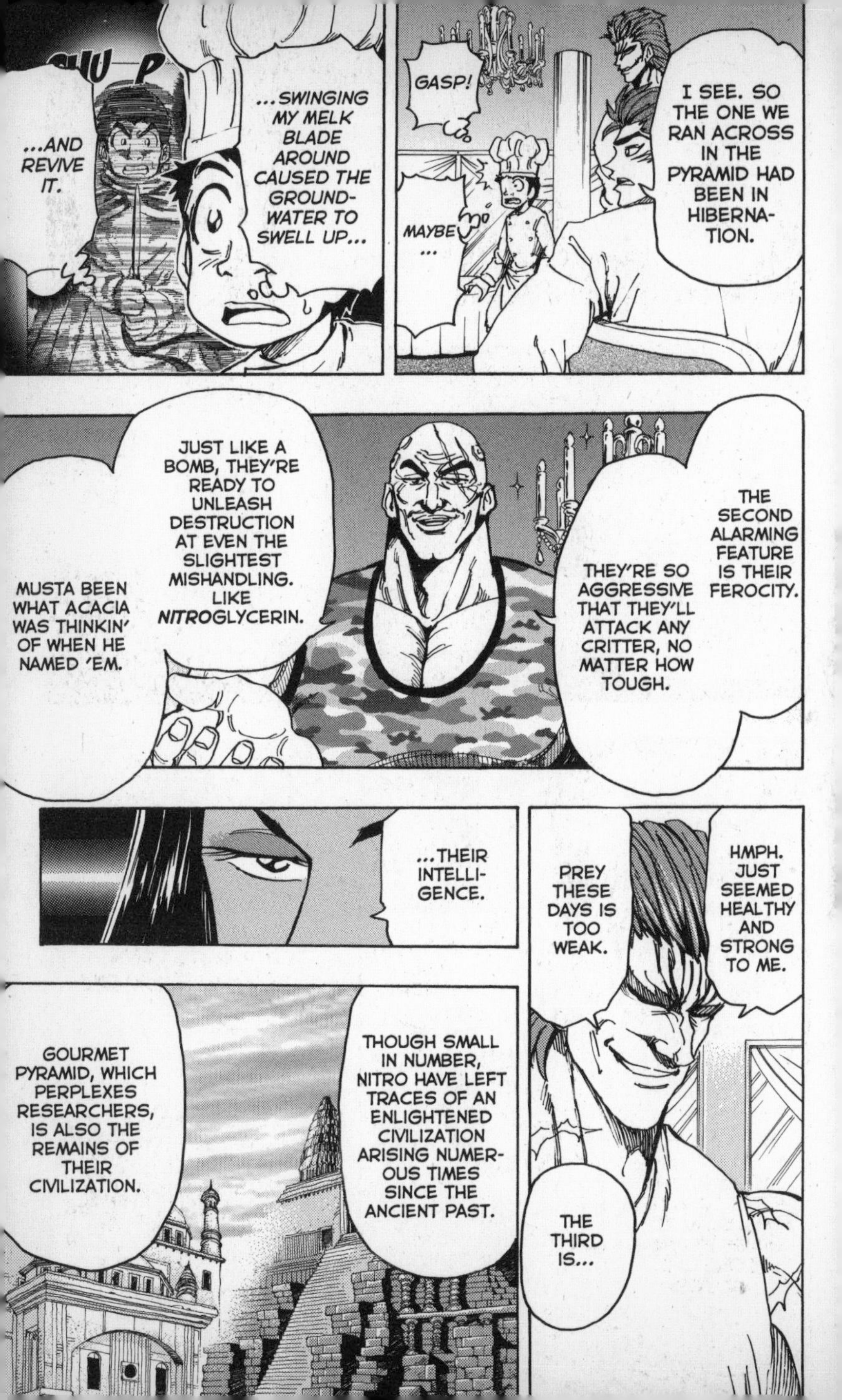
I SEE. SO THE ONE WE RAN ACROSS IN THE PYRAMID HAD BEEN IN HIBERNATION.
GASP!
MAYBE...
...SWINGING MY MELK BLADE AROUND CAUSED THE GROUNDWATER TO SWELL UP...
...AND REVIVE IT.
THE SECOND ALARMING FEATURE IS THEIR FEROCITY.
THEY'RE SO AGGRESSIVE THAT THEY'LL ATTACK ANY CRITTER, NO MATTER HOW TOUGH.
JUST LIKE A BOMB, THEY'RE READY TO UNLEASH DESTRUCTION AT EVEN THE SLIGHTEST MISHANDLING. LIKE *NITRO*GLYCERIN.
MUSTA BEEN WHAT ACACIA WAS THINKIN' OF WHEN HE NAMED 'EM.
HMPH. JUST SEEMED HEALTHY AND STRONG TO ME.
PREY THESE DAYS IS TOO WEAK.
THE THIRD IS...
...THEIR INTELLIGENCE.
THOUGH SMALL IN NUMBER, NITRO HAVE LEFT TRACES OF AN ENLIGHTENED CIVILIZATION ARISING NUMEROUS TIMES SINCE THE ANCIENT PAST.
GOURMET PYRAMID, WHICH PERPLEXES RESEARCHERS, IS ALSO THE REMAINS OF THEIR CIVILIZATION.

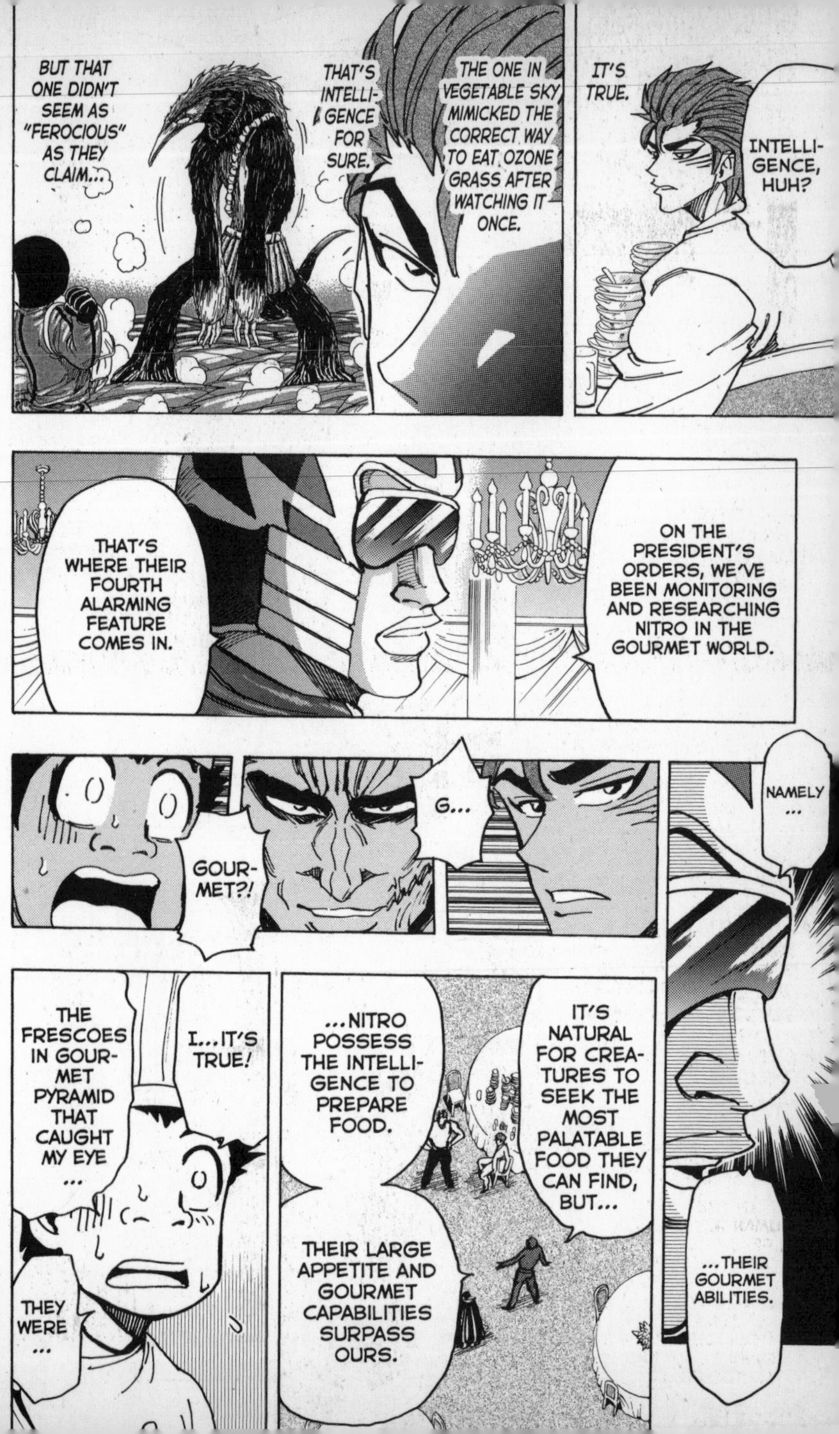
INTELLIGENCE, HUH?
IT'S TRUE.
THE ONE IN VEGETABLE SKY MIMICKED THE CORRECT WAY TO EAT OZONE GRASS AFTER WATCHING IT ONCE.
THAT'S INTELLIGENCE FOR SURE.
BUT THAT ONE DIDN'T SEEM AS "FEROCIOUS" AS THEY CLAIM...
ON THE PRESIDENT'S ORDERS, WE'VE BEEN MONITORING AND RESEARCHING NITRO IN THE GOURMET WORLD.
THAT'S WHERE THEIR FOURTH ALARMING FEATURE COMES IN.
NAMELY ...
...THEIR GOURMET ABILITIES.
G...
GOURMET?!
IT'S NATURAL FOR CREATURES TO SEEK THE MOST PALATABLE FOOD THEY CAN FIND, BUT...
...NITRO POSSESS THE INTELLIGENCE TO PREPARE FOOD.
THEIR LARGE APPETITE AND GOURMET CAPABILITIES SURPASS OURS.
I...IT'S TRUE!
THE FRESCOES IN GOURMET PYRAMID THAT CAUGHT MY EYE ...
THEY WERE ...

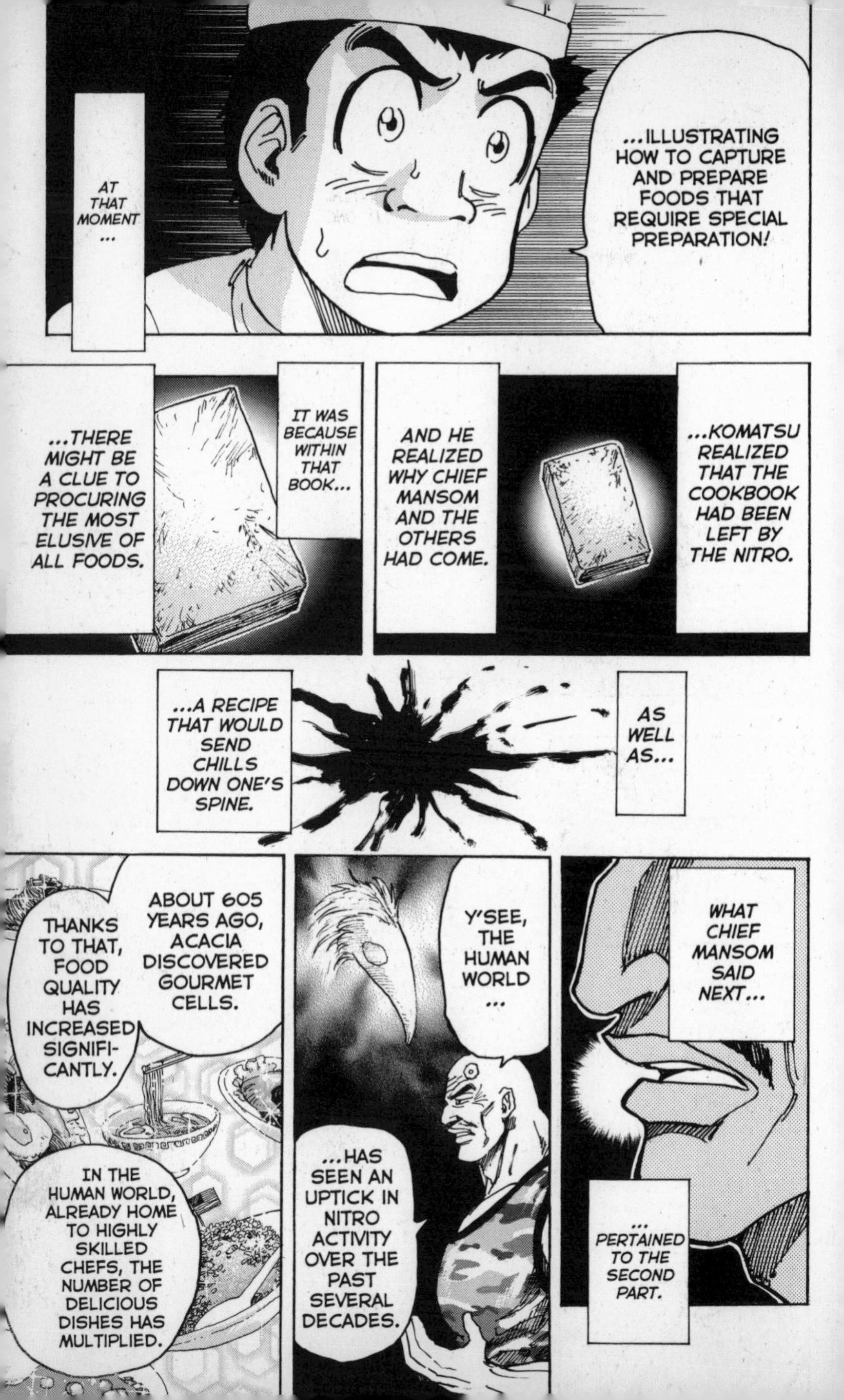
...ILLUSTRATING HOW TO CAPTURE AND PREPARE FOODS THAT REQUIRE SPECIAL PREPARATION!
AT THAT MOMENT...
...KOMATSU REALIZED THAT THE COOKBOOK HAD BEEN LEFT BY THE NITRO.
AND HE REALIZED WHY CHIEF MANSOM AND THE OTHERS HAD COME.
IT WAS BECAUSE WITHIN THAT BOOK...
...THERE MIGHT BE A CLUE TO PROCURING THE MOST ELUSIVE OF ALL FOODS.
AS WELL AS...
...A RECIPE THAT WOULD SEND CHILLS DOWN ONE'S SPINE.
WHAT CHIEF MANSOM SAID NEXT...
...PERTAINED TO THE SECOND PART.
Y'SEE, THE HUMAN WORLD...
...HAS SEEN AN UPTICK IN NITRO ACTIVITY OVER THE PAST SEVERAL DECADES.
ABOUT 605 YEARS AGO, ACACIA DISCOVERED GOURMET CELLS.
THANKS TO THAT, FOOD QUALITY HAS INCREASED SIGNIFI-CANTLY.
IN THE HUMAN WORLD, ALREADY HOME TO HIGHLY SKILLED CHEFS, THE NUMBER OF DELICIOUS DISHES HAS MULTIPLIED.

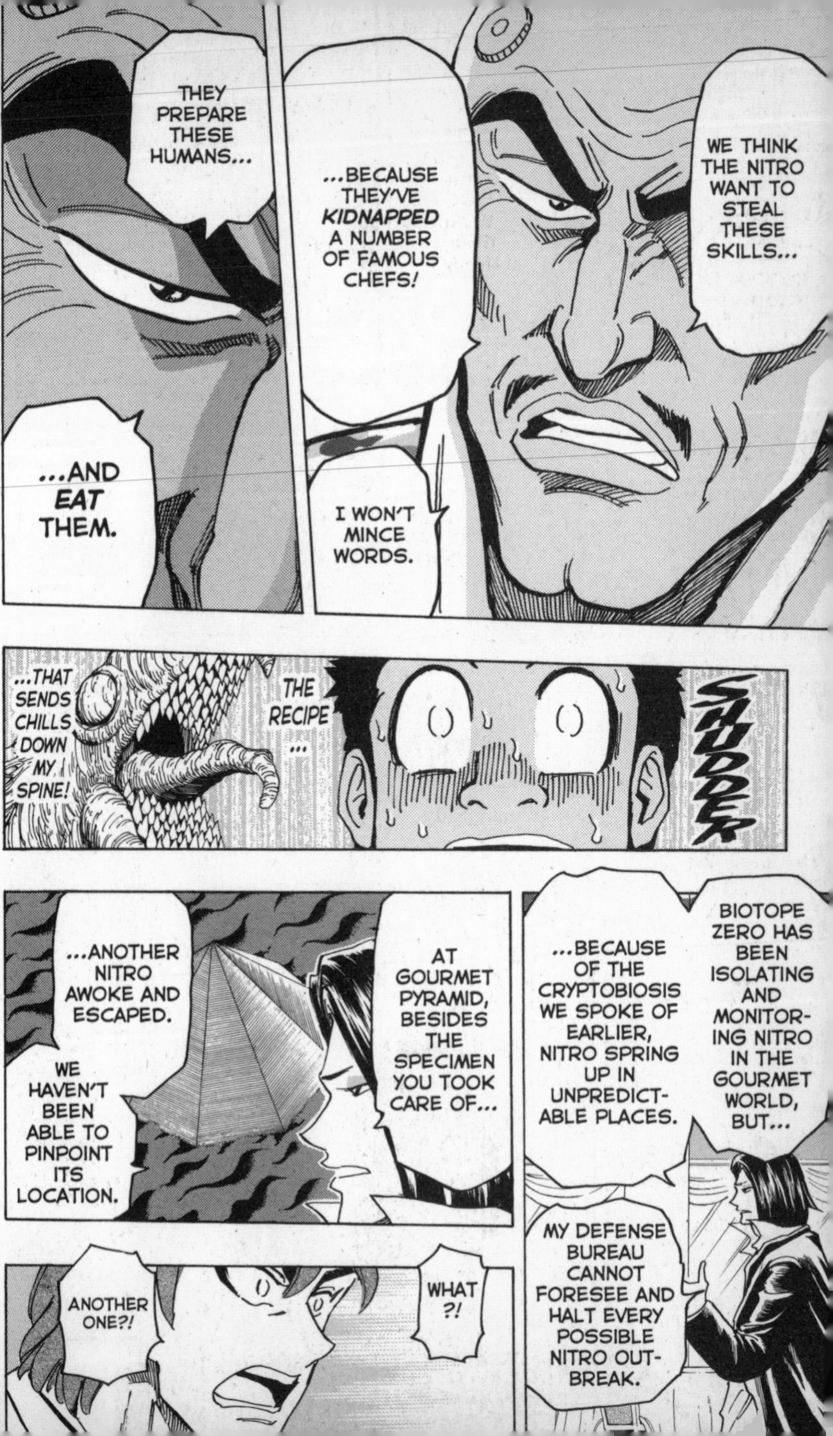
WE THINK THE NITRO WANT TO STEAL THESE SKILLS...
...BECAUSE THEY'VE KIDNAPPED A NUMBER OF FAMOUS CHEFS!
I WON'T MINCE WORDS.
THEY PREPARE THESE HUMANS...
...AND EAT THEM.
SHUDDER
THE RECIPE...
...THAT SENDS CHILLS DOWN MY SPINE!
BIOTOPE ZERO HAS BEEN ISOLATING AND MONITORING NITRO IN THE GOURMET WORLD, BUT...
...BECAUSE OF THE CRYPTOBIOSIS WE SPOKE OF EARLIER, NITRO SPRING UP IN UNPREDICTABLE PLACES.
MY DEFENSE BUREAU CANNOT FORESEE AND HALT EVERY POSSIBLE NITRO OUTBREAK.
AT GOURMET PYRAMID, BESIDES THE SPECIMEN YOU TOOK CARE OF...
...ANOTHER NITRO AWOKE AND ESCAPED.
WE HAVEN'T BEEN ABLE TO PINPOINT ITS LOCATION.
WHAT?!
ANOTHER ONE?!

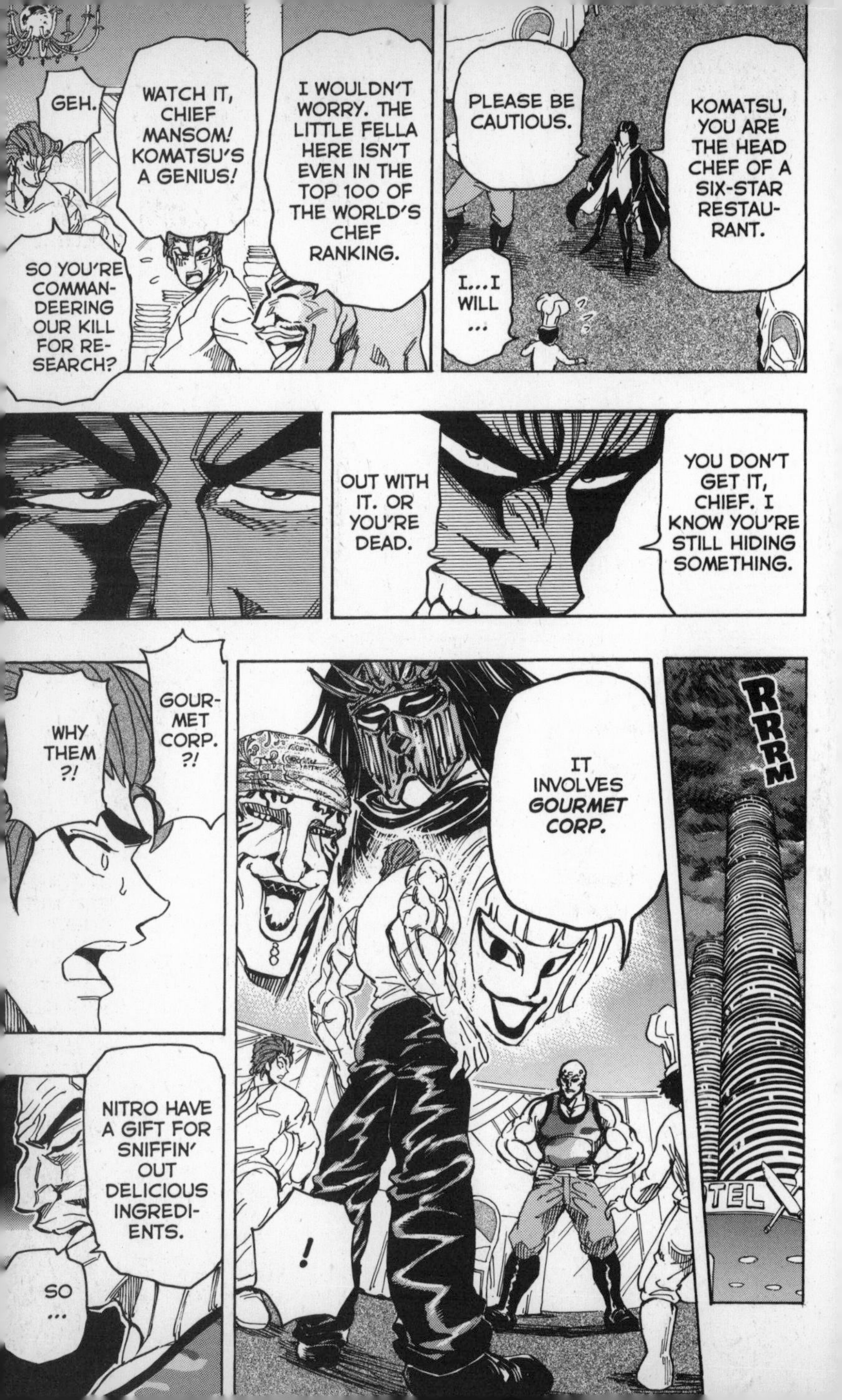

KOMATSU, YOU ARE THE HEAD CHEF OF A SIX-STAR RESTAURANT.
PLEASE BE CAUTIOUS.
I...I WILL ...
I WOULDN'T WORRY. THE LITTLE FELLA HERE ISN'T EVEN IN THE TOP 100 OF THE WORLD'S CHEF RANKING.
WATCH IT, CHIEF MANSOM! KOMATSU'S A GENIUS!
GEH.
SO YOU'RE COMMANDEERING OUR KILL FOR RESEARCH?
YOU DON'T GET IT, CHIEF. I KNOW YOU'RE STILL HIDING SOMETHING.
OUT WITH IT. OR YOU'RE DEAD.
RRRM
IT INVOLVES GOURMET CORP.
!
GOURMET CORP.?!
WHY THEM?!
NITRO HAVE A GIFT FOR SNIFFIN' OUT DELICIOUS INGREDIENTS.
SO ...

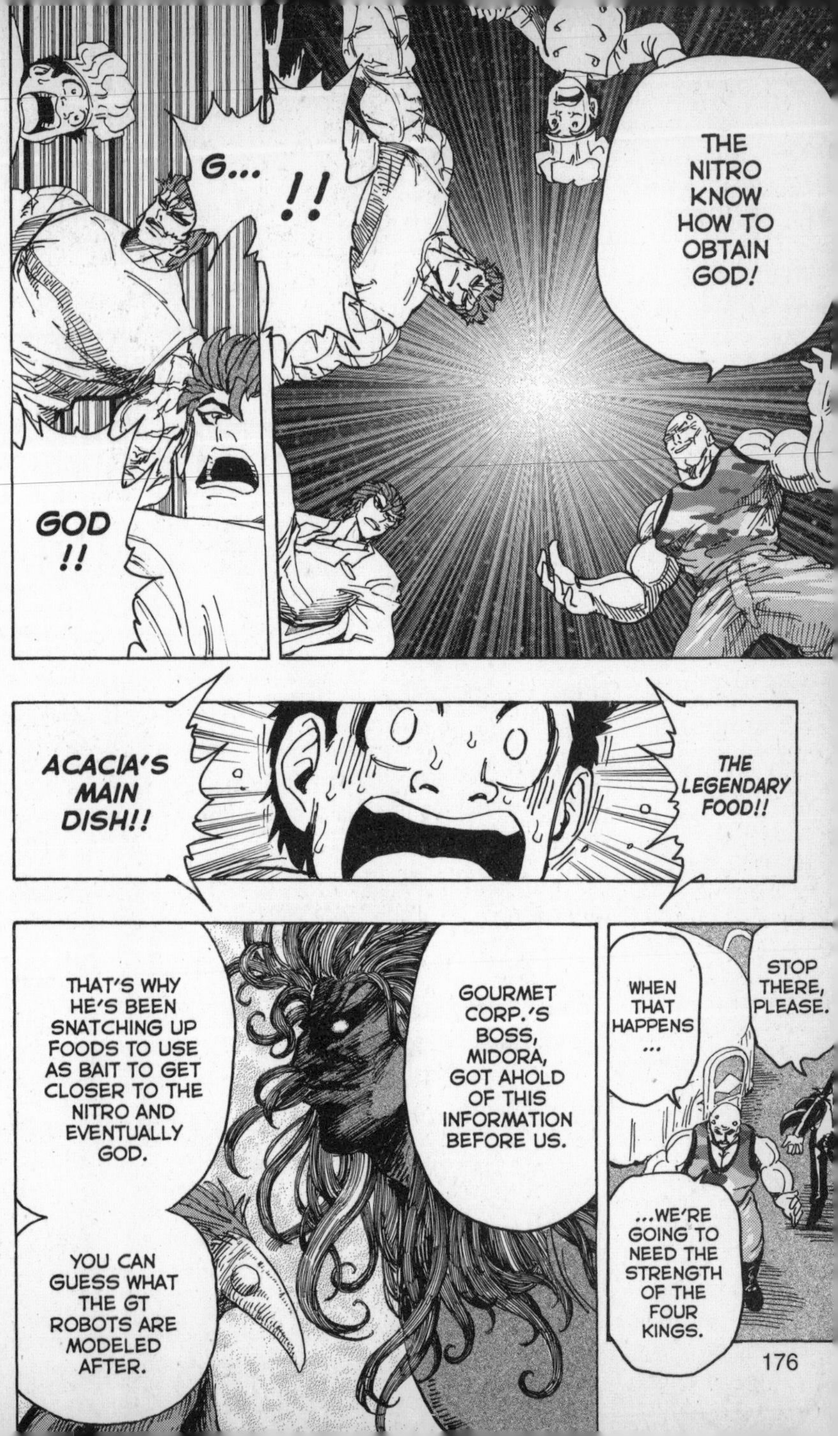
THE NITRO KNOW HOW TO OBTAIN GOD!
G... !!
GOD !!
THE LEGENDARY FOOD!!
ACACIA'S MAIN DISH!!
STOP THERE, PLEASE.
WHEN THAT HAPPENS ...
...WE'RE GOING TO NEED THE STRENGTH OF THE FOUR KINGS.
GOURMET CORP.'S BOSS, MIDORA, GOT AHOLD OF THIS INFORMATION BEFORE US.
THAT'S WHY HE'S BEEN SNATCHING UP FOODS TO USE AS BAIT TO GET CLOSER TO THE NITRO AND EVENTUALLY GOD.
YOU CAN GUESS WHAT THE GT ROBOTS ARE MODELED AFTER.

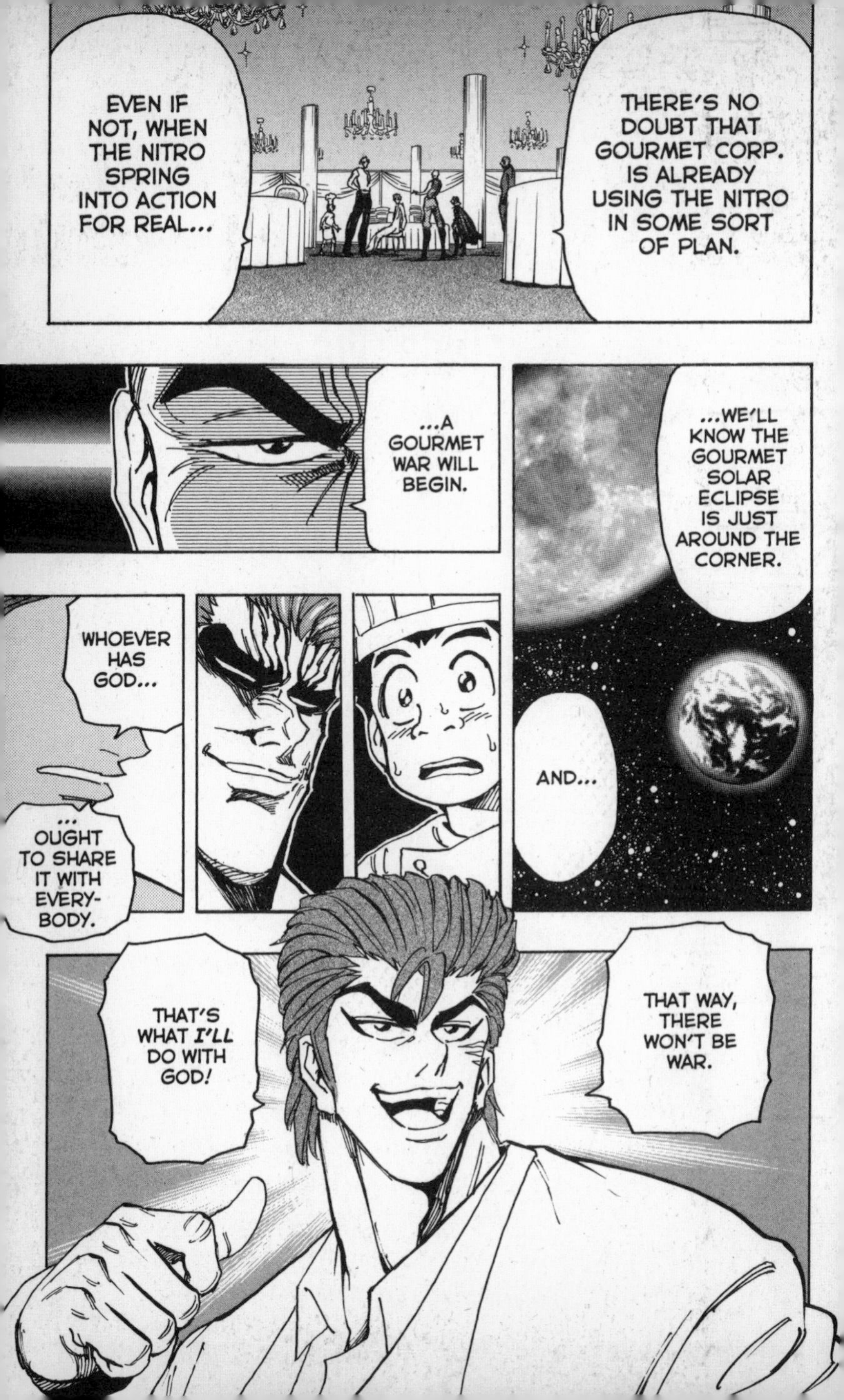
THERE'S NO DOUBT THAT GOURMET CORP. IS ALREADY USING THE NITRO IN SOME SORT OF PLAN.
EVEN IF NOT, WHEN THE NITRO SPRING INTO ACTION FOR REAL...
...WE'LL KNOW THE GOURMET SOLAR ECLIPSE IS JUST AROUND THE CORNER.
AND...
...A GOURMET WAR WILL BEGIN.
WHOEVER HAS GOD...
...OUGHT TO SHARE IT WITH EVERY-BODY.
THAT WAY, THERE WON'T BE WAR.
THAT'S WHAT *I'LL* DO WITH GOD!

TORIKO

GOURMET CHECKLIST

Vol. 165

GINGER PIG

(MAMMAL)

CAPTURE LEVEL: LESS THAN 1

HABITAT: ANYWHERE, CAN BE DOMESTICATED

LENGTH: 1 METER

HEIGHT: ---

WEIGHT: 150 KG

PRICE: 100 G / 500 YEN

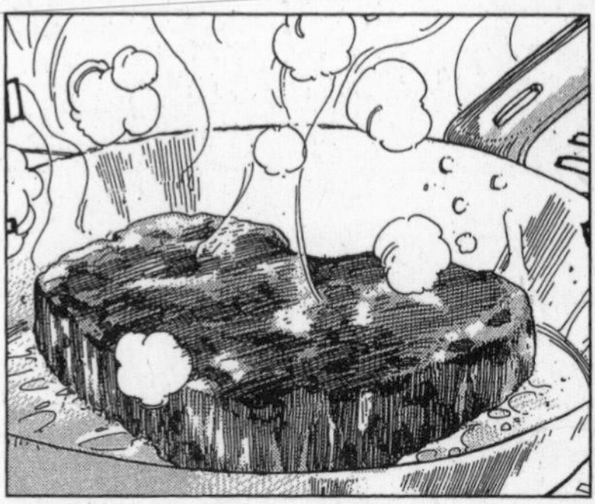

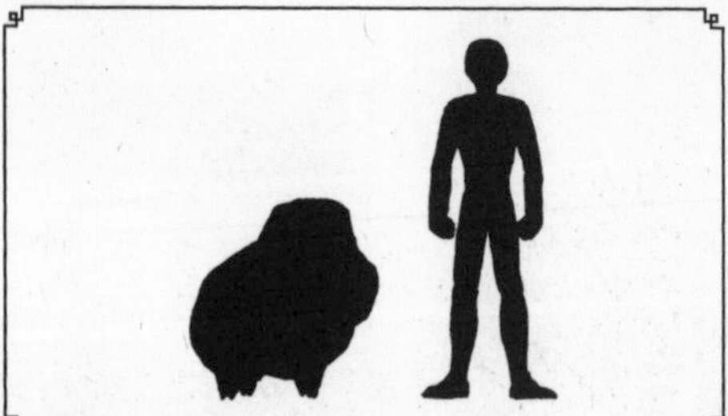

SCALE

A PIG THAT BECOMES GINGER-FLAVORED WHEN ITS FLESH IS GRILLED. THE GINGER PIG'S APPEARANCE IS EVEN GINGER-LIKE, MAKING IT A VERY BIZARRE PORKER. THEY'RE SURPRISINGLY EASY TO RAISE, EVEN IN A TYPICAL YARD. THEY'RE REASONABLY PRICED AND SOMETHING ANYONE CAN COOK, BUT TRYING TO PREPARE ONE PERFECTLY HAS BROUGHT MANY A CHEF TO TEARS.

GOURMET 144: REUNION WITH TERROR!!

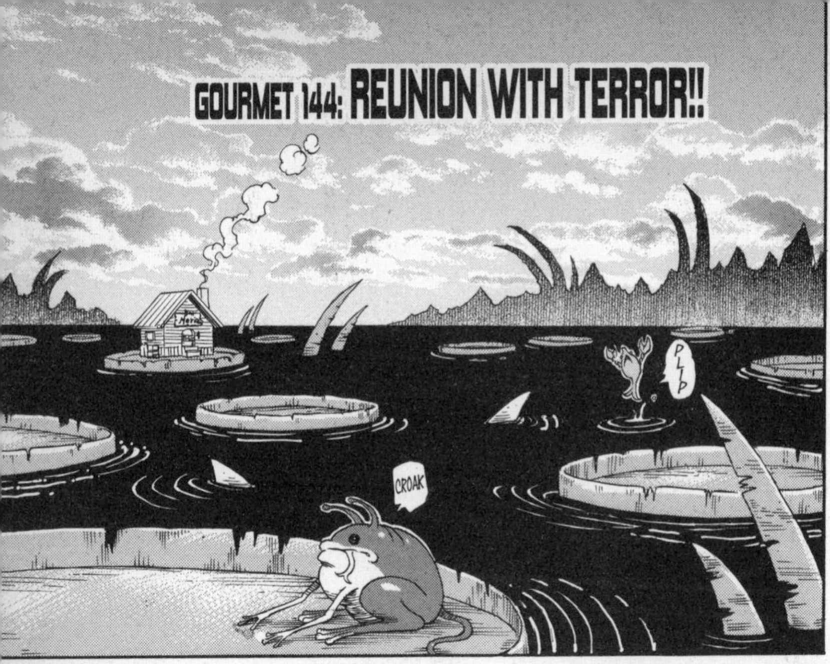
PLIP
CROAK

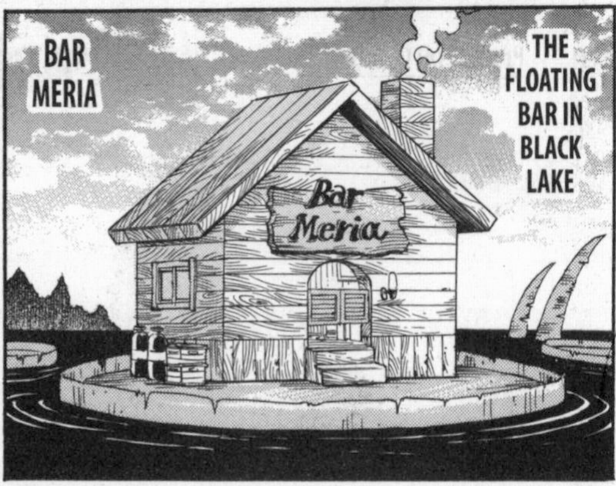
THE FLOATING BAR IN BLACK LAKE
BAR MERIA
Bar Meria

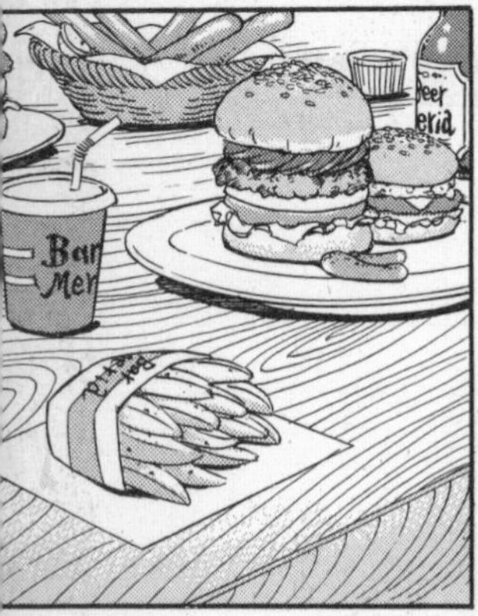

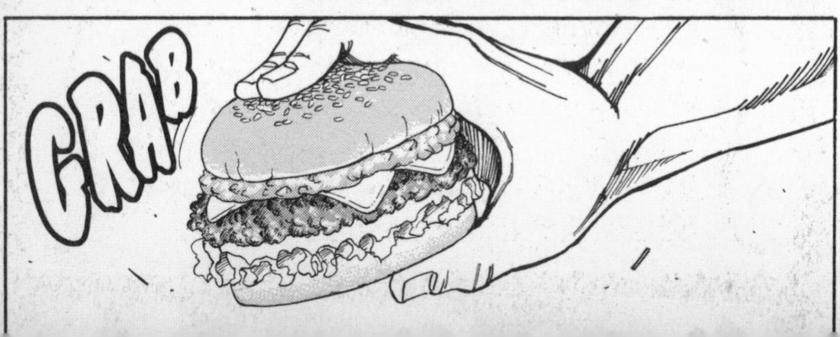
GRAB

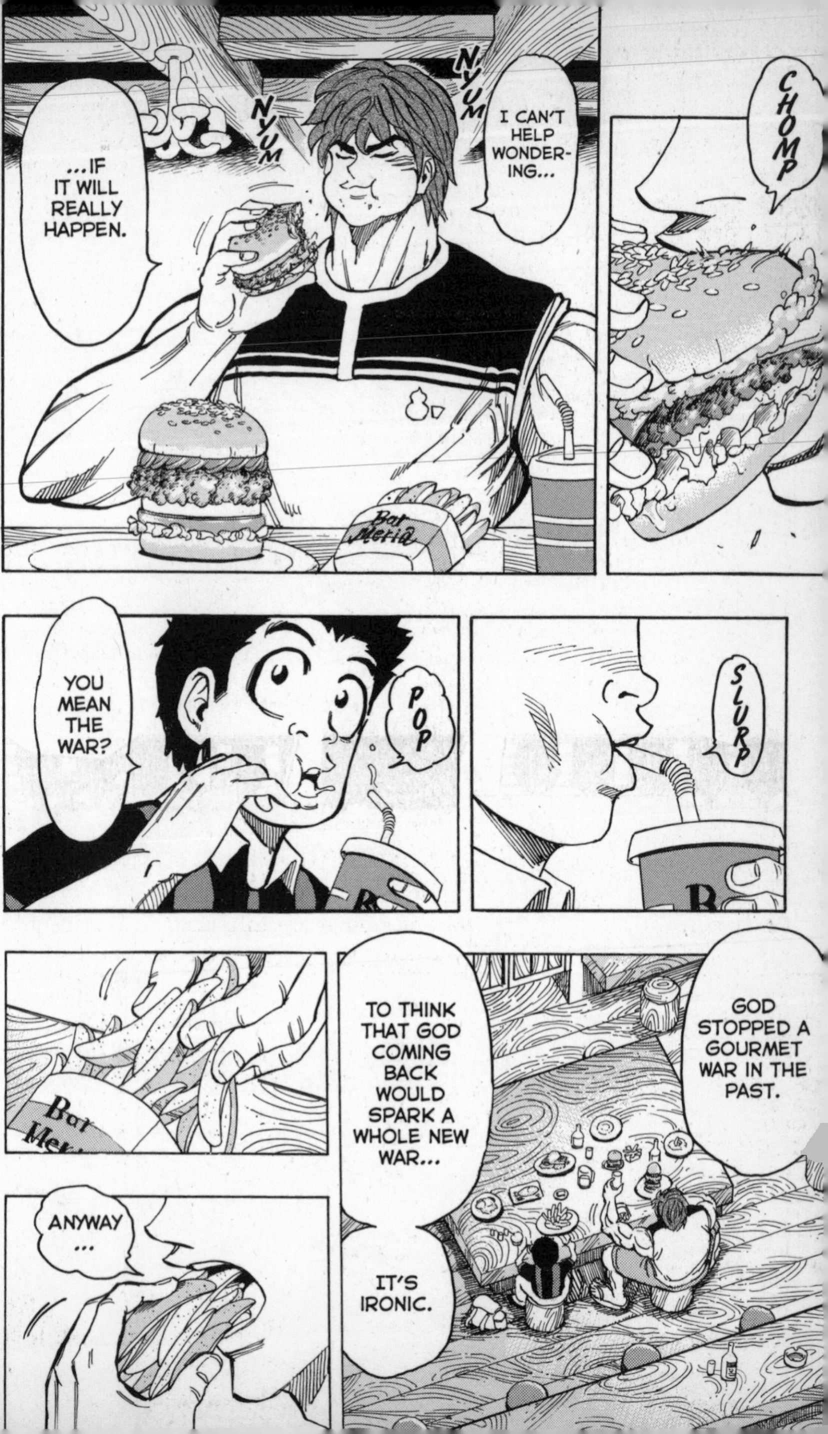
CHOMP
NYUM
I CAN'T HELP WONDERING...
NYUM
...IF IT WILL REALLY HAPPEN.
Bat Meria
SLURP
POP
YOU MEAN THE WAR?
GOD STOPPED A GOURMET WAR IN THE PAST.
TO THINK THAT GOD COMING BACK WOULD SPARK A WHOLE NEW WAR...
IT'S IRONIC.
ANYWAY...

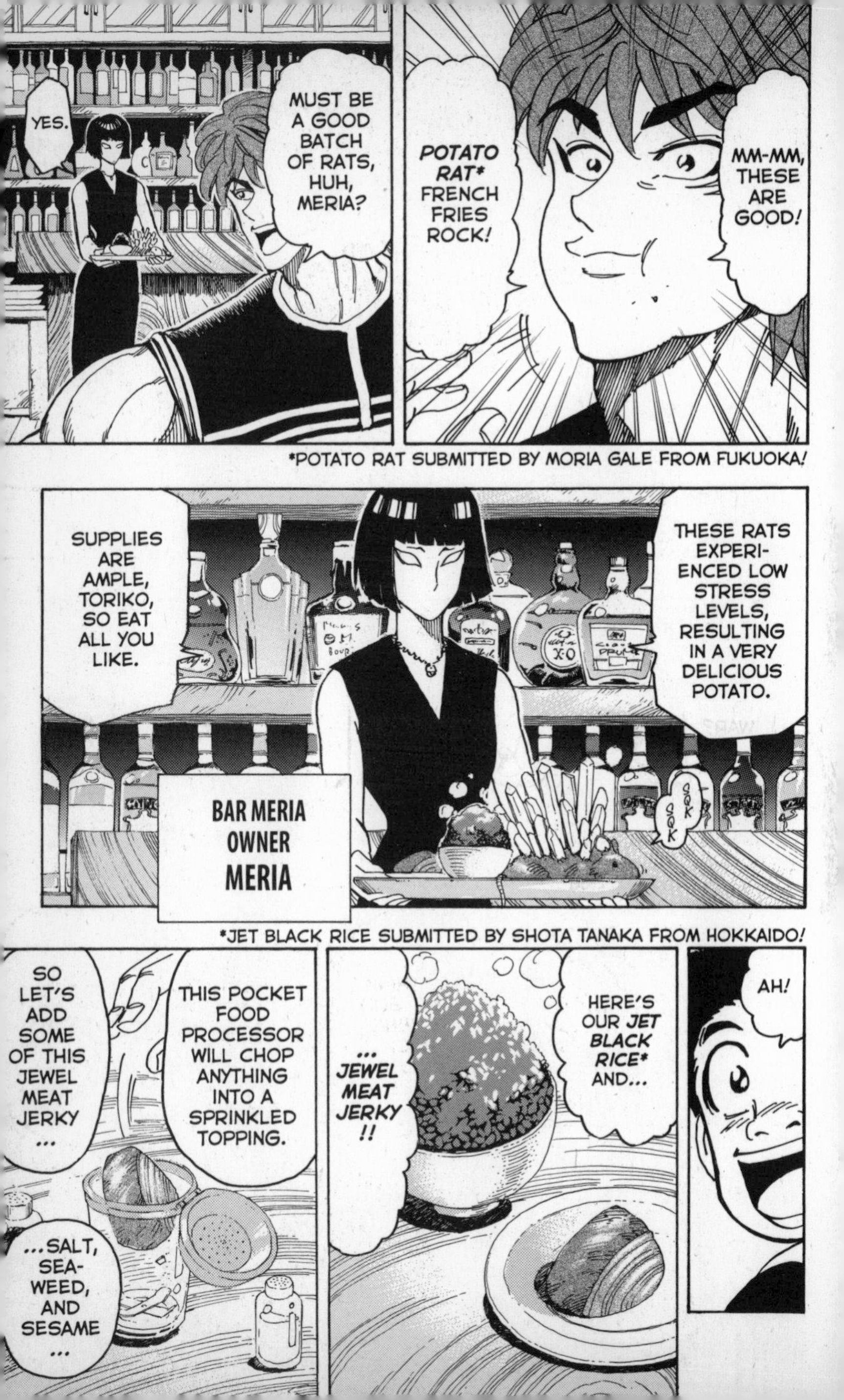
MM-MM, THESE ARE GOOD!
POTATO RAT* FRENCH FRIES ROCK!
MUST BE A GOOD BATCH OF RATS, HUH, MERIA?
YES.
*POTATO RAT SUBMITTED BY MORIA GALE FROM FUKUOKA!
THESE RATS EXPERI-ENCED LOW STRESS LEVELS, RESULTING IN A VERY DELICIOUS POTATO.
SQK SQK
SUPPLIES ARE AMPLE, TORIKO, SO EAT ALL YOU LIKE.
BAR MERIA OWNER MERIA
*JET BLACK RICE SUBMITTED BY SHOTA TANAKA FROM HOKKAIDO!
AH!
HERE'S OUR JET BLACK RICE* AND...
...JEWEL MEAT JERKY!!
THIS POCKET FOOD PROCESSOR WILL CHOP ANYTHING INTO A SPRINKLED TOPPING.
SO LET'S ADD SOME OF THIS JEWEL MEAT JERKY...
...SALT, SEA-WEED, AND SESAME...

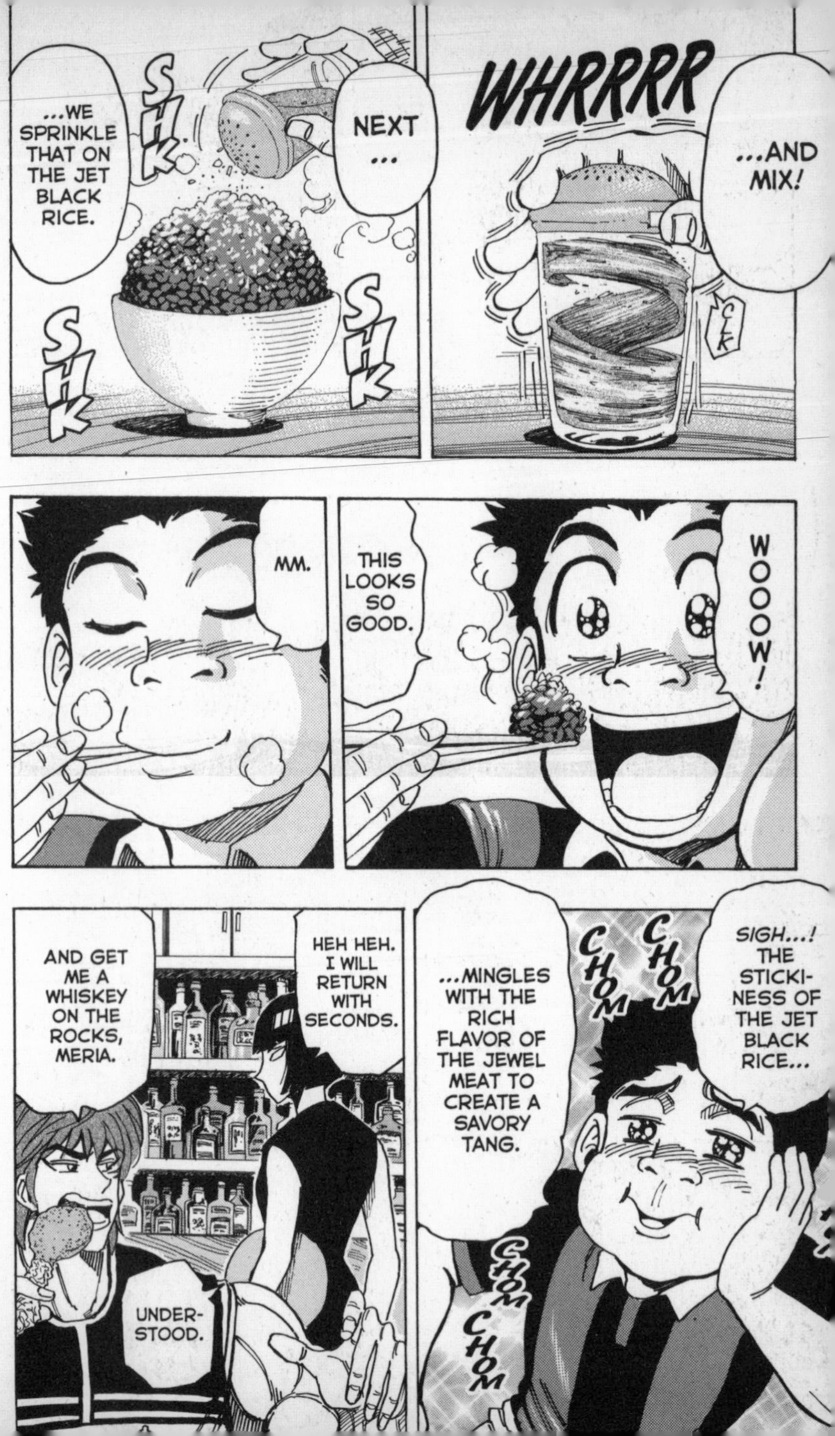
WHRRRR
...AND MIX!
CLK
NEXT...
...WE SPRINKLE THAT ON THE JET BLACK RICE.
SHK
SHK
SHK
WOOOOW!
THIS LOOKS SO GOOD.
MM.
CHOM CHOM
SIGH...! THE STICKINESS OF THE JET BLACK RICE...
...MINGLES WITH THE RICH FLAVOR OF THE JEWEL MEAT TO CREATE A SAVORY TANG.
CHOM CHOM
HEH HEH. I WILL RETURN WITH SECONDS.
AND GET ME A WHISKEY ON THE ROCKS, MERIA.
UNDER-STOOD.

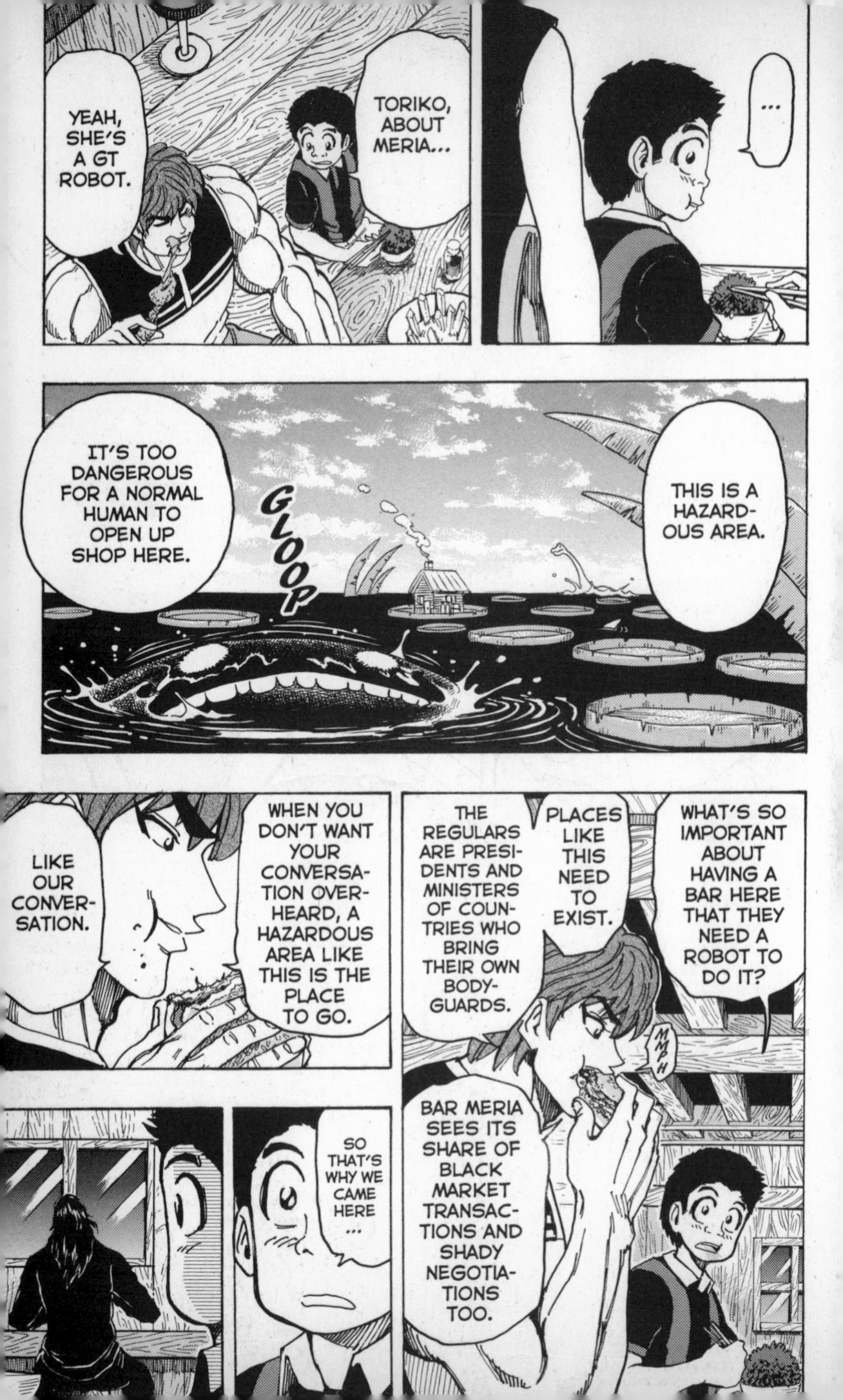
...
TORIKO, ABOUT MERIA...
YEAH, SHE'S A GT ROBOT.
THIS IS A HAZARDOUS AREA.
GLOOP
IT'S TOO DANGEROUS FOR A NORMAL HUMAN TO OPEN UP SHOP HERE.
WHAT'S SO IMPORTANT ABOUT HAVING A BAR HERE THAT THEY NEED A ROBOT TO DO IT?
PLACES LIKE THIS NEED TO EXIST.
THE REGULARS ARE PRESIDENTS AND MINISTERS OF COUNTRIES WHO BRING THEIR OWN BODYGUARDS.
MMPH
BAR MERIA SEES ITS SHARE OF BLACK MARKET TRANSACTIONS AND SHADY NEGOTIATIONS TOO.
WHEN YOU DON'T WANT YOUR CONVERSATION OVERHEARD, A HAZARDOUS AREA LIKE THIS IS THE PLACE TO GO.
LIKE OUR CONVERSATION.
SO THAT'S WHY WE CAME HERE...

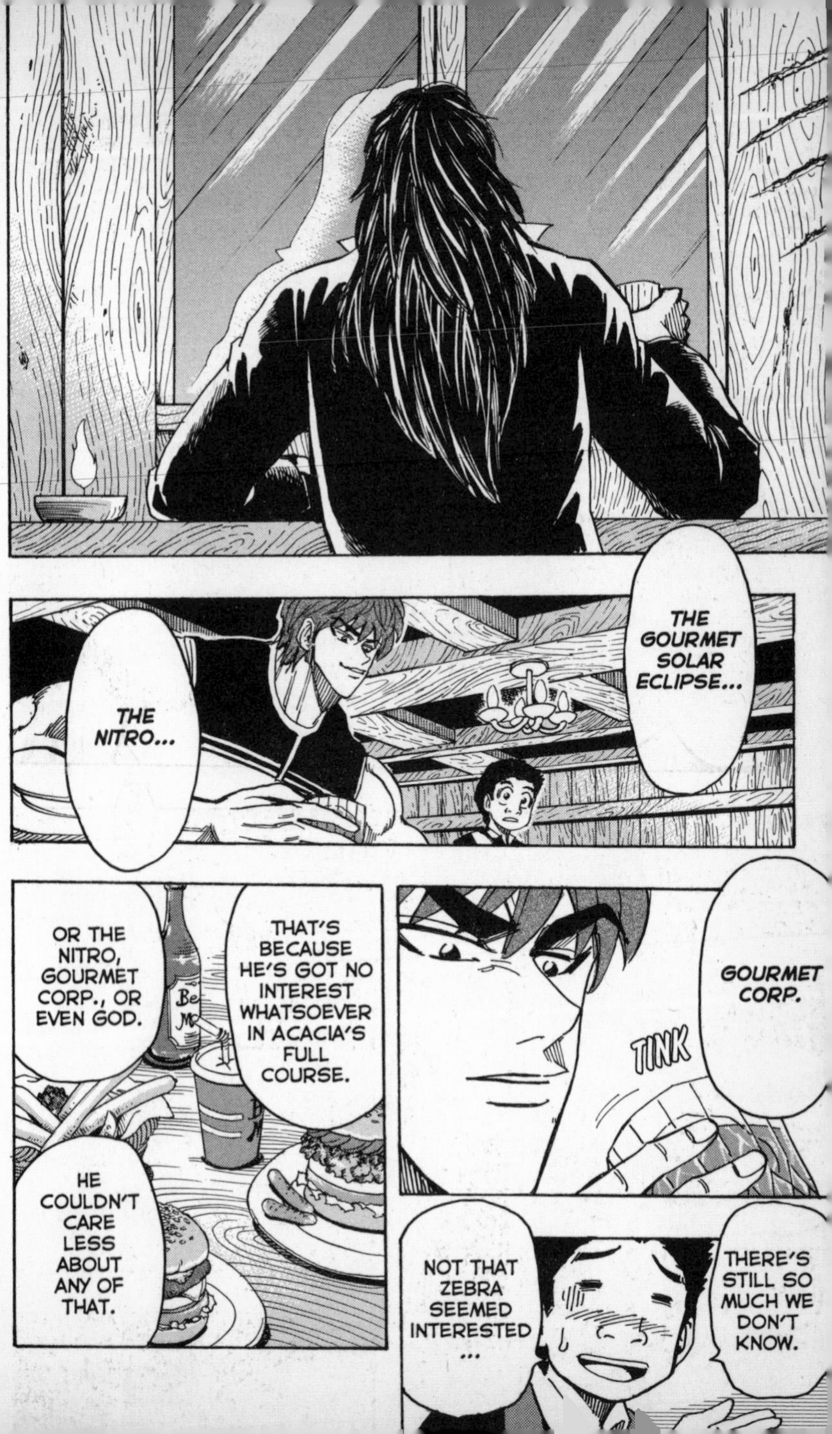
THE GOURMET SOLAR ECLIPSE...
THE NITRO...
GOURMET CORP.
TINK
THERE'S STILL SO MUCH WE DON'T KNOW.
NOT THAT ZEBRA SEEMED INTERESTED ...
THAT'S BECAUSE HE'S GOT NO INTEREST WHATSOEVER IN ACACIA'S FULL COURSE.
OR THE NITRO, GOURMET CORP., OR EVEN GOD.
HE COULDN'T CARE LESS ABOUT ANY OF THAT.

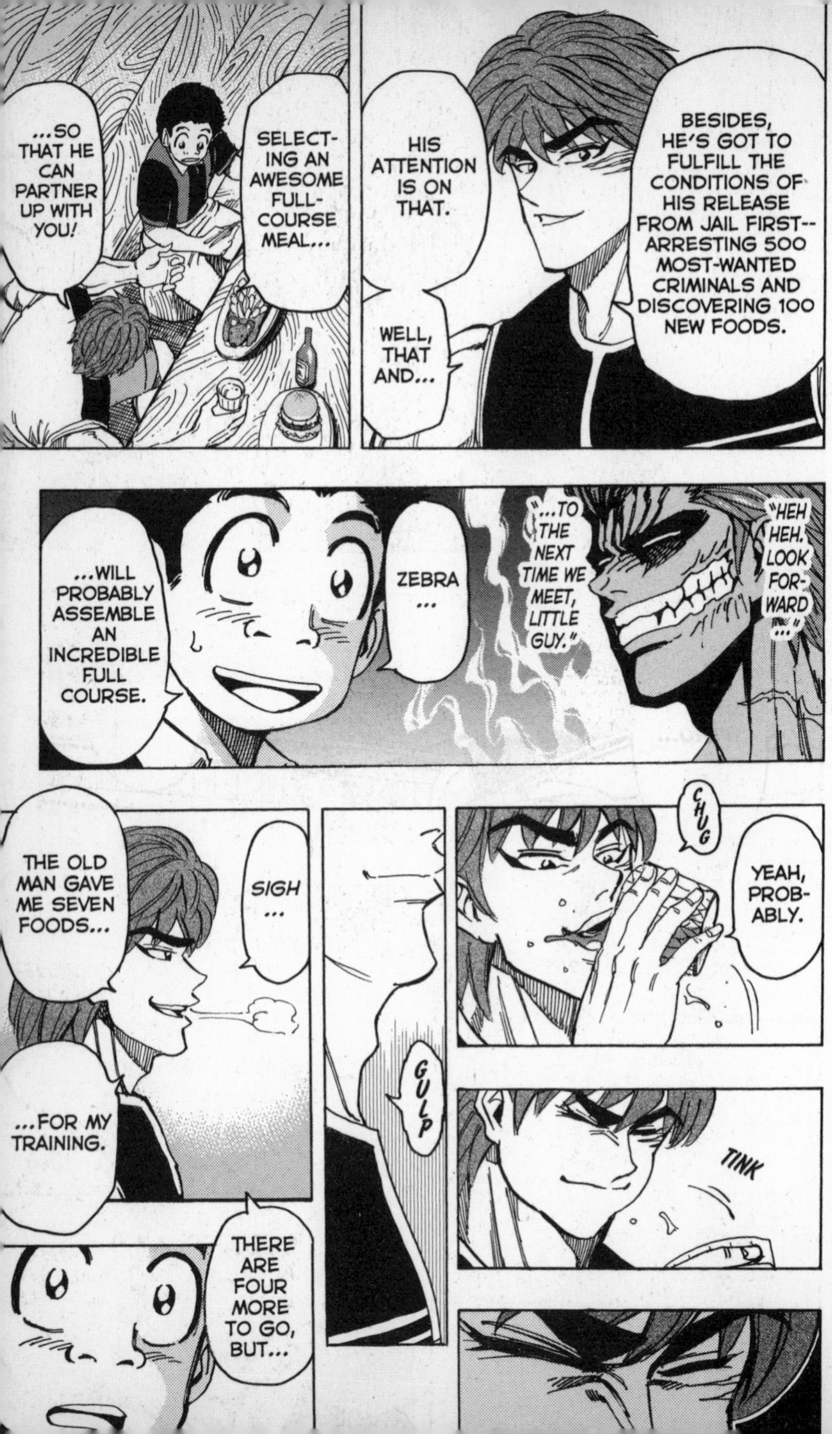
BESIDES, HE'S GOT TO FULFILL THE CONDITIONS OF HIS RELEASE FROM JAIL FIRST-- ARRESTING 500 MOST-WANTED CRIMINALS AND DISCOVERING 100 NEW FOODS.
HIS ATTENTION IS ON THAT.
WELL, THAT AND...
SELECTING AN AWESOME FULL-COURSE MEAL...
...SO THAT HE CAN PARTNER UP WITH YOU!
"HEH HEH. LOOK FORWARD..."
"...TO THE NEXT TIME WE MEET, LITTLE GUY."
ZEBRA...
...WILL PROBABLY ASSEMBLE AN INCREDIBLE FULL COURSE.
CHUG
YEAH, PROBABLY.
TINK
GULP
SIGH...
THE OLD MAN GAVE ME SEVEN FOODS...
...FOR MY TRAINING.
THERE ARE FOUR MORE TO GO, BUT...

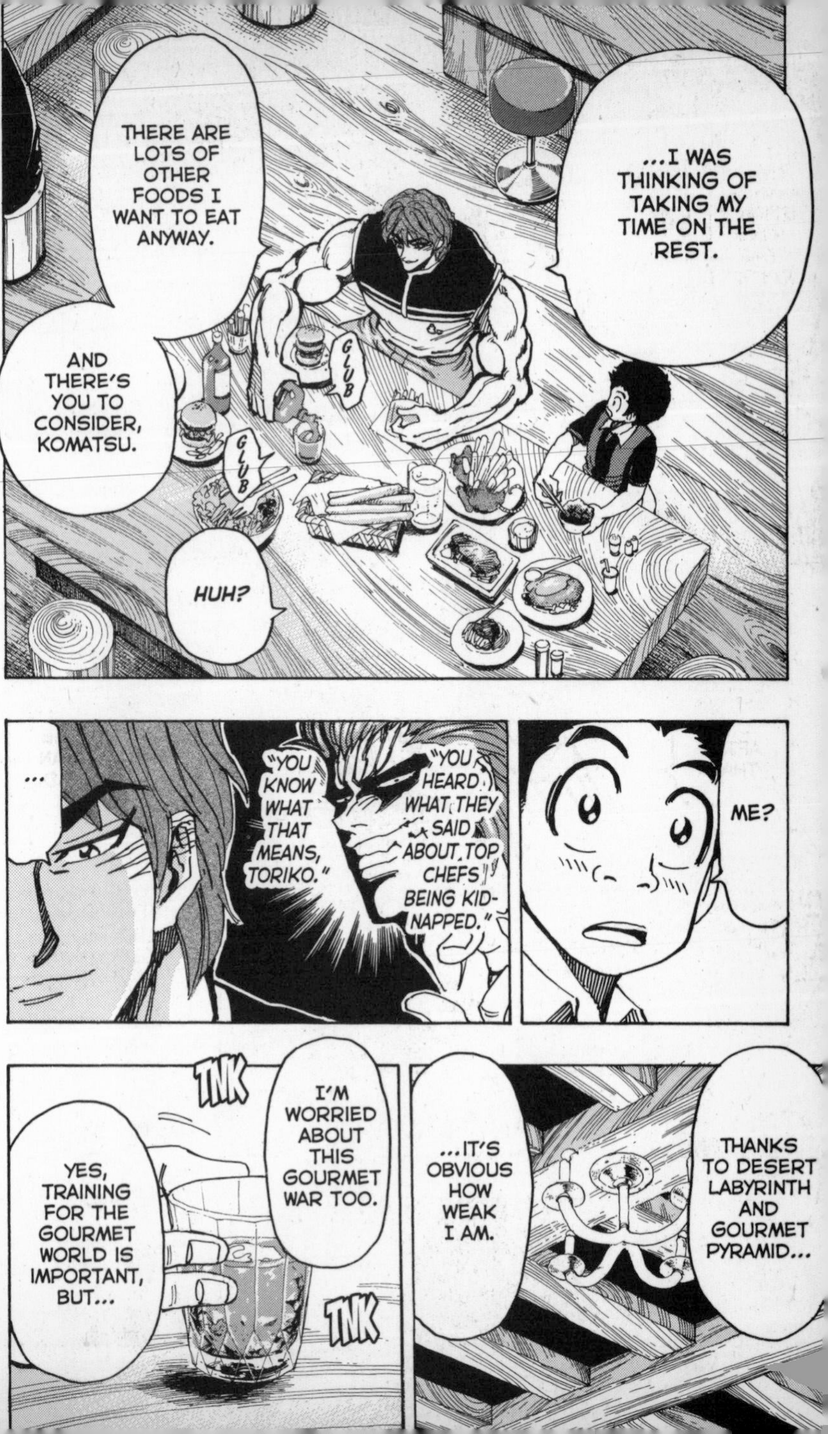
...I WAS THINKING OF TAKING MY TIME ON THE REST.
THERE ARE LOTS OF OTHER FOODS I WANT TO EAT ANYWAY.
GLUB
AND THERE'S YOU TO CONSIDER, KOMATSU.
GLUB
HUH?
ME?
"YOU HEARD WHAT THEY SAID ABOUT TOP CHEFS BEING KID-NAPPED."
"YOU KNOW WHAT THAT MEANS, TORIKO."
...
THANKS TO DESERT LABYRINTH AND GOURMET PYRAMID...
...IT'S OBVIOUS HOW WEAK I AM.
I'M WORRIED ABOUT THIS GOURMET WAR TOO.
TNK
YES, TRAINING FOR THE GOURMET WORLD IS IMPORTANT, BUT...
TNK

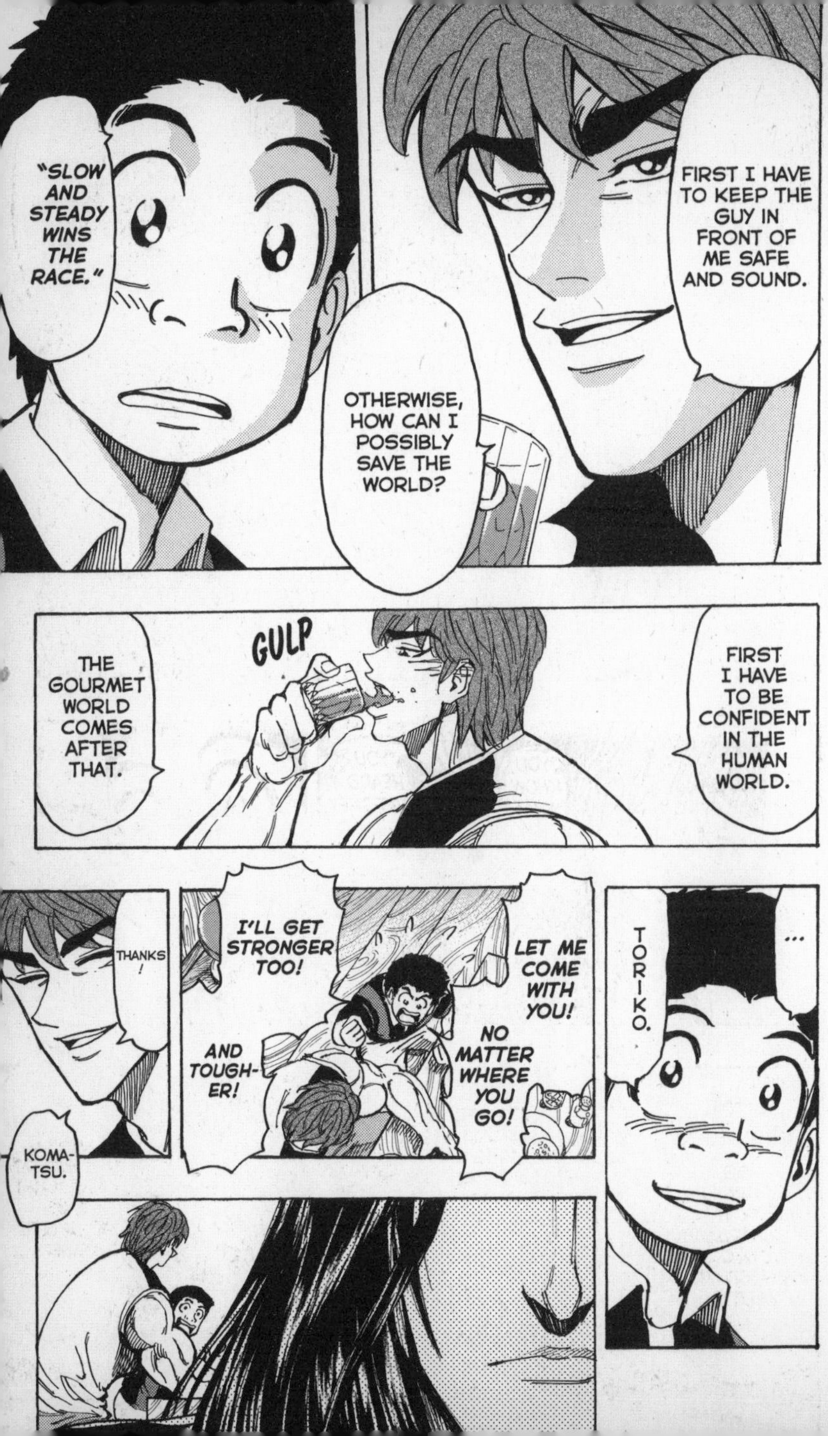
FIRST I HAVE TO KEEP THE GUY IN FRONT OF ME SAFE AND SOUND.
OTHERWISE, HOW CAN I POSSIBLY SAVE THE WORLD?
"SLOW AND STEADY WINS THE RACE."
FIRST I HAVE TO BE CONFIDENT IN THE HUMAN WORLD.
GULP
THE GOURMET WORLD COMES AFTER THAT.
...
TORIKO.
LET ME COME WITH YOU!
NO MATTER WHERE YOU GO!
I'LL GET STRONGER TOO!
AND TOUGHER!
THANKS!
KOMATSU.

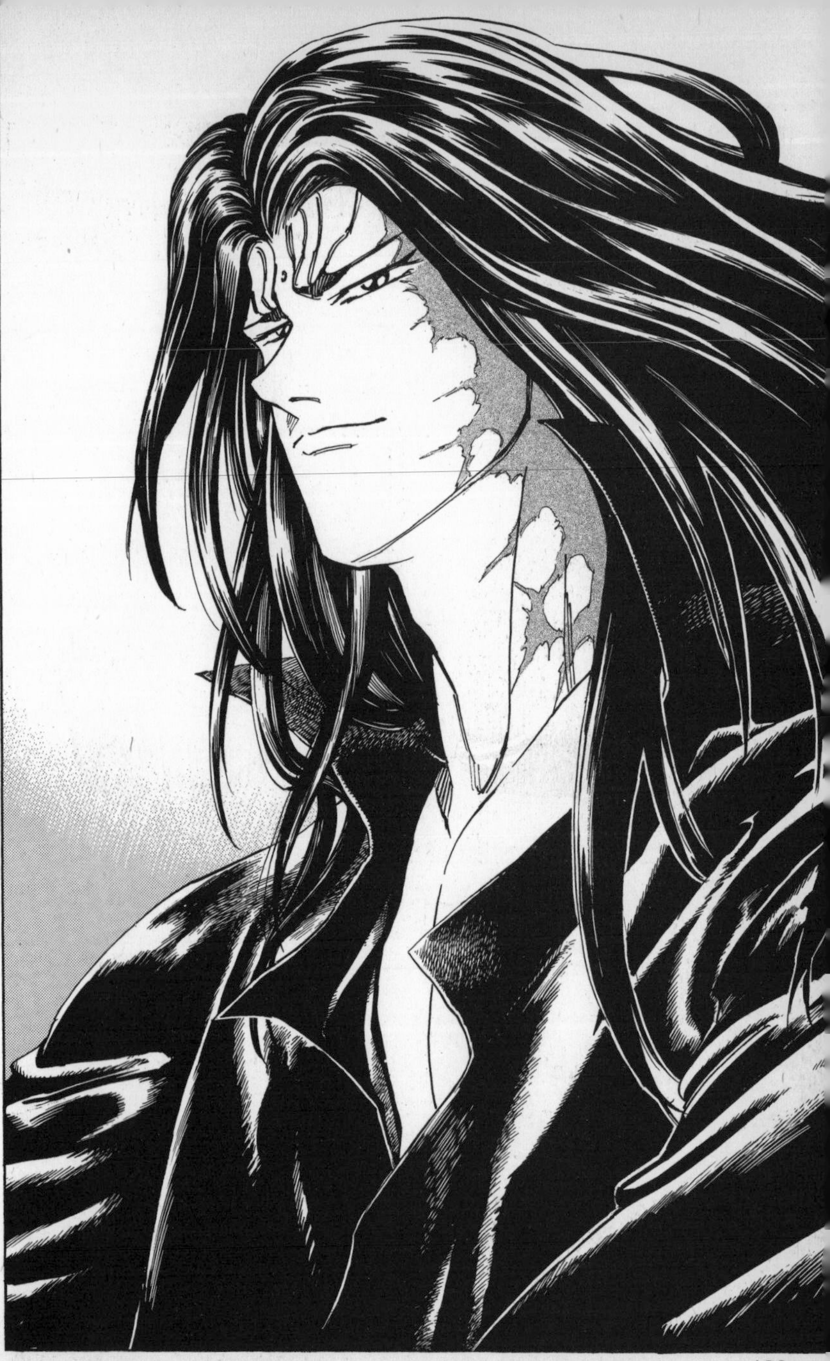

CLINK

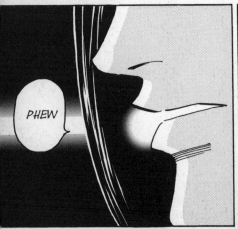

PHEW

TNK

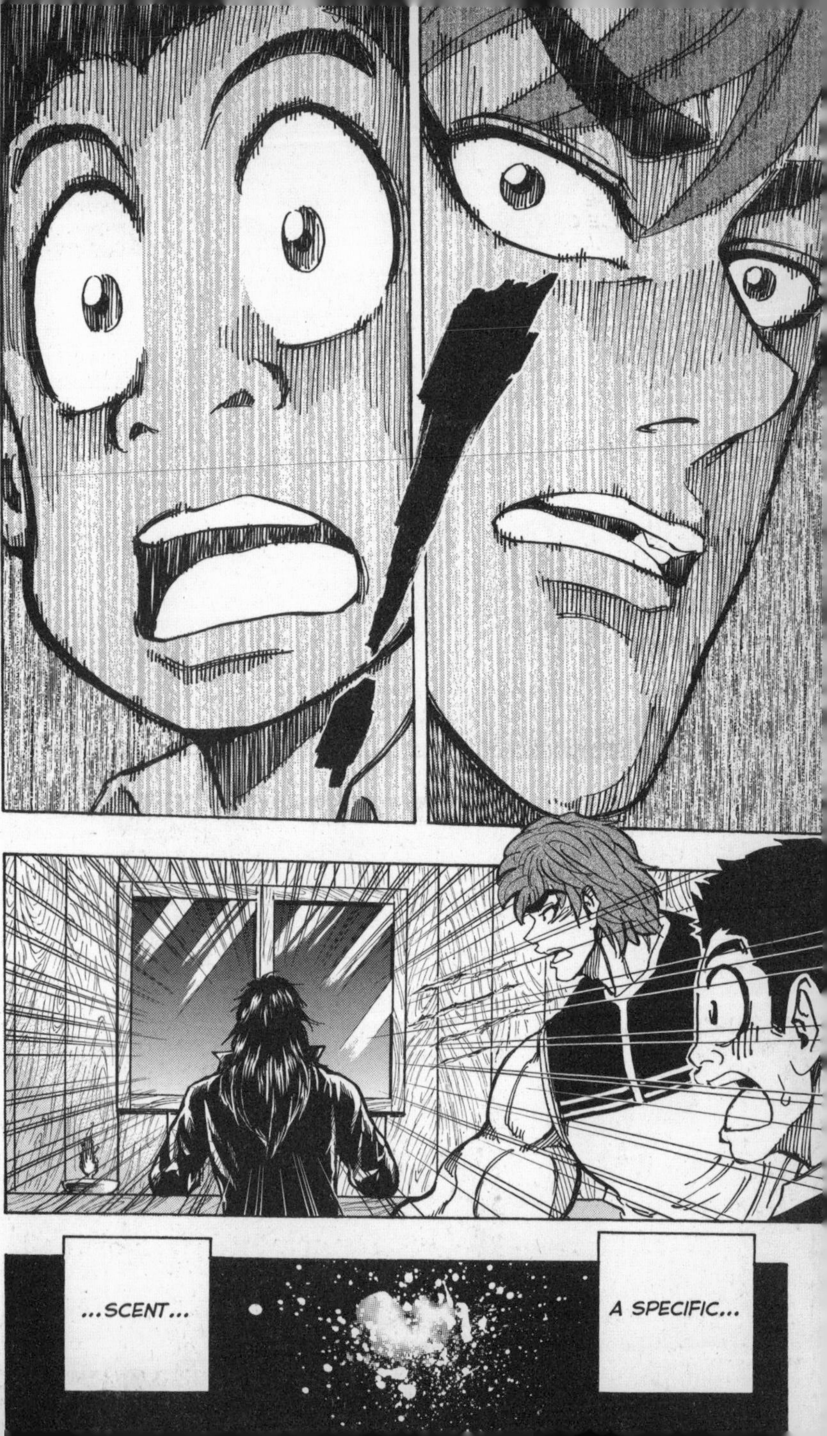
A SPECIFIC...
...SCENT...

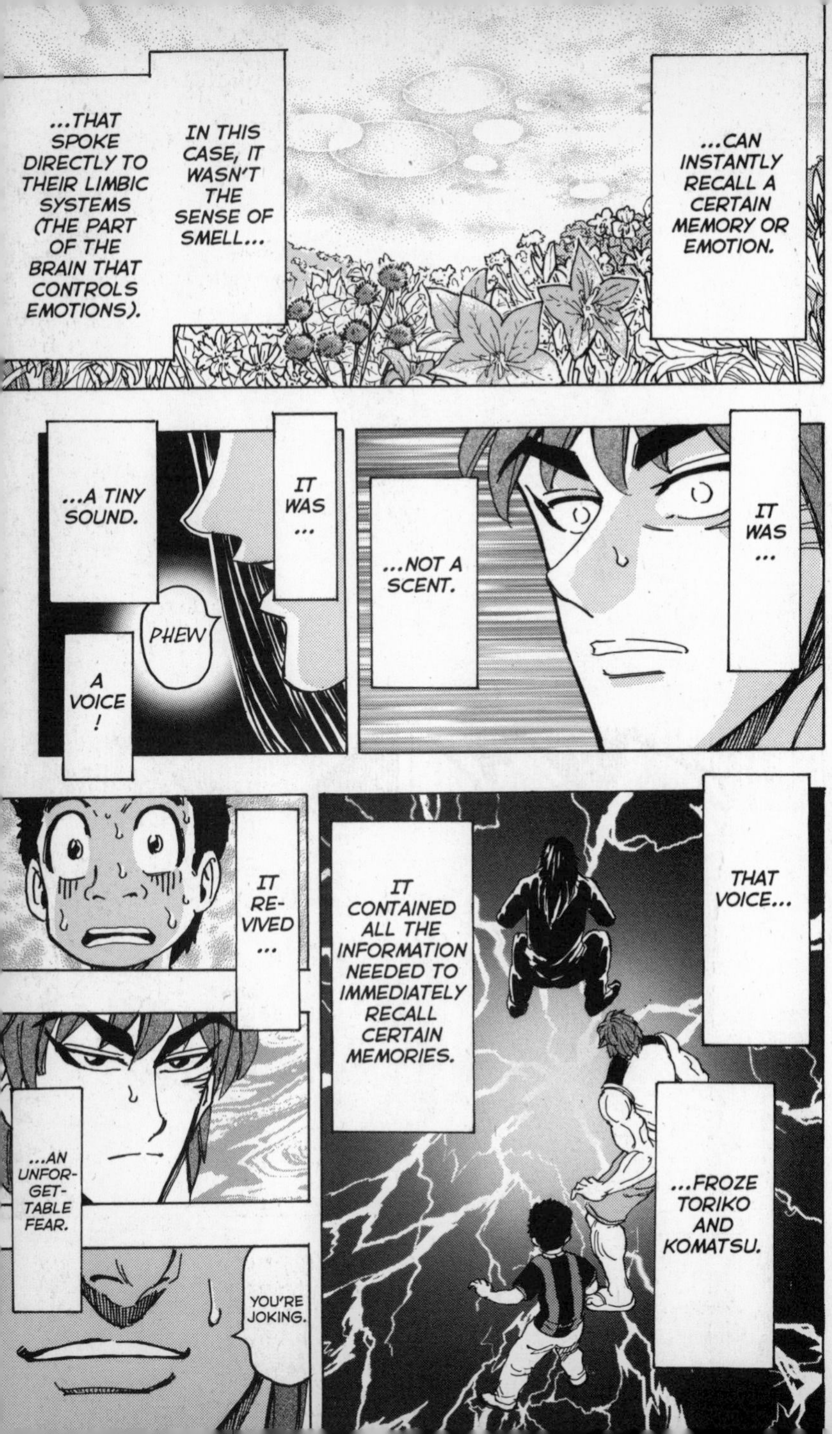
...CAN INSTANTLY RECALL A CERTAIN MEMORY OR EMOTION.
IN THIS CASE, IT WASN'T THE SENSE OF SMELL...
...THAT SPOKE DIRECTLY TO THEIR LIMBIC SYSTEMS (THE PART OF THE BRAIN THAT CONTROLS EMOTIONS).
IT WAS...
...NOT A SCENT.
IT WAS...
...A TINY SOUND.
PHEW
A VOICE!
THAT VOICE...
IT CONTAINED ALL THE INFORMATION NEEDED TO IMMEDIATELY RECALL CERTAIN MEMORIES.
...FROZE TORIKO AND KOMATSU.
IT REVIVED...
...AN UNFORGETTABLE FEAR.
YOU'RE JOKING.

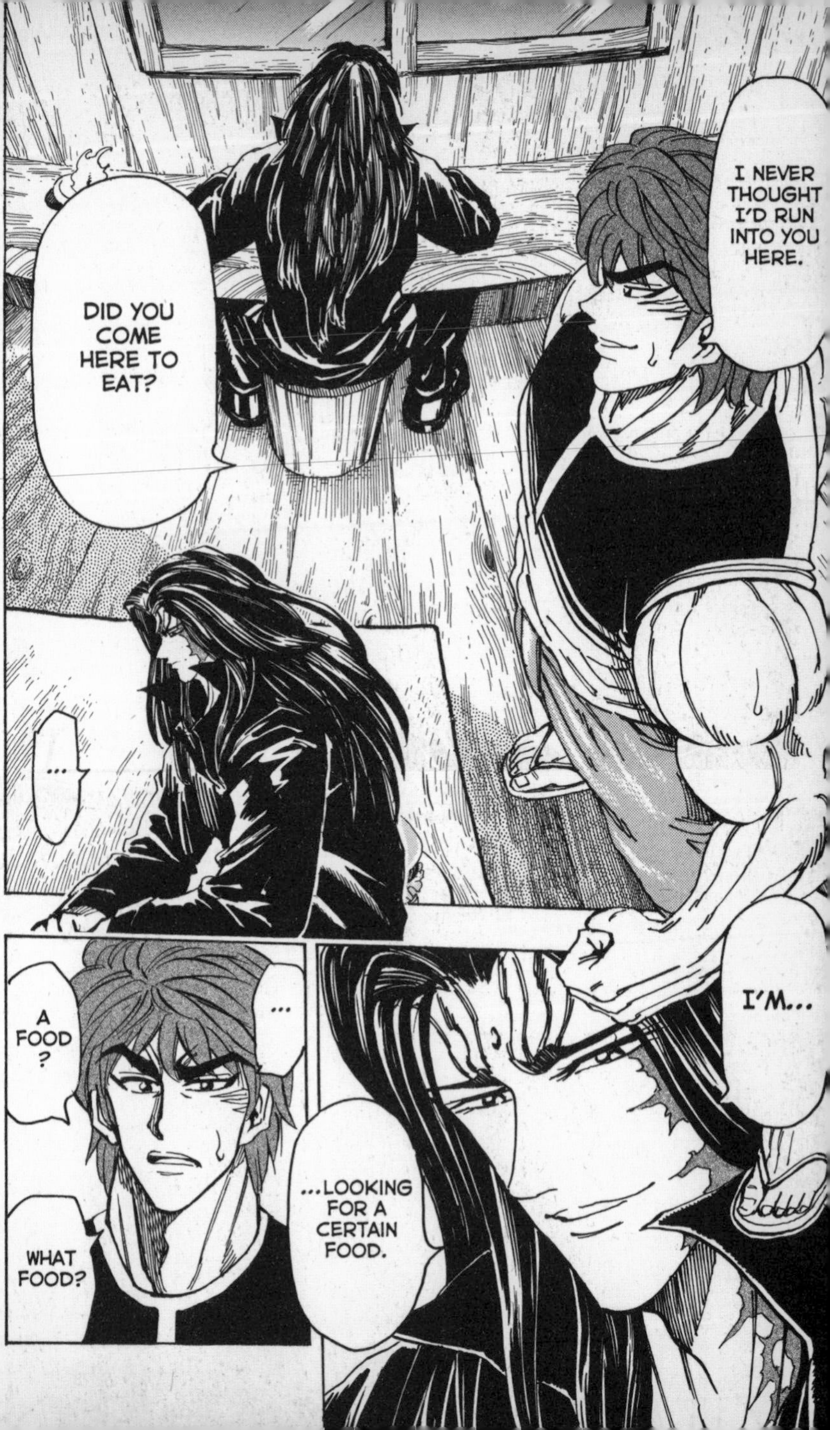
I NEVER THOUGHT I'D RUN INTO YOU HERE.
DID YOU COME HERE TO EAT?
...
I'M...
...LOOKING FOR A CERTAIN FOOD.
...
A FOOD?
WHAT FOOD?

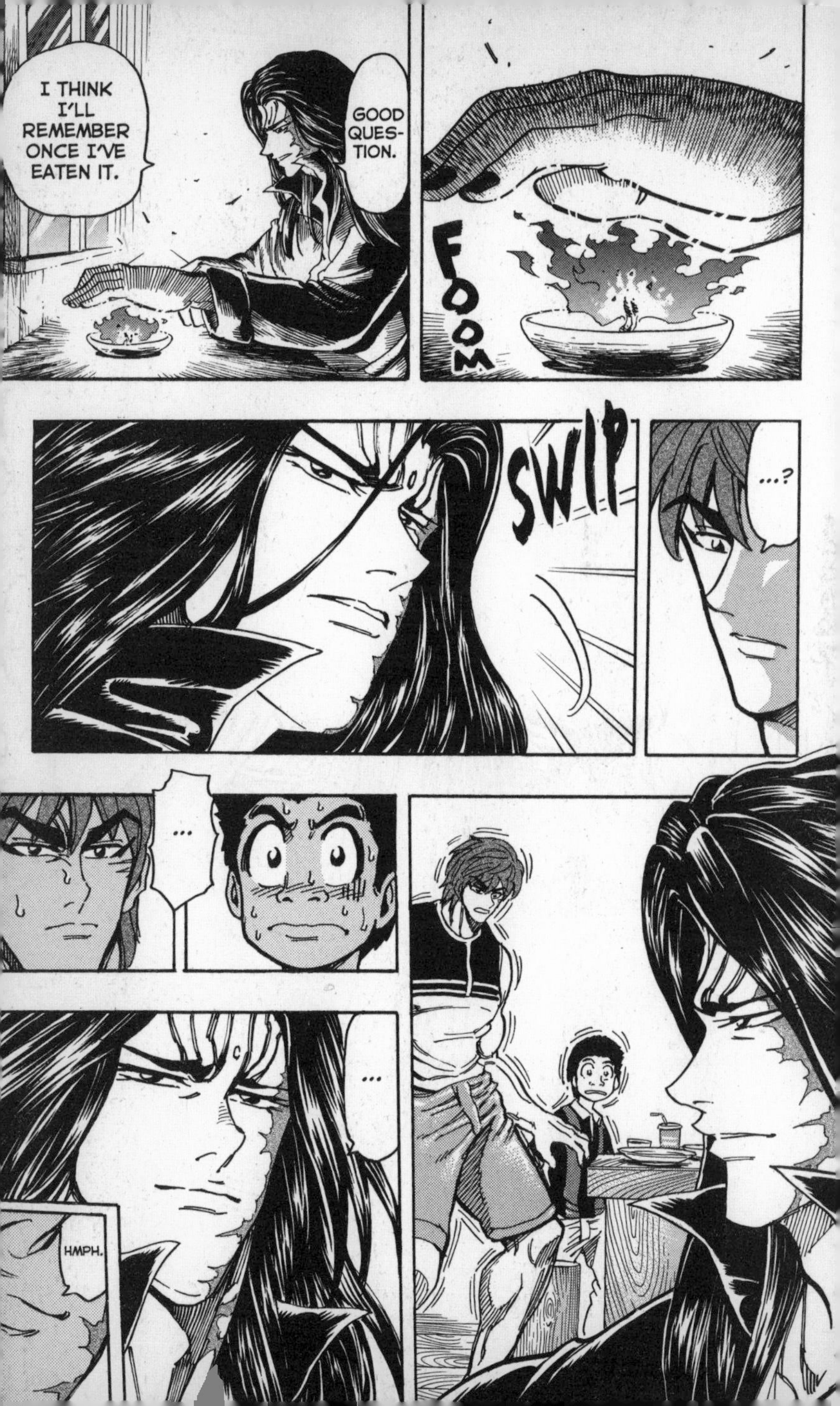
FOOM
GOOD QUES-TION.
I THINK I'LL REMEMBER ONCE I'VE EATEN IT.
...?
SWIP
...
...
HMPH.

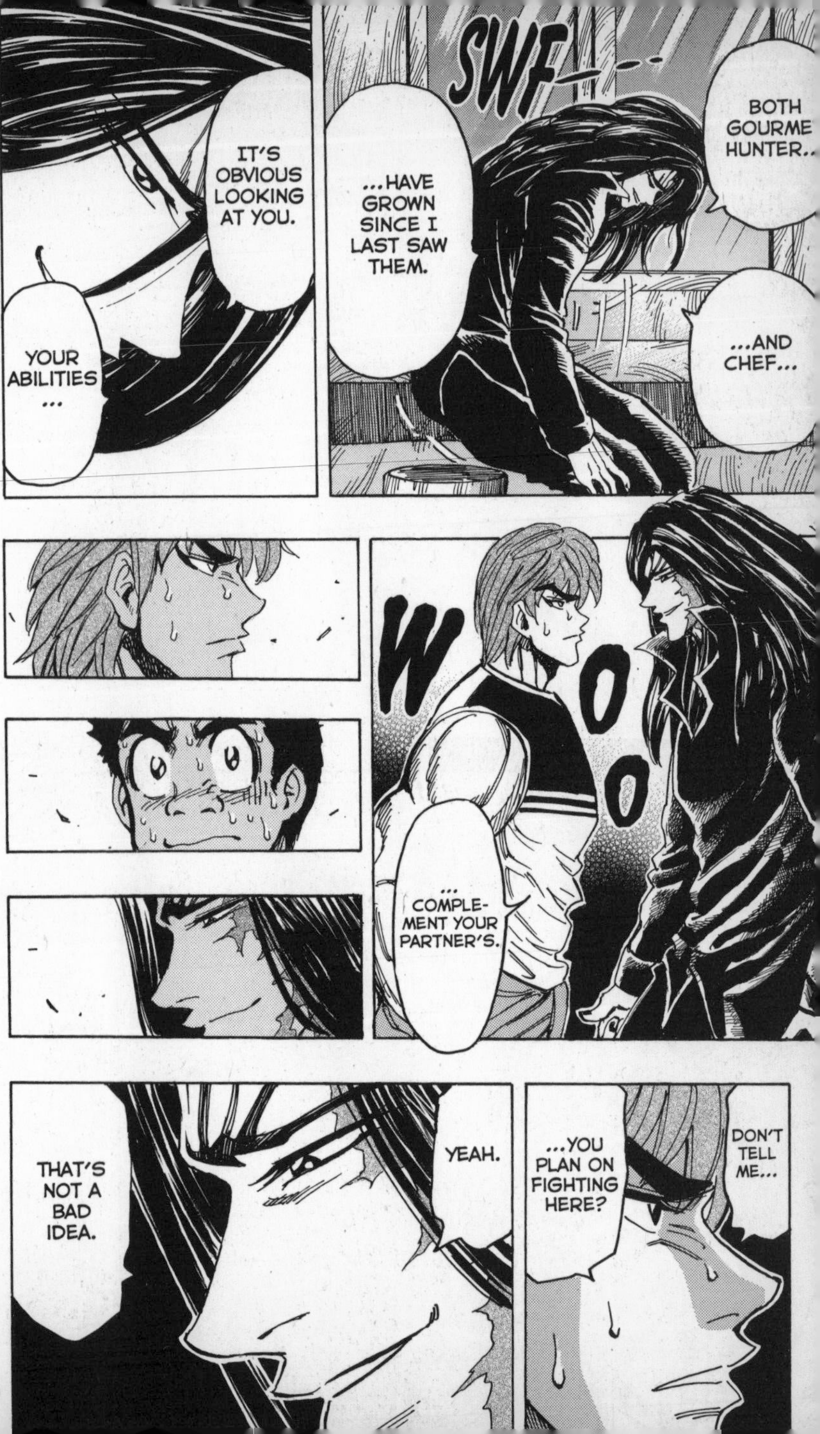
SWF
BOTH GOURME HUNTER...
...AND CHEF...
...HAVE GROWN SINCE I LAST SAW THEM.
IT'S OBVIOUS LOOKING AT YOU.
YOUR ABILITIES ...
WOO
... COMPLEMENT YOUR PARTNER'S.
DON'T TELL ME...
...YOU PLAN ON FIGHTING HERE?
YEAH.
THAT'S NOT A BAD IDEA.

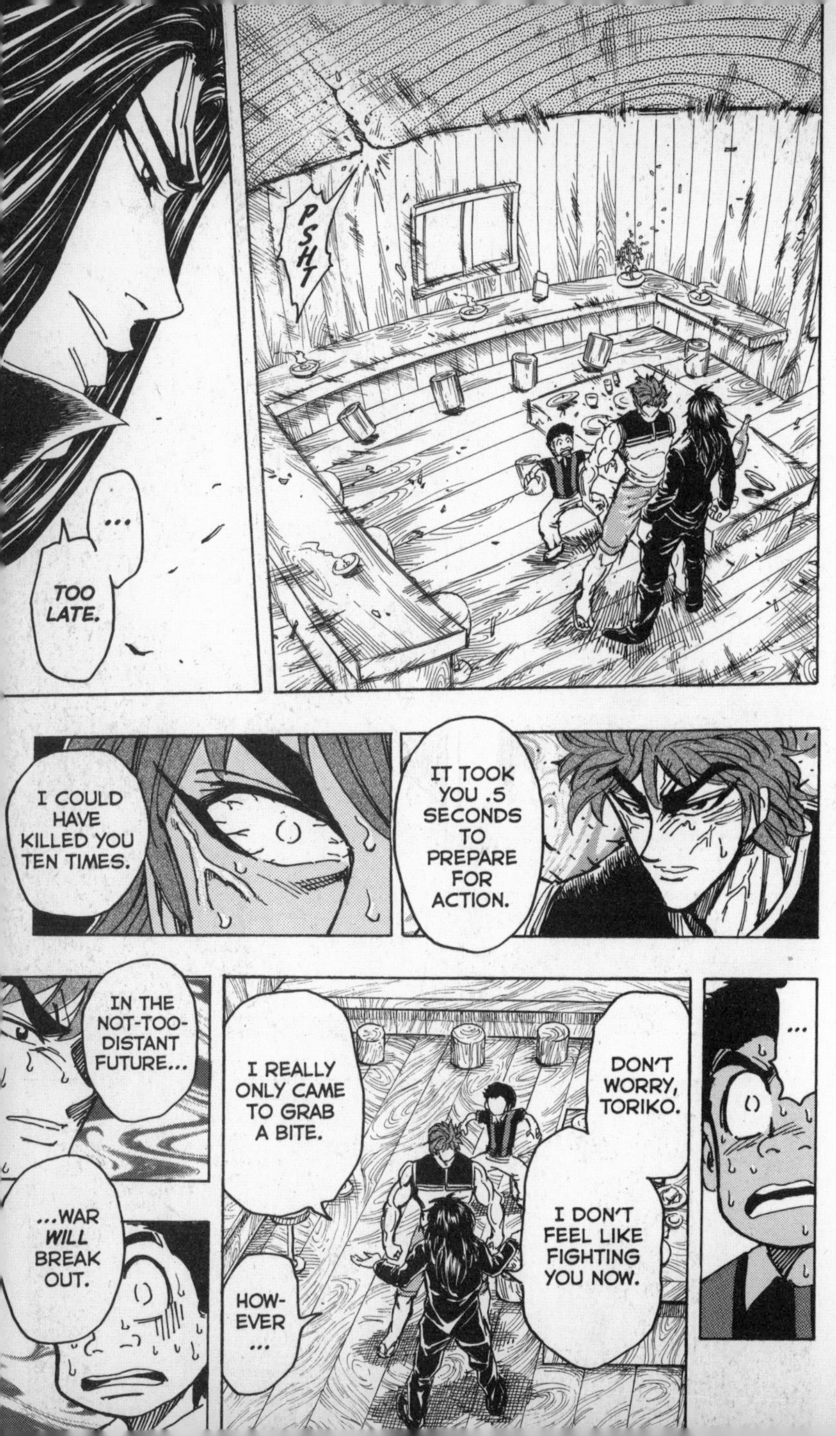
PSHT
...
TOO LATE.
IT TOOK YOU .5 SECONDS TO PREPARE FOR ACTION.
I COULD HAVE KILLED YOU TEN TIMES.
...
DON'T WORRY, TORIKO.
I REALLY ONLY CAME TO GRAB A BITE.
I DON'T FEEL LIKE FIGHTING YOU NOW.
HOW-EVER...
IN THE NOT-TOO-DISTANT FUTURE...
...WAR WILL BREAK OUT.

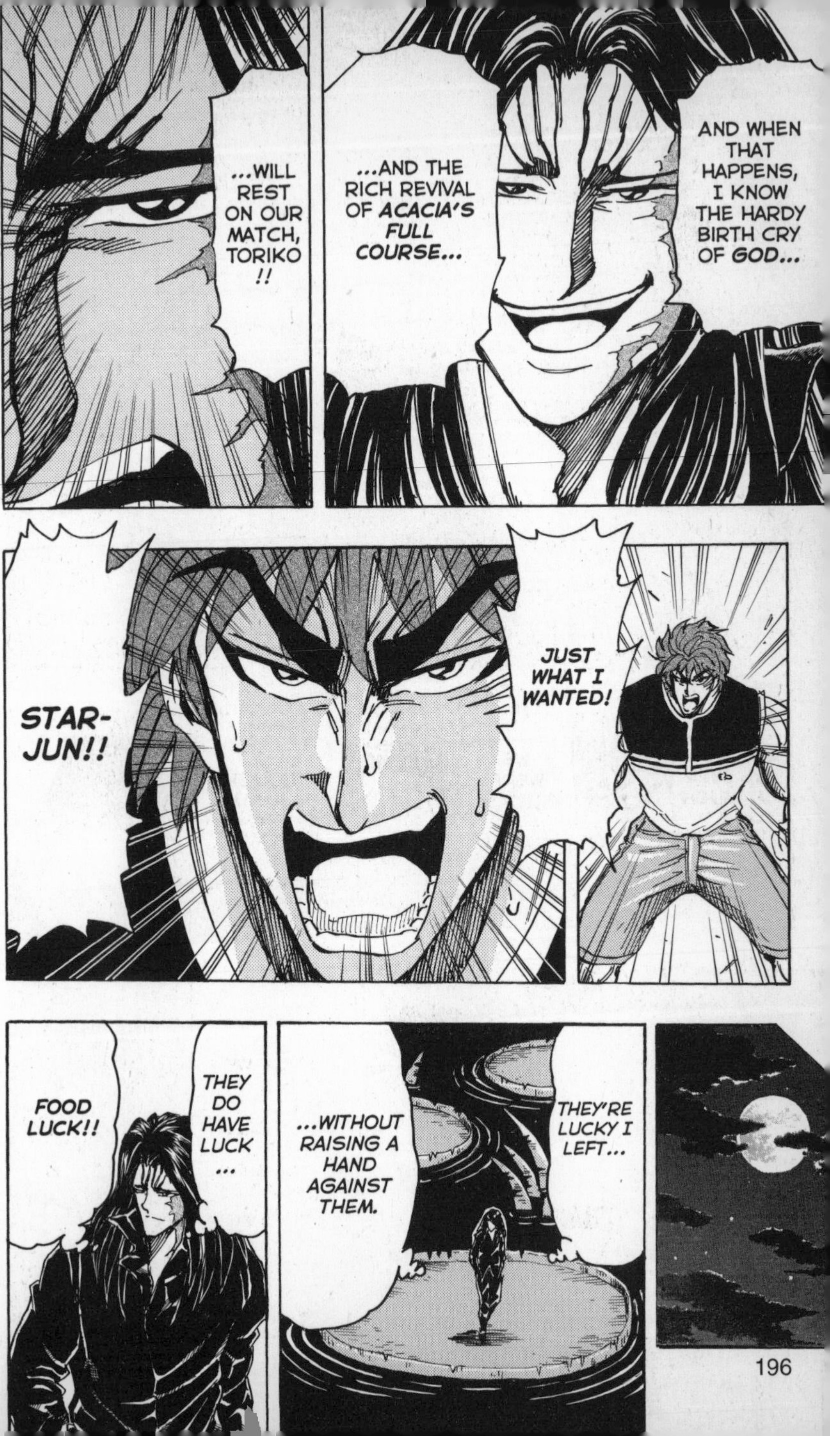
AND WHEN THAT HAPPENS, I KNOW THE HARDY BIRTH CRY OF *GOD*...
...AND THE RICH REVIVAL OF *ACACIA'S FULL COURSE*...
...WILL REST ON OUR MATCH, TORIKO!!
JUST WHAT I WANTED!
STAR-JUN!!
THEY'RE LUCKY I LEFT...
...WITHOUT RAISING A HAND AGAINST THEM.
THEY DO HAVE LUCK...
FOOD LUCK!!

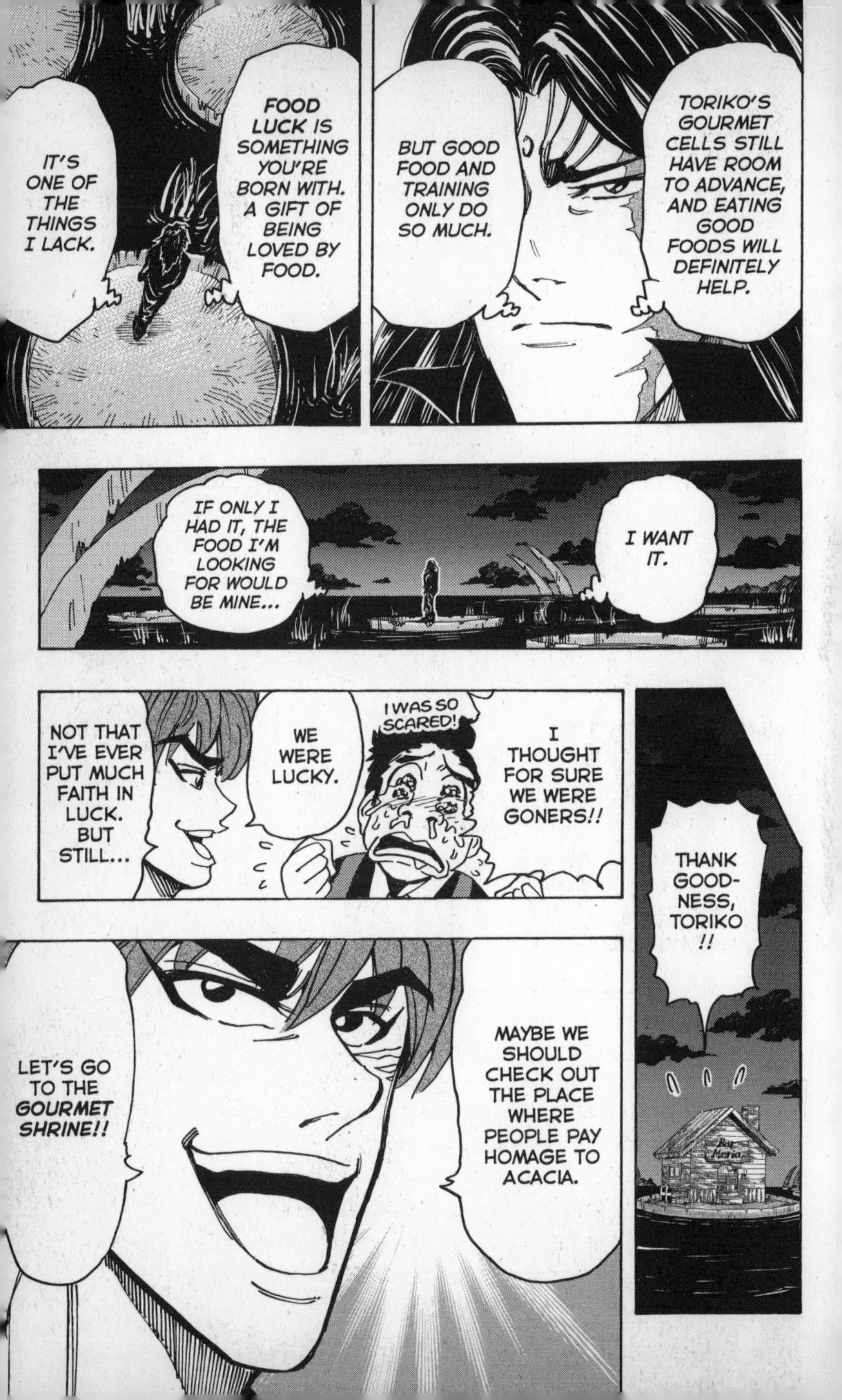
TORIKO'S GOURMET CELLS STILL HAVE ROOM TO ADVANCE, AND EATING GOOD FOODS WILL DEFINITELY HELP.
BUT GOOD FOOD AND TRAINING ONLY DO SO MUCH.
FOOD LUCK IS SOMETHING YOU'RE BORN WITH. A GIFT OF BEING LOVED BY FOOD.
IT'S ONE OF THE THINGS I LACK.
I WANT IT.
IF ONLY I HAD IT, THE FOOD I'M LOOKING FOR WOULD BE MINE...
THANK GOOD-NESS, TORIKO!!
I THOUGHT FOR SURE WE WERE GONERS!!
I WAS SO SCARED!
WE WERE LUCKY.
NOT THAT I'VE EVER PUT MUCH FAITH IN LUCK. BUT STILL...
MAYBE WE SHOULD CHECK OUT THE PLACE WHERE PEOPLE PAY HOMAGE TO ACACIA.
LET'S GO TO THE GOURMET SHRINE!!

TORIKO

GOURMET CHECKLIST

Vol. 166

 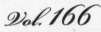

CORN ON THE BONE
(VEGETABLE)

CAPTURE LEVEL: 11

HABITAT: CORN FIELDS

LENGTH: 50 CM

HEIGHT: ---

WEIGHT: 2 KG

PRICE: 8,000 YEN PER EAR

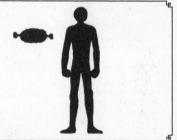

SCALE

AN ELUSIVE CORN THAT POPS UP IN ORDINARY CORN FIELDS ONCE A DECADE. CORN ON THE BONE CONCENTRATES TEN YEARS' WORTH OF NUTRIENTS IN ITS RICH FLAVOR. YOU CAN PASS IT OVER A LIGHT FLAME TO INCREASE ITS AROMA AND MAKE IT OVERFLOW WITH SAVORY JUICINESS. IT'S TOO APPETIZING TO PASS UP! FRESH GRILLED CORN ON THE BONE GETS ITS RIGHTFUL APPRECIATION WHEN SOLD BY OUTDOOR VENDORS EVERY YEAR AT THE IGO'S GOURMET FESTIVAL.

TORIKO

GOURMET CHECKLIST

Vol. 167

ROAST BANANA
(PLANT)

CAPTURE LEVEL: 1

HABITAT: ANYWHERE, READILY
AVAILABLE

LENGTH: 25 CM

HEIGHT: ---

WEIGHT: 150 G

PRICE: 10,000 YEN PER BANANA

SCALE

ROAST BANANAS GROW AT LOWER ALTITUDES THAN REGULAR BANANAS. THEY'RE DELICIOUS WHEN EATEN AS IS, BUT PASSING ONE OVER A FLAME WILL BRING OUT A MORE SAVORY AROMA AND TASTE! ROAST BANANA IS OFTEN SERVED LIGHTLY ROASTED WITH A BITE OF CAVIAR ON TOP. SO DELICIOUS YOU'LL BE SHOUTING "YUM!" IT'S ALSO ONE OF TORIKO'S FAVORITES.

TORIKO

GOURMET CHECKLIST

Vol.168

HAM SHELL
(UNKNOWN)

CAPTURE LEVEL: UNKNOWN

HABITAT: GOURMET WORLD

LENGTH: 20 CM

HEIGHT: ---

WEIGHT: 1 KG

PRICE: UNKNOWN

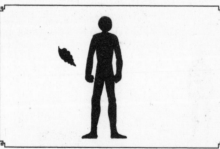

SCALE

A STRANGE FOOD THAT LIVES IN THE GOURMET WORLD'S UNDERGROUND FOREST. DETAILS REGARDING ITS BEHAVIOR, CAPTURE LEVEL, AND MORE ARE A COMPLETE MYSTERY. WHILE TORIKO WAS IN THE GOURMET WORLD, KNOCKING MASTER JIRO OFFERED HIM A TASTE, BUT TORIKO PUT HIS GLUTTONY ASIDE AND DECIDED TO HOLD OFF FROM EATING ANYTHING IN THE GOURMET WORLD UNTIL HE RETURNED WITH KOMATSU. THIS FOOD HARDENED TORIKO'S RESOLVE TO CONQUER THE GOURMET WORLD.

TORIKO

GOURMET CHECKLIST

Vol. 169
DON ACORN
(NUT)

CAPTURE LEVEL: LESS THAN 1

HABITAT: ANYWHERE, READILY

    AVAILABLE

LENGTH: 30 CM (MAXIMUM

    2 METERS)

HEIGHT: ---

WEIGHT: ROUGHLY 15 KG

    (WHEN 30 CM LONG)

PRICE: 3,600 YEN PER NUT

    (WHEN 30 CM LONG)

SCALE

A GIANT OAK NUT TOUTED AS THE KING OF ACORNS. IT HAS THE TOUGHEST
SHELL OF ANY ACORN, AND UNLESS YOU USE A SPECIAL HAMMER TO BREAK
IT, YOU RUN THE RISK OF SHATTERING YOUR KNIFE INSTEAD! THE NUTMEAT
INSIDE HAS A FRUITY FLAVOR AND IS POPULAR AS A NUT JUICE. THIS FOOD
IS RESPONSIBLE FOR BREAKING KOMATSU'S BELOVED KNIFE, BUT IN A WAY
IT IS ALSO RESPONSIBLE FOR HIS QUEST FOR MELK STARDUST. YOU COULD
SAY IT WAS LUCK A DON ACORN BROKE HIS KNIFE.

TORIKO

GOURMET CHECKLIST

Vol. 170

FURNIP

(MAMMAL)

CAPTURE LEVEL: 15

HABITAT: MELK MOUNTAIN AND MINES

LENGTH: 6 METERS

HEIGHT: ---

WEIGHT: 1.2 TONS

PRICE: NOT FIT FOR CONSUMPTION

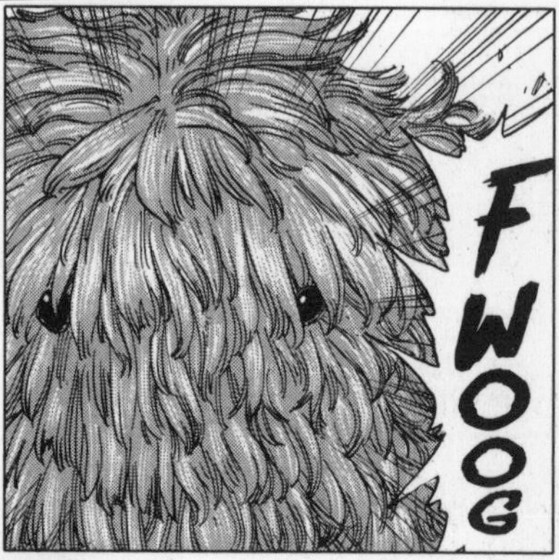
FWOOG

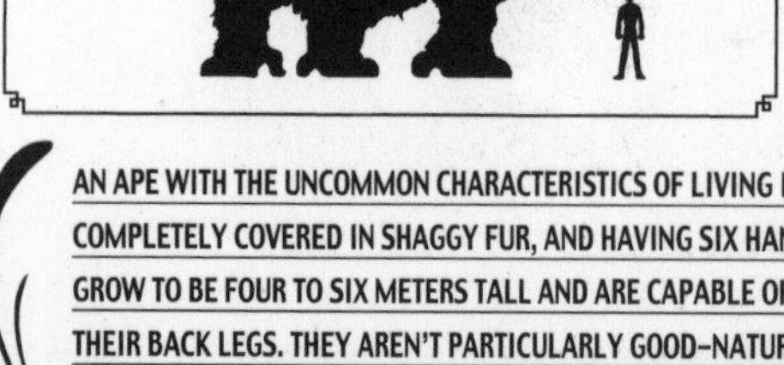

SCALE

AN APE WITH THE UNCOMMON CHARACTERISTICS OF LIVING IN MINES, BEING COMPLETELY COVERED IN SHAGGY FUR, AND HAVING SIX HANDS. FURNIPS CAN GROW TO BE FOUR TO SIX METERS TALL AND ARE CAPABLE OF WALKING ON THEIR BACK LEGS. THEY AREN'T PARTICULARLY GOOD-NATURED, BUT WITH TIME AND AFFECTION, IT'S NOT COMPLETELY OUT OF THE QUESTION TO DOMESTICATE THEM. THERE ARE EVEN "FURNIP HUNTERS" WHO TAME FURNIPS FOR THE PURPOSE OF SENDING THEM TO HIGH PLACES WHERE FRUITS GROW.

CHARACTER PROFILE

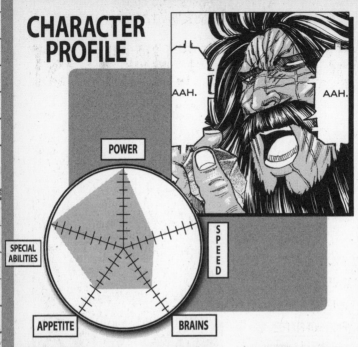

POWER

SPECIAL ABILITIES

SPEED

APPETITE

BRAINS

MELK (THE FIRST)

AGE: 72		**BIRTHDAY:** NOVEMBER 16	
BLOOD TYPE: AB		**SIGN:** SCORPIO	
HEIGHT: 270 CM		**WEIGHT:** 380 KG	
EYESIGHT: 20/10		**SHOE SIZE:** 60 CM	

SPECIAL MOVES/ABILITIES: ● Unknown

The world's best and most famous cutler. Not only does he craft and grind his knives, but he is skilled enough to gather high Capture Level raw materials and whetstones. Currently, he has given the "Melk" name over to his successor and is busy crafting the knife commissioned by IGO President Ichiryu to slice "Air," an ingredient used in Gourmet God Acacia's Salad Course. He's believed to be a hermit, but the truth is he just has an incredibly soft voice. He actually considers himself to be a bit of a chatterbox!

COMING NEXT VOLUME

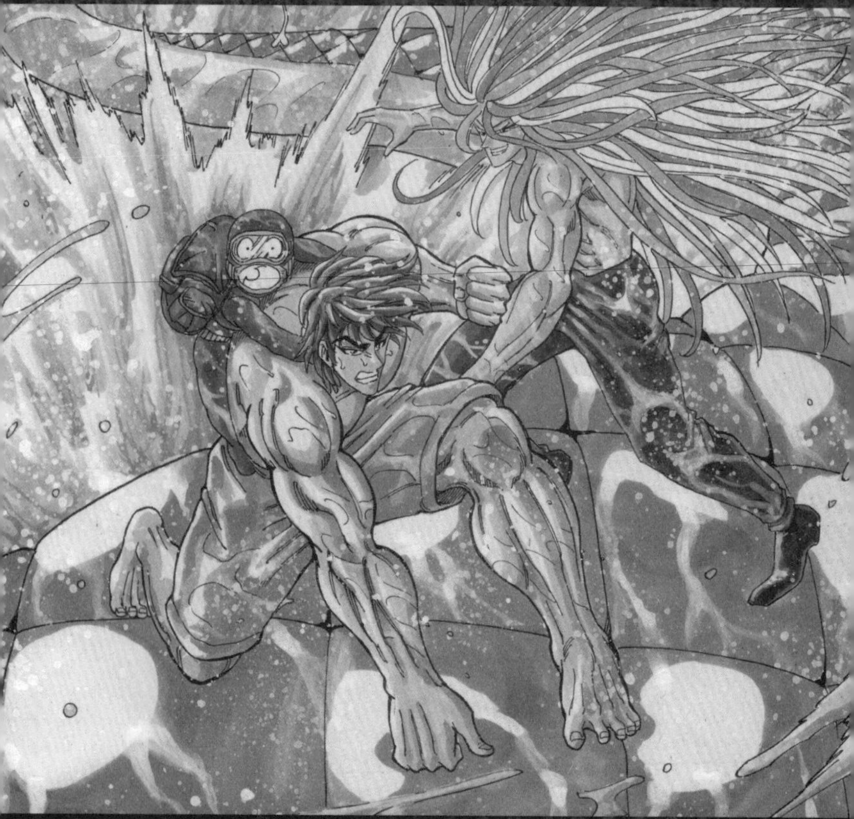

REUNION WITH TERROR

After a trip to the Gourmet Shrine, the place where Gourmet God Acacia's Full-Course Meal is honored, Toriko and Komatsu set their sights on the Shining Gourami. Since this glittering fish lives in one of the world's most humongous and deadly waterfalls, they enlist the help of a powered-up Sunny and his n[illegible] pet snake for a

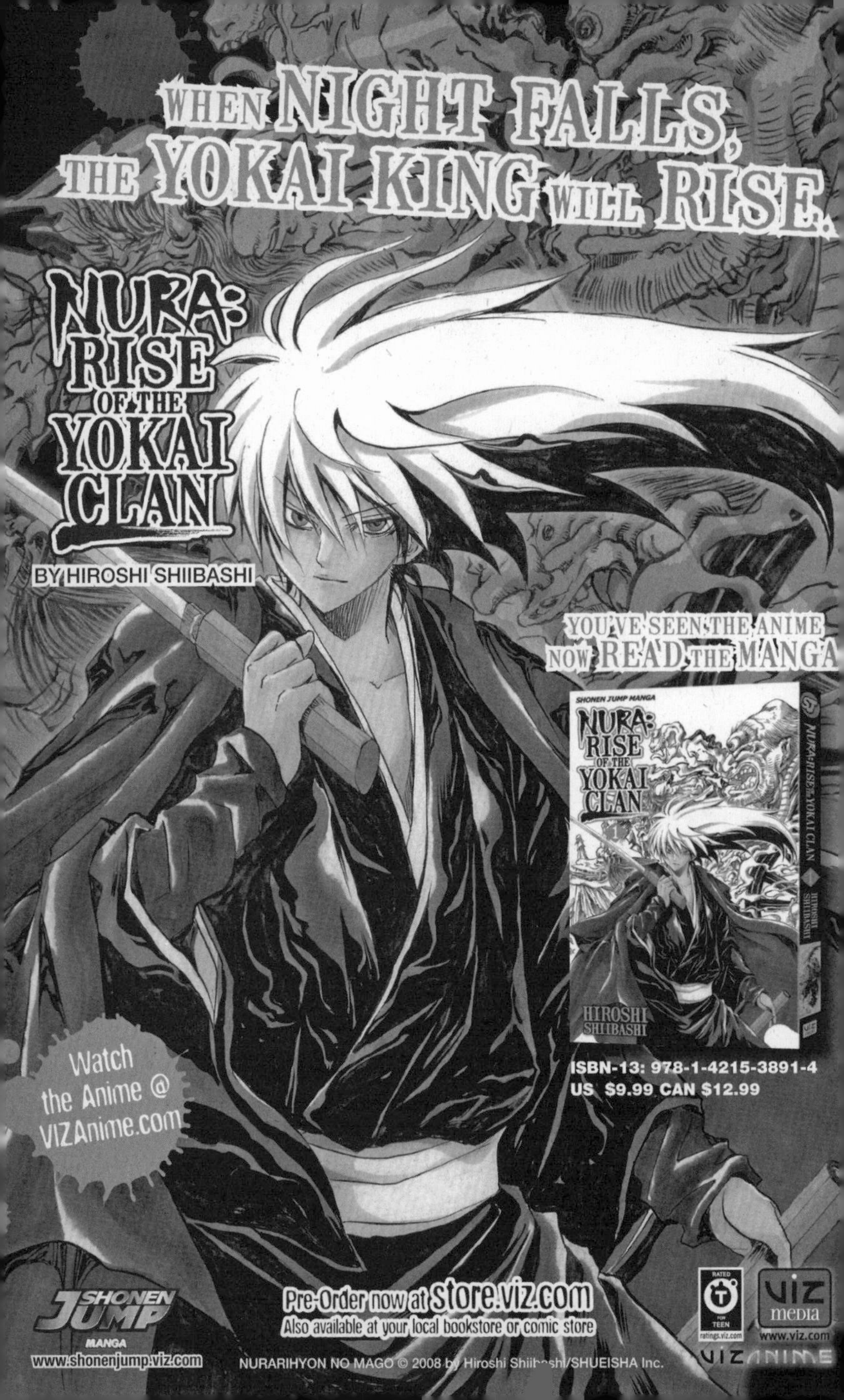
WHEN NIGHT FALLS,
THE YOKAI KING WILL RISE.
NURA: RISE OF THE YOKAI CLAN
BY HIROSHI SHIIBASHI
YOU'VE SEEN THE ANIME
NOW READ THE MANGA
SHONEN JUMP MANGA
NURA: RISE OF THE YOKAI CLAN
HIROSHI SHIIBASHI
ISBN-13: 978-1-4215-3891-4
US $9.99 CAN $12.99
Watch the Anime @ VIZAnime.com
SHONEN JUMP MANGA
www.shonenjump.viz.com
Pre-Order now at store.viz.com
Also available at your local bookstore or comic store
RATED T FOR TEEN
ratings.viz.com
VIZ media
www.viz.com
NURARIHYON NO MAGO © 2008 by Hiroshi Shiibashi/SHUEISHA Inc.

VIZMANGA
Read manga anytime, anywhere!

From our newest hit series to the classics you know and love, the best manga in the world is now available digitally. Buy a volume* of digital manga for your:

- iOS device (**iPad®, iPhone®, iPod® touch**) through the **VIZ Manga app**

- Android-powered device (**phone or tablet**) with a browser by visiting **VIZManga.com**

- **Mac or PC computer** by visiting **VIZManga.com**

VIZ Digital has loads to offer:

- 500+ ready-to-read volumes
- New volumes each week
- FREE previews
- Access on multiple devices! Create a log-in through the app so you buy a book once, and read it on your device of choice!*

To learn more, visit www.viz.com/apps

* Some series may not be available for multiple devices.
   Check the app on your device to find out what's available.

viz.com/apps

You're Reading in the Wrong Direction!!

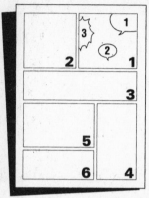

Whoops! Guess what? You're starting at the wrong end of the comic!

...It's true! In keeping with the original Japanese format, **Toriko** is meant to be read from right to left, starting in the upper-right corner.

Unlike English, which is read from left to right, Japanese is read from right to left, meaning that action, sound effects and word-balloon order are completely reversed... something which can make readers unfamiliar with Japanese feel pretty backwards themselves. For this reason, manga or Japanese comics published in the U.S. in English have sometimes been published "flopped"— that is, printed in exact reverse order, as though seen from the other side of a mirror.

By flopping pages, U.S. publishers can avoid confusing readers, but the compromise is not without its downside. For one thing, a character in a flopped manga series who once wore in the original Japanese version a T-shirt emblazoned with "M A Y" (as in "the merry month of") now wears one which reads "Y A M"! Additionally, many manga creators in Japan are themselves unhappy with the process, as some feel the mirror-imaging of their art skews their original intentions.

We are proud to bring you Mitsutoshi Shimabukuro's **Toriko** in the original unflopped format. For now, though, turn to the other side of the book and let the adventure begin...!

—Editor